W9-CTW-358

DATE DUE

			PRINTED IN U.S.A.

SOMETHING ABOUT THE AUTHOR

ISSN 0276-816X

SOMETHING ABOUT THE AUTHOR

**Facts and Pictures about Authors
and Illustrators of Books for Young People**

EDITED BY
ANNE COMMIRE

VOLUME 62

 **Gale Research Inc.** • *DETROIT* • *NEW YORK* • *LONDON*

Riverside Community College
Library
4800 Magnolia Avenue
Riverside, California 92506

Managing Editor: Anne Commire

Editors: Agnes Garrett, Helga P. McCue

Associate Editors: Elisa Ann Ferraro, Eunice L. Petrini

Assistant Editors: Marc Caplan, Marja T. Hiltunen, Linda Shedd

Sketchwriters: Kim Burdick, Yvette Burnham, Catherine Coray, Cathy Courtney,
Marguerite Feitlowitz, Mimi H. Hutson, Deborah Klezmer

Researcher: Catherine Ruello

Editorial Assistants: Joanne J. Ferraro, June Lee, Susan Pfanner

Production Manager: Mary Beth Trimper

External Production Assistant: Marilyn Jackman

Production Supervisor: Laura Bryant

Internal Production Associate: Louise Gagné

Art Director: Arthur Chartow

Keyliner: C. J. Jonik

Special acknowledgment is due to the members of the *Something about the Author Autobiography Series* staff
who assisted in the preparation of this volume.

While every effort has been made to ensure the reliability of the information presented in this
publication, Gale Research Inc. does not guarantee the accuracy of the data contained herein.
Gale accepts no payment for listing; and inclusion in the publication of any organization,
agency, institution, publication, service, or individual does not imply endorsement of the
editors or publisher.

Errors brought to the attention of the publisher and verified to the satisfaction of the publisher
will be corrected in future editions.

The paper used in this publication meets the minimum requirements
of American National Standard for Information Sciences—Permanence
Paper for Printed Library Materials, ANSI Z39.48-1984. ∞™

Copyright © 1990
Gale Research Inc.
835 Penobscot Bldg.
Detroit, MI 48226-4094

Library of Congress Catalog Card Number 72-27107

ISBN 0-8103-2272-2
ISSN 0276-816X

Printed in the United States

Published simultaneously in the United Kingdom
by Gale Research International Limited
(An affiliated company of Gale Research Inc.)

Contents

T

V

W

Introduction

As the only annually published ongoing reference series that deals with the lives and works of authors and illustrators of children's books, *Something about the Author (SATA)* is a unique source of information. The *SATA* series includes not only well-known authors and illustrators whose books are most widely read, but also those less prominent people whose works are just coming to be recognized. *SATA* is often the only readily available information source for less well-known writers or artists. You'll find *SATA* informative and entertaining whether you are:

—a student in junior high school (or perhaps one to two grades higher or lower) who needs information for a book report or some other assignment for an English class;

—a children's librarian who is searching for the answer to yet another question from a young reader or collecting background material to use for a story hour;

—an English teacher who is drawing up an assignment for your students or gathering information for a book talk;

—a student in a college of education or library science who is studying children's literature and reference sources in the field;

—a parent who is looking for a new way to interest your child in reading something more than the school curriculum prescribes;

—an adult who enjoys children's literature for its own sake, knowing that a good children's book has no age limits.

Scope

In *SATA* you will find detailed information about authors and illustrators who span the full time range of children's literature, from early figures like John Newbery and L. Frank Baum to contemporary figures like Judy Blume and Richard Peck. Authors in the series represent primarily English-speaking countries, particularly the United States, Canada, and the United Kingdom. Also included, however, are authors from around the world whose works are available in English translation, for example: from France, Jean and Laurent De Brunhoff; from Italy, Emanuele Luzzati; from the Netherlands, Jaap ter Haar; from Germany, James Krüss; from Norway, Babbis Friis-Baastad; from Japan, Toshiko Kanzawa; from the Soviet Union, Kornei Chukovsky; from Switzerland, Alois Carigiet, to name only a few. Also appearing in *SATA* are Newbery medalists from Hendrik Van Loon (1922) to Lois Lowry (1990). The writings represented in *SATA* include those created intentionally for children and young adults as well as those written for a general audience and known to interest younger readers. These writings cover the spectrum from picture books, humor, folk and fairy tales, animal stories, mystery and adventure, science fiction and fantasy, historical fiction, poetry and nonsense verse, to drama, biography, and nonfiction.

Information Features

In *SATA* you will find full-length entries that are being presented in the series for the first time. This volume, for example, marks the first full-length appearance of George Webbe Dasent, Gareth Floyd, A. B. Guthrie, Katharine Holabird, Elspeth Huxley, and John Jakes.

Obituaries have been included in *SATA* since Volume 20. An Obituary is intended not only as a death notice but also as a concise view of a person's life and work. Obituaries may appear for persons who have entries in earlier *SATA* volumes, as well as for people who have not yet appeared in the series. In this volume Obituaries mark the recent deaths of Frank Bonham, Guy Daniels, Frank Eyre, and Frances Clarke Sayers.

Revised Entries

Since Volume 25, each *SATA* volume also includes newly revised and updated entries for a selection of *SATA* listees (usually four to six) who remain of interest to today's readers and who have been active enough to require extensive revision of their earlier biographies. For example, when Beverly Cleary first appeared in *SATA* Volume 2, she was the author of twenty-one books for children and young adults and the recipient of numerous awards. By the time her updated sketch appeared in Volume 43 (a span of fifteen years), this creator of the indefatigable Ramona Quimby and other memorable characters had produced a dozen new titles and garnered nearly fifty additional awards, including the 1984 Newbery Medal.

The entry for a given biographee may be revised as often as there is substantial new information to provide. In this volume, look for revised entries on Lena Young de Grummond, Peter Dickinson, Rosa Guy, Kathleen Peyton, and Elizabeth George Speare.

Illustrations

While the textual information in *SATA* is its primary reason for existing, photographs and illustrations not only enliven the text but are an integral part of the information that *SATA* provides. Illustrations and text are wedded in such a special way in children's literature that artists and their works naturally occupy a prominent place among *SATA*'s listees. The illustrators that you'll find in the series include such past masters of children's book illustration as Randolph Caldecott, Walter Crane, Arthur Rackham, and Ernest H. Shepard, as well as such noted contemporary artists as Maurice Sendak, Edward Gorey, Tomie de Paola, and Margot Zemach. There are Caldecott medalists from Dorothy Lathrop (the first recipient in 1938) to Ed Young (the latest winner in 1990); cartoonists like Charles Schulz ("Peanuts"), Walt Kelly ("Pogo"), Hank Ketcham ("Dennis the Menace"), and Georges Rémi ("Tintin"); photographers like Jill Krementz, Tana Hoban, Bruce McMillan, and Bruce Curtis; and filmmakers like Walt Disney, Alfred Hitchcock, and Steven Spielberg.

In more than a dozen years of recording the metamorphosis of children's literature from the printed page to other media, *SATA* has become something of a repository of photographs that are unique in themselves and exist nowhere else as a group, particularly many of the classics of motion picture and stage history and photographs that have been specially loaned to us from private collections.

Index Policy

In response to suggestions from librarians, *SATA* indexes no longer appear in each volume but are included in each alternate (odd-numbered) volume of the series, beginning with Volume 57.

SATA continues to include two indexes that cumulate with each alternate volume: the **Illustrations Index,** arranged by the name of the illustrator, gives the number of the volume and page where the illustrator's work appears in the current volume as well as all preceding volumes in the series; the **Author Index** gives the number of the volume in which a person's Biographical Sketch, Brief Entry, or Obituary appears in the current volume as well as all preceding volumes in the series.

These indexes also include references to authors and illustrators who appear in *Yesterday's Authors of Books for Children* (described in detail below). Beginning with Volume 36, the *SATA* Author Index provides cross-references to authors who are included in Gale's *Children's Literature Review.* Starting with Volume 42, you will also find cross-references to authors who are included in the *Something about the Author Autobiography Series* (described in detail below).

What a *SATA* Entry Provides

Whether you're already familiar with the *SATA* series or just getting acquainted, you will want to be aware of the kind of information that an entry provides. In every *SATA* entry the editors attempt to give as complete a picture of the person's life and work as possible. In some cases that full range of information may simply be unavailable, or a biographee may choose not to reveal complete personal details. The information that the editors attempt to provide in every entry is arranged in the following categories:

1. The "head" of the entry gives

    —the most complete form of the name,
    —any part of the name not commonly used, included in parentheses,
    —birth and death dates, if known; a (?) indicates a discrepancy in published sources,
    —pseudonyms or name variants under which the person has had books published or is publicly known, in parentheses in the second line.

2. "Personal" section gives

    —date and place of birth and death,
    —parents' names and occupations,
    —name of spouse, date of marriage, and names of children,
    —educational institutions attended, degrees received, and dates,
    —religious and political affiliations,
    —agent's name and address,
    —home and/or office address.

3. "Career" section gives

    —name of employer, position, and dates for each career post,
    —military service,
    —memberships,
    —awards and honors.

4. "Writings" section gives

    —title, first publisher and date of publication, and illustration information for each book written; revised editions and other significant editions for books with particularly long publishing histories; genre, when known.

5. "Adaptations" section gives

    —title, major performers, producer, and date of all known reworkings of an author's material in another medium, like movies, filmstrips, television, recordings, plays, etc.

6. "Sidelights" section gives

    —commentary on the life or work of the biographee either directly from the person (and often written specifically for the *SATA* entry), or gathered from biographies, diaries, letters, interviews, or other published sources.

7. "For More Information See" section gives

    —books, feature articles, films, plays, and reviews in which the biographee's life or work has been treated.

How a *SATA* Entry Is Compiled

A *SATA* entry progresses through a series of steps. If the biographee is living, the *SATA* editors try to secure information directly from him or her through a questionnaire. From the information that the biographee supplies, the editors prepare an entry, filling in any essential missing details with research. The author or illustrator is then sent a copy of the entry to check for accuracy and completeness.

If the biographee is deceased or cannot be reached by questionnaire, the *SATA* editors examine a wide variety of published sources to gather information for an entry. Biographical sources are searched with the aid of Gale's *Biography and Genealogy Master Index*. Bibliographic sources like the *National Union Catalog*, the *Cumulative Book Index*, *American Book Publishing Record*, and the *British Museum Catalogue* are consulted, as are book reviews, feature articles, published interviews, and material sometimes obtained from the biographee's family, publishers, agent, or other associates.

For each entry presented in *SATA*, the editors also attempt to locate a photograph of the biographee as well as representative illustrations from his or her books. After surveying the available books which the biographee has written and/or illustrated, and then making a selection of appropriate photographs and illustrations, the editors request permission of the current copyright holders to reprint the material. In the case of older books for which the copyright may have passed through several hands, even locating the current copyright holder is often a long and involved process.

We invite you to examine the entire *SATA* series, starting with this volume. Described below are some of the people in Volume 62 that you may find particularly interesting.

Highlights of This Volume

PETER DICKINSON......was attending King's College in England when a tutor suggested that he join the staff of *Punch.* "On my way to the interview I was run into by a tram and arrived covered in blood." That was the beginning of a seventeen-year relationship with *Punch* as assistant editor and reviewer of crime novels. After several years on the job, Dickinson began doing some writing of his own. "There is this extraordinary feeling, when all one's contemporaries are brigadiers and bishops, that if one doesn't start being go-go, one will be went-went." His first novel, published in England as *Skin Deep,* won the Golden Dagger Award of the British Crime Writers and began Dickinson's career as an author of adult novels and children's adventure and fantasy books. "...The crucial thing for a writer is the ability to make up coherent worlds. I'm like a beachcomber walking along the shores of my imagination, picking up things and wondering what kinds of structures they could make. I want it to be an interesting structure, not a ramshackle, beachy thing. The imagination is like the sea, full of things you can't see but can possibly harvest and use....I have a function, like the village cobbler, and that is to tell stories. I am strongly against the religion in art, and the priesthood of artists. I am a cobbler. Given good leather I can make a comfortable shoe."

GARETH FLOYD......was born in 1940 during the first blitz on Liverpool and shortly thereafter moved with his parents to Whiston (Meyerside) "to escape the bombs falling on London....My early childhood recollections are of constant moving, and if memory serves correctly, I've had more than thirty addresses." Taking a position as an art teacher in a secondary school, Floyd "learned a lot, but, by God, I hated it....I was one of four young teachers who were all going through the same hell with physical threats by these sixteen-year-old boys....I left after a year. For years afterwards I still had nightmares and woke up in the night screaming their names." Many years later, having illustrated more than one hundred and thirty works, Floyd returned to teaching, finding that "The nice thing about teaching late in life is that you have learned a great deal by watching your own children grow up, which helped me relate to the chidren at school....Apart from my [early teaching days], I've never punished anyone. You learn to let go as you get older....There are two wonderful sounds for teachers to hear: the sound of running feet coming towards their classes and the sound of a class groaning as you tell them to pack up at the end of the lesson."

ROSA GUY......writes through a consciousness which rejects "the notion of the innocence of youth. The television sets in our living rooms projecting the global disasters caused by wars have robbed us of innocence; I reject a world where the young are sheltered in innocence while the youth of other nations are condemned to perpetual misery by the greed, or wrath, of their fathers; I reject the innocence of children whose fathers are more interested in building jails for minority youth of this nation instead of schools. I reject the pampering of babies as their parents vote for bombs instead of for books; I reject the ignorance of the heirs of Superman and Wonderwoman, who believe themselves inherently stronger and thus immune from catastrophies created by their forefathers, their fathers; I reject the young of each succeeding generation who dare to say: 'I don't understand *you* people....Do you see the way *they* act...?' They are us! Created by us for a society which suits our ignorance....I insist that Everychild go out into the world with this knowledge: there are no good guys. There are no bad guys. We are all good guys. We are all bad guys. And we are all responsible for each other."

PATRICIA MacLACHLAN......still has the story she wrote in grade school on a three by five card. It read: " 'My cats have names and seem happy. Often they play. The end.' My teacher was not impressed. I was discouraged, and I wrote in my diary: 'I shall not try to be a writer.' I was very fond of *shall* at age eight. I find the world *try* interesting. It did not occur to me then that everything in my diary was fiction, carefully orchestrated and embroidered tales of an exciting life—an unreal life. Or was it? The question of what was real and what was not fascinated me, and I spent lots of time asking people, becoming a general annoyance....I invented an imaginary friend named Mary who was real enough for me to insist that my parents set a place for her at the table. Mary was a free spirit. She talked me into drawing a snail on the living room wall, larger and larger, so that the room had to be repainted. She invited me to run away on a hot summer day to find a white horse. She lured me to the lake, unsupervised, to feed the ducks. My parents tolerated Mary with good humor, though I'm sure it was trying. Mary was ever present. 'Don't sit there,' I'd cry with alarm. 'Mary's there!' One of my early memories is of my father, negotiating with Mary for the couch after dinner. Then I went one step further. I invented Mary's mother, a freewheeling, permissive woman who, in my words, 'wanted Mary to be creative on the wall.' "

ROBERT NEWTON PECK......"didn't start out to write for any particular age group. If my books turn out to be right for teenagers, as well as adults and/or kids, it just happens that way. I can only write about what I know and I've never been shy about telling people what I know. As a matter of fact, when I told my mother, who is eighty-two, that three of my books were about to be published by a very important publishing house, she thought for a minute, looked up at me and said, 'Son, you always did have a lot to say.' " A "stubborn Vermonter who wears mule-ear boots, a ten-gallon hat" and what he likes to think of as "a country-boy grin," Peck acquired most of his wisdom from "a mother, a father, an aunt and a grandmother...none of whom could read or write....My grandmother, when I was a tadpole, led me to a pine. Reaching upward, she pulled a normal clump of five needles in order to place it upon the five fingers of my small hand. Grandmother pointed to the tree, then to me, so I would forever know that we are brothers....My three morning rules are these: Up at 6:00, breakfast at 6:15, and at 6:30...back to bed. But come to think about it, my life has been mostly work. I was a mite too busy for hopes, prayers, or dreams. So here's my personal [motto:] Wish not for apples. Grow strong trees."

KATHLEEN PEYTON......started her first book at age nine, "written in longhand, of course, and...called, I remember, 'Gray Star, the Story of a Race Horse.' It was in the first person. *I* was the race horse. After that I always had a book going....As soon as I finished one, I started another." Though often frustrated by the interruptions of daily life, Peyton has learned to work among the chaos. "I think now that if I only had a book to write, and nothing else to do, I would just sit and stare into space. To know that on Tuesday, for instance, Fred will call for coffee and chat at half-past ten, the butcher will interrupt at eleven fifteen and want to know what I shall want next Friday, and that I've got to get to the nearest shop, three miles away, to buy a loaf before it shuts at one, concentrates the mind wonderfully. My mother needs to talk to me at length twice a week at least, a pony needs shoeing (five miles there and five miles back and an hour in the middle), and in the summer the garden and the field are a full-time job (mine). It is no good at all pleading my vocation, for my only local claim to fame is not in writing but as secretary of the Pony Club...."

These are only a few of the authors and illustrators that you'll find in this volume. We hope you find all the entries in *SATA* both interesting and useful.

Yesterday's Authors of Books for Children

In a two-volume companion set to *SATA, Yesterday's Authors of Books for Children (YABC)* focuses on early authors and illustrators, from the beginnings of children's literature through 1960, whose books are still being read by children today. Here you will find "old favorites" like Hans Christian Andersen, J. M. Barrie, Kenneth Grahame, Betty MacDonald, A. A. Milne, Beatrix Potter, Samuel Clemens, Kate Greenaway, Rudyard Kipling, Robert Louis Stevenson, and many more.

Similar in format to *SATA, YABC* features bio-bibliographical entries that are divided into information categories such as Personal, Career, Writings, and Sidelights. The entries are further enhanced by book illustrations, author photos, movie stills, and many rare old photographs.

In Volume 2 you will find cumulative indexes to the authors and to the illustrations that appear in *YABC*. These listings can also be located in the *SATA* cumulative indexes.

By exploring both volumes of *YABC,* you will discover a special group of more than seventy authors and illustrators who represent some of the best in children's literature—individuals whose timeless works continue to delight children and adults of all ages. Other authors and illustrators from early children's literature are listed in *SATA,* starting with Volume 15.

Something about the Author Autobiography Series

You can complement the information in *SATA* with the *Something about the Author Autobiography Series (SAAS),* which provides autobiographical essays written by important current authors and illustrators of books for children and young adults. In every volume of *SAAS* you will find about twenty specially commissioned autobiographies, each accompanied by a selection of personal photographs supplied by the authors. The wide range of contemporary writers and artists who describe their lives and interests in the *Autobiography Series* includes Joan Aiken, Betsy Byars, Leonard Everett Fisher, Milton Meltzer, Maia Wojciechowska, and Jane Yolen, among others. Though the information presented in the autobiographies is as varied and unique as the authors, you can learn about the people and events that influenced these writers' early lives, how they began their careers, what problems they faced in becoming established in their professions, what prompted them to write or illustrate particular books, what they now find most challenging or rewarding in their lives, and what advice they may have for young people interested in following in their footsteps, among many other subjects.

Autobiographies included in the *SATA Autobiography Series* can be located through both the *SATA* cumulative index and the *SAAS* cumulative index, which lists not only the authors' names but also the subjects mentioned in their essays, such as titles of works and geographical and personal names.

The *SATA Autobiography Series* gives you the opportunity to view "close up" some of the fascinating people who are included in the *SATA* parent series. The combined *SATA* series makes available to you an unequaled range of comprehensive and in-depth information about the authors and illustrators of young people's literature.

Please write and tell us if we can make *SATA* even more helpful to you.

Acknowledgments

Grateful acknowledgment is made to the following publishers, authors, and artists for their kind permission to reproduce copyrighted material.

THE AMARYLLIS PRESS. Photographs by Hugo van Lawick from *Last Days in Eden* by Elspeth Huxley. Text copyright © 1984 by Elspeth Huxley. Photographs copyright © 1984 by Hugo van Lawick. Both reprinted by permission of The Amaryllis Press.

AMERICAN LIBRARY ASSOCIATION. Sidelight excerpts from *British Children's Authors* by Cornelia Jones and Olivia R. Way. Copyright © 1976 by American Library Association. Reprinted by permission of American Library Association.

ATHENEUM PUBLISHERS. Illustration by Angela Barrett from *The Dragon Wore Pink* by Christopher Hope. Text copyright © 1985 by Christopher Hope. Illustrations copyright © 1985 by Angela Barrett./ Illustration by Nina Winters from *Carrot Holes and Frisbee Trees* by N. M. Bodecker. Text copyright © 1983 by N. M. Bodecker. Illustrations copyright © 1983 by Nina Winters. Both reprinted by permission of Atheneum Publishers.

THE ATLANTIC MONTHLY PRESS. Illustration by Sarah Garland from *Going Shopping* by Sarah Garland. Copyright © 1982 by Sarah Garland. Reprinted by permission of The Atlantic Monthly Press.

BANTAM BOOKS, INC. Cover illustration from *The Big Sky* by A. B. Guthrie, Jr. Copyright 1947 by A. B. Guthrie, Jr. Cover illustration copyright © 1982 by Bantam Books, Inc./ Cover illustration by Max Ginsburg from *The Friends* by Rosa Guy. Text copyright © 1973 by Rosa Guy. Cover illustration copyright © 1983 by Max Ginsburg./ Sidelight excerpts from Preface to *Children of Longing* by Rosa Guy. All reprinted by permission of Bantam Books, Inc.

THE BOBBS-MERRILL COMPANY, INC. Illustration by Carol Nicklaus from *Raggedy Ann and Andy and How Raggedy Ann Was Born* by Stephanie Spinner. Copyright © 1982 by The Bobbs-Merrill Co., Inc. Reprinted by permission of The Bobbs-Merrill Company, Inc.

BRADBURY PRESS. Illustration by DyAnne DiSalvo-Ryan from *Saturday Belongs to Sara* by Cathy Warren. Text copyright © 1988 by Cathy Warren. Illustrations copyright © 1988 by DyAnne DiSalvo-Ryan. Reprinted by permission of Bradbury Press.

CAROL PUBLISHING GROUP. Cover design by Tim Gaydos from *The Virginian: A Horseman of the Plains* by Owen Wister. Copyright © 1984 by Citadel Press. Reprinted by permission of Carol Publishing Group.

T. Y. CROWELL, INC. Illustrations by John Stadler from *Words with Wrinkled Knees: Animal Poems* by Barbara Juster Esbensen. Text copyright © 1986 by Barbara Juster Esbensen. Illustrations copyright © 1986 by John Stadler. Reprinted by permission of T. Y. Crowell, Inc.

DELACORTE PRESS. Jacket illustration by Robert Chronister from *The Ups and Downs of Carl Davis III* by Rosa Guy. Text copyright © 1989 by Rosa Guy. Jacket illustration copyright © 1989 by Robert Chronister./ Jacket illustration by Stuart Kaufman and jacket design by Donna Jaseckas from *And I Heard a Bird Sing* by Rosa Guy. Text copyright © 1987 by Rosa Guy. Jacket illustration copyright © 1987 by Stuart Kaufman. Jacket design copyright © 1987 by Donna Jaseckas./ Jacket illustration by Chuck Gillies and jacket design by Lynn Andreozzi from *A Box of Nothing* by Peter Dickinson. Text copyright © 1985 by Peter Dickinson. Jacket illustration copyright © 1988 by Chuck Gillies./ Illustrations by Alan Lee from *Merlin Dreams* by Peter Dickinson. Text copyright © 1988 by Peter Dickinson. Illustrations copyright © 1988 by Alan Lee./ Jacket illustration by Leo and Diane Dillon from *Heartsease* by Peter Dickinson. Text copyright © 1969, 1986 by Peter Dickinson. Jacket illustration copyright © 1986 by Leo Dillon and Diane Dillon./ Jacket illustration from *Evergreen* by Belva Plain. Copyright © 1978 by Belva Plain./ Jacket illustration by Craig Nelson from *Eden Burning* by Belva Plain. Copyright © 1982 by Bar-Nan Creations, Inc. Jacket illustration copyright © 1982 by Craig Nelson. All reprinted by permission of Delacorte Press.

DELL PUBLISHING CO., INC. Cover illustration by Boris Vallejo from *The Girl Who Owned a City* by O. T. Nelson. Copyright © 1975 by Lerner Publications Co./ Illustration by Ted Lewin from *Soup for President* by Robert Newton Peck. Text copyright © 1978 by Robert Newton Peck. Illustrations copyright © 1978 by Alfred A. Knopf, Inc./ Cover illustration from *A Day No Pigs Would Die* by Robert Newton Peck. Copyright © 1972 by Robert Newton Peck./ Illustration by Pamela Johnson from *Trig Sees Red* by Robert Newton Peck. Copyright © 1978 by Robert Newton Peck./ Illustration by Charles Robinson from *Soup's Drum* by Robert Newton Peck. Text copyright © 1980 by Robert Newton Peck. Illustrations copyright © 1980 by Alfred A. Knopf, Inc./ Illustration by Charles C. Gehm from *Soup* by Robert Newton Peck. Copyright © 1974 by Robert Newton Peck./ Cover illustration from *The Devil's Children* by Peter Dickinson. Copyright © 1970, 1986 by Peter Dickinson./ Jacket illustration by Gehm from *The Disappearance* by Rosa Guy. Copyright © 1979 by Rosa Guy./ Cover illustration from *New Guys around the Block* by Rosa Guy. Copyright © 1983 by Rosa Guy./ Jacket illustration by Conway from *Paris, Pee Wee, and Big Dog* by Rosa Guy. Text copyright © 1984 by Rosa Guy. All reprinted by permission of Dell Publishing Co., Inc.

J. M. DENT & SONS LTD. Illustration by C. F. Tunnicliffe from *Letters from Skokholm* by Ronald M. Lockley. Reprinted by permission of J. M. Dent & Sons Ltd.

DE VORSS & CO. Illustration by David Stevens from *Making Music* by Eloise Franco. Copyright © 1976 by Eloise and Johan Franco. Reprinted by permission of De Vorss & Co.

DOUBLEDAY & CO., INC. Illustration by M. M. Kaye from *The Ordinary Princess* by M. M. Kaye. Copyright © 1980, 1984 by M. M. Kaye. Reprinted by permission of Doubleday & Co., Inc.

E. P. DUTTON, INC. Illustration by Penrod Scofield from *Isaac Bashevis Singer: The Story of a Storyteller* by Paul Kresh. Text copyright © 1984 by Paul Kresh. Illustrations copyright © 1984 by Penrod Scofield. Reprinted by permission of E. P. Dutton, Inc.

FABER & FABER LTD. Illustration by Gareth Floyd from *Gabrielle* by Kenneth Lillington. Text copyright © 1988 by Kenneth Lillington. Illustrations copyright © 1988 by Faber & Faber Ltd./ Frontispiece illustration by C. F. Tunnicliffe from *Salar the Salmon* by Henry Williamson. Both reprinted by permission of Faber & Faber Ltd.

FARRAR, STRAUS & GIROUX, INC. Illustration by Satoshi Kitamura from *When Sheep Cannot Sleep: The Counting Book* by Satoshi Kitamura. Copyright © 1986 by Satoshi Kitamura./ Jacket illustration by William Low from *Golden Girl* by Nancy Tilly. Text copyright © 1985 by Nancy Tilly. Jacket illustration copyright © 1985 by William Low. Both reprinted by permission of Farrar, Straus & Giroux, Inc.

VICTOR GOLLANCZ LTD. Sidelight excerpts by Ian Niall from *Portrait of a Country Artist: C. F. Tunnicliffe, R. A., 1901-1979*. Reprinted by permission of Victor Gollancz Ltd.

G. K. HALL & CO. Sidelight excerpts from *Presenting Rosa Guy* by Jerrie Norris. Copyright © 1988 by Twayne Publishers. Reprinted by permission of G. K. Hall & Co.

HARCOURT BRACE JOVANOVICH, INC. Jacket illustration by Paul Bacon from *Susanna of the Alamo: A True Story* by John Jakes. Text copyright © 1986 by John Jakes. Illustrations copyright © 1986 by Paul Bacon./ Jacket design by Paul Bacon from *North and South* by John Jakes. Copyright © 1982 by John Jakes./ Illustration by Richard Jesse Watson from *Tom Thumb*, retold by Richard Jesse Watson. Copyright © 1989 by Richard Jesse Watson./ Illustration by Richard Jesse Watson from *Bronwen, the Traw, and the Shape-Shifter* by James Dickey. Text copyright © 1986 by James Dickey. Illustrations copyright © 1986 by Richard Jesse Watson. All reprinted by permission of Harcourt Brace Jovanovich, Inc.

HARPER & ROW, PUBLISHERS, INC. Illustration by Emily Arnold McCully from *Joseph on the Subway Trains* by Kathleen Benson. Text copyright © 1981 by Kathleen Benson. Illustrations copyright © 1981 by Emily Arnold McCully./ Illustration by Wayne Anderson and design by Julie Harris and Steve Ridgeway from *The Flight of Dragons* by Peter Dickinson. Text copyright © 1979 by Peter Dickinson. Illustrations copyright © 1979 by Wayne Anderson./ Illustration by Lloyd Bloom from *Arthur, for the Very First Time* by Patricia MacLachlan. Text copyright © 1980 by Patricia MacLachlan. Illustrations © 1980 by Lloyd Bloom./ Jacket illustration by Arieh Zeldich from *Cassie Binegar* by Patricia MacLachlan. Text copyright © 1982 by Patricia MacLachlan. Jacket illustration copyright © 1982 by Arieh

Zeldich./ Illustration by Deborah Ray from *Through Grandpa's Eyes* by Patricia MacLachlan. Text copyright © 1979 by Patricia MacLachlan. Illustrations copyright © 1980 by Ray Studios, Inc./ Jacket illustration by Marcia Sewall from *Sarah, Plain and Tall* by Patricia MacLachlan. Copyright © 1985 by Patricia MacLachlan./ Illustration by Maria Pia Marrella from *Seven Kisses in a Row* by Patricia MacLachlan. Text copyright © 1983 by Patricia MacLachlan. Illustrations copyright © 1983 by Maria Pia Marrella./ Illustration by Kathy Jacobi from *Tomorrow's Wizard* by Patricia MacLachlan. Text copyright © 1982 by Patricia MacLachlan. Illustrations copyright © 1982 by Kathy Jacobi./ Jacket illustration by Ruth Sanderson from *The Facts and Fictions of Minna Pratt* by Patricia MacLachlan. Text copyright © 1988 by Patricia MacLachlan. Jacket illustration copyright © 1988 by Ruth Sanderson./ Jacket illustration by Ruth Sanderson from *Unclaimed Treasures* by Patricia MacLachlan. Text copyright © 1984 by Patricia MacLachlan. Jacket illustration copyright © 1984 by Ruth Sanderson. All reprinted by permission of Harper & Row, Publishers, Inc.

HENRY HOLT & CO., INC. Sidelight excerpts from *A Place for Noah* by Josh Greenfeld. Copyright © 1978 by Josh Greenfeld. Reprinted by permission of Henry Holt & Co., Inc.

THE HORN BOOK, INC. Sidelight excerpts from an article "Newbery Award Acceptance," by Elizabeth George Speare in *Horn Book* magazine, August, 1959, August, 1962./ Sidelight excerpts from an article "Laura Ingalls Wilder Award Acceptance," by Elizabeth George Speare in *Horn Book* magazine, July/August, 1989. Both reprinted by permission of The Horn Book, Inc.

HOUGHTON MIFFLIN CO. Jacket illustration by Arthur Shilstone from *Fair Land, Fair Land* by A. B. Guthrie, Jr. Text copyright © 1982 by A. B. Guthrie, Jr. Jacket illustration copyright © 1982 by Arthur Shilstone./ Jacket illustration by Wendell Minot from *The Last Valley* by A. B. Guthrie, Jr. Copyright © 1975 by A. B. Guthrie, Jr. Jacket illustration copyright © 1975 by Wendell Minot./ Jacket illustration from *The Witch of Blackbird Pond* by Elizabeth George Speare. Copyright © 1958 by Elizabeth George Speare./ Cover illustration from *The Bronze Bow* by Elizabeth George Speare. Copyright © 1961 by Elizabeth George Speare./ Illustrations by W. T. Mars from *Calico Captive* by Elizabeth George Speare. Copyright © 1957 by Elizabeth George Speare./ Jacket illustration by Marlies Najaka from *Ike and Poker* by Susan E. Kirby. Text copyright © 1983 by Susan E. Kirby. Jacket illustrations copyright © 1983 by Marlies Najaka. All reprinted by permission of Houghton Mifflin Co.

KESTREL BOOKS. Sidelight excerpts from "On Not Writing a Proper Book," in *The Thorny Paradise,* edited by Edward Blishen. Reprinted by permission of Kestrel Books.

ALFRED A. KNOPF, INC. Jacket illustration from *Millie's Boy* by Robert Newton Peck. Copyright © 1973 by Robert Newton Peck. Reprinted by permission of Alfred A. Knopf, Inc.

J. B. LIPPINCOTT CO. Sidelight excerpts from *A Sounding for Storytellers: New and Revised Essays on Contemporary Writers for Children* by John Rowe Townsend./ Sidelight excerpts from *A Sense of Story* by John Rowe Townsend./ Jacket illustration by John Quirk from *Good-bye, Glamour Girl* by Erika Tamar. Text copyright © 1984 by Erika Tamar. Jacket illustration copyright © 1984 by John Quirk and Harper & Row, Publishers, Inc. All reprinted by permission of J. B. Lippincott Co.

LITTLE, BROWN & CO., INC. Illustration by Adrienne Kennaway from *Hot Hippo* by Mwenye Hadithi. Copyright © 1986 by Bruce Hobson and Adrienne Kennaway./ Sidelight excerpts from "Superintendent Pibble," in *The Great Detectives* by Peter Dickinson. Edited by Otto Penzler./ Line drawing by Victor Ambrus and David Smee from *Chance, Luck, and Destiny* by Peter Dickinson. Copyright © 1976 by Peter Dickinson. All reprinted by permission of Little, Brown & Co., Inc.

MACMILLAN PUBLISHING CO. Illustration by Gareth Floyd from *Up the Pier* by Helen Cresswell. Copyright © 1971 by Helen Cresswell./ Illustration by Gareth Floyd from *The Night Watchman* by Helen Cresswell. Copyright © 1969 by Helen Cresswell./ Jacket illustration by Linda Benson from *Listen for Rachel* by Lou Kassem. Text copyright © 1986 by Lou Kassem. Jacket illustration copyright © 1986 by Linda Benson./ Jacket illustration by Steven Kuzma from *Witchery Hill* by Welwyn Wilton Katz. Text copyright © 1984 by Welwyn Wilton Katz. Jacket illustration copyright © 1984 by Steven Kuzma./ Jacket illustration from *The Cage* by Ruth Minsky Sender. Copyright © 1986 by Ruth Minsky Sender and Macmillan Publishing Co./ Illustration from *Roosevelt: The Story of a Friendship* by Owen Wister. Copyright 1930 by The Macmillan Company. All reprinted by permission of Macmillan Publishing Co.

NORTHLAND PRESS. Jacket illustration by David Jenny from *Big Sky, Fair Land: The Environmental Essays of A. B. Guthrie, Jr.* Commentary copyright © 1988 by David Petersen. Essays copyright © 1988 by A. B. Guthrie, Jr. Reprinted by permission of Northland Press.

W. W. NORTON & CO., INC. Sidelight excerpts from *A Nation of Sheep* by William Lederer./ Sidelight excerpts from Preface to *The Deceptive American* by William Lederer./ Sidelight excerpts from *Our Own Worst Enemy* by William Lederer./ Cover design by The Stimbans from *The Ugly American* by William J. Lederer and Eugene Burdick. Copyright © 1958 by William J. Lederer and Eugene Burdick./ Jacket illustration by Alan Haemer from *The Ugly American* by William J. Lederer and Eugene Burdick. Copyright © 1958 by William J. Lederer and Eugene Burdick. All reprinted by permission of W. W. Norton & Co., Inc.

ODDO PUBLISHING, INC. Illustration by Ian Hastings from *Rufus and Christopher and the Box of Laughter* by Ian Hastings. Copyright © 1972 by Oddo Publishing, Inc. Reprinted by permission of Oddo Publishing, Inc.

OXFORD UNIVERSITY PRESS, INC. Jacket illustration by Joy Barling from *Who, Sir? Me, Sir?* by K. M. Peyton. Copyright © 1983 by K. M. Peyton./ Illustration by Gareth Floyd from *Steam on the Line* by Philip Turner. Text copyright © 1968 by Philip Turner. Illustrations copyright © 1968 by Gareth Floyd./ Illustration by Victor G. Ambrus from *The Maplin Bird* by K. M. Peyton. Copyright © 1965 by K. M. Peyton./ Cover illustration by Tony Morris from *Pennington's Seventeenth Summer* by K. M. Peyton. Copyright © 1970 by K. M. Peyton./ Cover illustration by Robert Barrett from *The Edge of the Cloud* by K. M. Peyton. Text copyright © 1969 by K. M. Peyton. Cover illustration copyright © 1989 by Robert Barrett. All reprinted by permission of Oxford University Press, Inc.

PADDINGTON PRESS. Sidelight excerpts from *The Pied Pipers* by Justin Wintle and Emma Fisher. Reprinted by permission of Paddington Press.

PENGUIN BOOKS. Illustration by Victor G. Ambrus from *Flambards* by K. M. Peyton. Copyright © 1967 by K. M. Peyton./ Illustration by Victor G. Ambrus from *Flambards in Summer* by K. M. Peyton. Text copyright © 1969 by K. M. Peyton. Illustrations copyright © 1969 by Victor G. Ambrus./ Cover illustration by Richard Mantel/ Push Pin and cover design by Neil Stuart from *The Flame Trees of Thika* by Elspeth Huxley. Copyright © 1959 by Elspeth Huxley./ Cover illustration by Christoper Brown from *My Days: A Memoir* by R. K. Narayan. Copyright © 1973, 1974 by R. K. Narayan./ Cover illustration by Subrata Chowdhury and Sidelight excerpts from *A Writer's Nightmare: Selected Essays 1958-1988* by R. K. Narayan. Copyright © 1956, 1974, 1987 by R. K. Narayan./ Cover illustration by Christopher Brown from *A Tiger for Malgudi* by R. K. Narayan. Copyright © 1982, 1983 by R. K. Narayan./ Cover illustration by Christopher Brown from *Under the Banyan Tree* by R. K. Narayan. Copyright © 1985 by R. K. Narayan./ Cover illustration by Christopher Brown from *Talkative Man* by R. K. Narayan. Copyright © 1986 by R. K. Narayan./ Sidelight excerpts from *My Days* by R. K. Narayan./ Sidelight excerpts from Introduction to *Malgudi Days* by R. K. Narayan./ Sidelight excerpts from Introduction to *Under the Banyan Tree and Other Stories* by R. K. Narayan. All reprinted by permission of Penguin Books.

CLARKSON N. POTTER, INC. Jacket illustration by Dayal Kaur Khalsa and jacket design by Carl Barile and Sidelight excerpts from *Tales of a Gambling Grandma* by Dayal Kaur Khalsa. Copyright © 1986 by Dayal Kaur Khalsa./ Illustration by Helen Craig from *Alexander and the Dragon* by Katharine Holabird. Text copyright © 1988 by Katharine Holabird. Illustrations copyright © 1988 by Helen Craig./ Illustration by Helen Craig from *Angelina and the Princess* by Katharine Holabird. Text copyright © 1984 by Katharine Holabird. Illustrations copyright © 1984 by Helen Craig./ Illustration by Helen Craig from *Angelina's Birthday* by Katharine Holabird. Text copyright © 1989 by Katharine Holabird. Illustrations copyright © 1989 by Helen Craig./ Illustration by Helen Craig from *Angelina Ballerina* by Katharine Holabird. Text copyright © 1983 by Katharine Holabird. Illustrations copyright © 1983 by Helen Craig. All reprinted by permission of Clarkson N. Potter, Inc.

THE PUTNAM PUBLISHING GROUP, INC. Sidelight excerpts from "A Memoir," in *Popular Tales from the Norse* by George Webbe Dasent./ Illustration by Gillian Barlow from *East o' the Sun and West o' the Moon: An Old Norse Tale,* translated by Sir George Webbe Dasent. Copyright © 1988 by Gillian Barlow./ Illustration by Tomie de Paola from *The Cat on the Dovrefell: A Christmas Tale,* translated from the Norse by Sir George Webbe Dasent. Illustration copyright © 1979 by Tomie de Paola. All reprinted by permission of The Putnam Publishing Group, Inc.

RANDOM HOUSE, INC. Illustration by Charles Walker from *Life in Colonial America* by Elizabeth George Speare. Copyright © 1963 by Random House, Inc. Reprinted by permission of Random House, Inc.

ST. MARTIN'S PRESS, INC. Jacket illustration by Peter Goodfellow from *The Far Pavilions* by M. M. Kaye. Copyright © 1978 by M. M. Kaye./ Sidelight excerpts from *Death in Zanzibar* by M. M. Kaye. Both reprinted by permission of St. Martin's Press, Inc.

SIMON & SCHUSTER, INC. Illustration from *The War on Terrorism* by Michael Kronenwetter. Copyright © 1989 by The Westport Publishing Group./ Cover design by Push Pin Studios from *Mornings on Horseback* by David McCullough. Copyright © 1981 by David McCullough./ Photograph by Betsy Imershein from *Animal Doctor* by Betsy Imershein. Copyright © 1988 by Betsy Imershein. All reprinted by permission of Simon & Schuster, Inc.

STUDIO. Sidelight excerpts from *My Country Book* by C. F. Tunnicliffe. Reprinted by permission of Studio.

THOR PUBLISHING CO. Sidelight excerpts from *Self-Defense: A Basic Course* by Bruce Tegner. Copyright © 1979 by Bruce Tegner, Alice McGrath and Thor Publishing Co./ Sidelight excerpts and illustration from *Karate: Beginner to Black Belt* by Bruce Tegner. Copyright © 1982 by Bruce Tegner. Copyright © 1982, 1986 by Alice McGrath./ Illustration from *Aikido and Bokata* by Bruce Tegner. Copyright © 1983 by Bruce Tegner. Copyright © 1983, 1986 by Alice McGrath. All reprinted by permission of Thor Publishing Co.

UNIVERSITY OF CHICAGO PRESS. Sidelight excerpts from *Owen Wister Out West: His Journals and Letters* by Fanny Kemble Wister. Reprinted by permission of University of Chicago Press.

UNIVERSITY OF WYOMING. Photograph from American Heritage Center from *Owen Wister: Chronicler of the West, Gentleman of the East* by Darwin Payne. Copyright © 1985 by Darwin Payne. Reprinted by permission of University of Wyoming.

WALKER & CO. Illustration by William Sauts Bock from *Growing Up Indian* by Evelyn Wolfson. Text copyright © 1986 by Evelyn Wolfson. Illustrations copyright © 1986 by William Sauts Bock. Reprinted by permission of Walker & Co.

FRANKLIN WATTS, INC. Illustration by Anne Canevari Green from *Latchkey Kid* by Irene Cumming Kleeberg. Copyright © 1985 by Irene Cumming Kleeberg. Illustrations copyright © 1985 by Anne Canevari Green. Reprinted by permission of Franklin Watts, Inc.

Sidelight excerpts from an article "All about Caring," by Rosa Guy in *Top of the News,* Winter, 1983. Reprinted by permission of American Library Association./ Sidelight excerpts from an audio tape of a speech "Children's Writing Today for Tomorrow's Adults," by Rosa Guy in *Boston Globe,* November 4, 1984. Reprinted by permission of *Boston Globe.*/ Sidelight excerpts from an article "Fantasy: The Need for Realism," by Peter Dickinson in *Children's Literature in Education,* spring, 1986. Reprinted by permission of *Children's Literature in Education.*/ Sidelight excerpts from an article "John Jakes," by Robert Dahlin in *Publishers Weekly,* March 30, 1984. Copyright by Robert Dahlin. Reprinted by permission of Robert Dahlin./ Sidelight excerpts from *Out of Africa* by Karen Blixen. Reprinted by permission of The Folio Society./ Sidelight excerpts from an article in *The Village Voice* by Joe Levy. Reprinted by permission of Josh Greenfeld./ Sidelight excerpts from *Gallipot Eyes: A Wiltshire Diary* by Elspeth Huxley. Reprinted by permission of Elspeth Huxley./ Sidelight excerpts from *Spare-Time Article Writing for Money* by William Lederer. Reprinted by permission of William Lederer.

Sidelight excerpts from an article "Salute to Deeds of Non-Ugly Americans," by William Lederer and Eugene Burdick in *Life* magazine, December 7, 1959. Reprinted by permission of *Life* magazine./ Sidelight excerpts from an article "Making Crime Pay," by Caroline Moorehead in *London Times,* May 21, 1983. Reprinted by permission of *London Times.*/ Sidelight excerpts from an article "Facts and Fictions," by Patricia MacLachlan in *Horn Book* magazine, January/February, 1986. Reprinted by permission of Patricia MacLachlan./ Sidelight excerpts from an article "Corking Plotter," by Catherine Stott in *Manchester Guardian,* February 8, 1971. Reprinted by permission of *Manchester Guardian.*/ Illustration by Carol Nicklaus from *Harry the Hider* by Carol Nicklaus. Copyright © 1979 by Carol

Nicklaus. Reprinted by permission of The National Sobel Association./ Sidelight excerpts from an article "Behind the Bestsellers: M. M. Kaye," by Herbert Mitgang in *The New York Times Biographical Service.* Copyright © 1978 by The New York Times Co. Reprinted by permission of *The New York Times Biographical Service.*/ Sidelight excerpts from an article "Write, Research, Then Rewrite," by Eden Ross Lipson in *New York Times Book Review,* April 20, 1986. Reprinted by permission of The New York Times Co./ Sidelight excerpts from an article "A Valentine to Love," by Belva Plain in *Woman's Day,* February 16, 1988. Copyright © 1987, 1988 by Bar-Nan Creations, Inc. Reprinted by permission of Harold Ober Associates, Inc.

Sidelight excerpts from an article "The Fifties," by Belva Plain in *Woman's Day,* November 27, 1987. Copyright © 1987, 1988 by Bar-Nan Creations, Inc. Reprinted by permission of Harold Ober Associates, Inc./ Illustration by Gareth Floyd from *Flight to the Forest* by Barbara Willard. Copyright © 1967 by Barbara Willard. Reprinted by permission of Harold Ober Associates, Inc./ Sidelight excerpts from an article "John Jakes Has a Writing Fever," by Kirk Polking in *Writer's Digest,* January, 1977. Reprinted by permission of Kirk Polking./ Sidelight excerpts from an article "The B-B-B-Best Friend I Ever Had in the Navy," by William Lederer in *Reader's Digest,* December, 1957. Copyright © 1957 by Reader's Digest Association, Inc. Reprinted by permission of Reader's Digest Association, Inc./ Sidelight excerpts from an article "A Dramatic Sense of Age...A Sudden Sniff of Death," by Josh Greenfeld in *Today's Health,* March, 1973. Reprinted by permission of *Today's Health.*/ Photograph by Sean Hagerty from *Portrait of a Country Artist* by Ian Niall. Text copyright © 1980 by Ian Niall. Illustrations copyright © 1980 by The Tunnicliffe Trustees. Reprinted by permission of The Tunnicliffe Trustees.

Wood engraving by C. F. Tunnicliffe from *Portrait of a Country Artist* by Ian Niall. Text copyright © 1980 by Ian Niall. Illustrations copyright © 1980 by The Tunnicliffe Trustees. Reprinted by permission of The Tunnicliffe Trustees./ Photograph from *Portrait of a Country Artist* by Ian Niall. Text copyright © 1980 by Ian Niall. Illustrations copyright © 1980 by The Tunnicliffe Trustees. Reprinted by permission of The Tunnicliffe Trustees./ Sidelight excerpts from an article by Joe Levy in *The Village Voice,* July 28, 1975. Reprinted by permission of *The Village Voice.*/ Sidelight excerpts from an article "To Be a Writer: What Does It Take?" by John Jakes in *The Writer,* January, 1987. Reprinted by permission of *The Writer.*/ Sidelight excerpts from "Fiction Is Folks," by Robert Newton Peck in *Writer's Digest,* 1983. Reprinted by permission of *Writer's Digest.*

PHOTOGRAPH CREDITS

Phil Berger: Arlene Schulman; Charles Bohner: Copyright © 1985 by Kate Bohner; Barbara Cass-Beggs: Schiffer Photography Ltd.; Peter Dickinson: Jerry Bauer; Josh Greenfeld: Takashi Kato; Rosa Guy: Copyright © by Fern Logan; Jacqueline L. Harris: R. Martin; Katharine Holabird: Barbara Hayes; John Jakes: Copyright © by Bud Dunn; John Jakes with Paul Bacon: Zavell's Inc.; Welwyn Wilton Katz: Victor Aziz Photography Ltd.; William J. Lederer: Rosmarie Hausherr; Patricia MacLachlan: Judith Nulty; David McCullough: Copyright © 1982 by Alison Shaw; R. K. Narayan: Rajendra P. Battarai; Van Dyke Parks: Carl Studna; Kathleen Peyton: Copyright © by *Evening Echo*; Belva Plain: Copyright © by Francesco Scavullo; Robert Somerlott: Michael Snyder; George Steiner: Copyright © 1983 by Belsey; Erika Tamar: Ray Sapirstein; Nancy Tilly: Copyright © by John Rosenthal; Cathy Warren: Jim McGuire; Richard Jesse Watson: Sue Watson; Evelyn Wolfson: Copyright © 1989 by J and B Photo.

SOMETHING ABOUT THE AUTHOR

BALDWIN, Stan(ley C.) 1929-

PERSONAL: Born December 17, 1929, in Bend, Ore.; son of Leonard Rite (a cowboy) and Irma Mae (a homemaker; maiden name, Brown) Baldwin; married Marjorie Antoinette Iverson (a retailer), December 17, 1948; children: Kathleen (Mrs. Morton Holland), Krystal (Mrs. Arthur W. Brown), Steven, Karen (Mrs. David Kraus), Gregory Laverne Todd. *Education:* Attended Powellhurst College, 1947-48, Prairie Bible Institute, 1949-52, University of North Dakota, 1954, and Oregon State University, 1962. *Politics:* Independent. *Religion:* Interdenominational. *Home:* Milwaukee, Ore. *Office:* P.O. Box 101, Oregon City, Ore. 97045.

CAREER: Pastor of Calvary Community Church in Albany, Ore., 1955-62, of Baptist churches in Corvallis, Ore., 1962-65, and Burns, Ore., 1965-69, and of Village Church in Carol Stream, Ill., 1970-75; Scripture Press, Wheaton, Ill., editor of Victor Books and consulting editor for *Power for Living,* 1970-75; free-lance writer and lecturer, 1975—. *Member:* Oregon Association of Christian Writers (president, 1965-66, 1976-78, 1988—).

WRITINGS:

Will the Real Good Guys Please Stand?, Victor Books, 1971.
Games Satan Plays, Victor Books, 1971.
(With wife, Marjorie Baldwin) *Tough Questions Boys Ask,* Victor Books, 1972.
(With M. Baldwin) *Tough Questions Girls Ask,* Victor Books, 1972.
(With James D. Mallory) *The Kink and I,* Victor Books, 1973.
(With Hank Aaron and Jerry Jenkins) *Bad Henry: An Authorized Hank Aaron Story,* Chilton, 1974.
What Did Jesus Say about That?, Victor Books, 1975.
What Makes You So Special?, Baker Book, 1977.

(With Malcolm MacGregor) *Your Money Matters,* Bethany Fellowship, 1977.
(With Jerry Cook) *Love, Acceptance and Forgiveness,* Regal Books, 1979.
A True View of You, Regal Books, 1982, new edition published as *If I'm Created in God's Image, Why Does It Hurt to Look in the Mirror? A True View of You,* Aglow Publications, 1989.
How to Build Your Christian Character, Victor Books, 1982.
Bruised but Not Broken, Multnomah, 1985.
When Death Means Life, Multnomah, 1986.
The Overflowing Life, Revell, 1987.
Take This Job and Love It, Inter-Varsity, 1988.
(With J. Cook) *A Few Things I've Learned Since I Knew It All,* Word, 1989.

Contributor of articles and stories to periodicals, including *Christianity Today, Eternity, Moody Monthly,* and *Guideposts.*

WORK IN PROGRESS: A book entitled *Why Smart People Do Dumb Things.*

SIDELIGHTS: "I write as a ministry: to influence people, teach them, communicate truth to them. I suppose I'm nothing but a preacher at heart, only I've found a bigger pulpit—the printed page.

"It was an awesome experience for me, early in my career, to attend a Billy Graham crusade in Chicago and see 25,000 people gathered to hear the evangelist. I realized then that almost everything I wrote reaches an audience that large and maybe ten times larger.

1

STAN BALDWIN

"So I must write, I suspect, for the same reason Graham must preach. It's the most effective use I can make of my talents, and represents an opportunity I cannot neglect. How else could I reach such multitudes, including people who read only German, Spanish, French, Japanese, Indonesian, or half a dozen other languages into which at least some of my works have been translated?

"As a co-author, I am able also to provide an important service by teaming with people who have something vitally important to say but lack the skill or time to say it in writing. The large success of my books of this type has brought many people to seek my services as a co-author. I try to limit my involvement to those people with whom I feel a strong kinship.

"I find writing hard work. I'm an active person, and it's difficult to sit inside at a typewriter when the whole world beckons outside. Often I spend the earliest hours of my day writing and then give in to the call of other things. But I keep at the writing relentlessly, slow as the progress seems, because I know something worhwhile will eventually emerge.

"I have taught at writer's seminars and conferences all across the United States. In 1989 I organized and led the first Christian writer's conference in Nigeria, West Africa. Out of this has come the Christian Writers Association of Nigeria with chapters in five cities. This summer I will conduct both secular and Christian writing seminars in Bombay, India."

HOBBIES AND OTHER INTERESTS: Sports, fishing, property development, automobile mechanics, home and yard work, boating, water skiing, travel (has visited Mexico, Israel, Asia, Africa, and Europe).

BARTHELME, Donald 1931-1989

OBITUARY NOTICE—See sketch in *SATA* Volume 7: Born April 7, 1931, in Philadelphia, Pa.; died of cancer, July 23, 1989, in Houston, Tex. Museum director, educator, illustrator, journalist, editor, and author. Barthelme was a prizewinning writer best known for his minimalist short stories and novels. He turned to writing in the mid-1960s after stints as a newspaper reporter, art review editor, and museum director, and in the ensuing years earned great acclaim for his spare, quirky fiction. Barthelme became a member of the American Academy and Institute of Arts and Letters, taught at the City College of the City University of New York in the mid-1970s, and returned in the early 1980s to Houston, where he was Cullen Professor of English at the University of Houston. His self-illustrated book for children, *The Slightly Irregular Fire Engine; or, The Hithering Thithering Djinn,* received the National Book Award and was included on the Children's Book Showcase, both in 1972.

Among Barthelme's adult writings are the short-story collections *City Life,* which *Time* named a Best Book for 1971, and *Sixty Stories,* which was nominated in 1982 for both a National Book Critics Circle Award and PEN's William Faulkner Award, and the novels *Snow White, The Dead Father,* and *Paradise.* Barthelme was a regular contributor to *New Yorker, Atlantic Monthly* and *Paris Review.*

FOR MORE INFORMATION SEE:

Current Biography 1976, H. W. Wilson, 1977.
Contemporary Authors New Revision Series, Volume 20, Gale, 1987.
Who's Who in America 1988-1989, 45th edition, Marquis, 1988.
Stephen H. Gale, editor, *Encyclopedia of American Humorists,* Garland, 1988.

OBITUARIES

New York Times, July 24, 1989.
Detroit Free Press, July 25, 1989.
Times (London), July 25, 1989.
Washington Post, July 25, 1989.
Los Angeles Times, July 25, 1989.
Chicago Tribune, July 26, 1989.
Time, August 7, 1989 (p. 44).
School Library Journal, September, 1989 (p. 154).

BENSON, Kathleen 1947-

PERSONAL: Born February 10, 1947, in Keene, N.H.; daughter of Roland F. (a technical representative) and Margaret (a bookkeeper; maiden name, Bliss) Benson. *Education:* University of Connecticut, B.A., 1969. *Residence and office:* New York, N.Y.

CAREER: Museum of the City of New York, New York, N.Y., associate head of education, 1969—. Member of board of directors, Children's Book Review Service.

Member: Phi Beta Kappa, Phi Kappa Phi, Mortar Board. *Awards, honors:* Deems Taylor Award from the American Society of Composers, Authors, and Publishers, 1979, and selected one of New York Public Library's Books for the Teen Age, 1980, both for *Scott Joplin: The Man Who Made Ragtime; The Sixties Reader* was selected one of the Best Books for Young Adults by the *Journal of Youth Services in Libraries,* 1989.

WRITINGS:

(With Jim Haskins and Ellen Inkelis) *The Great American Crazies,* Condor, 1977.
(With J. Haskins) *Scott Joplin: The Man Who Made Ragtime,* Doubleday, 1978.
(With J. Haskins) *The Stevie Wonder Scrapbook,* Grosset, 1978.
A Man Called Martin Luther, Concordia, 1980.
Joseph on the Subway Trains (illustrated by Emily Arnold McCully), Addison-Wesley, 1981.
(With J. Haskins) *Lena: A Personal and Professional Biography of Lena Horne,* Stein & Day, 1983.
(With J. Haskins) *Nat King Cole: An Intimate Biography,* Stein & Day, 1984.
(With J. Haskins) *Space Challenger: The Story of Guion Bluford,* Carolrhoda, 1984.
(With J. Haskins) *The Sixties Reader,* Viking, 1988.

Contributor of articles to *Now* and of crossword puzzles to newspapers.

Joseph watched her out of the corner of his eye. (From *Joseph and the Subway Trains* by Kathleen Benson. Illustrated by Emily Arnold McCully.)

WORK IN PROGRESS: A history of Black Americans for young people.

SIDELIGHTS: "Research fascinates me. Nothing is more exciting than making a discovery about which no one else knows; for example, identifying Scott Joplin's German music professor or mentor. My advice to aspiring writers is to read as much really good writing as possible and always to keep trying."

FOR MORE INFORMATION SEE:

Washington Post, July 24, 1978.

BERGER, Phil 1942-

PERSONAL: Born April 1, 1942, in Brooklyn, N.Y.; son of of Jack (a grocer) and Fanny (Finkelstein) Berger; married Leslie Brooks (an actress). *Education:* Johns Hopkins University, B.A. (cum laude), 1964. *Residence:* New York, N.Y.

CAREER: Greenwich Time (newspaper), Greenwich, Conn., reporter, summers, 1963-64; Associated Press, Atlanta, Ga., newsman, 1964; *Sport* (magazine), New York, N.Y., associate editor, 1966-67; free-lance writer, 1966-85; *New York Times,* New York, N.Y., reporter, 1986—. *Military service:* U.S. Army Reserve, 1967-71, active duty, 1965-66. *Awards, honors:* Annual Charlies Comedy Award for Best Book on the Field of Stand-up Comedy from the Association of Comedy Artists, 1987, for *The Last Laugh.*

WRITINGS:

Championship Teams of the NFL, Random House, 1968.
Heroes of Pro Basketball, Random House, 1968.
Great Moments in Pro Football, Messner, 1969.
Joe Namath: Maverick Quarterback, Cowles, 1969.
Miracle on Thirty-Third Street: The New York Knickerbockers' Championship Season, Simon & Schuster, 1970.
Great Running Backs in Pro Football, Messner, 1970.
More Championship Teams of the NFL, Random House, 1974.
The Last Laugh: The World of the Standup Comics, Morrow, 1975.
(With Larry Borstein) *The Boys of Indy,* Corwin, 1977.
Where Are They Now?: Yesterday's Sports Heroes Today, Popular Library, 1978.
The State-of-the-Art Robot Catalog, Dodd, 1984.
Deadly Kisses (mystery), Charter Books, 1984.
Blood Season: Tyson and the World of Boxing, Morrow, 1989.
Big Time (novel), Taylor, 1990.

Contributor of more than three hundred stories and articles to periodicals, including *New York, National Observer, Playboy, Penthouse, New York Times Magazine, Cavalier, Look, Worlds of Tomorrow, Sport, Pageant, Parade, Johns Hopkins, Village Voice* and *New York Post.*

HOBBIES AND OTHER INTERESTS: Reading, basketball, distance running, New York City.

FOR MORE INFORMATION SEE:

New York Times, October 22, 1970.

PHIL BERGER

New York Post, February 8, 1971.
San Francisco Chronicle, April 9, 1975.

BIAL, Morrison David 1917-

PERSONAL: Surname is pronounced "Beal"; born August 29, 1917, in New York, N.Y.; son of Jacob (a diamond setter) and Carrie (Dash) Bial; married Dorothy Berman, November 6, 1954; children: Daniel, Anne Rachel. *Education:* Brooklyn College (now of the City University of New York), B.A., 1941; Jewish Institute of Religion, Rabbi, 1945, M.H.L., 1946. *Religion:* Jewish. *Home:* 1812 S.E. 38th Court, Ocala, Fla. 32671.

CAREER: Rabbi, Temple Emanuel, Lynbrook, N.Y., 1944-46, Beth Shalom Temple, Brooklyn, N.Y., 1946-50, Free Synagogue, Mt. Vernon, N.Y., 1950-52, Temple Sinai, Summit, N.J., 1953-85, Temple Beth Shalom, Ocala, Fla., 1985—. Instructor at Hebrew Union College, beginning 1956. *Awards, honors:* D.D. from Jewish Institute of Religion, 1970.

WRITINGS:

The Passover Story, Behrman, 1951.
The Hanukkah Story (juvenile), Behrman, 1952.
An Offering of Prayer, Temple Sinai (Summit, N.J.), 1962.
(With Solomon Simon) *The Rabbis' Bible,* Behrman, Volume I, 1966, Volume II, 1969.

In 1943 a very large transport of Jews was being sent from France to concentration camps. (Illustration by David Stone Martin from *The Holocaust: A History of Courage and Resistance* by Bea Stadtler. Edited by Morrison David Bial.)

Liberal Judaism at Home: The Practices of Modern Judaism, Temple Sinai, 1967, revised edition, Union of American Hebrew Congregations, 1971.
Questions You Asked, Behrman, 1972.
(Editor) Bea Stadtler, *The Holocaust: A History of Courage and Resistance* (illustrated by David S. Martin), Behrman, 1974.
Your Jewish Child, Union of American Hebrew Congregations, 1978.

POEMS FOR CANTATAS; ALL BY A. W. BINDER

Israel Reborn, Bloch Publishing, 1949.
Hanukkah of the Maccabees, Transcontinental, 1950.
Passover into Freedom, Transcontinental, 1951.

Contributor of articles and reviews to magazines.

BLANK, Clarissa Mabel 1915-1965 (Clair Blank)

PERSONAL: Born August 5, 1915, in Allentown, Pa.; died August 15, 1965, in Philadelphia, Pa.; daughter of Edgar H. (a loom fixer) and Bessie Blank; married George E. Moyer, 1943; children: John, Robert. *Education:* Attended Pierce Business College.

CLAIR BLANK

CAREER: Author. Keystone Pipeline, Philadelphia, Pa., typist and secretary, until 1946.

WRITINGS:

UNDER NAME CLAIR BLANK; "BEVERLY GRAY COLLEGE MYSTERY" SERIES

Beverly Gray, Freshman, Burt, 1934.
Beverly Gray, Sophomore, Burt, 1934.
Beverly Gray, Junior, Burt, 1934.
Beverly Gray, Senior, Burt, 1934.
Beverly Gray's Career, Burt, 1935.
Beverly Gray at the World's Fair, Burt, 1935.
Beverly Gray on a World Cruise, Burt, 1936.
Beverly Gray in the Orient, Burt, 1937.
Beverly Gray on a Treasure Hunt, Grosset, 1938.
Beverly Gray's Return, Grosset, 1939.
Beverly Gray, Reporter, Grosset, 1940.
Beverly Gray's Romance, Grosset, 1941.
Beverly Gray's Quest, Grosset, 1942.
Beverly Gray's Problem, Grosset, 1943.
Beverly Gray's Adventure, Grosset, 1944.
Beverly Gray's Challenge, Grosset, 1945.
Beverly Gray's Journey, Grosset, 1946.
Beverly Gray's Assignment, Grosset, 1947.
Beverly Gray's Mystery, Grosset, 1948.
Beverly Gray's Vacation, Grosset, 1949.
Beverly Gray's Fortune, Grosset, 1950.
Beverly Gray's Secret, Grosset, 1951.

Beverly Gray's Island Mystery, Grosset, 1952.
Beverly Gray's Discovery, Grosset, 1953.
Beverly Gray's Scoop, Grosset, 1954.
Beverly Gray's Surprise, Grosset, 1955.

UNDER NAME CLAIR BLANK; "ADVENTURE GIRLS" SERIES

The Adventure Girls at K Bar O, Burt, 1936.
The Adventure Girls at Happiness House, Burt, 1936.
The Adventure Girls in the Air, Burt, 1936.

OTHER

Lover Come Back, Gramercy, 1940.

Contributor to magazines.

SIDELIGHTS: Despite authoring the successful "Beverly Gray Mystery" series, which by 1955 amounted to twenty-six volumes, Clair Blank faded into almost total obscurity after her death in 1965.

Blank was born in Allentown, Pennsylvania on August 5, 1915 and moved, at the age of ten, with her family to Philadelphia. Blank's father had been a loom fixer for a silk mill and later worked for a clothing plant.

The year after her graduation from high school, Blank published the first four books of the "Beverly Gray Mystery" series. Virtually the only documented evidence of her literary existence occurred at this time, in the form of local newspaper clippings such as:

GIRL AUTHOR FORMER ALLENTOWN
SCHOOL GIRL

"A story-writer at nineteen with a record of never having had a manuscript rejected and the author as well of a series of books for girls which has had a large sale is the achievement of Miss Clair Blank, former Allentown schoolgirl.

"The young woman, who is the daughter of Mr. and Mrs. Edgar Blank, resided in this city until eight years ago when the family removed to Philadelphia. She continued her schooling in that city and graduated from the Philadelphia High School with honors.

"Since then she has devoted her time to the writing of juvenile literature. Four books of 50,000 words each are entitled *Beverly Gray, Freshman, Beverly Gray, Sophomore, Beverly Gray, Junior* and *Beverly Gray, Senior.* They have run into large sale, being published by a New York publication house.

"She recently sold a manuscript to a leading magazine and is now working on a new series of books for girls.

"Miss Blank is a niece of Mr. and Mrs. John Gillespie, 426 Chestnut Street."[1]

After the sale of *Beverly Gray, Freshman,* her publisher, A. L. Burt Company, immediately wanted the next three books in the series, and wanted them quickly. Another contributing factor to Blank's obscurity was that she was writing for a publisher who was more concerned with satisfying word-count requirements than literary quality or the promotion of a particular author, as is demonstrated by their letter to her:

"Dear Miss Blank:

"We wish to report that we have had your manuscript entitled *Beverly Gray, Freshman,* read, and our reader reports as follows:

"'A very good story, well told, full of good adventures, with a very good atmosphere all through—but only 41,500 words.'

"As we wrote you under date of November 29th, it is necessary that juvenile manuscripts contain at least *50,000* words.

"If it is agreeable to you to lengthen this manuscript to the required number of words, we would agree to pay you our regular price of One Hundred and Seventy-five Dollars (175.00 dollars) for all rights in same, provided you can also supply us with additional manuscripts of 50,000 words each, for

> *Beverly Gray, Sophomore,* and
> *Beverly Gray, Junior,*

not later than March 1st of this year, and will give us *Beverly Gray, Senior* at a later date, for publication next year, and for which we will pay you 175.00 dollars each for all rights.

"May we hear from you promptly regarding the above? Thanking you, we remain

"Yours very truly,

"A. L. BURT COMPANY."[1]

Nonetheless, Blank thrived under such adverse conditions and met all that was required of her, beginning a second series of books with the publication of *Adventure Girls at the K Bar O.* After receiving the manuscript, her publisher immediately sent her the following: "Regarding your manuscript *The Adventures at the K Bar O,* is it not your intention to write a *series* called the 'Adventure Girls?' If so, how soon could we have two additional stories to add to the present one you have submitted, and how soon could you send us a synopsis of the books? .... If we decide on this series, would you not consider 150 dollars for each story? This price is what we are now paying for juvenile new books. Our plans would be to bring this out as early as possible.

"Also, don't you think it advisable if we go ahead with a new series, to use your same pen name, CLAIR BLANK? There are many authors who, when writing a different series, would rather write under a nom de plume, but as we have met with such success with your 'Beverly Gray' series, we think this might help in a new series."[1]

During this time, Blank attended Pierce Business College which led to a job as typist at the Keystone Pipeline, a subsidiary of the Atlantic Refinery Company. With the start of World War II, Blank joined AWVS, a group of volunteer women who drove on-leave Army officers. It was during this time that Blank met George Moyer, her future husband. They married in 1943.

In 1946 Blank quit her job to devote more time to her family. She had a son in 1947 and one in 1953. Friends remembered her as fun-loving and sociable; she often enjoyed weekend excursions to New York and summers with family members in Wildwood, New Jersey.

Blank died on August 15, 1965, in Philadelphia at the age of fifty.

FOOTNOTE SOURCES:

[1]Anita Susan Grossman, "The Mystery of Clair Blank," *Yellowback Library,* January, 1989.

BOHNER, Charles (Henry) 1927-

PERSONAL: Born November 23, 1927, in Wilmington, Del.; son of Charles H. (a clergyman) and Frances Gilmore (a businesswoman; maiden name, Ramsey) Bohner; married Jean Astolfi, 1961 (divorced, 1988); children: Christine Ramsey, Charles Russell, Catherine Russell. *Education:* Syracuse University, B.A., 1950; University of Pennsylvania, M.A., 1952, Ph.D., 1957. *Home:* 61 Kells Ave., Newark, Del. 19711. *Agent:* Ann Elmo, Ann Elmo Agency, Inc., 60 East 42nd St., New York, N.Y. 10165. *Office:* Department of English, University of Delaware, Newark, Del. 19711.

CAREER: Syracuse University, Syracuse, N.Y., instructor in English, 1952-54; University of Delaware, Newark, Del., instructor, 1955-58, assistant professor, 1958-62, director of American Studies Program, 1958-68, associate professor, 1962-66, professor of English, 1966—, chairman of department, 1969-76. *Military service:* U.S. Army, 1946-47. *Member:* Modern Language Association of America, College English Association, American Studies Association of the Middle Atlantic States. *Awards, honors:* U.S. State Department Grant for Lecturing in Germany, Yugoslavia, Ireland, Finland, and Norway, 1965; Notable Children's Trade Book in the Field of Social Studies from the National Council for Social Studies and the Children's Book Council, 1985, and one of Child Study Association of America's Children's Books of the Year, 1986, both for *Bold Journey.*

WRITINGS:

John Pendleton Kennedy: Gentleman from Baltimore, Johns Hopkins Press, 1961.
Robert Penn Warren, Twayne, 1964, revised edition, 1981.
Bold Journey: West with Lewis and Clark, Houghton, 1985.
Classic Short Fiction, Prentice-Hall, 1985, 2nd edition, 1989.

CHARLES BOHNER

Contributor of articles and reviews to literature journals.

BONHAM, Frank 1914-1989

OBITUARY NOTICE—See sketch in *SATA* Volume 49: Born February 25, 1914, in Los Angeles, Calif.; died 1989. Author. Bonham never held a job due to chronic asthma. He wrote primarily Western novels for adults for twenty years before turning exclusively to children's literature. His works for children were often aimed at minorities. *Durango Street* was an ALA Notable Book in 1965 and won the George C. Stone Award for its depiction of life in the Watts Ghetto of Los Angeles. *The Nitty Gritty* and *Mystery of the Fat Cat,* which was an Edgar Allan Poe runnerup in 1969, also dealt with delinquency and ghetto problems. Other Edgar Allan Poe runnerups were *Honor Bound* (1963) and *Mystery of the Red Tide* (1966). *Gimmee an H, Gimmee an E, Gimmee an L, Gimmee a P* explored the problems of teenage suicide. In 1980 Bonham received the Southern California Council on Literature for Children and Young Adults Award for his body of work.

In addition to novels and short stories, Bonham wrote screenplays for the television programs "Wells Fargo," "Restless Guns," "Shotgun Slade," and "Death Valley Days."

FOR MORE INFORMATION SEE:

Lee Bennett Hopkins, *More Books by More People,* Citation, 1974.
D. L. Kirkpatrick, *Twentieth-Century Children's Writers,* St. Martin's, 1978, 2nd edition, 1983.
Contemporary Authors New Revision Series, Volume 4, Gale, 1981.
Authors and Artist for Young Adults, Volume 1, Gale, 1989.

OBITUARIES

School Library Journal, April, 1989 (p. 24).

BOUR, Daniele 1939-

PERSONAL: Born August 16, 1939, in Chaumont, France; daughter of Fernand (a shopkeeper) and Marguerite (a shopkeeper; maiden name, Pabst) Gustin; married Louis Bour (a publicist), July 11, 1960; children: Laura, Celine, Martin. *Education:* Ecole des Beaux Arts de Nancy, C.A.F.A.S., 1961. *Religion:* Catholic. *Home and Office:* Place du Village, Vandelainville 54890, Onville, France.

CAREER: Illustrator of children's books and maker of rag dolls. *Awards, honors:* Aiglon d'Or (Young Golden Eagle Award) from the Festival of Nice, 1973, for *Au fil des jours;* Medaille de Bronze de Leipzig, 1974, and Hans Christian Andersen Award from the International Board on Books for Young People, both for *Un Hiver dans la vie de gros ours.*

WRITINGS:

Au fil des jours (title means 'Day after Day'), Grasset, 1972.
My Family and Me, A. & C. Black, 1974.
La Maison du matin au soir (self-illustrated), Editions du Centurion, 1978, published as *The House from Morning to Night,* Kane/Miller, 1985.

DANIELE BOUR

ILLUSTRATOR

J. Brisville, *Un hiver dans la vie de gros ours,* Grasset, 1973, published as *Big Bear,* translated by Anita Mondello, Prentice-Hall, 1977.
Jean-Claude Brisville, *The Bear and the Nobody Boy,* English text by Peggy Blakeley, A. & C. Black, 1975.
Nicole Russell Bedford, *Le joyeux fantome,* Grasset, published as *The Joyful Ghost,* W. H. Allen, 1977.
Jean Joubert, *Le voyage a Poudrenville: Conte-Poeme* (title means "The Trip to Powderville"), J. P. DeLarge (Paris), 1977.
J. Brisville, *Oleg le leopard des neiges,* Grasset, published as *Oleg, the Snow Leopard,* translated by Anthea Bell, Gollancz, 1978.
Jacques Chessex, *La petite fille et le chat sauvage,* Grasset, published as *Mary and the Wild Cat,* Gollancz, 1980.
J. Brisville, *Oleg retrouve son royaume,* Grasset, published as *King Oleg,* Gollancz, 1982.
Laurence Ottenheimer, *Le livre de l'hiver,* Gallimard, published as *Winter,* adapted and edited by Alex Campbell, Methuen, 1984.

"LITTLE BROWN BEAR" SERIES; ALL BY CLAUDE LEBRUN

Petit Ours Brun dit non, Pomme d'Api Bayard, 1979, published as *Little Brown Bear Says No,* Barrons, 1982.
Petit Ours Brun est malade, Pomme d'Api Bayard, 1979, published as *Little Brown Bear Is Ill,* Barrons, 1982.
Petit Ours Brun se Lave, Pomme d'Api Bayard, 1979, published as *Little Brown Bear Takes a Bath,* Barrons, 1982.
Petit Ours Brun s'habille, Pomme d'Api Bayard, 1979, published as *Little Brown Bear Gets Dressed,* Barrons, 1982.
Petit Ours Brun se reville, Pomme d'Api Bayard, 1982, published as *Little Brown Bear Wakes Up,* Barrons, 1982.
Little Brown Bear Is Cross, Methuen, 1982.
Little Brown Bear Won't Eat!, Methuen, 1982.

Little Brown Bear's Story, Methuen, 1982.
Little Brown Bear's Tricycle, Methuen, 1982.
Little Brown Bear's Walk, Methuen, 1982.
Little Brown Bear's Cold, Methuen, 1982.
Little Brown Bear's Playtime, Methuen, 1983.
Little Brown Bear's Snowball, Methuen, 1983.
Little Brown Bear Can Cook, Methuen, 1983.
Little Brown Bear Is Big!, Methuen, 1983.
Little Brown Bear's Bad Day, Methuen, 1983.
Little Brown Bear's Breakfast Egg, Methuen, 1983.

Also illustrator of *Le renard qui disait non a la lune* (title means "The Fox Who Said No to the Moon") Grasset; *Boucle d'or et les trois ours* (title means "Goldilocks and the Three Bears"), Delarge; *La poule a trouve un clairon* (title means "The Hen Found a Bugle"), Gallimard; *Pierrot ou les secrets de la nuit* (title means "Pierrot; or, The Secrets of the Night"), Gallimard; *Adele Lapinou,* Editions de l'Amitie; *La cave* (title means "The Cellar"), J. P. DeLarge; *Le lait pour tout les petits* (title means "Milk for All the Little Ones"), Gallimard; *Les contes de Perrault* (title means "Perrault's Fairytales"), Grasset; *A loisir* (title means "At Leisure"), Hachette Classiques; *Les contes d'Andersen* (title means "Andersen's Fairytales"), Grasset; *Noel poesies comptines* (title means "Christmas"), Gallimard; *Noeuf l'oeuf* (title means "The Egg"), Grasset. Also illustrator of book covers for the "Folio Junior" books, Gallimard.

WORK IN PROGRESS: Lesanimaux sous la terre (title means "Animals Underground"), for Gallimard; *Les fables de la Fontaine* (title means "Lafontaine's Fables"), for Grasset.

SIDELIGHTS: "I live with my husband and our three children in a small village of a hundred and fifty inhabitants. My husband works as a publicist in Metz, a larger town near our village, my eldest daughter Laura is also an illustrator. Celine goes to the Arts Decorations School in Strasbourg, and Martin is an apprentice publicist with his father. Outside of illustrating children's books, I take care of the house and the garden. I also bake my own bread. We have two horses, a cat, a dog, and some chickens. We all like nature very much, and we all like the Canadian painter Robert Bateman."

HOBBIES AND OTHER INTERESTS: Gardening, baking, animals, nature.

BROWNLEE, Walter D. 1930-

PERSONAL: Born September 9, 1930, in Hartlepool, England; son of Mark (an engineer) and Elizabeth Jane (a housewife; maiden name, Boagey) Brownlee; married Joyce Cynthia Harrison (a teacher), July 30, 1960; children: Neville. *Education:* South Shields Nautical College, Second Officer's Certificate, 1952, Chief Officer's Certificate, 1955, Master Mariner, 1958; Sunderland College of Education, Teaching Certificate, 1961. *Home:* 23 Valley Gardens, Eaglescliffe, Cleveland TS16 OLY, England.

CAREER: Served in British Merchantile Marine, 1948-58; became master mariner. Teacher at various primary schools in North of England, 1961-66; Thornaby Church of England Primary School, Cleveland, England, deputy headmaster, 1964-66; Ragworth Primary School, Stockton, Cleveland, headmaster, 1969-74; Stockton Teachers' Center, Cleveland, principal, 1974-81; *Warrior* Preservation Trust, Hartlepool, Cleveland, ships' historian, 1979-81, historian, 1981-87; Hartlepool Ship Restoration Co. Ltd., Hartlepool, ships' historian, 1987—. *C.S.S. Alabama* Project, Birkenhead, Wirral, England, advisor.

WRITINGS:

The White Dove (novel), Evans Brothers, 1966, Houghton, 1968.
The First Ships Round the World, Cambridge University Press, 1974, Lerner, 1977.
The Navy That Beat Napoleon, Cambridge University Press, 1980, Lerner, 1982.
Warrior: The First Modern Battleship, Cambridge University Press, 1985.

Brownlee's books have been translated into Dutch and Spanish. Contributor to periodicals, including *Scientific American* and *Teachers World.*

SIDELIGHTS: "The most interesting phase of my career came when old hulk *H.M.S. Warrior,* the 1860 iron clad battleship, arrived in Hartlepool for restoration. I was seconded from the education service to serve as historian on the world's largest historical ship restoration. The task brought together all my experience as a sea captain, educationalist, archaeologist, and historian. I left the education service to take on the task full time in 1981. I met the Duke of Edinburgh three times and he kindly wrote a forward for the book I wrote on the *Warrior.*

"When *Warrior* left for her permanent berth in Portsmouth, the Preservation Trust was reformed into a company that offered to make replicas of any ancient vessel from Roman grain ships to clipper ships. At the moment two eighteenth-century sailing ships are nearing completion for a new dockland complex near Tower Bridge in London. Other projects are under discussion, though my own personal dream would be to rebuild the whole Confederate Navy from the Civil War period. The recent heavy workload in historical research for these ships has left me little time for writing.

"All my books have been aimed at presenting in a palatable form the results of historical research to first the younger generation and secondly to the public in general.

"*The White Dove* was written for a class of ten-year-old children and I recreated the area in which they lived as it would have been in the time of the Norman conquest. I also used it as a means of 'de-romanticizing' the outlaw or 'Robin Hood' myth.

"The other books are simply trying to present an accurate perception of naval history using my experience at sea and as an historian. My motivation comes from my discovery that seamen rarely write about the sea and ships, whereas historians write a great deal, but, not being seamen, they often get it wrong.

"I do not believe I am a natural writer. It takes me a long time to develop a theme for a book and then even longer to write, and rewrite, then rewrite again. By the time the editor starts making suggested alterations, I have lost interest, mainly because the whole writing process has taken about two years, at least.

WALTER D. BROWNLEE

"Like many before me, I aim to settle down to do more writing when I retire. I also know this may mean I may never manage to produce another book—but at least I will try."

Brownlee has held an International Glider Pilots "A" License since 1948.

HOBBIES AND OTHER INTERESTS: Photography, archaeology, historical research, war games.

CASS-BEGGS, Barbara 1904-

PERSONAL: Born November 10, 1904, in Nottingham, England; daughter of Bingley (a clergyman) and Eva (a musician; maiden name, Marks) Cass; married David Norman Beggs, December 17, 1932 (died, 1986); children: Rosemary Cass-Beggs Burstall, Ruth Cass-Beggs Smith, Mi-

chael. *Education:* Royal College of Music, London, graduate, L.R.A.M., A.R.C.M., G.R.S.M., 1930. *Politics:* Labour. *Religion:* Unitarian. *Home:* The Little Studio, 8 Chenier, Hull, Quebec, Canada J8X 1E5.

CAREER: Student Christian Movement Choir All Hallows, London, England, music director, 1929-38; Harrow County Day School, Harrow, Middlesex, England, music teacher, 1929-32; Victory Air Craft, Malton, England, in personnel, 1943-45; University Settlement Music School, Toronto, Ontario, Canada, director, 1945-52; Regina Conservatory of Music, Regina, Saskatchewan, Canada, music teacher, 1955; Algonquin Community College, Ottawa, Ontario, teacher of music, 1967; Douglas Community College, Vancouver, British Columbia, music lecturer, 1973; Heritage College, Hull, Quebec, teacher of music, 1987—. Has conducted song and lecture recitals in London, Oxford, and Toronto, and private music classes for young children and for mothers and babies.

Lecturer and organizes workshops and conferences related to music and the young child. Founder, Saskatchewan Junior Concert Society. Member of Planned Parenthood, Ottawa.

MEMBER: Canadian Listen Like Learn Music Association (founder and director), Canadian Folk Music Society (board member; honorary life member), International Society for Music Education, Canadian Authors Association. *Awards, honors:* Children's Service Award from the Association for Early Childhood Education of Ontario, 1982; Planned Parenthood Award, 1988; Community Health Clinic Regina Award, 1989.

WRITINGS:

(With Edith Fowke) *A Reference List of Canadian Folk Songs,* Canadian Folk Music Society, 1958, revised edition, 1973.

Eight Saskatchewan Folk Songs, Canadian Music Sales, 1963.

A Christmas Festival Pageant, Waterloo Music, 1964.

Seven Metis Songs, Berandol Music, 1967.

(With son, Michael Cass-Beggs) *Folk Lullabies,* Oak Publishing, 1969.

To Listen, To Like, To Learn (illustrated by Susan Fothergill and with photographs by Ian Wilson), Peter Martin, 1975.

(Selector) *Canadian Folk Songs for the Young* (illustrated by John Robertson), J. J. Douglas, 1975.

Your Baby Needs Music, Douglas & MacIntyre, 1978, 2nd edition, Addison-Wesley, 1990.

BARBARA CASS-BEGGS

Folk Carols for Young Children, Ward Lock Educational, 1980.

A Music Calendar of Festivals: Folk Songs of Feast-Days and Holidays from around the World, Ward Lock Educational, 1983.

Your Baby's Day, Tumblehome Books, 1987.

Your Child Needs Music, Frederick Harris, 1987.

Contributor of articles to periodicals, including *World's Children, Canadian Camping, Community Courier, Parents Co-operative Preschool International, British Columbia Music Educator, Journal of the Association for the Care of Children's Health, Preschool Music Association, British Journal of Music Therapy, Canadian Music Educator Journal, Ontario Music Educator,* and *Royal College of Music.*

ADAPTATIONS:

"Saskatchewan Folk Songs" (record), Folkways Records, 1963.

"Your Baby Needs Music" (cassette), Cass-Beggs Productions, 1980.

"Listen Like Learn" (videocassette), Peter Martin Associates, 1986.

WORK IN PROGRESS: An autobiography.

SIDELIGHTS: "I always enjoyed English literature as a subject and became interested in young children when I began to teach in Sunday school at the age of eleven.

"After high school I studied to work with children of nursery school age. I took the first part of the Archbishop's diploma which qualified me for Sunday school work. (My father and head mistress of my high school encouraged this interest.) When my godmother gave me enough money to finance my college education I at once applied to the Royal College of Music. My real desire always was to be a musician—a singer, and later, a teacher with special interest in the young child.

"I needed to earn my living so I had to teach, as solo singing did not pay well enough. In any case I found that I enjoyed teaching students and children more than I enjoyed performing.

"I only wrote books when I could not find a book which suited my purpose. One needs to research one's subject and I think I spent more time on research for the "Baby" books and *A Music Calendar of Festivals* than any of the others. I wrote my memoirs because when my husband died I wanted to re-think our lives together.

"Putting our names together signified our equalized view of marriage. We were both concerned with the upbringing of our children, encouraging them to make participation in the arts part of their life and to become informed about such topics as sex, politics, and religion.

"My advice to young people is to consider what you can *contribute* to the world—not what you expect to *get*. To do as far as possible what you *enjoy* doing. (You will do it much better and contribute more than if you do a job you dislike or do not think worthwhile.) Money is useful but enough to 'live on' is enough, to collect *more* than you need is unnecessary and makes for a wasteful life. People and your relationship with them plus the enjoyment of nature, the arts, and the many joys which life has to offer, makes for a worthwhile life, and hence, a happy life. *Don't* consider that you have to be a success!

"Through the 'Listen Like Learn,' my teacher training courses; the music conferences I have organized, 'Music for the Young Child' and 'Why the Arts Belong in Music Education'; and papers presented at the International Society for Music Education, I was asked to Vienna, Austria to train teachers and to Jerusalem and Haifa to give classes as well as train teachers. I hope to return to Israel this fall to oversee the publication of my book *Your Baby Needs Music* in Hebrew."

HOBBIES AND OTHER INTERESTS: Reading, travel, gardening, personal living.

CAVALLARO, Ann (Abelson) 1918-
(Ann Abelson)

PERSONAL: Born in 1918, in New Haven, Conn.; daughter of Louis and Berthe (Adler) Abelson; married Alfonso Cavallaro, 1942 (divorced, 1983); children: Leonard. *Education:* Albertus Magnus College, B.A., 1940; Yale University, M.A., 1955. *Home:* 41 Jones Hill Rd., 215, West Haven, Conn. 06516.

CAREER: Connecticut Division of Child Welfare, social worker in adoption and child guidance, 1942-45, 1953-58; West Haven Schools, Conn., guidance director, 1958-81; writer, 1981—. *Member:* American Personnel and Guidance Association, Connecticut Personnel and Guidance Association, PEN. *Awards, honors:* Grant from the National Endowment for the Arts.

WRITINGS:

Angels' Metal, Harcourt, 1947.
The Little Conquerors, Random House, 1960.
The Physician's Associate: A New Career in Health Care (young adult), Elsevier-Nelson, 1978.
Careers in Food Services (young adult), Elsevier-Nelson, 1981.
Blimp (young adult novel), Lodestar, 1983.

Contributor of stories and articles to periodicals and professional journals.

COX, (Christopher) Barry 1931-

PERSONAL: Born July 29, 1931, in London, England; son of Herbert Ernest (a civil servant) and May (a pianist; maiden name, Bell) Cox; married Sheila Morgan (a secretary), April 6, 1961; children: Timothy David, Sally Ann, Justin Daniel. *Education:* Balliol College, Oxford, B.A. (with first class honors), 1953; St. John's College, Cambridge, Ph.D., 1956. *Home:* "Conifers," Grange Rd., Leatherhead, Surrey, England. *Office:* Division of Biosphere Sciences, King's College, Campden Hill Rd., London W8 7AH, England.

CAREER: University of London, King's College, London, England, lecturer, 1956-66, senior lecturer, 1966-69, reader, 1969-76, professor of zoology, 1976—; assistant principal, 1989—. Chairman, Epsom-Ewell Consultative Committee; vice-chairman, Governors of Epsom High School. *Member:* Palaeontological Association (vice-president, 1980-82),

Epsom Protection Society (chairman). *Awards, honors:* Harkness Fellow of Commonwealth Fund, Harvard University, 1959-60; Outstanding Science Book from the National Science Teachers Association, 1976, for *The Prehistoric World;* Fulbright Travel Scholarship to Stanford University, 1988.

WRITINGS:

Prehistoric Animals, Hamlyn, 1969, Bantam, 1971.
(With I. N. Healey and P. D. Moore) *Biogeography: An Ecological and Evolutionary Approach,* Blackwell Scientific Publications, 1973, 4th edition (with P. D. Moore), 1985.
The Prehistoric World, Samson Lowe, 1975, F. Watts, 1976.
Life Long Ago, Macmillan Educational, 1978.
Prehistoric Life, Macmillan, 1978.
Dinosaurs (illustrated by Denys Ovenden), Fontana, 1979, reissued, James Service Ltd., 1985.
Illustrated Encyclopedia of Prehistorical Animals, Macmillan, 1988.
(With D. Attenborough, P. D. Moore, and P. J. Whitfield) *Atlas of the Living World,* Weidenfeld & Nicholson, 1989.

WORK IN PROGRESS: Research on historical biogeography and its relationship to continental drift, and on the structures and evolution of fossil amphibians and reptiles; with P. D. Moore preparing the 5th edition of *Biogeography.*

SIDELIGHTS: "My father's work as a civil servant meant that we moved around Britain several times, and because of the war, I went to seven different schools—not a recipe for happiness! I was also an only child, frequently ill with asthma, and spent long periods in bed. So I read avidly and widely, from archaeology to zoology. I later realized that, in all areas, it was the historic aspect that most intrigued me, from the links between different languages to the history of man's various civilizations or the evolution of living things.

"At school, I was at first a classicist, learning Latin and Greek (as well as French and German), but I was uncertain what to do next (at sixteen). In fact, I only became a scientist because the biology master thought that I had done well at that subject some years earlier and asked for me to be put in his form!

"I soon found biology an enjoyable and easy subject, and went to Oxford University to study zoology, intending to specialize in marine zoology. But my old interest in evolution and fossils was re-kindled by an excellent Oxford lecturer in that subject. He arranged for me to go on to Cambridge University to do a Ph.D. under the supervision of Dr. Rex Parrington, who was then one of Britain's leading vertebrate palaeontologists. Later, I was fortunate in being awarded a Harkness Fund Fellowship to study for a year at Harvard University with Dr. Al Romer, who was a marvellously warm and kind individual as well as being a brilliant palaeontologist, known all over the world.

"My earliest research was on the dicynodonts, a specialized group of herbivores in the mammal-like reptile group (the major group from which mammals evolved). After finding very similar species when collecting in Central Africa and Argentina, I became interested in the relationship between the distributions of fossil vertebrate animals and the changing pattern of geography caused by continental drift. So began my interest in historical biogeography, which gradually extended to a synthesis of the history of animal and plant life on each of the world's continents as they separated and moved across the face of the earth. I have developed this story in the various editions of my student textbook, *Biogeography,* with my botanical colleague, Peter Moore.

"I am interested in, and enjoy, teaching as well as research, and I especially enjoy trying to make students think for themselves. I have never tried to write especially for children, in the sense of writing for immature minds. I don't think there's any real difference between the intellectual abilities of someone of twelve and someone of twenty, except their different levels of factual knowledge. So the challenge is to present the scientific facts and problems in simple language, cutting out the jargon and unnecessary technicalities. And sometimes you end up understanding things better yourself as a result!

"It has been especially interesting to see the varying ways in which, over the last twenty years, different research workers have changed their views on the interpretation of biogeographic patterns from those based on the old stabilist-earth concept to the new moving-continents picture. Not surprisingly, the senior workers, already firmly committed to the older assumptions, often found the most difficulty in this. There's a moral here for us all!

"I have travelled fairly widely, having been on collecting expeditions for fossil vertebrates to Central Africa (Zambia and Tanzania), the Andes of north-west Argentina, northern Brazil, and Australia, as well as having spent two years in the U.S."

HOBBIES AND OTHER INTERESTS: Tennis, archaeology and linguistics of the Middle East.

CURTIS, Philip (Delacourt) 1920-

PERSONAL: Born June 23, 1920, in Westcliff, England; son of Harold (a headmaster) and Pauline (a teacher; maiden name, Saundes) Curtis; married Elsa Schroer; children: John, Elizabeth. *Education:* Attended Eastbourne Training College for Teachers, 1948-49. *Home:* 224 Station Rd., Leigh-on-Sea, Essex SS9 3BS, England.

CAREER: Worked as teacher until 1968, deputy headmaster, 1968-81, and headmaster, 1981—. *Member:* Society of Authors.

WRITINGS:

FOR CHILDREN

Mr. Browser and the Brain Sharpeners (illustrated by Tony Ross), Andersen Press, 1979, published as *Invasion of the Brain Sharpeners,* Knopf, 1981.
Mr. Browser Meets the Burrowers (illustrated by T. Ross), Andersen Press, 1980, published as *Invasion from below the Earth,* Knopf, 1981.
Mr. Browser and the Comet Crisis (illustrated by T. Ross), Andersen Press, 1981.
The Revenge of the Brain Sharpeners (illustrated by T. Ross), Andersen Press, 1982.
Mr. Browser and the Mini-Meteorites (illustrated by T. Ross), Andersen Press, 1983.

Beware of the Brain Sharpeners (illustrated by T. Ross), Andersen Press, 1983.
A Party for Lester (illustrated by Sarah Parker), Andersen Press, 1984.
Mr. Browser in the Space Museum (illustrated by T. Ross), Andersen Press, 1984.
The Quest of the Quidnuncs (illustrated by T. Ross), Andersen Press, 1984.
The Toothless Wonder in the Tower (illustrated by Govinder Ram), Andersen Press, 1986.

Also author of *Bewitched by the Brain Sharpeners,* 1985; *A Gift from Another Fantasy,* 1986; *The Brain Sharpeners Abroad,* 1987; and *Chaos Comes to Chirry Chase,* 1988. *Mr. Browser and the Brain Sharpeners* has been published in Germany, Spain, Japan, Holland, and Denmark. Contributor of short stories, plays, and articles to British magazines.

WORK IN PROGRESS: A collection of stories for children; *The Toothless Wonder and the Double Agent* and *Mr. Browser and the Space Maggots.*

SIDELIGHTS: "My books have arisen, I hope, from a desire, as a teacher, to represent a realistic view of school life, mixed with fantasy and influenced, perhaps, by admiration of various writers of humor. I have traveled in India and Pakistan (which provided background for *The Revenge of the Brain Sharpeners*) and Europe."

PHILIP CURTIS

FOR MORE INFORMATION SEE:

Listener, November 8, 1979.
Observer, March 1, 1981.
Times Educational Supplement, May 22, 1981.
Times Literary Supplement, November 20, 1981.

DANIELS, Guy 1919-1989

OBITUARY NOTICE—See sketch in *SATA* Volume 11: Born May 11, 1919, in Gilmore City, Iowa; died of prostate cancer, February 24, 1989, in Manhattan, N.Y. Educator, civil servant, translator, poet, and novelist. Specializing in the writings of Russian dissidents, Daniels translated more than forty works from French and Russian into English. After holding posts as language instructor with Trans-World Airlines and research analyst with the National Security Agency, he became a full-time writer and translator in 1952. He translated a number of children's books, including *Ivan the Fool and Other Tales of Leo Tolstoy,* Mikhalkov's *Let's Fight and Other Russian Fables,* Chekov's i Wolf and the Mutt, and Colette Portal's *The Beauty of Birth.* In addition to translating *The Complete Plays of Vladimir Mayakovsky,* Daniels translated his tale *Timothy's Horse,* which was selected one of *New York Times* Best Illustrated Children's Books of the Year in 1970. Daniels is also known for his translation of *The Autobiography of Sergei Prokofiev,* his translations of Stendhal's *Racine and Shakespeare,* and Andre Shakharov's *My Country and the World.* Daniels published his own poetry in *Poems and Translations* and wrote a novel, *Progress, U.S.A.*

FOR MORE INFORMATION SEE:

Contemporary Authors, Volume 21-24R, Gale, 1969.
Childhood in Poetry, 1st supplement, Gale, 1972.
Who's Who in the East 1974-1975, 14th edition, Marquis, 1973.
Martha E. Ward and Dorothy A. Marquardt, *Authors of Books for Young People,* supplement to 2nd edition, Scarecrow, 1979.

OBITUARIES

New York Times, March 1, 1989 (p. B-8).
Chicago Tribune, March 5, 1989.

DANN, Max 1955-

PERSONAL: Born July 7, 1955, in Melbourne, Australia; son of Wal (an auto electrician) and Sheila (Simpson) Dann; married Carol Pelham-Thorman (an artist), March 15, 1984. *Education:* Attended schools in Australia. *Office:* c/o Oxford University Press, GPO Box 2784Y, Melbourne, Victoria 3001, Australia.

CAREER: Writer. Has worked as a carpenter's apprentice, handyman, factory worker, and gardener. *Awards, honors:* Winner of *Age* short story competition, 1982, for "Love among the Moccasins"; Junior Book of the Year Medal from the Children's Book Council of Australia, 1984, for *Bernice Knows Best;* Children's Book Council of Australia High Commendation, 1984, for *Going Bananas.*

WRITINGS:

JUVENILE

Adventures with My Worst Best Friend (illustrated by Graeme Base), Oxford University Press, 1982.
Bernice Knows Best (illustrated by Ann James), Oxford University Press, 1983.
Going Bananas (illustrated by Terry Denton), Oxford University Press, 1983.
Ernest Pickle's Remarkable Robot: Featuring Glen's Recipes (illustrated by David Pearson), Oxford University Press, 1984.
One Night at Lotte's House (illustrated by D. Pearson), Oxford University Press, 1985, published as *One Night at Lottie's House,* 1987.
(With Robin Klein) *The Lonely Hearts Club,* Oxford University Press, 1985.
Clark, Penguin, 1987.
Horrible Humans: A Field Guide, Methuen, 1987.
The All-Amazing Ha Ha Book, Oxford University Press, 1987.

ADULT FICTION

The Onion Man, Penguin, 1988.

Work represented in anthologies, including *Australian Short Stories.* Author of television scripts for episodes of "Not Suitable for Adults," and "Fast Lane." Contributor to newspapers.

WORK IN PROGRESS: "Spotswood," a film script; a children's novel.

SIDELIGHTS: "The first important thing to happen to me was that I grew up in the western suburbs of Melbourne. This gave me the basics of life. The second important thing was that I left the western suburbs of Melbourne. Real, lower-class, eccentric people interest me. I write humor because I feel comfortable with it. If I tried to write any other way, it would probably be unbearable.

"I left school when I was fifteen. I found it a lengthy enough disruption to my life without continuing it even further. Some people get a lot out of school. I always felt, and continue to feel, that what I actually learned in school I could have managed in half the time.

"I became interested in writing when I was seventeen, largely because I didn't seem to be able to do anything else. Not that I could write any better, but that was something I only began to realize a few years later.

"Originally all I wanted to write was science fiction. I spent three years in the beginning writing nothing else. It was never publishable, and I doubt if I ever will have anything resembling science fiction published. Whenever I try and write anything dramatic, I always seem to spoil it by inserting a few jokes."

DASENT, George Webbe 1817-1896

PERSONAL: Born May 22, 1817, in St. Vincent, West Indies; died June 11, 1896, in Ascot, Berkshire, England; son of John Roche (an attorney-general) and Charlotte Martha (Irwin) Dasent; married Frances Louisa Delane, April 4, 1846; children: John Roche, George William Manuel, Arthur

She came to a great farm-house, where an old hag of the Trolls lived with her daughter. (Illustration by Theodor Kittelsen from *East o' the Sun and West o' the Moon* by Peter Christen Asbjoernsen and Joergen Moe, compiled by George Webbe Dasent.)

Irwin, Frances Emily Mary. *Education:* Attended King's College; Magdalen Hall, B.A., 1840, M.A., 1843, D.C.L., 1852.

CAREER: British scholar, author, translator, and civil servant. Secretary to British envoy, Stockholm, Sweden, 1840-44; *Times,* London, England, assistant editor, 1845-70; called to the Bar 1852; King's College, London, professor of English literature and modern history, 1853-66; civil service commissioner, 1870-92. Member of Royal Commission on Historical Manuscripts. *Member:* Atheneum Club, Cosmopolitan Club. *Awards, honors:* Knight of the Danish Order of Dannebrog; Knighted, 1876, for his services to literature.

WRITINGS:

(Translator) *The Prose; or, Younger Edda from the Old Norse,* Boho's Antiquarian Library, 1842.

(Translator) *A Grammar of the Icelandic or Old Norse Tongue from the Swedish of Erasmus Rask,* W. Pickering, 1843, new edition, Benjamins (Amsterdam), 1976.

Theophilus in Icelandic, Low German, and Other Tongues from MSS. in the Royal Library, Stockholm, [England], 1845.

Popular Tales from the Norse (Being Translations from the Norske Folkeeventyr of P. C. Asbjoernsen and J. Moe) With an Introductory Essay on the Origin and Diffusion of Popular Tales, Edmonston & Douglas, 1859, Putnam, 1888, [other editions published as *A Selection from the*

Norse Tales for the Use of Children, Edmonston & Douglas, 1861; *Popular Tales from the Norse,* with a memoir by Arthur Irwin Dasent, Putnam, 1904; *The Blue Belt and More Fairy Stories,* J. Birch, 1906; *Tales from the Norse,* Blackie & Son, 1906; *Norse Wonder Tales* (illustrated by Willy Pogany), Collins, 1909; *Norse Fairy Tales,* selected and adapted by F. J. Simmons (illustrated by Reginald L. Knowles and Horace J. Knowles), Lippincott, 1910; *East of the Sun and West of the Moon: Old Tales from the North* (illustrated by Kay Nielsen), Hodder & Stoughton, 1914; *East of the Sun and West of the Moon: Twenty-one Norwegian Folk Tales* (edited and illustrated by Ingri d'Aulaire and Edgar Parin d'Aulaire), Viking, 1969; *Popular Tales from the Norse by Peter Christen Asbjoernsen and Joergen I. Moe* (illustrated by William Stobbs), Bodley Head, 1969; *East o' the Sun and West o' the Moon: Fifty-nine Norwegian Folk Tales from the Collection of Peter Christen Asbjoernsen and Joergen Moe* (illustrated by Theodor Kittelsen, Alf Rolfsen, and others), Dover, 1970; *East o' the Sun, West o' the Moon: An Old Norse Tale* (illustrated by Gillian Barlow), Philomel, 1988].

The Story of Burnt Njal; or, Life in Iceland at the End of the Tenth Century from the Icelandic of the Njals Saga, two volumes, [Edinburgh], 1861, Grant Richards, 1900, reissued, Arden Library, 1979 [other editions published as *Heroes of Iceland,* adapted by Allen French, Little, Brown, 1905; *The Story of Burnt Njal,* Dutton, 1911, reissued, 1931, Biblio Distributors, 1971].

The Story of Gisli the Outlaw from the Icelandic, Lippincott, 1866, another edition published as *Gisli the Outlaw,* retold by A. E. Sims, 1909.

Annals of an Eventful Life (autobiographical novel), three volumes, Hurst & Blackett, 1870, revised fifth edition, 1870.

Three to One; or, Some Passages Out of the Life of Amicia, Lady Sweetapple (novel), three volumes, Chapman & Hall, 1872, published as *Lady Sweetapple; or, Three to One,* Appleton, 1876.

Jest and Earnest: A Collection of Essays and Reviews, two volumes, Chapman & Hall, 1873.

Half a Life (novel), three volumes, Chapman & Hall, 1874.

(Translator) P. C. Asbjoernsen, *Tales from the Fjeld: A Second Series of Popular Tales,* [London], 1874, new edition with a preface by his son, John Roche, 1903, reissued, Ayer, 1969, published as *Tales from the Fjeld* (illustrated by Moyr Smith), Blom, 1970.

(Editor) *Introduction and Life to R. Cleasby's Icelandic English Dictionary,* Clarendon, 1874.

The Vikings of the Baltic: A Tale of the North in the Tenth Century (novel), three volumes, Chapman & Hall, 1875.

(Translator) *Icelandic Sagas and Other Historical Documents on the British Isles,* Volume I: *Orkneyinga Saga and Magnus Saga,* Volume II: *Hakonar Saga with Fragment of Magnus Saga,* Volume III: *Orkneyinger's Saga,* Volume IV: *Saga of Hacon and a Fragment of the Saga of Magnus,* [England], 1887-94, reissued, Kraus Reprint.

(Translator) *Princess of Glass Hill and Other Fairy Stories,* J. Birch, 1905.

Shortshanks, the Giant Killer and Other Fairy Stories, J. Birch, 1905.

A Collection of Popular Tales from the Norse and North German, Norroena Society, 1911.

A. Pitt-Kethley (reteller) *Tales from the Norse,* Routledge & Sons, 1915.

(Translator) *Mother Roundabouts Daughter,* Oxford University Press, 1918.

Children's Holiday Stories (includes selections from Dasent's *Norske Folkeeventyr*), Sphinx, 1921.

Tales of the Norseman [and] *The Saga of Gisli the Outlaw,* Collins, 1928.

E. E. Reynolds, selector, *Fifteen Norse Tales* (illustrated by Doris Paithorpe), T. Nelson, 1931.

Tales from the Norse, T. Nelson, 1933.

Virginia Haviland, editor, *Favorite Fairy Tales Told in Norway,* Bodley Head, 1967.

(Translator) *The Cat on the Dovrefell: A Christmas Tale* (illustrated by Tomie de Paola), Putnam, 1979.

Contributor to *Edinburgh Review, Quarterly Review,* and *Fraser's.*

ADAPTATIONS:

Greysteel; or, The Bearsarks Come to Surnadale (an opera in one act; based on *Gisli the Outlaw*), W. C. Leng, 1906.

SIDELIGHTS: George Webbe Dasent was born on **May 22, 1817,** on the island of St. Vincent in the West Indies. The Dasent family, believed to have been of Norman-French extraction, owned property in the West Indies since the Restoration. "[It] was really a lovely spot, shaded by trees of all kinds ... nutmegs from the Moluccas, bread-fruit from Otaheite, betel-palms from Madras—in fact, all kinds of rare shrubs and trees grew thickly about that ridge. Then there were the trees of the country: cocoanut, palm, tamarind, mango, huge plum-trees, Indian figs, hard woods,

She took her eldest sister, and put her head on her shoulders. (Illustration by Alf Rolfsen from "The Old Dame and Her Hen" in *East o' the Sun and West o' the Moon* by Peter Christen Asbjoernsen and Joergen Moe, compiled by George Webbe Dasent.)

greenheart, locust, and mahogany. Great creepers; all the passion-flowers, from the huge grenadilla down to the tiniest passiflora. Over head, by day, soared the man-of-war bird, a kind of albatross, and lower down flew wild pigeons and ring-doves. The caves of the house were lined with humming-birds' nests, much in the same way as our martin builds at home; and here, too, was the perpetual swallow. If the scene was gay by day, it was more brilliant by night. As soon as the sun fell—and in those islands he literally falls; he does not set or sink; he rushes to his rest in the ocean as though worn out with his hot day's work, and, as Coleridge says:

"'At one step comes the night'—

"then the landscape was lit by countless fire-flies, chiefly of two kinds: the lesser winking and twinkling in their light, starting in fitful radiance from every branch; the larger flying straight through the air with a fixed glare—insect mete-ors—till they rested amid the leaves and veiled their light. To a child who had nothing to think of except objects of sense, [this] was an earthly paradise.

"The people, too, the slaves, were good people. Grown children, black Irishmen,—call them anything you please that expresses cleverness and carelessness. How should it be otherwise? They were well fed, well clothed, and not over-worked. There was a hospital on the estate, and a doctor who lived in it. A church, too.

"English ideas of slavery are unfortunately taken from Cuba and the United States, where it was the interest of owners to work their slaves to death in order to save the expense of supporting them in an old age. But this is to confound the slave-trade with slavery .... It was the interest of no West Indian proprietor to over-work his slaves; on the contrary, he had everything to gain by taking the greatest care of them. To me, who went constantly among them, they seemed as happy as birds. They were always singing, and their Crop Over Festival was a far more heartfelt rejoicing than so many of our mock Harvest Homes. On those occasions every man, woman, and child that could crawl, walk, or creep, came up to the 'great house,' clad in their best—the men in broadcloth and brass buttons,—those who could afford it; the rest in drill or pilot cloth. The women in the gayest cotton prints, their heads tastefully tied with Madras handkerchiefs.

"They marched to an awful music, far exceeding anything that our marrow-bones and cleavers could ever perform. It was a mingling of tom-toms and conches, huge shells which, when properly played by Tritons, may be very melodious, but which, with a negro's breath in them, utter a most unearthly sound. It beats, in fact, any of those German bands which make the squares of the metropolis hideous in the summer months. Those were the male performers; the women had 'shake-shakes,' as they called them, gourds or calabashes, filled with small round red seeds with black eyes. Each of them, like a grain of powder, as Coleridge says of Frenchmen, was contemptible, but five hundred 'shake-shakes' all shaken at once, let me tell you, produced a dry, hoarse sound, something like the crash which Virgil describes as issuing from the Italian hills when the dry boughs and leaves were stirred by the coming storm."[1]

In **1830** Dasent was sent to Westminster School in England. "When I went to Westminster the school was full, and full of boys of good family. There were Byngs, Grosvenors, Pagets, Lennoxes, Pettys—all the old Whig families. There was the grand old Abbey, with its fighting-green, in which there were

"Can this be me now?" said Grizzel. (Illustration by Henrik Soerensen from "Goosey Grizzle" in *East o' the Sun and West o' the Moon* by Peter Christen Asbjoernsen and Joergen Moe, compiled by George Webbe Dasent.)

still, fights. Then, too, there was hockey round the Cloisters—very bad for the monuments of the dead, but very good for the bones of the living.

"It was a custom of the school that between Christmas and Easter subjects were given out each week on which any boy, who chose, might write an epigram, and if he thought it good enough he might run up with it to the headmaster's desk, and read it out aloud. If it were bad he was treated with derision; if it were good the headmaster dipped his hand in a bag and gave him some silver pennies. I got some more than once, and I have them still. They were all the prizes I ever got at Westminster."[1]

While Dasent was at Westminster, his father died. With the emancipation of the slaves sometime later, the West Indian proprietors found it increasingly difficult to live on their estates. "Real rain came with Emancipation. I know it is the fashion to talk of the generosity of England to the West Indian proprietors. Generosity! A highwayman is generous when, after robbing a traveller of a hundred sovereigns, he throws him two or three pieces to take him on to the next

town. Very generous, no doubt to put your hands into the pocket of a man and take out a pound, and then to put half-a-crown into it! That was about what the twenty millions came to. Slavery was, no doubt, a great evil-greater to the proprietors than to any one else; but the way in which it was done away was the first step to that great march of sentimental humbug which has been going on in England ever since. Solid and old-established interests are sacrificed to the sentiment and clamour of a clique, who gratify their sentiment very often at the expense of the class against which the outcry is raised, and fill their own pockets into the bargain.

"But, fair or unfair, there could be no doubt of the consequences to the proprietors.

"The slaves had passed from apprenticeship to complete freedom, for which they were about as fit as children to keep house. In any temperate clime they would have been forced to work for existence, but in the West Indies a man can sit down for a month and supply himself with food by mere tickling the soil with a hoe for half-a-day. Then, too, wife-working is a great institution, especially for a negro, and very often the men did no work at all, but made their wives put in their provisions. As for the children, negroes were never very good fathers or mothers. They were as the hen pheasants who are above hatching their own eggs, and must have Dorking hens to take the labour off their hands. The fine ladies of ornithology, they bring up their children by the help of others. In the case of the negroes this was an evil inherited from the old system. The slaves were so accustomed to see their children taken care of from their birth at the pains and expense of the proprietor, that they altogether neglected the duties of parents.

"Of course, this dry-nursing by the owner ceased with slavery; but the habits of a century cannot be made to cease by Act of Parliament."[1]

Dasent studied for a short time at King's College, London, and in **1840** graduated from Magdalen Hall, Oxford. "However, I went up to Oxford, and I always look back upon those three years as the happiest of my life. I left Westminster scholar enough to pass Littlego and Greats with little trouble. The *Bible,*—that stumbling-block in the way of 'Greats,' that book utterly impossible to be crammed up in six weeks,—that had been made safe by my mother and my aunt. Don't laugh, you enlightened people, who know how to do without the *Bible*. Don't think me a fool for being taught the *Bible* almost by heart by two weak women. I say the *Bible* so learnt is a pearl beyond price, a book full of touching memories, of recollections which sweep across the soul, soothing all the tempests of passion—oil, balm, manna, spices, call it what you will. Let no one mock me for knowing the *Bible*."[1]

Dasent's son, Arthur, wrote in his memoirs: "After going down from the university [father] spent some little time in London, where his mother had now removed from the West Indies. Delane [his life-long friend and future brother-in-law, whom he had first met at King's College], who about this time was established in the editorial chair of the *Times,* was in constant association with him, and it was at this early period of his career that Dasent began to write articles for the paper which he afterwards served so faithfully and so well in an official capacity."[2]

Dasent next went to Stockholm as secretary to the British Envoy. Arthur Dasent wrote: "In these days of rapid railway travelling, when the Swedish capital has been brought within

He set off down the road. (Illustration by Erik Werenskiold from "Why the Sea Is Salt" in *East o' the Sun and West o' the Moon* by Peter Christen Asbjoernsen and Joergen Moe, compiled by George Webbe Dasent.)

fifty hours of London, it is interesting to read the description given by him in his MS. diary of the dangers and difficulties attending a journey to northern Europe during the bitter winter of 1840-41.

"After taking leave of his mother, on New Year's Day 1841, he, the only cabin passenger in the ship, embarked on the *City of Hamburg,* lying off the Tower Stairs, and reached Cuxhaven on the 4th of January, posting the seventy miles on to Hamburg in twenty-nine hours!

"Thence the Copenhagen diligence crawled at a snail's pace through Holstein till a heavy fall of snow compelled him to take to a sledge, 'escorted,' the diary tells us, 'by a band of the most savage peasantry it is possible to conceive.' The Danish capital was not reached till the 14th of the month; and here he learnt from Sir Henry Wynn, to whom he brought letters of introduction, that he had missed the diligence for Stockholm by a day. In spite, however, of the extreme cold then prevailing, Dasent, whose impetuous nature was always impatient of delay, again resorted to an open sledge contrary to Wynn's advice, and reaching Elsinore he bargained for a boat to carry him to Helsingborg."[2] Dasent landed safely in Sweden, twenty-five days after he had boarded a ship on the Thames.

In **1842** Dasent published his first translation, *The Prose; or, Younger Edda.* His translation from the Swedish of Rask's *A*

Grammar of the Icelandic or Old Norse Tongue followed. In its preface he wrote: "This Translation was undertaken to further my own studies in the Old Norse, it has been lately revised, or rather rewritten, and is now offered to the English reader in the hope that it may excite attention toward a language and literature, of vast importance to the English student, but hitherto little understood or valued in England.

"Putting aside the study of Old Norse for the sake of its magnificent Literature, and considering it merely as an accessory help for the English student, we shall find it of immense advantage, not only in tracing the rise of words and idioms, but still more in clearing up many dark points in our early History; in fact so highly do I value it in this respect, that I cannot imagine it possible to write a satisfactory History of the Anglo Saxon Period without a thorough knowledge of the Old Norse Literature."[3]

In **1845** Dasent joined Delane as assistant editor of the *Times* and the following year married his sister, Fanny, with whom he was to have three sons and a daughter. In 1852 he was called to the bar and a year later was appointed professor of English literature and modern history at King's College.

In the introduction on the migration of tales from Asia to northern Europe, Dasent wrote: "The Norsemen came from the East, and brought a common stock of tradition with them. Settled in the Scandinavian peninsula, they developed themselves through Heathenism, Romanism, and Lutheranism, in a locality little exposed to foreign influence, so that even now the Daleman in Norway or Sweden may be reckoned among the most primitive examples left of peasant life. We should expect, then, that these Popular Tales, which, for the sake of those ignorant in such matters, it may be remarked, had never been collected or reduced to writing till within the last few years, would present a faithful picture of the national consciousness, or, perhaps, to speak more correctly, of that half consciousness out of which the heart of any people speaks in its abundance. Besides those world-old affinities and primaeval parallelisms, besides those dreamy recollections of its old home in the East, we should expect to find its later history, after the great migration, still more distinctly reflected; to discover heathen gods masked in the garb of Christian saints; and thus to see the proof that a nation more easily changes the form than the essence of its faith, and clings with a toughness which endures for centuries to what it has once learned to believe.

"The notion of the arch-enemy of God and man, of a fallen angel, to whom power was permitted at certain times for an all-wise purpose by the Great Ruler of the universe, was as foreign to the heathendom of our ancestors as his name was outlandish and strange to their tongue. This notion Christianity brought with it from the East; and though it is a plant which has struck deep roots, grown distorted and awry, and borne a bitter crop of superstition, it required all the authority of the Church to prepare the soil at first for its reception.

"The frequent transformation of men into beasts, in these tales, is another striking feature. This power the gods of the Norseman possessed in common with those of all other mythologies. Europa and her Bull, Leda and her Swan, will occur at once to the reader's mind; and to come to closer resemblances, just as Athene appears in the Odyssey as an eagle or a swallow perched on the roof of the hall, so Odin flies off as a falcon, and Loki takes the form of a horse or bird. This was only part of that omnipotence which all gods enjoy. But the belief that men, under certain conditions, could also take the shape of animals, is primaeval, and the traditions of every race can tell of such transformations.

"But we should ill understand the spirit of the Norsemen, if we supposed that these transformations into beasts were all that the national heart has to tell of beasts and their doings, or that, when they appear, they do so merely as men-beasts, without any power or virtue of their own. From the earliest times, side by side with those productions of the human mind which speak of the dealings of men with men, there has grown up a stock of traditions about animals and their relations with one another, which form a true Beast Epic, and is full of the liveliest traits of nature. Here too, it was reserved for Grimm to restore these traditions to their true place in the history of the human mind, and to show that the poetry which treats of them is neither satirical nor didactic, though it may contain touches of both these artificial kinds of composition, but, on the contrary, purely and intensely natural. It is Epic, in short, springing out of that deep love of nature and close observation of the habits of animals which is only possible in an early and simple stage of society."[4]

Dasent placed the origin of hell in the figure of Hel, a stern and grim goddess fated to outlive the Frost Giants, who owned that part of the universe that had not been seized by Odin. Hel was made queen of an icy place, where she received those who died of sickness and old age, though she was not originally an evil spirit. "When Christianity came in and ejected Odin and his crew of false divinities, declaring them to be lying gods and demons, then Hel fell with the rest; but fulfilling her fate, outlived them. From a person she became a place, and all the Northern nations, from the Goth to the Norseman, agreed in believing Hell to be the abode of the devil and his wicked spirits, the place prepared from the beginning for the everlasting torments of the damned."[4]

Of the role women played in Norse society Dasent noted: "In all ages and in all races this belief in sorcery has existed. Men and women practised it alike, but in all times female sorcerers have predominated. This was natural enough. In those days women were priestesses; they collected drugs and simples; women alone knew the virtues of plants. Those soft hands spun linen, made lint, and bound wounds. Women in the earliest times with which we are acquainted with our forefathers, alone knew how to read and write, they only could carve the mystic runes, they only could chant the charms so potent to allay the wounded warrior's smart and pain. The men were busy out of doors with ploughing, hunting, barter, and war. In such an age the sex which possessed by natural right booklearning, physic, soothsaying, and incantation, even when they used these mysteries for good purposes, were but a step from sin."[4]

To a second edition of the Norse tales Dasent appended Ananzi stories told by the Blacks of the West Indies. In 1861 he published a translation of the Icelandic saga *The Story of Burnt Njal.*

In **1866** he published another translation from the Icelandic, *Gisli the Outlaw.* In 1870 appeared, first anonymously, his autobiographical novel *Annals of an Eventful Life,* and in the same year he resigned from the *Times* and accepted a civil commissionership. His son recalled: "Though it was a great wrench to him to sever his long connection with Delane at the *Times* Office, and an immediate loss of income, after some hesitation he accepted the post on the advice of his family. No longer constrained to work every night into the small hours of the morning, he was now free to go more into London society; and bringing to it, as he did, a well-stored mind, a fund of native humour, great capacity for enjoyment, and rare conversational powers, he became one of its recognised favourites, and a welcome guest, like Delane himself, at its dinner-tables."[2]

Jest and Earnest, a collection of essays and reviews, appeared in **1873.** Among the subjects were the history of England and the English language and travels to Denmark and Germany. "For what is the English language? To some it is a gorgeous Mosaic—a pattern of rare stones, delicately arranged and adjusted; to others a monstrous patchwork, which the nation, as it has hurried along the path of time, has snatched up and pieced together in no order and after no law or rule. It is the glory of far-sighted philologists and the confusion and despair of purists and precisians. There can be no doubt, however, that the language of a nation will be always a reflex and representation of the nation itself. The history of the one will be in some sort the history of the other. No country has received so many foreigners into her bosom as England; no spot on the earth's surface has ever seen such a succession of races and masters as this island—now, it is true, all fused into one harmonious whole, and welded by time and trouble into a distinct nationality, but once at internecine feud the one with the other, each striving to secure for itself what was destined to remain their common inheritance. What wonder, then, that the English is, as the dictionaries and grammarians tell us, 'a composite language.'"[5]

Then the white bear rose up and growled, and hunted the whole pack of them out-of-doors, both great and small.

(Detail from *The Cat on the Dovrefell: A Christmas Tale,* translated from the Norse by George Webbe Dasent. Illustrated by Tomie de Paola.)

A translation of a second series of popular stories, *Tales from the Fjeld* by Asbjoernsen and Moe, appeared in 1874. On **June 27th, 1876,** on Mr. Disraeli's recommendation, Dasent received the honour of knighthood 'for public services.' He was already a Knight of the Danish Order of the Dannebrog; another compliment which he received from the Danes was a silver drinking-horn, shaped like a Viking ship, in recognition of his services to Northern literature.

In **1890** Dasent's country house burned to the ground and with it an extensive library. With "characteristic energy" according to Arthur, his father took to the task of rebuilding his destroyed house.

In **1894** Dasent's translation of the Orkney and Hacon Sagas was published. In the revisions he had received assistance from his eldest son, John. His health failing, Dasent spent the last year and a half of his life confined to his room. He died

June 11, 1896. Recalled Arthur, "He passed away, surrounded by his family, at his house at Tower Hill, overlooking the wild landscape of Bagshot Heath, and the woodlands of Swinley which he loved so well.

"On the Monday following his remains were quietly interred in the picturesque churchyard of the old forest parish of Easthampstead, where, too, his life-long friend, John Delane, rests from his labours."[2]

FOOTNOTE SOURCES

[1]George Webbe Dasent, *Annals of an Eventful Life,* three volumes, Hurst & Blackett, 1870.
[2]"A Memoir by Arthur Irwin Dasent," *Popular Tales from the Norse,* by G. W. Dasent, Putnam, 1912.
[3]G. W. Dasent, "Translator's Preface," in Rasmus Kristian Rask's *A Grammar of the Icelandic or Old Norse Tongue,* Benjamins (Amsterdam), 1976.

"Good evening to you!" said the White Bear. (Illustration by Gillian Barlow from *East o' the Sun and West o' the Moon: An Old Norse Tale* by Peter Christen Asbjoernsen and Joergen Moe, translated by George Webbe Dasent.)

⁴G. W. Dasent, *A Collection of Popular Tales from the Norse and North German,* Norroena Society, 1911.

⁵G. W. Dasent, *Jest and Earnest,* two volumes, Chapman & Hall, 1873.

FOR MORE INFORMATION SEE:

Biographical Dictionary and Synopsis of Books, Werner, 1902, reissued, Gale, 1965.

Stanley J. Kunitz, editor, *British Authors of the Nineteenth Century,* H. W. Wilson, 1936.

The Oxford Companion to English Literature, Harvey House, 1967.

New Century Handbook of English Literature, Barnhart, 1967.

Brian Doyle, editor, *The Who's Who of Children's Literature,* Schocken, 1968.

Every Man's Dictionary of Literary Biography, English and American, third edition, Browning, 1969.

Randolph Quirk, *The Linguist and the English Language,* Edward Arnold, 1974.

Humphrey Carpenter and Mari Prichard, *The Oxford Companion to Children's Literature,* Oxford University Press, 1984.

OBITUARIES:

New York Times, June 13, 1896.

LENA YOUNG de GRUMMOND

de GRUMMOND, Lena Young (?)-1989

PERSONAL: Born in Centerville, La.,; died April 26, 1989; daughter of William J. (a merchant) and Amy (Etienne) Young; married Will White de Grummond (deceased); children: Jewel Lynn (Mrs. Richard K. Delaune), Will White. *Education:* Southwestern Louisiana Institute of Liberal and Technical Learning (now University of Southwestern Louisiana), B.A., 1929; Louisiana State University, B.S., 1939, M.S., Ph.D., 1956. *Religion:* Protestant. *Residence:* Hattiesburg, Miss.

CAREER: St. Mary Parish, La., teacher; Louisiana State Library, Baton Rouge, La., staff member, 1937-38; Centerville High School, Centerville, La., teacher and librarian, 1938-44; Sulphur High School, Sulphur, La., librarian, 1944-47; Terrebonne High School, Houma, La., librarian, 1947-49; Louisiana Department of Education, Baton Rouge, state supervisor of school libraries, 1950-65; University of Southern Mississippi, Hattiesburg, professor of library science, 1965-70. Founder, De Grummond Collection at the University of Southern Mississippi, 1966. Book reviewer. Member of East Baton Rouge Community Service Commission. *Member:* National League of American Pen Women, American Library Association (former council member), Louisiana Library Association, Mississippi Library Association, Deep South Writers Conference (director, 1962-64, president, 1970-72), Louisiana Genealogical and Historical Society (program chairperson, 1962-63), Louisiana Historical Society, Louisiana Folklore Society, Delta Kappa Gamma, Theta Sigma Phi, Phi Kappa Phi.

AWARDS, HONORS: Modisette Award for Best School Library, 1959; honored by J. B. Lippincott, 1963, for the publication of *Jeb Stuart;* University of Southern Mississippi Collection of Original Manuscripts and Illustrations for Children's Books named Lena Young de Grummond Collection, 1970; Phi Lambda Pi National Award, 1972; Golden Deeds Award from the Mississippi Exchange Club (Hattiesburg), 1984; honored by the Randolph Caldecott Society of America, 1988, for contributions to the world of children's literature.

WRITINGS:

(With Minns S. Robertson) *How to Have What You Want in Your Future,* privately printed, 1959.

(With daughter, Lynn de Grummond Delaune) *Jeff Davis: Confederate Boy,* Bobbs-Merrill, 1960.

Books Suitable for Use in Schools, Grades 1-12, Louisiana Department of Education, 1961.

(With L. Delaune) *Jeb Stuart,* Lippincott, 1962, reissued, Pelican Press, 1979.

(With L. Delaune) *Babe Didrikson: Girl Athlete,* Bobbs-Merrill, 1963.

(With L. Delaune) *Jean Felix Picard: Boy Balloonist,* Bobbs-Merrill, 1968.

Contributor of articles to professional journals, including *Education* and *Louisiana English Journal.*

SIDELIGHTS: Lena Young de Grummond's career in library science began after her husband, Will de Grummond, an engineer with the U.S. Corps of Engineers, died in a drowning accident. Because education was one of the only careers open to women, she taught school while pursuing a master's degree from Louisiana State University. One of her

De Grummond presents the 1970 USM Medallion to Ernest H. Shepard, while Mrs. Shepard looks on. (Photograph courtesy of McCain Library and Archives, University of Southern Mississippi.)

classmates, Laura Boddie Jones Bowers, recalled: "Lena and I were classmates in Library School during the 1936-37 session. Her daughter, Jewel Lynn was a university freshman. I had just graduated from Newcomb, so daughter and I were much nearer the same age than mother and I. Although our entire class looked on Lena as a sort of 'little mother,' I don't think we ever considered the age difference at all, so perfectly did she fit into our group."[1]

After completing her requirements for the degree, de Grummond served as librarian in Sulphur and Houma, Louisiana. Her work was so distinguished that she soon drew the attention of Louisiana state authorities. She rose to the position of the state's assistant librarian, and in 1950 moved into the top post, where responsibility for restructuring the school library system was placed largely in her hands. De Grummond earned a reputation for her devotion to the job; she usually arrived at work by 5:00 A.M. and visited every school in the state each year.

In 1956 de Grummond earned her Ph.D. in library science from Lousiana State University at the same time her son, Will, received his B.S. degree.

Her first book, with Minns S. Robertson, titled *How to Have What You Want in Your Future,* a nonfiction guide to personal finances, was published in 1959. This book was followed by four biographies, all co-authored with her daughter, Lynn Delaune.

While serving as supervisor of libraries, de Grummond began making contacts with children's authors in Louisiana. One such writer, Mary Alice Fontenot, recalled, "My first encounter with Lena Y. de Grummond was in 1961. I was at the editor's desk at the Rayne (La.) *Acadian-Tribune* when I received her phone call from Baton Rouge. She identified herself by name and position . . . and then proceeded to tell me that she wanted to introduce my first published book, *Clovis Crawfish and His Friends,* to elementary school children. 'We are in need of more material that reflects Louisiana's unique culture,' she explained. 'Young children have so few books that deal with their own state.' With this kind of encouragement, I wrote another book, then another, and another . . . .

"Each new book brought a warm note of encouragement from Lena."[2]

In June, 1965, de Grummond retired. Within a few months, she assumed teaching duties at the University of Southern Mississippi at Hattiesburg. While instructing teachers and librarians on children's literature, de Grummond developed the idea for a special collection devoted exclusively to her field of expertise. The two goals of the project were to demonstrate the physical and creative development of children's books, and to provide a permanent archive for researchers, authors, and publishers involved with juvenile literature.

De Grummond approached the University with her ideas and received approval, but no offer of financial assistance from the university librarian, Dr. Warren Tracy. Undaunted, she began a letter writing campaign with authors, illustrators, and publishers. A typical request included a paragraph that read: "We are ordering copies of your books, but we lack those materials which enrich a collection—manuscripts of published books, illustrations, 'dummies,' scripts, sketches, rough notes, etc. Would you please help us with some of yours? We want to set up a collection of your materials in your name. (Such gifts are tax deductible, you know.)"[3]

De Grummond's enthusiasm for her work was such that at one point she was mailing over four hundred handwritten letters per week.

In 1969 the first annual Children's Book Festival was held at the university. This yearly two-day event features speeches from outstanding contributors to the field of children's literature. The highlight of the festival is the presentation of the university's silver medallion to one individual. Each of the medallions is uniquely designed with input from the recipient, and all contributors to the collection receive copies of the annual medallions. The first award was presented to Lois Lenski; other winners have included E. H. Shepard, Roger Duvoisin, Marcia Brown, Lynd Ward, Taro Yashima, Barbara Cooney, Scott O'Dell and Lee Bennett Hopkins.

Because of administrative rules, de Grummond was forced to retire as professor in 1970. In honor of her work, the Children's Literature Research Collection was officially renamed the de Grummond Collection. On the day after her retirement, she returned to work with the collection full-time, without pay. That same year, she travelled to England to personally award E. H. Shepard with his silver medallion.

Recognizing the geographic isolation of the collection, in 1973 de Grummond instituted traveling exhibits of archive materials. There were soon five such exhibits, which logged thousands of miles through fifteen states. "This collection was created for children. I refuse to have it hidden away in a vault only to be plundered through by elderly scholars. These materials should be where children can see and enjoy them."[2]

De Grummond herself eventually visited thirty-five states as well as foreign countries on behalf of the Collection, all the while strengthening her personal contacts with authors and illustrators. She developed a particular fondness for British illustrator, Edward Ardizzone. Politely declining her solicitation of his work, the artist invited de Grummond for tea in London. She accepted Ardizzone's invitation, and returned to Mississippi with his illustrations for Paula Fox's *A Likely Place.*

At this point, the Collection had grown to fill a second floor wing of the University library. In 1976 it was estimated that the archive housed two thousand authors' manuscripts, over nine thousand pieces of original artwork, more than two hundred authors and artists' dummies, and as many as twenty-seven hundred photographs. The largest single donation was a sixty-foot circus mural done in collage by Esphyr Slobodkina; the painting was based on two of Slobodkina's books, *Pezzo the Peddlar and the Circus Elephant* and *Caps for Sale.* Other contemporary artists and writers in the collection include Robert Quackenbush, Daniel S. Halacy, Miriam Chaikin, Richard Armour, Syd Hoff, and Charlotte Zolotow.

Although the de Grummond Collection focuses primarily on materials created after 1920, it has also acquired a significant number of historical artifacts. The highlights among these antiques include two horn books (sixteenth-century children's primers protected by a sheet of transparent horn), a collection of twelve hundred mid-nineteenth-century printers proofs from McLoughlin Brothers, six Randolph Caldecott wood blocks, a sixteenth-century copy of Aesop's Fables in Greek and Latin, and two groups of nineteenth-century American dolls.

Lena Young de Grummond died peacefully in her sleep on the night of April 26, 1989, the Year of the Young Reader. "Working at a job which you truly enjoy is more satisfying than any paid position. But my interests do not begin and end with the library. Most of all, I like people."[4]

FOOTNOTE SOURCES

[1]"Remembrances of Lena Y. de Grummond," *Juvenile Miscellany,* spring, 1990.
[2]"Remembrances of Lena Y. de Grummond," *Juvenile Miscellany,* summer, 1989.
[3]Eleanor Graham Vance, "Resource Library for Children," *Christian Science Monitor,* April 15, 1972.
[4]Louise Munro Foley, "The de Grummond Collection: A Working Library," *Horn Book,* December, 1976.

FOR MORE INFORMATION SEE:

Baton Rouge State Times, March 22, 1963.
Juvenile Miscellany, summer, 1970, spring, 1972.
Dorothy A. Marquardt and Martha E. Ward, *Authors of Books for Young People,* 2nd edition, Scarecrow, 1971.
St. Augustine Record, March 25, 1988.

OBITUARIES

School Library Journal, September, 1989 (p. 154).

DICKINSON, Peter (Malcolm de Brissac) 1927-

PERSONAL: Born December 16, 1927, in Livingstone, Northern Rhodesia (now Zambia); son of Richard Sebastian Willoughby (a colonial civil servant) and Nancy (a sculptor; maiden name, Lovemore) Dickinson; married Mary Rose Barnard (an artist; died, 1988), April 20, 1953; children: Philippa, Polly, John, James. *Education:* King's College, Cambridge, B.A., 1951; *Politics:* "Leftist." *Religion:* "Lapsed Anglican." *Home and office:* 61A Ormiston Grove, London W12 0JP, England. *Agent:* A.P. Watt Ltd., 20 John St., London WC1N 2DR, England; Georges Borchardt Inc., 136 East 57th St., New York, N.Y. 10022.

CAREER: Punch, London, England, assistant editor and reviewer, 1952-69; writer of novels and juvenile books, 1968—. *Military service:* British Army, 1946-48.

PETER DICKINSON

AWARDS, HONORS: British Crime Writer's Association Award for Best Mystery of the Year, 1968, for *Skin Deep,* and 1969, for *A Pride of Heroes; Guardian* Award Commendation, 1970, for *Heartsease,* and 1973, for *The Dancing Bear;* Carnegie Medal Commendation from the British Library Association 1970, for *The Devil's Children,* 1972, for *The Dancing Bear,* and 1976, for *The Blue Hawk; The Dancing Bear* was selected one of Child Study Association of America's Children's Books of the Year, 1973, *Chance, Luck and Destiny,* 1976, and *The Devil's Children, Heartsease,* and *The Weathermonger,* 1987; *Guardian* Award, 1977, for *The Blue Hawk; Boston Globe-Horn Book* Award for Nonfiction, 1977, for *Chance, Luck and Destiny;* Whitbread Award, 1979, for *Tulku;* Carnegie Medal from the British Library Association, 1979, for *Tulku,* and 1980, for *City of Gold and Other Stories from the Old Testament;* Mother Goose Award Runner-up from the Books for Children Book Club, 1979, for *Hepzibah.*

Kate Greenaway Medal High Commendation from the British Library Association, 1980, and Bologna Children's Book Fair Prize for Graphics for Youth, 1982, both for *City of Gold and Other Stories from the Old Testament;* International Board on Books for Young People Honor List, 1982, for *Tulku; The Iron Lion* was selected one of *New York Times* Notable Books, 1984; *Boston Globe-Horn Book* Award Fiction Honor Book, 1989, for *Eva.*

WRITINGS:

"CHANGES" TRILOGY; FOR YOUNG PEOPLE

The Weathermonger, Gollancz, 1968, Little, Brown, 1969.
Heartsease (Junior Literary Guild selection; illustrated by Robert Hales), Gollancz, 1969, U.S. edition (illustrated by Nathan Goldstein), Little, Brown, 1969.

The Devil's Children (Junior Literary Guild selection; illustrated by R. Hales), Little, Brown, 1970.
The Changes (omnibus edition), Gollancz, 1975, Delacorte, 1986.

OTHER; FOR YOUNG PEOPLE

Emma Tupper's Diary (ALA Notable Book; Junior Literary Guild selection; illustrated by David Omar White), Little Brown, 1971.
The Dancing Bear (ALA Notable Book; illustrated by David Smee), Gollancz, 1972, Little, Brown, 1973.
The Iron Lion (illustrated by Marc Brown), Little, Brown, 1972, new edition (illustrated by Pauline Baynes), Blackie, 1983, Peter Bedrick, 1984.
The Gift (illustrated by Gareth Floyd), Gollancz, 1973, Little, Brown, 1974.
Chance, Luck and Destiny (miscellany; illustrated by D. Smee and Victor Ambrus), Gollancz, 1975, Little, Brown, 1976.
(Editor) *Presto! Humorous Bits and Pieces,* Hutchinson, 1975.
The Blue Hawk (*Horn Book* honor list; illustrated by D. Smee), Little, Brown, 1976.
Annerton Pit (*Horn Book* honor list), Little, Brown, 1977.
Hepzibah (illustrated by Sue Porter), Eel Pie, 1978, Godine, 1980.
Tulku (*Horn Book* honor list), Dutton, 1979.
The Flight of Dragons (illustrated by Wayne Anderson), Harper, 1979.
City of Gold and Other Stories from the Old Testament (illustrated by Michael Foreman), Pantheon, 1980.
The Seventh Raven (*Horn Book* honor list), Dutton, 1981.
Giant Cold (illustrated by Alan E. Cober), Gollancz, 1983, Dutton, 1984.
Healer (ALA Notable Book), Gollancz, 1983, Delacorte, 1985.
A Box of Nothing (illustrated by I. Newsham), Gollancz, 1985, Delacorte, 1988.
Mole Hole (illustrated by Jean Claverie), Peter Bedrick, 1987.
Merlin Dreams (illustrated by Alan Lee), Delacorte, 1988.
Eva (ALA Notable Book), Gollancz, 1988, Delacorte, 1989.

TELEVISION SERIES; JUVENILE

"Mandog," British Broadcasting Corporation, 1972.

ADULT NOVELS

The Glass Sided Ants' Nest, Harper, 1968 (published in England as *Skin Deep,* Hodder & Stoughton, 1968).
The Old English Peep Show, Harper, 1969 (published in England as *A Pride of Heroes,* Hodder & Stoughton, 1969).
The Sinful Stones, Harper, 1970 (published in England as *The Seals,* Hodder & Stoughton, 1970).
Sleep and His Brother, Harper, 1971.
The Lizard in the Cup, Harper, 1972.
The Green Gene, Pantheon, 1973.
The Poison Oracle, Pantheon, 1974, large print edition, J. Curley, 1984.
The Lively Dead, Pantheon, 1975.
King and Joker, Pantheon, 1976.
Walking Dead, Hodder & Stoughton, 1977, Pantheon, 1978.
One Foot in the Grave, Hodder & Stoughton, 1979, Pantheon, 1980.
A Summer in the Twenties, Pantheon, 1981.
The Last House-Party, Pantheon, 1982.
Hindsight, Bodley Head, 1983, large print edition, J. Curley, 1984.
Death of a Unicorn, Pantheon, 1984.
Tefuga, Pantheon, 1986.

The turrets of her castle rose above tree-tops. (Illustration by Alan Lee from *Merlin Dreams* by Peter Dickinson.)

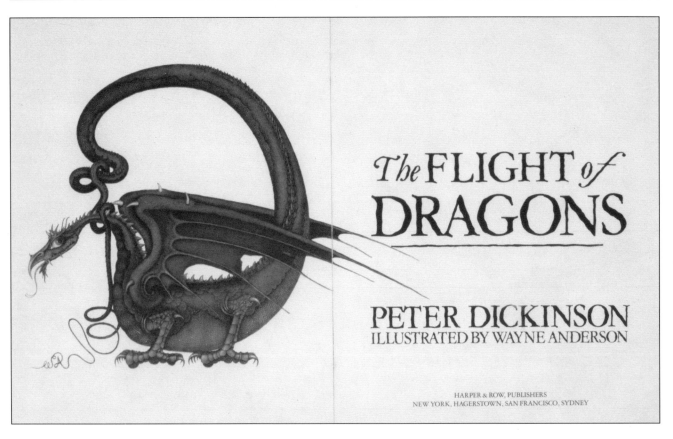

(From *The Flight of Dragons* by Peter Dickinson. Illustrated by Wayne Anderson.)

Perfect Gallows, Pantheon, 1987.
Skeleton in Waiting, Bodley Head, 1989, Pantheon, 1990.

Contributor to periodicals, including *Punch, Atlantic,* and *Tatler.*

ADAPTATIONS:

"The Flight of Dragons" (animated film), ABC-TV, January 1, 1982.
"A Box of Nothing" (cassette), G. K. Hall, 1988.

BBC produced a television serial based on the "Changes" trilogy, 1975.

WORK IN PROGRESS: Ak, a novel about a boy's adventures in the aftermath of an African guerrilla war.

SIDELIGHTS: Dickinson was born **December 16, 1927,** in Livingstone, Northern Rhodesia, now Zambia. His father was a civil servant and his mother the daughter of a South African farmer who raised sheep and ostriches. Of four brothers, Dickinson was second oldest. The family moved to England when Dickinson was seven, only to see their father die shortly thereafter.

In **1941** he won a scholarship to Eton College in Buckinghamshire where he was a " . . . bottom scholar of the worst year" and an " . . . intellectual and a lout . . . . I only did one thing worthwhile. When my turn came to beat a boy, I refused. I was too squeamish."[1]

1946-1948. Served as a district signals officer in the British Army.

1951. Dickinson graduated with a B.A. from King's College, Oxford. Because he was becoming " . . . worse and worse at writing Latin,"[1] he changed to English literature. A tutor suggested that he join the staff of *Punch,* which was looking for new writers. "They had suddenly noticed that their youngest member of staff was forty. On my way to the interview I was run into by a tram and arrived covered in blood."[1] That was the beginning of a seventeen-year career at *Punch* as assistant editor and reviewer of crime novels, often reading as many as thirty thrillers a month.

After many years at *Punch,* the day came when he felt the need to do some writing of his own. "There is this extraordinary feeling, when all one's contemporaries are brigadiers and bishops, that if one doesn't start being go-go, one will be went-went. I had a picture of a tribesman lying dead on a bare floor in a room in London, with a lamp at his feet and a wake going on around him, and from that I got this corking idea which you could hardly go wrong with, provided you could make up a tribe realistically."[2]

This idea grew into his first novel, *Skin Deep.* "I think there is a strong element of lying fallow; that there is an awful lot of stuff which you happen to know which is lying around in your mind in a rather untidy way. People who start being brilliant writers at twenty simply haven't got the store of rather trivial experience that I have, and the oddities of knowledge, even if they have gone up the Orinoco in a canoe. This is what does give the reader an impression of richness, and I always try to give them more than their money's worth."[2]

Skin Deep, which was titled *The Glass Sided Ants' Nest* in the United States, introduced one of Dickinson's strongest characters, James Willoughby Pibble, a detective who inhabited six Dickinson thrillers. This first novel won the Golden Dagger Award of the British Crime Writers.

It all became like the nightmares you have again and again. (Jacket illustration by Leo and Diane Dillon from *Heartsease* by Peter Dickinson.)

At once the whole group began to move. (From *The Devil's Children* by Peter Dickinson.)

Dickinson began to write novel after novel on the kitchen table of his North Kensington home. It was here that he penned his first children's novel, *The Weathermonger,* which began the "Changes" trilogy about an alternative present time when Britons reject machinery and return to ignorance and superstition. Written in reverse order, the first book tells how the time of the Changes ended, while the others follow different groups of children through earlier periods. The Changes are explained as the effect of the reawakening of the great magician, Merlin, thus influencing the times.

1969. Dickinson published *Heartsease,* the second in the "Changes" trilogy, detailing the middle period. He also published his second adult crime novel, *A Pride of Heroes,* published as *The Old English Peep Show* in the United States. It, too, won a Golden Dagger Award, an unprecedented honor for a beginning writer. Dickinson jokes about it: "It was probably all a ghastly error. If you get one ghastly error you can say 'that's life.' If you get two ghastly errors you have to say 'that's a computer.'"[2]

1970. *The Devil's Children,* the third in the "Changes" trilogy but the earliest period chronologically, was published.

1971. Dickinson continued writing for adults and children. *Emma Tupper's Diary,* a children's adventure/fantasy, was inspired by a vacation he spent in Western Scotland near Loch Morar when he was eighteen. It is about a hoax to

disguise a miniature submarine as a sea monster in order to bring more tourists to the loch, but Emma and her cousins discover that there's a real monster in the loch. Dickinson recalls his childhood visit to Scotland. "There was supposed to be a monster in the loch, though it was never a famous one, like the Loch Ness Monster. And my friends' grandfather had been a Victorian inventor, though he never built a submarine. All the rest of *Emma Tupper's Diary* just came to me out of the blue. One moment my mind was blank, and the next I had a whole book ready to write.

"It can't have been quite like that. I had to pester crusty old naval officers about early submarines, and what it felt like to risk your life in that sort of primitive iron bubble. And I know that quite early on I realized that this was a good chance to write, without preaching, about the way Man is destroying species after species of his fellow creatures. And I also remember enjoying the chance to tease the Scots a bit. But mostly, given my first idea, one thing seemed to follow from another in a perfectly logical order, and all I had to do was write it down."[3]

He also wrote a crime novel for adults that year, *Sleep and His Brother.* "It's perhaps not up to the standard of my others, but it's still better than most detective stories that get published. There is a problem with crime writing. Those who treat it as just that are really rather boring. It's like someone who writes a sonnet and is pleased with himself when he's got fourteen lines that rhyme and scan. It is really a form in whose curious conventions you do something quite different but if

The hoofbeats dwindled into the forest, into silence. Then huntsmen and villagers, waiting out of sight beyond the forest, heard a voice like the snarl of trumpets, a man's shout and a crash. Then silence once more.

The trackers followed the hoofprints deep into the dark wood. They found Sir Brangwyn's body under an oak tree, pierced through from side to side. His horse they caught wandering close by.

Rhiannon came out of the forest at sunset. What had she seen and heard? What fiery eye, what silvery mane? What challenge and what charge? She would not say.

Only when her mother and father came home, set free by Sir Brangwyn's heir, she told them something. They had taken her to her bed and were standing looking down at her, full of their happiness in being all three together again, and home, when she whispered four words.

"Unicorns have parents too."

(From *Merlin Dreams* by Peter Dickinson. Illustrated by Alan Lee.)

you stretch the form too far then you've written the fifteenth line to your sonnet. So the money's worth is the detective story; the bonus you get from me is a much greater flavour."[2]

1972. Dickinson wrote a television series for children entitled "Mandog," and wrote *The Lizard in the Cup,* his fifth and at the time last book with the Pibble character. Pibble finally had to retire, both because he was aging and because Dickinson needed a change. He describes Pibble as "an elderly, intelligent man, refreshing in that he is clearly not a great lover, not a strong personality but fairly easily brow-beaten. Not the kind of hero normally found in thrillers, nor a nit-picking drunk who passes for an anti-hero. Likeable, unintentionally cuddly.

"I suppose he is like what a fairly unambitious man would like to think of himself as, towards the end of his working life; honourable but having resigned himself to the fact that he is not the tops."[2]

"He was a copper's copper, and that's almost true. He was very good at his paperwork, for instance. He had a darn quick memory, especially for faces and places. He had a nose, too—I don't mean he was an intuitive copper—there wasn't much of the Maigret about him—but he was especially good about which areas of a case to bear down on. He didn't neglect the others, and he was damn quick to change his tack if something new cropped up to shed a fresh light on things; in fact the best part about working with him was that he had no

vanity at all—he'd never impose his own view on a case because it was his. For himself, he was a worrier, but he was easygoing about other people. One or two of his colleagues put his back up for no reason that I could see, but on the whole practically everybody liked him.

"It seems funny to me . . . to be writing about old Pibble like this, as if he were real. I don't think many writers— perhaps only the great ones—start with totally solid characters in their heads. Usually, with a major character, you have certain ideas about him/her which you embody in characteristics. Then you find yourself adding twiddly bits, sometimes for fun, sometimes for plot, judging what to say by a vague notion of 'rightness' for that particular person. If your invention is of a piece you finish up with a real-seeming character. That's how Pibble evolved. I simply wanted a detective who was not at all James Bondish, was unsexy, easily browbeaten, intelligent, fallible. Then he became real-seeming. That, I suppose, is why I stopped writing about him. You can't go on creating somebody when he's already created. Five books is a lot to live through. If he wasn't solid by then he never would be."[4] He makes one final appearance as a resident of a nursing home who stumbled upon a crime in *One Foot in the Grave.*

1975. *The Changes,* an omnibus edition of the trilogy, was published and arranged in chronological order, rather than the order in which it was written.

(From the animated movie "The Flight of Dragons," produced by Rankin Bass, 1982. Movie still courtesy of Telepictures Corp.)

Dickinson has continued to write both adult thrillers and children's adventure and fantasy books which are sometimes described as science fiction. "I think of myself as writing science fiction with the science left out. I try to write proper detective stories, with clues and solutions, which work in the traditional way, but also provide something extra by way of ideas, without getting portentous about it. My books have tended to deal with closed worlds—partly because that makes it easier to limit suspects, etc. (as in the good old snowbound country house), and partly because it allows me to give the inhabitants of that closed world a definite twist which sets them apart from the outside world. For my main characters I like competent women and weedy men, and tend to overpopulate my books with grotesques."[5]

Children's books "... are easier to write, as it is easier to cook a good breakfast than a good dinner."[2]

"My purpose in writing a children's book is to tell a story, and everything else is secondary to that; but when secondary considerations arise they have to be properly dealt with. Apart from that I like my stories exciting and as different as possible from the one I wrote last time. When I write for children I'm conscious of doing a different sort of thing from what I do when I write for adults, but that doesn't mean I'm writing down. Place and feel, even of imaginary landscapes, are important to me, nuances of character less so. Most of my books have an element of fantasy in them, but where this

happens I try to deal with the subject in as practical and logical a way as possible."[6]

"All fiction is a map, which we need our imaginations to read. The most elaborate and detailed fiction will always be far, far simpler and more schematic than the real world. Fiction shrinks the real world into a book, flattens it into the two dimensions of print on paper, lays it out so that we can follow the routes through its landscape without moving from our chairs. Mainstream fiction mostly provides us with maps of landscapes that cannot easily be explored by any other means, such as the hidden country of fear behind a smiling face, or the multidimensional communications network, mostly glances and silences, that both joins and separates the members of a family.

"But fantasy fiction doesn't and shouldn't do this .... Fantasy is the poetry of ideas. We tend to be told that the prime aim of fantasy is to arouse a sense of wonder. It is an ambiguous phrase. If you take wonder to mean awe, and the marvellous, then I think it isn't true, and even if it were it wouldn't get us very far. It might have been true once, when our ancestors listened open-mouthed to the travellers' tales. But if we take wonder to mean speculation, then I think we are on to something. That's the beginning. Speculation begins with 'If.' It goes on from there and discovers new worlds. It's the going on that matters.

He was approached by a short, bald man wearing a white raincoat. (Illustration by Victor Ambrus and David Smee from *Chance, Luck and Destiny* by Peter Dickinson.)

"It is essential that the invented world should be so constructed that it is coherent on its own terms. We know the world, as I have said, not by individual perceptions but by the coherence of our perceptions. This is how we learn, how we expand our understanding. What fantasy literature is doing is providing us with maps of coherences, which we may imaginatively follow. That is what I meant when I said that fantasy is the poetry of ideas. Not only the poetry of 'If.' Stories which are just one astonishing invention after another are fundamentally boring. We need the poetry of 'Then.' One astonishing consequence is worth twenty unconnected marvels.

"Children are of course learning machines, despite appearances to the contrary on occasion. The reason why we have such an absurdly long childhood and adolescence compared with the rest of the animals is that we are genetically programmed to do a great deal of learning. And almost the chief thing we have to learn is this basic matter of coherence. How the real world fits together in space and in time. Particularly in time. I believe our sense of time differentiates us from the animals much more than the self-awareness I mentioned earlier. It is in the dimension of time that cause follows effect. It is in the dimension of time that coherent worlds evolve. And it is the intuitive understanding of such coherences that equips us to cope with the immensely complex real world we live in."[7]

"I was raised with religion, read the *Bible* when I was about nine, but am completely without faith. But I write a lot about cults and isolating kinds of faith in both the adult and the children's books.

"It's all very instinctive. I try to find a voice in my head. I write the books first, then do the research, then rewrite them. I'm so bad at research because everything I want to know seems to fall between the Dewey numerals. I do less research than most writers, and I do it partly to find areas on which I feel confident rather than write from the facts . . . . I regard myself as a feminine chap. I love cooking, bake the bread, love to hold a baby on my hip. If I had one wish, it would be to be a woman, just briefly . . . . But I write in the women's voices for a technical reason as well—the reader is unlikely to mistake you for the character.

"I believe the crucial thing for a writer is the ability to make up coherent worlds. I'm like a beachcomber walking along the shores of my imagination, picking up things and wondering what kinds of structures they could make. I want it to be an interesting structure, not a ramshackle, beachy thing. The imagination is like the sea, full of things you can't see but can possibly harvest and use."[8]

"When I'm on form, I think my books are a pleasure to read. If critics wanted to do a hatchet job on me they'd say that they lacked a true emotional core. That I'm frightened of emotion.

"I'm really a poet. I'm almost cursed with too great a facility with verse. On form I can talk in heroic couplets. I'm about twenty years behind. I've just discovered that Auden is relatively easy to understand.

"I grow bored with my own company. I eke out spare time with games of solitaire, keeping the more intellectually demanding for special occasions. We don't entertain much, or go to the theatre or the cinema. I find I overreact violently to other people's emotions. Nor do I read fiction. If it's good, it makes me jealous. If it's bad, cross."[1]

"I've read practically no modern fiction. I am, in a highbrow sense, almost illiterate . . . not totally since I've read everything by anyone who's dead, but I think it is a very rare person who can write satisfyingly in a genre which he himself does not enjoy. I like plots and stories and well-made plays. I dream in plots, and have been known to wake up shouting. 'I simply will not dream these dreadful cliches.'"[2]

Dickinson usually writes from nine-thirty to twelve-thirty in the morning, then gardens. He moves between his apartment in London and his Victorian dower house in Hampshire. A tall man, over six feet, he is known for his booming voice. "I prefer not to think, let alone write, coherently about how I do what I do, or why, or even for whom. Part of the reason will be obvious to anyone who has ever had an on day at some sport, say tennis: the moment you start to wonder what you're doing right your game goes to pieces. Another part of the reason is that I might grow to the shape of my theories. One of the pleasures of writing for children is that it is a sufficiently small world for a single writer to be able to explore large districts of it. The Stevenson of *Treasure Island* is, I suppose, my Socrates and the Kipling of *Rewards and Fairies* my Plato. But though I am aware of working inside a strong tradition I regard myself as a primitive. I have a function, like the village cobbler, and that is to tell stories. Everything else is subservient to that.

"If I fight shy of positive notions about my writing, I do have one fairly coherent negative belief. It's about what I'm not

There was nowhere to hide. (Jacket illustration by Chuck Gillies from *A Box of Nothing* by Peter Dickinson.)

doing. I am not whittling rungs for the great ladder that leads up to Lawrence and Proust. I think children read differently from adults, and have a different use for books. (I also think that many adults have never learnt to read the way adults are supposed to, which accounts in part for the decline of the novel.) To me the great ladder tradition is something of a tyranny. So if, for instance, the intricate development and exploration of character plays no great part in my stories, that's because I don't think it is a proper element in the genre. People have to have characters, of course, in the same way that priests have to have theologies; but if I get it right then the person is there in the book, clear and rounded-seeming, and the reader acknowledges her existence and gets on with the story.

"Finally, I am strongly against the religion of art, and the priesthood of artists. I am a cobbler. Given good leather I can make a comfortable shoe."[9]

FOOTNOTE SOURCES

[1]Caroline Moorehead, "Making Crime Pay," *Times* (London), May 21, 1983. Amended by P. Dickinson.
[2]Catherine Stott, "Corking Plotter," *Manchester Guardian* (England), February 8, 1971.
[3]*Junior Literary Guild,* September, 1971.
[4]Peter Dickinson, "Superintendent Pibble," *The Great Detectives,* edited by Otto Penzler, Little, Brown, 1978.
[5]John M. Reilly, editor, *Twentieth-Century Crime and Mystery Writers,* Macmillan, 1980.
[6]D. L. Kirkpatrick, *Twentieth-Century Children's Writers,* St. Martin's, 1978.
[7]P. Dickinson, "Fantasy: The Need for Realism," *Children's Literature in Education,* spring, 1986.
[8]Eden Ross Lipson, "Write, Research, Then Rewrite," *New York Times Book Review,* April 20, 1986. Amended by P. Dickinson.
[9]John Rowe Townsend, *A Sounding of Storytellers: New and Revised Essays on Contemporary Writers for Children,* Lippincott, 1979.

FOR MORE INFORMATION SEE:

Chicago Tribune Children's Book World, November 8, 1970.
Horn Book, April, 1970, December, 1970, July/August, 1989 (p. 487).
Peter Dickinson, "Meet Your Author," *Cricket,* March, 1975.
Doris de Montreville and Elizabeth D. Crawford, *Fourth Book of Junior Authors and Illustrators,* H. W. Wilson, 1978.
Peter Nicholls, editor, *The Science Fiction Encyclopedia,* Doubleday, 1979.
Armchair Detective, summer, 1980 (p. 185ff).
D. L. Kirkpatrick, editor, *Twentieth-Century Children's Writers,* St. Martin's, 1983.
Time, February 1, 1988 (p. 65).

ESBENSEN, Barbara J(uster) 1925-

PERSONAL: Born April 28, 1925, in Madison, Wis.; daughter of Eugene M. (a physician) and Isabel S. (a singer; maiden name, Sinaiko) Juster; married Thorwald S. Esbensen (a developer of educational programs for microcomputers), June 24, 1953; children: Julie Esbensen Simons, Peter (deceased), Daniel, Jane Esbensen Moore, George, Kai.

BARBARA J. ESBENSEN

Education: University of Wisconsin, B.S., 1947. *Home:* 5602 Dalrymple Rd., Edina, Minn. 55424.

CAREER: Madison Public Schools, Madison, Wis., art teacher, 1947-49; Shorewood Hills Schools, Shorewood Hills, Wis., art teacher, 1949-50; South Shore Community School, Port Wing, Wis., art and creative writing teacher, 1953-56; Trust Territory of the Pacific Islands, Truk, Eastern Caroline Islands, art and creative writing teacher, 1956-58; Eureka Public Schools, Eureka, Calif., elementary school teacher, 1960-63; College of St. Scholastica, Duluth, Minn., art and creative writing methods teacher, 1964-66; writer. *Member:* Academy of American Poets, Poetry Society of America, Society of Children's Book Writers. *Awards, honors:* Teacher's Choice from the National Council of Teachers of English, 1987, for *Words with Wrinkled Knees,* and 1988, for *The Star Maiden;* Minnesota Book Award, 1988, for *The Star Maiden;* Notable Children's Trade Book in the Field of Social Studies from the National Council for Social Studies and the Children's Book Council, 1989, for *Ladder to the Sky.*

WRITINGS:

Swing around the Sun, Lerner, 1965.
A Celebration of Bees, Winston, 1975.
Cold Stars and Fireflies: Poems of the Four Seasons (illustrated by Susan Bonners), Crowell, 1984.
Words with Wrinkled Knees: Animal Poems (illustrated by John Stadler), Crowell, 1986.
(Reteller) *The Star Maiden: An Ojibway Tale* (illustrated by Helen K. Davie), Little, Brown, 1988.
(Reteller) *Ladder to the Sky: How the Gift of Healing Came to the Ojibway Nation* (illustrated by H. K. Davie), Little, Brown, 1989.

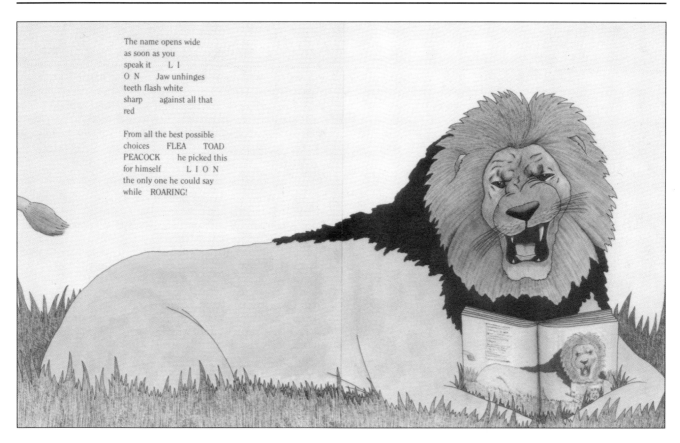

The name opens wide
as soon as you
speak it   L I
O N   Jaw unhinges
teeth flash white
sharp   against all that
red

From all the best possible
choices   FLEA   TOAD
PEACOCK   he picked this
for himself   L I O N
the only one he could say
while   ROARING!

(From *Words with Wrinkled Knees: Animal Poems* by Barbara Juster Esbensen. Illustrated by John Stadler.)

Great Northern Diver: The Loon (illustrated by Mary B. Brown), Little, Brown, 1990.
Who Shrank My Grandmother's House? (illustrated by Eric Beddows), Crowell, in press.
Tiger with Wings: The Great Horned Owl (illustrated by M. B. Brown), Orchard Books, in press.

CONTRIBUTOR TO ANTHOLOGIES

Myra Cohn Livingston, *Thanksgiving Poems,* Holiday House, 1985.
M. C. Livingston, *Poems for Jewish Holidays,* Holiday House, 1986.
M. C. Livingston, *Valentine Poems,* Holiday House, 1987.
Caroline Bauer, *Windy Day Stories and Poems,* Lippincott, 1988.
M. C. Livingston, *Halloween Poems,* Holiday House, 1989.
Bobbye S. Goldstein, *Bear in Mind,* Viking/Kestrel, 1989.

WORK IN PROGRESS: Dance with Me: Poems, for Crowell; reteller of *The Blind Boy and the Loon* (working title), for Little, Brown; *The Night Rainbow* (working title), historical fiction, for Orchard Books.

SIDELIGHTS: "From the age of ten, when I discovered that I couldn't bear to be without a book to read, I have considered myself a writer. My parents were not interested in my stories or poems, but became excited when teachers began to tell them, 'Barbara is certainly a good little artist.' Not until 1939, when I was fourteen and Russia invaded Finland, did I 'become' a writer. I was so upset at that international event that I wrote an anti-war poem and showed it to my English teacher the next day. She was a journalist and a published poet. 'Barbara,' she said, 'you are a *writer.*' From that moment, even though I took many art courses, majored in art

at the University of Wisconsin, and taught art for years, I thought of myself as '*A WRITER.*' She has seen *all* of my writing since 'that day.' Her name is Eulalie Beffel.

"It was my early reading of the L. M. Montgomery books that gave me the courage to play with words. *Anne of Green Gables* and the 'Emily' books made a terrific impression on me. Like Emily, I named my favorite 'reading-tree,' my bedroom, and a special place down by the lake, where I sat on the breakwater and thought about 'scope for the imagination.' My bedroom faced west and I called it 'Castle Afterglow.' I made a colorful sign for my door. It had a sunset with dark words crayoned over the pink; 'Welcome to Castle Afterglow: Keep Out.'

"Writing is my great joy. I have had six children, and children delight me as much as writing does. I want to be surrounded by flowers, so I am an enthusiastic gardener. I sing in a chorale—music is important to our family—and wish I had practiced the piano. My mother *said* I'd be sorry, and she was right!

"The poetry of Amy Lowell, Stephen Vincent Benet, and Sara Teasdale made me into a poet in 1941. Their use of language was the big revelation to me: Thomas Wolfe had me in a state of shock!

"In all my books I want to use language that will place an IMAGE in the reader's mind. Words can be combined in fresh, unexpected ways and when this happens, the result is a quiet explosion of delight for the reader. Whether I am writing prose or poetry, I like to find those word combinations and then watch the sentences catch fire and shower down sparks!"

HOBBIES AND OTHER INTERESTS: Music, singing in a chorale group, gardening, the natural world.

FOR MORE INFORMATION SEE:

CODA: Poets and Writers 1989-1990, Poets & Writers, 1990.

COLLECTIONS

Central Missouri State University Collection of Literature for Children, Warrensburg, Mo.
Kerlan Collection at the University of Minnesota.

EYRE, Frank 1910-1988

OBITUARY NOTICE: Born November 21, 1910, in Manchester, England; died March 7, 1988, on his yacht in Australia. Free-lance author, critic, editor, and publisher. Eyre published several books of poetry, and, as a result of his experience with the National Fire Service in England, published two books for young people, *Fire Service Today* and *Business of a Fireman.* From 1945 to 1949 he was managing editor of the Children's Book Department at Amen House, London, for the Oxford University Press. During this period the first volumes of the *Oxford Junior Encyclopedia* were published.

After moving to Australia, Eyre became general manager for Oxford University Press until his retirement in 1975. In this capacity he was instrumental in developing Australian children's literature, serving as a member of the Children's Book Council of Australia and as chairman of the committee which produced the *Books for Children* booklist. Ever enthusiastic about children's books, Eyre set up the Little Bookroom in 1960, and urged Australian children's books to retain their distinctive Australian flavor. In 1952 he published *Twentieth-Century Children's Books,* which was revised in 1973 as *British Children's Books in the Twentieth Century.*

FOR MORE INFORMATION SEE:

Humphrey Carpenter and Mari Pritchard, editors, *Oxford Companion to Children's Literature,* Oxford University Press, 1984.

OBITUARIES

Reading Time, Volume 32, number 2 (p. 2).

FLOYD, Gareth 1940-

PERSONAL: Born December 11, 1940, in Whiston, Lancashire, England; son of Leonard Sidney (an engineer) and Anne Harriet (a stenographer; maiden name, Smith) Floyd; married Penelope Dean (a nurse), August, 1965; children: Emma, Megan. *Education:* Attended Lowestoft School of Art, 1958-60; Guildford School of Art, National Diploma in Design, 1962; Brighton School of Art, Art Teacher's Certificate, 1963. *Politics:* Liberal. *Home:* 32 Wodeland Ave., Guildford, Surry GU2 5JZ, England.

CAREER: St. Joseph's School, Orpington, Kent, England, art teacher, 1963-64; Leicester College of Art, England, art teacher, 1964-66; free-lance illustrator, 1967—; free-lance model maker, 1981—. St. Catherines School, Bramley, En-

gland, art teacher, 1985—, art and design department head, 1987—. Artist for the British Broadcasting Corporation's "Jackanory" television show, London, 1972-84, 1990—. Served as town councillor for St. Nicolas Ward, and county councillor for Guildford South. *Awards, honors:* Carnegie Medal Honor Book from the British Library Association, 1969, for *The Night Watchmen;* Carnegie Medal High Commendation, 1971, for *Up the Pier; Book World's* Spring Book Festival Award Honor Book, 1973, for *The Writing on the Hearth.*

ILLUSTRATOR:

Marigold Hunt, *Patrick: A Patron Saint Book,* Sheed & Ward, 1964.
John Rackham, *Watch on Pier,* J. Cape, 1964.
Ray Pope, *Strosa Light,* Hart-Davis, 1965.
Rabina Beckles Wilson, *Anchors Wharf,* Hart-Davis, 1965.
Falcon Travis, *Grand Howl,* Brockhampton, 1965.
Eleanor Spence, *The Year of the Currawong,* Oxford University Press, 1965.
Sheena Porter, *The Knockers,* Oxford University Press, 1965.
Richard Parker, *Second Hand Family,* Brockhampton, 1965.
F. Travis, *Tawny Talent,* Brockhampton, 1966.
N. D. Smith, *Discovering Flight,* University of London Press, 1966, Dufour, 1968.
J. D. Bentley, *Leif Ericsson and the North Atlantic,* Hulton, 1967.
John Sanders, *Manchester,* Hart-Davis, 1967.
Daniel Roberts, *Roller Skate War,* Methuen, 1967.
F. Travis, *Tawny Trail,* Brockhampton, 1967.
Paul Buddee, *The Unwilling Adventurers,* Beaver Books, 1967.
R. Pope, *Salvage from Strosa,* Hart-Davis, 1967.
Nicholas Tyndall, *Prison People,* Educational Explorers, 1967.
Barbara Willard, *The Grove of Green Holly,* Longman, 1967.

GARETH FLOYD

Gilia came in carrying a big bunch of holly. (Illustration by Gareth Floyd from *Flight to the Forest* by Barbara Willard.)

Ronald Welch, *The Hawk,* Oxford University Press, 1967, Abelard, 1969.

B. Willard, *Flight to the Forest,* Doubleday, 1967.

Martin Ballard, *The Emir's Son,* Constable, 1967.

Harry Fleming, *One Exciting Day,* Brockhampton, 1967.

B. Willard, *Royal Rosie,* Hutchinson, 1968.

Jane Louise Curry, *The Sleepers,* Harcourt, 1968.

Philip Turner, *Steam on the Line,* World Publishing, 1968.

Richard Armstrong, *The Mutineers,* Dent, 1968.

Mary Leonore Murphy, *Douglas Can't Read,* Educational Explorers, 1968.

Ian Serraillier, *Havelock the Warrior,* Hamish Hamilton, 1968.

Helen Cresswell, *The Signposters,* Faber, 1968.

Geraldine Kaye, *Tawno the Gypsy Boy,* Brockhampton, 1968.

Michael Brown, editor, *Small Boat Adventures,* Hamish Hamilton, 1968.

Carol Beach York, *The Blue Umbrella,* Angus & Robertson, 1969.

R. P. A. Edwards, *The Tower Block,* Burke Books, 1969.

R. P. A. Edwards, *The Bypass,* Burke Books, 1969.

R. P. A. Edwards, *The New Town,* Burke Books, 1969.

R. P. A. Edwards, *The Branch Line,* Burke Books, 1969.

J. Sanders, *Birmingham,* Longman, 1969.

R. D. Lobban, *The Clansmen,* University of London Press, 1969.

H. Cresswell, *The Nightwatchmen,* Faber, 1969.

J. L. Curry, *The Change Child,* Harcourt, 1969.

John Hampden, *The Yellow Dragon,* Deutsch, 1969.

Leonard Wibberley, *Beyond Hawaii,* Macdonald, 1969.

R. Pope, *Desperate Breakaway,* Hart-Davis, 1969.

H. Cresswell, *A Game of Catch,* Chatto, Boyd & Oliver, 1969.

Betsy Byars, *The Midnight Fox,* Faber, 1970.

Charles Dickens, *Great Expectations,* abridged by Rosemary Manning, American Educational, 1970.

R. Pope, *Telford and the American Visitor,* Macdonald, 1970.

R. Pope, *Model Railway Men,* Macdonald, 1970.

M. Ballard, *Era Histories* (six volumes), Methuen, 1970.

B. Willard, *Lark and the Laurel,* Longman, 1970.

Sybil Allen and Roma Tomalty, *The Guardian Sword,* Abelard, 1970.

Audrey Weigh, *Bahama Adventure,* Abelard, 1970.

Clifford B. Hicks, *Alvin Fernald: Mayor for a Day,* Macdonald & James, 1970.

Molly Hunter, *The Bodach,* Blackie, 1970.

Joseph E. Chipperfield, *Storm Island,* Hutchinson Australia, 1970.

P. D. Pemberton, *Richard's M-Class Cows,* Faber, 1971.

Cynthia Harnett, *The Writing on the Hearth,* Methuen, 1971, Viking, 1973, new edition, Lerner, 1984.

R. Pope, *Model Railway Men Take Over,* Macdonald, 1971.

John Kitching, *Anyway,* Macmillan, 1971.

H. Cresswell, *Up the Pier,* Faber, 1971, Macmillan, 1972.

Catherine Storr, *Kate and the Island,* Faber, 1972.

G. Kaye, *Nowhere to Stop,* Brockhampton, 1972.

David Oakden, *Five Clues to the Dragon,* Brockhampton, 1972.

Mary Cockett, *Boat Girl,* Chatto, Boyd & Oliver, 1972.

V. Wear and F. Wear, *Hidden Germs of the Cote d'Opale,* Elmtree Books, 1972.

John Mendes, *Finch's London,* Elmtree Books, 1972.

Geoffrey Palmer, *A Year of Festivals,* Warne, 1972.

Eleis Dillon, *The Five-Hundred,* Hamish Hamilton, 1972.

Edmund Bohan, *The Buckler,* Hutchinson, 1972.

Catherine Sefton, *In a Blue Velvet Dress,* Faber, 1972.

Margaret J. Baker, *The Sand Bird,* T. Nelson, 1973.

Christobel Mattingly, *The Battle of the Galah Trees,* Brockhampton, 1973.

Peter Dickinson, *The Gift,* Gollancz, 1973.

Deji Lewis, *Tunde on the Run,* University of London Press, 1973.

Howard Pyle, *The Merry Adventures of Robin Hood,* Collins, 1973.

Meta Mayne Reid, *The Plotters of Pollnashee,* Lutterworth, 1973.

Lavinia Derwent, *The Boy in the Bible,* Blackie, 1973.

Douglas Botting, *The Pirates of the Spanish Main,* Longman, 1973.

R. L. Scott-Buccleuch, *The Promise,* Heinemann, 1974.

R. Parker, *He Is Your Brother,* Brockhampton, 1974.

Lawrence Meynell, *The Great Cup Tie,* Kaye & Ward, 1974.

Mary Schraeder, *Hey Robin Hide,* Kaye & Ward, 1974.

James Reeves, *Two Greedy Bears,* Hamish Hamilton, 1974.

R. Pope, *Telford Saves the Line,* Macdonald, 1974.

Irma Chilton, *The Hundred,* Macmillan, 1974.

J. Hampden, *The Donkey and the Hobgoblin,* Deutsch, 1974.

J. Kitching, *One from Three Makes None,* Macmillan, 1974.

Margaret J. Baker, *Lock, Stock and Barrel,* Methuen, 1974.

Rupert Swindells, *A Candle in the Night,* David & Charles, 1974.

Miss Read, *Animal Boy,* Pelham Books, 1975.

Ann Turnball, *The Wolf King,* Kestrel, 1975.

Cecil Maiden, *Castle Dangerous,* Pelham Books, 1975.

Alan C. Jenkins, *The Man Who Rode a Tiger,* Hamish Hamilton, 1975.

G. Kaye, *Billy-Boy,* Brockhampton, 1975.

Bill Naughton, *The Goalkeeper's Revenge and Other Stories,* Heinemann, 1976.

B. Willard, *The Miller's Boy,* Kestrel, 1976.

He stole by a complicated zigzag route. (Illustration by Gareth Floyd from *The Nightwatchmen* by Helen Cresswell.)

Helen Soloman, *The Time Junction,* Good Reading, 1976.

Penelope Lively, *The Whispering Knights,* Dutton, 1976.

Margaret Greaves, *Nothing Ever Happens on Sundays* (adapted from the television show "Jackanory"), British Broadcasting Corp. (BBC), 1976.

R. Pope, *Telford Goes Dutch,* Macdonald, 1976.

Joyce Gard, *The Hagwaste Donkeys,* Pelham Books, 1976.

M. Cockett, *Backyard Bird Hospital,* Hodder & Stoughton, 1976.

G. Kaye, *Children of the Turnpike,* Hodder & Stoughton, 1976.

Michael Hardcastle, *Holiday House,* Benn, 1977.

M. Hardcastle, *Fire on the Sea,* Benn, 1977.

M. Hardcastle, *Strong Arm,* Benn, 1977.

M. Hardcastle, *Crash Car,* Benn, 1977.

David Howarth, *1066: Year of the Conquest,* Collins, 1977.

Jubilee Jackanory (anthology), BBC, 1977.

R. Pope, *Telford Tells the Truth,* Mcdonald & James, 1977.

R. Pope, *Telford and the Ffestiniog Railway,* Macdonald & James, 1977.

Nora Rock, *Horses for the King,* Hamish Hamilton, 1978.

Joan de Hamel, *Take the Long Path,* Lutterworth, 1978.

Catherine Storr, *Kate and the Island,* Faber, 1978.

R. Pope, *Model Railwaymen in America,* Macdonald, 1978.

Frances Hodgson Burnett, *The Secret Garden,* Octopus Books, 1978.

F. H. Burnett, *Little Princess,* Octopus Books, 1978.

F. H. Burnett, *Little Lord Fauntleroy,* Octopus Books, 1978.

H. Soloman, *Stranded at Stafna,* Good Reading, 1979.

Ruth Dallas, *Shining Rivers,* Methuen, 1979.

Clare Cooper, *David's Ghost,* Hodder & Stoughton, 1980.

Aidan Chambers, *Ghosts That Haunt You,* Kestrel, 1980.

M. Greaves, *The Snake Whistle,* BBC, 1980.

Angela Grunsell, *Jackdaw, Jackdaw,* Macmillan Educational, 1980.

Ron Grunsell, *Stan the Stammerer,* Macmillan, 1980.

Pamela Oldfield, *A Bed for Buffy,* Macmillan, 1980.

Eileen Molony, *Giant, Spriggan, and Bucaboo,* Kaye & Ward, 1981.

Gillian Cross, *Save Our School,* Methuen, 1981.

C. Storr, *February Yowler,* Faber, 1982.

P. Dickinson, *The Gift,* Penguin, 1982.

G. Cross, *The Mintyglo Kid,* Methuen, 1983.

Jenny Butterworth, *The House in the Woods,* Kaye & Ward, 1984.

Michael Morpurgo, *Little Foxes,* Kaye & Ward, 1984.

Annabel Farjeon, *The Lucky Ones,* Kaye & Ward, 1984.

Charlotte Gerlings, *The Spangler's Gang,* Hodder & Stoughton, 1985.

G. Cross, *Swimmathon!,* Methuen, 1986.

Kenneth Lillington, *The Hallowe'en Cat,* Faber, 1987.

K. Lillington, *Gabrielle,* Faber, 1988.

Kevin Crossley-Holland, *Wulf,* Faber, 1988.

K. Lillington, *Real Life Dinosaur and Other Stories,* Faber, 1990.

Also illustrator of "Sparks" reading series, Stage Two, Three, and Four, by R. M. Fisher, published by Blackie, and of school pamphlets and paperbacks and book jackets. Contributor of illustrations to periodicals, including *Cricket.*

SIDELIGHTS: "I was born in 1940 during the first blitz on Liverpool, shortly after my parents moved to Whiston [Merseyside] to escape the bombs falling on London. My father worked as an engineer for a dust collecting company in munitions factories (now called air conditioning), a job which took him all over the country. My early childhood recollections are of constant moving, and if memory serves correctly, I've had more than thirty addresses.

"When I was six we went to live with my grandparents who were running a post office and store in a fascinating village called Homersfield in Suffolk. Unfortunately my mother and my grandmother didn't get along, and we ended up having to move into an old hospital site on an ex-American airbase. We had the run of four huge Nisson huts sectioned off to create bedrooms. School was six miles away but rarely attended during that winter of 1947. Snow drifted to the top of the door that year and we were unable to get out." A pot-boiler stove in the middle of the room was the only source of heat and it was so cold, recalled Floyd, that "We children cried all the time."

Apart from the cold, however, the airbase, the runways, and the many old buildings provided thrilling adventures and

His face was alert and watchful now. (Illustration by Gareth Floyd from *Up the Pier* by Helen Cresswell.)

explorations for the children. "Walls were still covered with pin-up posters, airplanes were decorated with glamorous women and devils riding bombs. Some of those images were a bit frightening for a kid."

Later that year the family moved from the airbase into a house in Halesworth, Suffolk, a situation which reestablished stability of home and school for young Floyd. "My father tired of roaming around and decided to settle down. He landed a job as a tinsmith for the United Dairies, soldering damaged milk churns in a fume-filled workshop. The upside was that he would bring home extra pieces of tin and make models for me. Some of my most precious memories are of my father building a marvelous battleship that I treasured more than anything and a go-cart that became one of the greatest toys I ever had.

"After we settled down I was able to enjoy my schooldays thoroughly in a Catholic school run by two old ladies. They let us have free rein to make models and paint and draw. It was wonderful. Three or four days were spent making model airplanes and then we'd smash them in about three seconds when we tried to fly them—a very disappointing business. I built an intricate cardboard model of a monastery, forts and castles, lorries. This was an activity much encouraged by my parents.

"I became a passionate reader in primary school. I'd burst out into uncontrollable laughter with a book about a koala bear called Wumpus. I was a very down to earth sort of chap and always preferred non-fiction."

Floyd's artistic skills were demonstrated at an early age. "At the Sir John Leman Grammar School in Beecles, Suffolk, I was greatly encouraged by my art master, Robert White. I won national prizes for the Royal Drawing Society including the Gold, Silver, and Bronze Stars."

It was decided to enroll him into an art school at Lowestoft. "Coming from a fairly straight-laced school into a studio

atmosphere felt slightly bohemian. The two primary buildings of Lowestoft were located at different ends of the town, separated by a river and a swing bridge which was always a good excuse for being late. I spent two years learning a bit of everything, the equivalent of what is now called the 'Foundation Year.'"

In 1958 Floyd moved with his parents to Dorking in the south of England where his father took a job running a farm for a convent and Floyd enrolled at Guildford School of Art to earn the National Diploma in Design. "When I went for my interview at Guildford the principal, Alan Coleman, looked at my work and said, 'You're going to be an illustrator, that's quite obvious.' Since most students were doing graphics, I more or less worked on my own. I did book jackets and read Faulkner and Hemingway because they were good to illustrate. Most of my time was spent rushing 'round filling up sketchbooks and preparing work for my final exam. My teachers were the illustrators Nigel Lambourne and Ian Ribbons.

"I was also taught graphics by an eccentric Polish chap named J. B. Karo. I tried to avoid imitating techniques of teachers with a very strong style. Some of my drawings were included in a traveling exhibition of National Diploma of Design work—quite a distinction.

"One of the staff at Guildford organized a painting trip to France in 1961. It was my first time abroad and proved to be a wonderful experience. I determined to learn the language, bought a dictionary and have had a passion for languages ever since.

"We drove to the South of France in an old Morris Minor to a little village near Avignon where we stayed for about two months. Like little Van Goghs we were supposed to paint the landscape and the old chapels. Instead I spent my time drawing street scenes. I was fascinated by the little French car called *deux cheveaux,* the houses with their chicken sheds, women in their widow's weeds, gypsies, and cowboys. I was far more interested in the realities of present life than in the historical side of things. From there I went to Paris and lived on a houseboat for three weeks teaching a boy English. We didn't get on!'' Floyd returned to France several times during his student years.

In 1962 he enrolled at the Brighton School of Art on the Sussex coast for a one-year teacher training course. "We studied all the aspects of teaching, including child psychology and participated in group therapy. A lot of it was quite new to me. Although I thought I understood how a child's mind worked, it wasn't until it was put to me formally that I realized that all children want to excel, want to be loved and recognized for their worth and not be subject to criticism. It was very useful training and helped me later when I started teaching.

"I always loved the practical, mechanical side of things, and in Brighton I was able to experiment with that. As part of a project for a car design, I built a model car. I tried my hand at photography and weaving. I wove a green herringbone for a suit. The wind went straight through it, but it was hard-wearing and I was very proud of myself for having made it. As a hobby I played the guitar and made my own lute (it never worked very well). I also got involved in politics for the first time at Brighton as a student rep on the Student Union, which gave me an interest in debate." It was a time for searching and exploring to see which area of the arts most fascinated him.

The seaside architecture of Brighton and the Royal Pavillion, in particular, appealed to him. He spent his hours sketching street scenes, much as he had done in Southern France. "I filled sketchbooks with drawings of the lads who rode around

Floyd, cycle racing in Wantage, Berkshire, 1980.

on Vespa and Lambretta motor scooters covered with horns and lights.

"I lived in an old lodging house in Clifton Terrace along with ten old ladies retired from colonial life in India. It was as if they had been stuck in aspic. They wore the clothing of the 1920s, complete with headband and a kiss curl on the fore-head.

"I would travel to London on my Lambretta scooter to see Le Corbusier shows, classic impressionist exhibitions, and the prints at the Victoria Albert Museum. The Tate Gallery was, to me, the hub of the universe. I always loved the Pre-Raphaelites and the nineteenth- and early twentieth-century painters. Paul Nash was one of my favorites. Stanley Spencer's black scribbly pen and ink self-portrait had an enormous influence on me as a student. I always wanted to draw like that."

In 1963, Floyd left Brighton and began his career as an art teacher. "My parents words were ringing in my ear: 'You've got to get a proper job.' I was hired as full-time art teacher at St. Joseph's, a Catholic boys' school in Orpington [Kent]. I learned a lot, but, by God, I hated it. It was a secondary modern school and most of the boys were sons of Irish laborers who worked on a local trading estate. The students were not very bright, although in the end I did get to like some of them.

"I was one of four young teachers who were all going through the same hell with physical threats by these sixteen-year-old boys. It came down to the simple equation of them or me, and I determined that it wasn't going to be me. I had never hit anyone before that, but I resorted to socking them in the face. I was appalled and always ill because I was under so much strain. I left after a year. For years afterwards I still had nightmares and woke up in the night screaming their names."

That same year, Floyd met his future wife, Penelope (Penny) Dean. "One Saturday night, I said to my brother, 'Let's go to Guildford and pick up a couple of birds [girls].' We pressed our trousers and headed for a cafe notorious for picking up *au pair* girls. We had been there for an hour when two girls came in and sat next to us. I thought I'd try to invite them for a drink, and much to my surprise they accepted.

"It took me about three weeks to summon the courage to ask Penny to marry me, but I would have proposed that very night if I had been brave enough. We saved up for about eighteen months and got married in August, 1965. Our daughter, Emma, was born nine months after our honey-moon. Penny and I seemed to have nothing in common except this great bond and after all these years, I'm still a complete drooling passionate fool about her. As far as I'm concerned, it's the greatest love story ever told."

Floyd was offered a job to teach illustration at Leicester College of Art through Jerzy Karo, who had taught him at Guildford. "By the time I joined the staff at Leicester I was already getting some illustration work from publishers. When I got my first illustration job for Jonathan Cape I was overjoyed and, at the same time absolutely terrified. It was a boy's story about a flying car which needed black and white drawings as well as a jacket in color. I went over and over the text and redid the drawings again and again. It was an ordeal but I finished it and was paid ninety pounds which, to me, was a king's ransom.

Floyd's 1989 sketch of one of the ladies of Clifton Terrace.

"One thing led to another and my work with books gradually increased. At the same time I was getting fed up with my teaching post because I had so little to do. I asked Karo if I could possibly go part-time for the same salary and he suggested I become a free-lance illustrator. I did, and I've never regretted it since.

"In 1970 my second daughter, Megan, was born."

Floyd moved to Guildford with his family in 1968 to begin his career as a free-lance illustrator. "I've never found a book I couldn't illustrate. Sometimes it felt as though it wouldn't work and I had to start all over again. Sleeping on it is a good philosophy, as is leaving and coming back to it later. I usually do my best work under the pressure of deadline. I work fast in my fairly sketchy style, although I can be rather hackneyed with too many of the children I draw looking the same.

"I've always admired people who can draw many different characters: Ernest Shepard's drawings for *Winnie the Pooh,* for instance. He has a wonderful capacity for simple images that are varied. Over the years my drawings have improved and I've become more skillful at drawing more accurately (one has to unlearn so many tricks and bad habits from the early days).

"My drawings are always inspired by the text. I read it once, then go through it again very carefully for details. I look for the specifics in a character—whether he has brown or blond hair, whether he wears a particular jacket. Quite often the text is so graphic that I don't want to illustrate it. For instance, to draw a fight scene already described by the author would be redundant. Instead, I may do a landscape or some other setting which will fit the book.

"Over the years I have accumulated mental pictures and can usually retrieve one from my brain cells. I prefer my memory to photographs, although I'm sometimes given them to work from. Most of the people I put in the illustrations are a blend of real and imagined—it's a subliminal thing. Having done a lot of sketchbook work throughout my life, my mental image of things is almost better than reality. But one still needs to cull from nature.

"My daughters claim that I always put them in my drawings, but I don't think I do. They are quite funny about my work and like to knock me down in a joking sort of way. Across our garden wall are the playing fields of the school they attended. In the summer I used to siesta on a deck chair and hear my children playing in the field. Their friends would ask, 'What does your dad do; he's always lying in the garden asleep?' And my daughters would answer, 'Oh, you know, he is out of work.' But I think they have always been secretly proud to have a father who has his name in books and on television.

"I've worked with several authors and have had good relationships with some, but quite often publishers try to keep us apart because it's less trouble for them. Nevertheless, I got to meet Helen Cresswell after I had illustrated a couple of her books, as well as Barbara Willard with whom I got on terribly well. I love her stories. I have not illustrated many of them, but did a lot of jackets for her. I also got on well by letter with Ray Pope, who did a very popular series about a boy who had model railways in which the little men came alive. Ray was a lorry driver and died tragically of a heart attack when he was only forty-six.

"I've rarely turned work down, although I did reject a hideous racist South African text on political grounds. I'm pretty good at self-discipline, since there's nothing like knowing that you've got a mortgage to pay, a wife and two children to support to get you going."

Another source of income for Floyd has been his work for television, particularly for the famous BBC children's series, "Jackanory." "The BBC people, who had seen a book I illustrated, asked if I'd like to work on 'Jackanory.' It ran every weekday evening for about twenty minutes during which the presenter read a story interspersed with still illustrations. Each story was spread over five episodes and required about sixty pictures. I used to do about two Jackanory commissions a year. Among the stories I did were 'Stig of the Dump,' and 'The Railway Children.' I also did a lot of Helen Cresswell's texts. Nineteen-seventy-seven was the Jubilee Year and the BBC commissioned special stories and a book in which I was involved as well.

"Drawing for television is quite different. My usual style had been to draw in pen, then in color in a sort of pen-wash drawing. That technique presented a problem on television where you tend to get a strobing of lines, the effect of lines crossing. When lines are at a right angle with one another there is no difficulty, but when the angles are similar it doesn't work. You can see it, for instance, when someone in the studio wears a jazzy suit or Prince of Wales check. The horizontal lines on the screen begin to coalesce with the lines of the suit and you get a vibrating effect. A more painterly style is often more suitable for television illustrations.

"Television scale is larger and calls for a bigger sweep. For 'Jackanory' I did big, loose drawings and colored them in afterwards. And because dull colors come up brighter on TV, I usually did washy sort of drawings that came up strong.

"The directors of 'Jackanory' were quite specific about the passages they wanted illustrated, though I often could control it and they'd agree to change it. It's not easy to finish sixty pictures on a tight schedule, and you can't be late with material for television. I had to fight my way back to the drawing board each time. Once the drawings were done I had to go to the studios and spend about three days altering details. The job was well paid and that was good incentive. I was given much work because I was reliable and always turned the goods in on time. I had heard many stories of illustrators who couldn't take the strain. The producer would have to finish the drawings because the artist was too traumatized to go on. I worked on 'Jackanory' for twelve years and was in shock when they cut it off. It was rather like being an actor in a long-running series which suddenly ends. It has now restarted and I have just done one of the first stories, 'The Finding,' by Nina Bawden."

In the late 1970s when his income from illustration began to decline, Floyd was able to turn his love of model-making into financial rewards. "One of my undying passions had always been making models, particularly aircraft and railway engines. I began making model ships for a shop in Putney, and eventually built models for the Arabs and the oil industry—mostly freighters and roll-on, roll-off ferries. I also did oil rigs and oil rig support ships which have lots of railings and cranes. The railings are only about a centimeter high and extremely intricate. They are made with fuse wire wound up and down on a board with nails on it, then stuck together.

Many of my models have ended up in showrooms, museums, and boardrooms throughout the world.

"When the shipping industry started to fall away I turned to making model railway engines for men who have their own model railway. Over the years I have developed my own model railway that runs from one room in my basement to another. Miniaturization has kept me on the straight and narrow and away from ale houses and loose women. I think everyone should have a hobby or an interest that is a passion."

Floyd's move to Guildford also coincided with his involvement in local politics. "I've always had a strong attachment to Guildford ever since I first cycled here as a student. There are wonderful medieval and Georgian buildings intermingled, and the cobbled high street is a classic blissful English scene. I always remember my first view of the high street with the river at the bottom and a green clump of trees at the top of the downs—an absolutely superb vista.

"After Penny and I moved here in 1968, we got involved in local amenity groups. The town center was riddled with parking and demolition problems. They started to put dreadful modern shops up, and I felt very strongly that the character of Guildford should be preserved. In 1971 it was suggested that I stand for election to the Borough Council; I agreed rather reluctantly. I stood as a candidate for the

Tom eased back on the regulator and gave a blast on the whistle. (Illustration by Gareth Floyd from *Steam on the Line* by Philip Turner.)

After school . . . he began trailing Gabrielle. (Illustration by Gareth Floyd from *Gabrielle* by Kenneth Lillington.)

Liberal party and, to my amazement, I won. It was one of my greatest thrills because a Liberal had never won before." This was the beginning of Floyd's involvement with local government. In 1973 he won a seat in Guildford's County Council, sitting on the education planning committees, and the parliamentary circuit. His experience with politics was "rather like a good book: I've read it and enjoyed it but wouldn't want to begin it again."

In 1985 Floyd returned to his career of art teacher. "I wasn't earning enough money as an illustrator or as a model maker to make it viable. I applied for a part-time job at St. Catherine's girls' school in Bramley. To my amazement I was shortlisted, then appointed. When the head of the department left eighteen months later I was given her job.

"It was a complete change of existence and quite enjoyable to be able to share all the things I had learned over the years. I've always tackled everything with enthusiasm and it's been an interesting process. I developed the course to include craft, design, model making, technology, and photography. It's easier to teach techniques than fine art because art is so subjective.

"The nice things about teaching late in life is that you have learned a great deal by watching your own children grow up, which helped me relate to the children at school. Many young teachers can't claim this experience and feel apprehensive, relying heavily on what I call silly and petty discipline. Apart

from my teaching days at Orpington, I've never punished anyone. You learn to let go as you get older.

"In a sense, teaching is terribly arrogant. Ruskin said that you don't have to teach your pupils, they just have to bathe in your presence. It's actually quite a profound statement. Every year I show a new crop of girls my sketchbooks because they are always interested in learning how to go about the process of observing and understanding.

"The school in which I teach is very academic. Most of the girls will go on to Oxford, Cambridge, or some other university. Art, with its strains of bohemia, is not valid for university entrance qualifications. Consequently, in the sixth grade form my students tend to shy away from it. Art is downgraded by many parents because 'there is no money in it.' I always reinforce the notion that if you're talented and hard working (the crucial part), there is a wonderful life ahead of you. The most marvelous thing is to take a piece of paper, a nib, and some ink and create something worth enough money to bring up a family.

"There are two wonderful sounds for teachers to hear: the sound of running feet coming towards their classes and the sound of a class groaning as you tell them to pack up at the end of the lesson."

Floyd continues to illustrate books and to make models along with his duties as a teacher. "A lot of the illustration work I do nowadays is for school books, particularly for Macmillan. However, I'm doing some books for Faber in the vein of children's adventure stories. I also illustrate the General Certificate of Secondary Education Life Skills papers, designed for children who are often not of the highest intelligence to give them the chance to pass an exam. The drawings have to be about modern-day youth, which today requires multi-ethnic pictures. You have to be careful that you get the character correct. If you draw an Asian, a Chinese, or a black youth, you've got to employ all your skills to make them blend in to make them believable. I became quite good at that kind of drawing and get a lot of work in that direction.

"One Life Skills paper was about a boy who wanted to be a window cleaner and the board was quite pleased to see that I had chosen to make him a punk instead of the usual well-dressed young lad. They liked down-to-earth style that illustrates different aspects of life. You have to keep an eye on current trends, but can't become too outrageous because the drawings will be dated very quickly."

Floyd is contented with his accomplishments. "I've got models all over the world and illustrations for people to see. I am privileged to have been chosen for the work, and it is marvelous to have given pleasure and have been creative."[1]

FOOTNOTE SOURCES:

[1]Based on an interview by Cathy Courtney for *Something about the Author.*

FOR MORE INFORMATION SEE:

Lee Kingman and others, compilers, *Illustrators of Children's Books: 1967-1976,* Horn Book, 1978.
Brigid Peppin and Lucy Micklethwait, *Dictionary of British Book Illustrators,* John Murray, 1983.

FRANCO, Eloise (Bauder) 1910-

PERSONAL: Born July 13, 1910, in Berkeley, Calif.; daughter of Ira James (a tree surgeon) and Ellen McKay (a teacher and governess; maiden name, Hensel) Bauder; married Tikhon I. Lavrischeff (a teacher and research professor at the University of Alaska), May 11, 1931 (died, December 5, 1937); married Johan Franco (a composer), March 28, 1948 (died April 14, 1988); children: John T., David T. *Education:* Santa Rosa Junior College, certificate, 1929; attended University of California at Berkeley, 1931, and National Academy of Broadcasting, Washington, D.C., 1940-46. *Home:* 403 Lake Dr., Virginia Beach, Va. 23451.

CAREER: Office of Indian Affairs, Kanakanak, and Hoonah, Alas., teacher, 1931; Library of Congress, Washington, D.C., research assistant, 1937; Federal Housing Administration, Washington, D.C., clerk, 1938; U.S. Government War Department, Washington, D.C., in charge of section for congressional and secret mail, 1940-48; *Searchlight* (magazine), Virginia Beach, Va., editor, 1948-56; Virginia Beach Public Library, Virginia Beach, Va., children's librarian assistant, 1950; Sarah Sadler School of Dance, Virginia Beach, secretary and receptionist, 1957. Lecturer. Volunteer teacher's aide, Project Head Start, Tidewater Rehabilitation Institute, and Tidewater Association for Retarded Children. *Awards, honors:* International Delius Award from the Delius Society, 1975, for "Ode."

WRITINGS:

Sing, My Soul! (poems; adult), Poetry Press, 1957.
Journey into a Strange Land (adult), Richard R. Smith, 1958.
Little Stories (juvenile; illustrated by Rein Bredius), Christopher Publishing House, 1970.
(With husband, Johan Franco) *Making Music: Teaching Children the Conscious Use of Inspiration* (illustrated by David Stevens), De Vorss, 1976.
The Young Look (juvenile; illustrated by J. Marianne Moll), De Vorss, 1979.

Also author in collaboration with J. Franco of song lyrics, and of juvenile plays, including "The Prince and the Prophecy," and "The Mystery of the Giant's Castle"; a juvenile ballet titled "The Pine Needles That Wanted to Dance"; an Easter cantata, "As the Prophets Foretold"; and a Christmas oratorio, "The Stars Look Down." Contributor of articles to *Mind Digest, Rosicrucian Digest, Treasure Trove, Unity,* and *Aspire.*

ADAPTATIONS:

"Making Music" (television series), WHRO-TV (PBS), Norfolk, Va., 1979.

SIDELIGHTS: "I call the University of California my 'family campus,' for I was born in Berkeley a few blocks from Sather Gate, entrance to the University; my mother attended before me and my son after me. I met my first husband there, where he earned his Ed.D. My second husband, Johan Franco, has joined us as he was awarded posthumously the University of California Berkeley Medal.

"When I taught Aleut and Eskimo children in the Department of the Interior School in Kanakanak, Alaska, their ages

Eloise and Johan Franco

were eight to eighteen in the third grade. This was in 1931 and I am sure educational advantages have since improved. In Hoonah, on Chichagof Island, it was not unusual for the boys to take two years to complete an elementary school grade, for they were needed to help with the family industry, fishing.

"During this time I wrote an Easter cantata, 'As the Prophets Foretold' and 'rearranged' some Russian religious and folk music to go with the text. Then Dr. Lavrischeff was transferred to the Library of Congress and shortly afterward passed away. It was then I was grateful my parents had insisted I take typing in high school, for then I could pass the civil service examination, ensuring support for myself and the boys. During World War II I was in charge of the War Department Section handling congressional and secret mail. During this time I was a member of Pen Women and the Writers' Guild.

"Shortly after the war I met Johan Franco, who had come to Washington to give a private lecture on the Count Saint Germain. I showed him the cantata and he did not like the music, but he did like me! We were married on March 28, 1948. We had just celebrated our fortieth wedding anniversary when he passed away in April, 1988.

"We had moved to Virginia Beach in order for me to edit the newly formed magazine of the Association for Research and Enlightenment founded by Edgar Cayce. I named the magazine *Searchlight*. I left it after several years to continue my own writing. It was then I wrote the oratorio, 'The Stars Look Down,' only portions of which have as yet been performed, although Johan's music for it is highly praised.

"I am naturally a spiritual person and agree with Johan that in any art form one should rely upon inspiration. In fact, the purpose of our *Making Music* is to teach children the conscious use of inspiration. *Little Stories* has been described as 'expressing the simple truths of life with an exquisite, delicate simplicity.' Of *The Young Look*, it is said the book provides 'the most basic principles of truth in a very subtle yet most explicit way.'

"I do try to be open for inspiration always and trust the Inner Guidance."

HOBBIES AND OTHER INTERESTS: Gardening.

FRANCO, Johan (Henri Gustave) 1908-1988

PERSONAL: Born July 12, 1908, in Zaandam, Netherlands; died April 14, 1988, in Virginia Beach, Va.; came to the United States in 1934, naturalized citizen, 1942; son of S. (an architect) and Margaretha J. E. C. (an artist; maiden name, Gosschalk) Franco; married Eloise Bauder Lavrischeff (a writer), March 28, 1948; stepchildren: John T., David T. *Education:* The Hague, graduated, 1929; studied musical composition with Willem Pijper. *Politics:* "Unaffiliated." *Religion:* Protestant. *Residence:* Virginia Beach, Va.

CAREER: Musical composer, 1932-88. Judge, National Guild of Piano Teachers, for twenty years. *Military service:* U. S. Army Air Forces, 1942-43. *Member:* Guild of Carillonneurs in North America (associate member), Broadcast Music, Inc., American Composers Alliance, Guilde des Carillonneurs de France, Southeastern Composer's League (charter member; treasurer). *Awards, honors:* First Delius

Award from the Delius Society, 1974, for "Ode"; University of California Berkeley Medal, 1988, for distinguished service to the carillon.

WRITINGS:

The Bacon Shakespeare Identities Revealed by Their Handwritings (booklet), Russell F. Moore, 1947.
(With wife, Eloise Franco) *Making Music: Teaching Children the Conscious Use of Inspiration* (illustrated by David Stevens), De Vorss, 1976.

Contributor of articles to periodicals, including *Musical America, Musical Quarterly, Cyclopedia of Music and Musicians, Nieuwe Rotterdamsche Courant, Rosicrucian Digest, Norfolk Virginian Pilot, Musical Courier,* and *Norfolk Ledger Dispatch.* Composer of 584 musical compositions including five symphonies, cantatas, works for solo instruments, children's plays, songs, and duets. Records include "The Virgin Queen's Dream Monologue," "The Cosmos," "As the Prophets Foretold," "Theater Music," and "Seven Biblical Sketches."

ADAPTATIONS:

"Making Music" (eleven-part television series), WHRO-TV (PBS), Norfolk, Va., 1979.

SIDELIGHTS: The first known work of Johan Franco (which he labelled "Opus 2"—although number one and no others so labelled have been found) was entitled "Fantasy about Princess Erea." It is dated January 19, 1909. He was ten-and-a-half years old.

While attending the first college of The Hague, Franco appeared repeatedly as piano soloist with the college orchestra. In 1929, after graduation, he studied privately with Willem Pijper, one of Holland's foremost composers and started his career as a composer with a sonatina for piano. His "First Symphony" premiered in Rotterdam in 1934.

Franco records have been played by many radio stations here and abroad (programs are now being listed as *in memoriam*). His compositions, performed in Europe, Japan, and Australia as well as the United States and Canada, have been described as composed by a person with a refined and artistic nature, a remarkable sense for color and sound, as well as an independence of conception which is far from ordinary.

Naturalized in 1942, Franco served in the American Armed Forces during World War II. On March 28, 1948, he married Eloise Bauder Lavrischeff, author and lecturer; they then described themselves as "Words and Music."

In spite of Holland's being known for its many carillons, it was not until 1949 that Franco wrote his first piece for the tuned bells of the American carillon, "Hymn to the Sun." Since then his compositions have been played on the carillons of many churches, including Riverside Church in New York and, on tour, the cathedrals of Great Britain with the Everyman Players, and at many universities and private institutions.

At the time of his death from a heart attack, Franco had composed 222 works for the carillon. The Guild of Carillonneurs in North America honored Franco by making him an associate member and said of his compositions, "It

We need to be concerned with the effects of polluting the water and the air. (Illustration by David Stevens from *Making Music* by Eloise Franco. Music by Johan Franco.)

takes a non-carillonneur to write significant music for the instrument."

Johan Franco commented: "I have learned to rely exclusively on Inspiration. All else is mere scaffolding."

HOBBIES AND OTHER INTERESTS: Travel, stereo photography.

FOR MORE INFORMATION SEE:

So Practical a Contribution, National Orchestral Association, 1930-40.
American Composers Alliance Bulletin, Volume VIII, number 3, Volume XIII, number 3.
Bulletin of the Guild of Carillonneurs in North America, Volume XVII, number 1, 1966.
Virginian-Pilot and Ledger-Star (obituary), April 16, 1988 (p. B3).

COLLECTIONS

Moldenhauer Archives, Northwestern University, Evanston, Ill.

GARLAND, Sarah 1944-

PERSONAL: Born April 9, 1944, in Hertfordshire, England; daughter of Richard A. (a writer) and Charlotte (a writer; maiden name, Woodyatt) Hough; married David Anthony Garland (an artist), May 30, 1964; children: William, Laura, Kitty, Jack. *Education:* Attended Bedales School, Hampshire, England. *Home and office:* 1 The Forge, Chedworth, Gloucestershire, England. *Agent:* Laura Cecil, 11 Alwyne Villas, London, England.

CAREER: Author and illustrator. *Awards, honors: Having a Picnic* was selected one of Child Study Association of America's Children's Books of the Year, 1986; *All Gone!* and *Oh, No!* were both shortlisted for Best Baby Books, 1990.

WRITINGS:

Rose and Her Bath, Faber, 1970.
Peter Rabbit's Gardening Book (illustrated by Beatrix Potter; diagrams by Garland), Warne, 1983.

ALL SELF-ILLUSTRATED

Rose, the Bath and the Merboy, Faber, 1970.
The Joss Bird, Scribner, 1975.
Henry and Fowler, Scribner, 1976.
Potter Brownware, Scribner, 1977.
The Seaside Christmas Tree, Bodley Head, 1980.
Going Shopping, Bodley Head, 1982, Little, Brown, 1985.
Tex the Cowboy, Collins, 1983.
Tex and Gloria, Collins, 1983.
Tex and Bad Hank, Collins, 1983.
Tex the Champion, Collins, 1983.
Doing the Washing, Bodley Head, 1983.
Having a Picnic, Bodley Head, 1984, Little, Brown, 1985.
Coming to Tea, Bodley Head, 1985.
Sam's the Name, Walker, 1987.
Sam's Cat, Walker, 1987.
Super Sam, Walker, 1987.
Sam and Joe, Walker, 1987.
Polly's Puffin, Bodley Head, 1988, Greenwillow, 1989.
Tom's Pocket, Reinhardt, 1989.
All Gone!, Reinhardt, 1989, Viking, 1990.
Oh, No!, Reinhardt, 1989, Viking, 1990.

Also illustrator of *Uncle Bolpenny Tries Things Out,* Faber.

SIDELIGHTS: "I write and draw about the domestic life of my family and friends, so my characters are generally cheerful, improvident, rather untidy, often distracted. The children tend to cope with the vagaries of their parents fairly well and get on with their independent and interesting lives despite, rather than because of, parental interruptions. I also write adult books on herbs and spices and herb gardening and work as a journalist."

(From *Going Shopping* by Sarah Garland. Illustrated by the author.)

FOR MORE INFORMATION SEE:

COLLECTIONS

De Grummond Collection at the University of Southern Mississippi.

GASCOIGNE, Bamber 1935-

PERSONAL: Born January 24, 1935, in London, England; son of Derich (a businessman) and Midi (O'Neill) Gascoigne; married Christina Ditchburn (a photographer), May 10, 1965. *Education:* Attended Magdalene College, Cambridge, 1955-58. *Politics:* "Middle of the road." *Religion:* Agnostic. *Home:* London, England. *Agent:* Curtis Brown Ltd., 162-168 Regent St., London W1R 5TB, England.

CAREER: Author and lyricist. Drama critic for *Spectator,* London, England, 1961-63, and *Observer,* London, 1963-64; also writes for television, and has appeared weekly on television as chairman of "University Challenge" program, Granada Television, Manchester, England, 1962-87; presenter of thirteen-part television documentary series, "The Christians," 1977, six-part television series, "Victorian Values," 1987, twelve-part television series "Man and Music," 1987-88, and six-part television series, "The Great Moghuls," 1990. *Member:* Royal Society of Literature (fellow).

WRITINGS:

JUVENILE FICTION

Why the Rope Went Tight (illustrated with photographs by wife, Christina Gascoigne), Lothrop, 1981.
Fearless Freddy's Sunken Treasure (illustrated with photographs by C. Gascoigne), Methuen, 1982.
Fearless Freddy's Magic Wish (illustrated with photographs by C. Gascoigne), Methuen, 1982.

OTHER

Twentieth-Century Drama, Hutchinson, 1962.

World Theatre: An Illustrated History, Little, Brown, 1968.
The Great Moghuls (history; illustrated with photographs by C. Gascoigne), Harper, 1971.
Murgatreud's Empire (fiction), Viking, 1972.
The Dynasties and Treasures of China (history; illustrated with photographs by C. Gascoigne and Derrick Witty), Viking, 1973 (published in England as *The Treasures and Dynasties of China,* Cape, 1973.)
The Heyday (fiction), Cape, 1973, Viking, 1974.
Ticker Khan (fiction), Cape, 1974, Simon & Schuster, 1975.
The Christians (illustrated with photographs by C. Gascoigne), Morrow, 1977.
(With Jonathan Ditchburn) *Images of Richmond: A Survey of the Topographical Prints of Richmond in Surrey up to the Year 1900,* St. Helena Press, 1978.
(With J. Ditchburn, Harriet George, and Peter George) *Images of Twickenham: With Hampton and Teddington,* St. Helena Press, 1982.
Quest for the Golden Hare (nonfiction), Cape, 1983, Salem House, 1984.
(Editor with C. Gascoigne) *Aesop's Fables,* Hamish Hamilton, 1984.
Cod Streuth (fiction), J. Cape, 1986, Ballantine, 1986.
How to Identify Prints: A Complete Guide to Manual and Mechanical Processes from Woodcut to Ink-Jet, Thames & Hudson, 1987.

PLAYS

"Share My Lettuce," first produced at Cambridge University, February, 1957.
"The Feydeau Farce of 1909," first produced in Greenwich, England at Greenwich Theatre, 1971, revised version retitled "Big in Brazil," first produced in London, England at Old Vic Theatre, September, 1984.

WORK IN PROGRESS: An encyclopedia about life, past and present, in the British Isles.

SIDELIGHTS: "I have done far too many different things, as a glance at my list of books and programmes will reveal, but that is what I love about being a freelance. You never know what will get you going next. My first children's book

BAMBER GASCOIGNE

came about because a personal friend, a successful children's publisher, Sebastian Walker, said that all that mattered was getting a young child to turn the page. So I thought, what better than a line of tension moving on in the pictures from one page to the next? And so came the idea of *Why the Rope Went Tight,* with a rope stretching all the way round a circus tent. Then my next children's character, Fearless Freddy Frog, came into being because my wife said one day that she fancied painting a frog water-skiing. What next? Who knows? That's the fun of it."

FOR MORE INFORMATION SEE:

Book World, December 1, 1968, December 5, 1971.
Spectator, December 20, 1968.
Books Abroad, summer, 1969.
New Statesman, November 5, 1971.
Times Literary Supplement, December 5, 1971, March 19, 1982, May 30, 1986.
Virginia Quarterly Review, winter, 1972.
New York Times Book Review, May 3, 1987.

GOLDSMITH, Ruth M. 1919-

PERSONAL: Born March 12, 1919, in North Stonington, Conn.; daughter of Thurman Park (a physician) and Harriet (Miner) Maine; married Charles Goldsmith, July 14, 1945. *Education:* Smith College, A.B., 1940; attended University of Paris, 1938-39. *Religion:* Protestant. *Residence:* Sarasota, Fla.

CAREER: Worked in publishing in New York, 1940-42; worked for the United States government in economic warfare in Spain and Washington, D.C., 1942-47. *Member:* Authors Guild.

WRITINGS:

Phoebe Takes Charge, Atheneum, 1983.

Contributor of short stories to periodicals, including *Magazine of Fantasy and Science Fiction, Atlantic,* and *North American Review.*

WORK IN PROGRESS: Research on the 1950s.

SIDELIGHTS: "The background that *Phoebe Takes Charge* sprang from was the small village in southeastern Connecticut where I grew up. Our schoolhouse had two rooms, with grades one through three on one side, and four through eight on the other. The school bell was a real bell with a long rope that the two teachers pulled on to ring. On Halloween nights the older boys turned the bell upside down as a prank. An impressive character from those days was Robert the Bruce, hiding in his cave, watching the spider rebuild his web over and over when it was destroyed, trying again and again. I was also partial to fairy godmothers, and still am.

"The village had once been a busy center, but had declined, leaving large, handsome houses along the road, many with acres of open space at the back, like playgrounds with stone walls and brooks. It was also left with a large and handsome granite library with lions out front. I'd have to admit that I preferred turning cartwheels on its lawn to spending much time in its awesome interior. But I was always interested in words, and what the arrangement of them said and didn't say. At some time in this early part of my life I decided I wanted to be a writer. I know I felt then, and still do, that children know a lot more than they're credited for. And a lot of it they have to keep to themselves.

RUTH M. GOLDSMITH

"I think readers are special people, who meet other people, places, and problems through the mind and imagination. And that's important to understanding."

HOBBIES AND OTHER INTERESTS: Watercolor painting.

GREEN, Anne Canevari 1943-

PERSONAL: Born December 17, 1943, in Norwalk, Conn.; daughter of Louis J. (a purchasing manager) and Helen (a stenographer and homemaker; maiden name, Smith) Canevari; married Monte Green (a high school math teacher), November 14, 1971. *Education:* College of New Rochelle, B.A., 1965. *Home and office:* Riverdale, N.Y.

CAREER: McGraw-Hill Book Co., New York, N.Y., secretary, 1965-67, senior book designer, 1968-80; Reuben Donnelley Corp., New York, N.Y., secretary, 1967-68; free-lance illustrator, 1980—. Chairman, Tree Committee, Riverdale Nature Preservancy; member of New York City Street Tree Consortium. *Exhibitions:* "Learning Materials Show," American Institute of Graphic Arts, 1975; "Cover Show," American Institute of Graphic Arts, 1981. *Member:* Freedom Writers, Amnesty International. *Awards, honors:* Award for Book Design from the American Institute of Graphic Arts Learning Materials Show, 1975, for *Concepts of Contemorary Astronomy;* *Art Direction* Magazine Creativity Award, 1978, for winning entry in "Creativity 78" show; Printing Industries of America Graphic Arts Award, 1979-80, for two covers, *Physics in Everyday Life* and *Retailing;* Cover Show Award from the American Institute of Graphic Arts, 1981, for cover of *Lauer: Structural Engineering for Architects; Latch-Key Kid, How to Run a Meeting,* and *Computer Maintenance* were each selected one of Child Study Association of America's Children's Books of the Year, all 1986.

ANNE CANEVARI GREEN

ILLUSTRATOR:

Ernst L. Wynder, editor, *The Book of Health* (adult), F. Watts, 1981.
Barbara Curry, *Model Historical Aircraft,* F. Watts, 1982.
Edward Stoddard, *Magic,* revised edition, F. Watts, 1983.
Christopher Lampton, *Space Science: A Reference First Book,* F. Watts, 1983.
Gilda Berger, *Religion,* F. Watts, 1983.
Melvin Berger, *Energy,* F. Watts, 1983.
H. H. Carey and Judith E. Greenberg, *How to Read a Newspaper,* F. Watts, 1983.
M. Berger, *Sports,* F. Watts, 1983.
Robert E. Dunbar, *The Heart and Circulatory System,* F. Watts, 1984.
Vivian Dubrovin, *Write Your Own Story,* F. Watts, 1984.
Bertha Davis, *How to Take a Test,* F. Watts, 1984.
Fern G. Brown, *Etiquette,* F. Watts, 1985.
David Guy Powers and Mary K. Harmon, *How to Run a Meeting,* F. Watts, 1985.
Judith Streb, *Holiday Parties,* F. Watts, 1985.
B. Davis, *How to Write a Composition,* F. Watts, 1985.
Irene Cumming Kleeberg, *Latch-Key Kid,* F. Watts, 1985.
D. J. Herda, *Computer Maintenance,* F. Watts, 1985.
George S. Fichter, *Cells,* F. Watts, 1986.
James B. Meigs and Jennifer Stern, *Make Your Own Music Video,* F. Watts, 1986.
Roy A. Gallant, *The Rise of Mammals,* F. Watts, 1986.

Sue R. Brandt, *How to Write a Report,* revised edition, F. Watts, 1986.
Ormond McGill, *Balancing Magic and Other Tricks,* F. Watts, 1986.
Lawrence B. White and Ray Broekel, *Optical Illusions,* F. Watts, 1986.
Paula Linden and Susan Gross, *The Mommy Manager* (adult), F. Watts, 1987.
M. Berger, *The Artificial Heart,* F. Watts, 1987.
Albert Stwertka, *Recent Revolution in Mathematics,* F. Watts, 1987.
Scanzoni and Scanzoni, *Men, Women, and Change,* 3rd edition, McGraw, 1987.
Nelson L. Novick and Maury Solomon, editors, *Skin Care for Teens,* F. Watts, 1988.
Beth Smith, *Castles,* F. Watts, 1988.
I. C. Kleeberg, *Fund Raising,* F. Watts, 1988.
Linda DeWitt, *Eagles, Hawks, and Other Birds of Prey,* F. Watts, 1989.
M. Berger, *Our Atomic World,* F. Watts, 1989.
Florence Mischel, *How to Write a Letter,* revised edition, F. Watts, 1988.
Patricia Ryon Quiri, *Dating,* F. Watts, 1989.
Isabel Burk Mazzenga, *Compromise or Confrontation,* F. Watts, 1989.
Kenneth L. Packer, *Puberty,* F. Watts, 1989.

Time outside doing whatever you want is good for you. (From *Latch-Key Kid* by Irene Cumming Kleeberg. Illustrated by Anne Canevari Green.)

Sommers, *Model Voices,* McGraw, 1989.
Frances S. Dayee, *Babysitting,* F. Watts, 1990.
Jeffrey Katzer, *Evaluating Information,* McGraw, 1990.
Thomas Rockwell, *How to Get Fabulously Rich,* F. Watts, 1990.

SIDELIGHTS: "Drawing and lettering constantly during my childhood was fun, but I was convinced I had to do something loathsome to actually make a living. So I didn't even take art courses in high school. I resigned myself to majoring in English in college and did pretty well until one night I found myself having to memorize a list of mythological figures from fifteenth-century literature, among which were creatures who dropped out of the sky in leather bags! The next day, I signed up for a basic drawing course, and the minute I stepped into that room and smelled pencils, chalk, plaster, and fixative spray, I knew I was 'home.'

"Upon graduating, however, I discovered that I was trained only as a fine artist, not for a career in commercial art. Three weeks of pounding pavements looking for *any* art job proved fruitless, so one day I walked into a personnel agency that had advertised for someone to write letters. I had given up on art. But they happened to have a secretarial job in the art department of McGraw-Hill Publishers! I grabbed it and stayed for the next fifteen years, learning how to spec type, do mechanicals, color separations, design brochures and textbooks, then book covers—my dream come true, almost.

"Meanwhile, a friend from McGraw-Hill had become an art director at Franklin Watts and began giving me some free-lance drawing jobs that I found so thrilling I could barely keep my mind on my regular job. After much discussion, my husband quit his teaching job to handle the business end and I quit my job to become a full-time illustrator. At first I took any job that was offered, but now take only what I love—full-color illustrated covers, medical and scientific illustrations for textbooks, spot drawings, chapter opening drawings, and cartoons. My favorites are lighthearted cartoon-like illustrations which are used in serious books for young readers.

"I thought at one time that I'd like to be a full-time cartoonist. Reading the biography of a successful cartoonist one day, however, I came across this chilling phrase: 'If you can't think of five cartoons while taking a walk down the block, you're in the wrong business.' Well, my rate was about one a month, so I discarded that idea and now confine my cartooning to illustrating reference books (such as *Latch-Key Kid* and *How to Write a Report*) where the subject is serious but needs lightening up, and where the material itself provides the germ of a cartoon idea. It's challenging, fun, and the authors are usually delighted that their instructional text has been sprinkled with humor.

"My favorite medium for covers is colored pencil because you have such complete control, but I've sometimes become impatient with the fact that you must often add four or five layers of color to each area to achieve the color you want—very time consuming. I do quite a bit of work with Color-Aid papers now, because of their rich colors and the fact that you can add colored-pencil highlights and shadows directly onto the paper. This is lots of fun and you get richer colors much faster. When I travel, though, (I stay in Santa Monica, California for several weeks each year) I do all my drawings in good old colored pencils, because all I need is a backpack full of bristol board, pencils, sharpener, eraser, and a small camp stool. No fuss or mess.

"This may not be what young people want to hear, but I've found that in this business reliability is almost as important as talent. I've known a few superstar designers who can get away with holding up a book's bound-book date because they just 'cannot create' until everyone is screaming at them, but they are the exception. A reputation for lateness and flightiness does not make the client eager to call you back, no matter how wonderful your work is.

"If you are a self-starter, however, organized and reasonably disciplined, free-lance illustration is a joy.

"Environmental causes are my third love (along with drawing and, of course, my husband!). I am an officer of the Riverdale Nature Preservancy, which spearheads efforts in my neighborhood to prevent the needless destruction of trees and natural habitats, and also educates people about local environmental issues. I have just written and illustrated a booklet entitled 'How to Save Trees during Construction,' which the Preservancy will be printing and distributing to local builders and developers. Many developers don't realize that healthy, mature trees add to the value of their properties, and this booklet tells them which trees to preserve and how not to injure them during the construction process.

"I also formed a volunteer committee in my co-op (412 apartments) which took over all landscaping of our grounds. Using all organic methods (composting, no pesticides or herbicides), we planted new flower beds, pruned trees and shrubs, maintained lawns, filled the outdoor pool area with tubs of flowers, and introduced a year-round 'indoor garden' in the lobby and mailroom."

GREENFELD, Josh 1928-

PERSONAL: Born February 27, 1928, in Malden, Mass.; son of Nathan Samuel (in business) and Kate (a homemaker; maiden name, Hellerman) Greenfeld; married Foumiko Kometani (an artist and writer), September 30, 1960; children: Karl Taro, Noah Jiro. *Education:* Attended Brooklyn College, 1944-46; University of Michigan, B.A., 1949; Columbia University, M.A., 1953. *Office:* 15215 Sunset Blvd., Pacific Palisades, Calif. 90272.

CAREER: Free-lance writer, 1956—. *Military service:* U.S. Army, achieved rank of corporal, 1953-55. *Member:* PEN, Writers Guild, Academy of Motion Picture Arts and Sciences, Dramatists Guild. *Awards, honors:* Ford Foundation Grant, 1959; Guggenheim Foundation Fellowship, 1960; Best Magazine Article of the Year from the Society of Magazine Writers, 1970, for "A Child Called Noah"; Academy Award Nomination for Best Screenplay, 1974, for "Harry and Tonto"; Christopher Award, 1974, for *Harry and Tonto,* 1979, for *A Place for Noah,* and 1980, for "Lovey: A Circle of Children, Part II."

WRITINGS:

NOVELS

O for a Master of Magic, World Publishing, 1968.
(With Paul Mazursky) *Harry and Tonto,* Saturday Review Press, 1974, large print edition, G. K. Hall, 1974.
The Return of Mr. Hollywood, Doubleday, 1984.
What Happened Was This, Carroll & Graf, 1990.

NONFICTION

A Child Called Noah: A Family Journey, Holt, 1972.
A Place for Noah, Holt, 1978.
A Client Called Noah: A Family Journey Continued, Holt, 1986.

OTHER

Clandestine on the Morning Line: A Play in Three Acts (first produced in Washington, D.C. at Arena Stage, 1959, produced off-Broadway, 1961), Dramatists Play Service, 1961.
"I Have a Dream" (play), first produced in Washington, D.C., 1976.
"Lovey: A Circle of Children, Part II" (television movie), CBS-TV, 1978.
"Oh God! Book II" (screenplay), Warner Bros., 1980.

Contributor to periodicals, including *Time, New York Times Book Review, Newsweek, Washington Post, Chicago Sun-Times, Commonweal, Village Voice, New York, Life, New York Times Magazine, Esquire,* and *Reporter.*

ADAPTATIONS:

(Adapter with Paul Mazursky), "Harry and Tonto" (motion picture), starring Art Carney, directed by P. Mazursky, Twentieth Century-Fox, 1974.

WORK IN PROGRESS: A novel dealing with the court-martial of an American GI in Germany for going AWOL from a special service entertainment unit during peace time.

SIDELIGHTS: Josh Greenfeld was born on February 27, 1928 in Malden, Massachusetts. "My family moved to New York ... when I was ten years old. I grew up in the East Flatbush section of Brooklyn, a step up from the ghettos of Brownsville and Williamsburg for Jews in the 1930s and 1940s."[1]

In a nostalgic trip back to the old neighborhood in the seventies, Greenfeld found "The nameplates in the apartment house cluster I once lived in were now a commingling of Danielses and Williamses along with Feinsteins and Landaus. The avenue corner featured two real estate offices, where once had stood a delicatessen and a grocery. A kosher butcher shop was a few doors down from a mini-market advertising collard greens. The one remaining delicatessen had two waiters, one black and one white .... Candy stores had all but vanished; yet drugstores and dry-cleaning establishments seemed to endure. The lots that had been vacant along the business-avenue block had developed into buildings but at the same time many of the old storefronts were boarded up. The effect was that of a rotting mouth containing new bridgework. There were other paradoxes: The streets seemed wider, from sidewalk to sidewalk, yet the distances between streets seemed shorter. The schoolyard in which I used to play ball—and shoot craps—looked neglected, grass and weeds had sprung up between the concrete boxes; yet there were nets on the basketball hoops—something we

JOSH GREENFELD

never had. I walked past the local Jewish Center; the huge Honor Roll for those who'd served in World War II was gone, but the same rabbi who presided at my Bar Mitzvah was still in charge. My brief moment of *deja vu* in front of the Jewish Center was interrupted by a flashing sense of the present—cops frisking a black against the side of a car."[1]

After he graduated from high school Greenfeld thought he " . . . would go swaggering into the world. Instead, I was in the subbasement of the post office, in the bag room, checking empty bags under a light-bulb lamp for contents left in by mistake—a kind of lower depths of monotony. For me the summer would end and I would start college but I wondered how the regulars could do it, day after day, without the promise of an end. And they even had had to pass a Civil Service exam to do it."[1]

Between 1944 and 1946 Greenfeld attended Brooklyn College; he received his B.A. from the University of Michigan in 1949 and his M.A. in 1953 from Columbia University. "In the winter of 1953 [I was] living in a fifteen-dollar-a-month cold-water apartment in Greenwich Village. I had been trying to tear myself away from my family—and my family away from me—so that I could become my own man, and, perhaps more important, my own image of a writer—free, independent, and broke."[1]

Greenfeld served as a corporal in the U. S. Army from 1953 to 1955, after which he began to work as a free-lance writer. On September 30, 1960 he married Foumiko Kometani, a painter and writer. "Clandestine on the Morning Line," his

play about a seventeen-year-old pregnant girl looking for the father of her child, was produced at Arena Stage in Washington D.C. in 1959, and off-Broadway in 1961. From 1962-1965 he lived in Japan, where his first son, Karl, was born. His first novel, *O for a Master of Magic,* was published in 1968. Throughout the sixties Greenfeld was a prolific magazine journalist and book reviewer.

On July 1, 1966 Greenfeld's second son was born. Noah suffers from autism. "After living the Bohemian life during my twenties, I decided that perhaps the middle-class way was the way for me; that the realities of its rewards were worth the surrender of my illusions; that it was better to have a family and children than to write seriously and have a life in art. Noah mocks that decision. I have been dealt the joker in the bourgeois deck. And I wonder if it is because I violated a fundamental law: I made a move which was alien to my natural tendencies; I tried to play a game I was not meant to play.

"So much for cosmic musings.

"But encircling [Noah] with an Orwellian word such as *autism*—one that cosmeticizes rather than communicates—is no help. As a writer I should have known to be wary of so murky a word, of any attempt to conquer with language an uncharted province of science.

"Yet, ironically, just as autism does not really exist as a unique and disparate form of brain damage, the games some people play with the term are only too real, and the effects of

Son, Noah Greenfeld

its use are all too damaging. Thus, many psychogenic-oriented professionals have managed to keep an organic malady within their own alleged esoteric expertise. Thus, certain parents of brain-damaged and retarded children—unable to face the realities and stigmas of the old words—have found an elitist designation, or diagnosis, for their children, requiring more funding, more staffing, more attention.

"But, to me, by far the cruelest effect of the glamorous term *autism* is the specious hope it promises for a miraculous cure."[1]

A Child Called Noah, published in 1972, was followed by *A Place for Noah* and *A Client Called Noah,* all autobiographical, all culled from the journals Greenfeld kept of family life. "I've always considered my journal to be my warm-up. And the great irony of my writing career is that the material I have culled from those warmup exercises for my Noah books has made me better known than any of my writing 'events' themselves. It is as if I am an artist with a reputation based on my palette rather than my paintings. But I still continue to chip away at novels and screenplays and theatre works, anyway.

"Since my three Noah books are all autobiographical I think it would be presumptuous—and dangerous—to talk in any greater detail about myself.... I have always believed in 'the tale and not the teller.' And writing the Noah books has served me well in that respect."

In his introduction to *A Place for Noah* Greenfeld wrote: "What is my attitude toward Noah? How do I view him? I think, put simply, I view him as a responsibility, someone I have to take care of—almost like a job that has to be done. Because if we don't do the job, who will? It's our job by elimination. And I mean job, just a job. I am no Job and Noah is no great affliction and neither of us is part of any cosmic test-or otherworldly joke."

Greenfeld is gratified that his "Noah" books have helped numerous families of the developmentally disabled. "They know that they are not alone and that they have nothing to be ashamed of. Their journey, actually, is a very common one. Indeed, I would venture to say that the developmentally disabled comprise one of the single largest minorities in our country—and also the one that is most discriminated against and abused."

From his novel *Harry and Tonto* Greenfeld adapted a screenplay with Paul Mazursky, who also directed the movie. "I modeled the plot on *King Lear,* and put the cat in so the old man would have somebody to talk to. I was going to use a dog, but a dog would have stolen the picture."[2]

The movie received the Christopher Award and an Academy Award nomination for Best Screenplay. Before the award ceremony, he thought: "Thankfully, the Academy Award hullabaloo will be over . . . and I'll get back to being a normal human being. I don't think I'd be going if Foumi hadn't bought the dress. I know I don't have a chance to win. I know it really doesn't matter very much in the scheme of things

(From the movie "Harry and Tonto," starring Art Carney. Co-scripted by Greenfeld, it was produced by Twentieth Century-Fox in 1974.)

even if I were to win. I am angry at the base element in myself for getting caught up in the sweepstakelike excitement of the whole thing. I like to think I am above and beyond such nonsense. But obviously I'm not. I want to win."[1]

After the award ceremony, he thought: "Needless to say, I did not win. That was expected. But I was also bored. And that was unexpected. I rented a tuxedo and rode a Cadillac limousine downtown just to be part of the studio audience of a TV show. In the rain. During the dinner hour. Next time I'll just watch the show in my bathrobe. How's that for being a sore loser?

"But Art Carney did win Best Actor for the picture."[1]

"If I'd done a cops and robbers movie, a genre movie, then it would do me some good. They have a very narrow vision—if it's the '30s, get me Bob Towne; if it's the '60s, get me Gloria and Willard Huyck ('American Graffiti'). That's what they call an idea around here. Paris in the '20s, Chicago in the '40s. If they ever get another movie about an old man and a cat, they'll come to me. 'Harry and Tonto' is a movie the studio can be proud of, but what does that mean? If we could come up with a Yiddish word that means *success d'estime,* we could revolutionize Hollywood.

"Look. If you're a serious writer, a serious artist, you don't write for the screen. How can you get involved in ensemble

stuff? You sit down, and you write a book. You write for movies because you want to be a director, or because the money is good, or because it's easy. It's physically possible to write a screenplay in two weeks; I don't think you can write a novel in two weeks. A screenplay is much less writing. It's 120 pages with a tab key.

"Hollywood ruins writers, right? Take Faulkner. He was the guy who everybody said was not affected by all this. He was [there] fifteen years: they put him on Biblical movies. Highblown dialogue. And he never wrote anything great after."[3]

"I Have a Dream," Greenfeld's play based on the life and words of Martin Luther King, was produced in 1976. "I went to Washington for the opening of 'I Have a Dream.' all the technical cues—the complete sound track—that the director had kept telling me not to worry about should have been worried about a lot more. But that's show business. The audience loved it.

"I was very moved on opening night too. Especially when Coretta King came onstage during the curtain calls and joined the cast in singing 'We Shall Overcome.' And at the party afterward, when I was introduced to Coretta, she turned away from the leaders and dignitaries clustered about her and embraced me with tears in her eyes.

(From the movie "Oh God! Book II," starring George Burns, produced by Warner Bros., 1980.)

"As always, though, the best part of being away was coming back. How I loved the moment I walked in the door last night. The cat eyed me strangely, Noah shyly, Karl expectantly (he knew I would have gifts for him), and Foumi with quiet delight. I hugged and kissed everyone, the paterfamilias home again. Life in Washington without them had been mostly an empty hotel room and long, solitary walks."[1]

Then the play opened on Broadway, "... and I wasn't there. Not because of Noah. But because of the carpetbagging director and producers. I couldn't decide what would be worse—celebrating or commiserating with them.

"Meanwhile, my lawyer has called from New York to tell me that the first reviews have been raves, that the play should do well during its ten-week run."[1]

Greenfeld wrote the script for the television film "Lovey: Circle of Children, Part Two" and the screenplay for "Oh God! Book II." His novel *The Return of Mr. Hollywood,* about a philandering and devious film director with a taste for drugs who returns to Brooklyn for the funeral of his mother, was published in 1984.

"I look like what I am, a writer in [his] sixties who wonders how he suddenly changed from a young adult to a senior citizen without scarcely noticing the passage of time."

FOOTNOTE SOURCES

[1]Josh Greenfeld, *A Place for Noah,* Holt, 1978.
[2]R. Z. Sheppard, "For Better and for Worse," *Time,* April 10, 1978.
[3]*Village Voice,* July 28, 1975.

FOR MORE INFORMATION SEE:

New Yorker, November 11, 1961.
Mademoiselle, March, 1969 (p. 206ff).
Harper's, September, 1972 (p. 108ff).
Today's Health, March, 1973 (p. 44ff).
New York Times Book Review, May 19, 1974, February 15, 1987 (section VII, p. 1).
New Republic, September 14, 1974 (p. 20).
Time, October 4, 1976 (p. 100).
Esquire, February, 1978 (p. 80ff).
Michael Rubin, *Men without Masks,* Addison-Wesley, 1980.
Time, May 7, 1984 (p. 114ff).
Los Angeles Times Magazine, June 12, 1988.

GUTHRIE, A(lfred) B(ertram), Jr. 1901-

PERSONAL: Born January 13, 1901, in Bedford, Ind.; son of Alfred Bertram (an educator) and June (a housewife; maiden name, Thomas) Guthrie; married Harriet Larson, June 25, 1931 (divorced, 1963); married Carol Bischman (a housewife), April 3, 1969; children: (first marriage) Alfred Bertram III, Helen Guthrie Atwood. *Education:* Attended University of Washington, Seattle, 1919-20; University of Montana, A.B., 1923; Harvard University, graduate study, 1944-45. *Politics:* Independent. *Home and office:* The Barn, Star Rte., Box 30, Choteau, Mont. 59422. *Agent:* Brandt & Brandt, 101 Park Ave., New York, N.Y. 10017.

CAREER: Lexington Leader, Lexington, Ky., reporter, 1926-29, city editor and editorial writer, 1929-45, executive editor, 1945-47; writer, 1944—; University of Kentucky, Lexington, teacher of creative writing, 1947-52. *Awards, honors:* Litt.D., University of Montana, 1949, and Montana State University, 1977; Pulitzer Prize for Fiction, 1950, for *The Way West;* Boys' Club Junior Book Award, 1951, for *The Big Sky: An Edition for Younger Readers;* Western Heritage Wrangler Award, 1970, and selected one of *School Library Journal*'s Best Books for Spring, 1971, both for *Arfive;* Distinguished Achievement Award from the Western Literature Association, 1972; Dr. of Humane Letters, Indiana State University, 1975, and College of Idaho, 1986; Golden Saddleman Award from the Western Writers of America, 1978; Distinguished Contribution Award from the State of Indiana, 1979, for contributions to literature; Commemorative Award from the Commonwealth of Kentucky, 1979, for contributions to literature; Montana Governor's Award for Distinguished Achievement in Arts, 1982; Kentucky Journalism Hall of Fame, 1983; Literary Contribution Award from the Northern Plains Library Association, 1987.

WRITINGS:

Murders at Moon Dance, Dutton, 1943.
The Big Sky, Sloane, 1947, published as *The Big Sky: An Edition for Younger Readers* (illustrated by Jacob Landau), Sloane, 1950.
The Way West, Sloane, 1949.
These Thousand Hills, Houghton, 1956, new edition, Gregg, 1979.
The Big It and Other Stories, Houghton, 1960, published as *Mountain Medicine,* Pocket Books, 1961.
The Blue Hen's Chick (autobiography), McGraw, 1965.

A. B. GUTHRIE, JR.

It was no more than a shadow passing in shadows, but he saw it. (From *The Big Sky* by A. B. Guthrie, Jr.)

Arfive, Houghton, 1970.
Wild Pitch, Houghton, 1973.
Once upon a Pond, Mountain Press, 1973.
The Last Valley, Houghton, 1975.
The Genuine Article, Houghton, 1977.
No Second Wind, Houghton, 1980.
Fair Land, Fair Land, Houghton, 1982.
Playing Catch-Up, Houghton, 1985.
Four Miles from Far Mountain (poems), Kutenai Press, 1987.
Big Sky, Fair Land (essays), Northland Press, 1988.
Murder in the Cotswolds, Houghton, 1989.

SCREENPLAYS

"Shane," Paramount, 1953.
"The Kentuckian," United Artists, 1955.

Contributor of articles and stories to periodicals, including *Esquire, Holiday, Atlantic Monthly,* and *Harper's.*

ADAPTATIONS:

MOTION PICTURES

"The Big Sky," RKO, 1952.
"These Thousand Hills," Twentieth Century-Fox, 1959.

(From the movie "Shane," starring Alan Ladd and Brandon de Wilde, produced by Paramount Pictures, 1953.)

"The Way West," United Artists, 1967.

RECORDS

"The Big Sky," Caedmon.

WORK IN PROGRESS: A manual on writing fiction.

SIDELIGHTS: A. B. Guthrie was born on January 13, 1901 in Bedford, Indiana. The family moved to Choteau, Montana where he spent his childhood. "The thing I remember most is boys walking on stilts, all kinds of stilts. Sometimes high, but usually they were about a foot and a half off the ground. We'd strap them around the knees and clomp around all day.

"Now kids grow up with computer games and television and are not left to their own devices. We went fishing, hunting, swimming—the water was so cold at times, we'd come out blue and shivering until we warmed ourselves around the fires we built on the banks." Guthrie is saddened that children today are not involved with the great outdoors he so much enjoyed as a youngster. It is vital, he feels, that they become acquainted with the fauna and flora that surrounds their natural environment.

The town was not his town anymore, the world not his world. (Jacket illustration by Wendell Minor from *The Last Valley* by A. B. Guthrie, Jr.)

Reading was also an important aspect of Guthrie's boyhood. His father, an educator, and his mother, a college graduate, shared a great love and respect for books and poetry. "My father would read Dickens to us, and the 'Jungle Books,' classics of that kind. As a matter of fact, I still have Robert Frost's first volume, which my father bought in 1914." He learned to love Latin. "It was invaluable in learning the structure of English and the origin of words, as well." He was also involved in school sports and considered himself a "trifle better than mediocre."

But at a young age, Guthrie had already experienced the harshness of the times in which he lived. Altogether, six of his siblings died during infancy, a cruel reality which much affected him in later years when his own children became sick. "I was sure they would die, too, because that seemed to be inevitable in our family. We had none of those magical remedies (antibiotics) and the old fashioned ones didn't work, especially when it involved bronchitis and pneumonia."

In 1915, Guthrie started working part-time on the *Chocteau Ancatha* weekly newspaper. "I found this job very useful later when I began my own work on a daily paper. I learned how to read type upside down, how to make-up and operate a Linotype by myself. I'd go down and help the printers. All that helped me when I got into real newspaper work. The printers respected the fact that I knew something about what they did."

After four years, he entered the University of Washington, but left after a year. "I was a little country boy and the school was too damn big for me. I also didn't like Seattle, with it's constant rain, something the Seattle people called 'liquid sunshine.' Days would pass before I saw the sun again. I couldn't stand it."

In 1920, Guthrie entered the University of Montana. "Dean A. L. Stone, the head of the journalism department, was establishing quite a reputation and I wanted to be a journalist. The University of Montana was much smaller, which I liked. You get to know the professors in small schools. In big schools teaching assistants do most of the work.

"I had a fine teacher named H. G. Merrian who had an interesting knowledge of what good writing was. I remember once when I read him the first paragraph of *A Summit of the Years* by John Burroughs. When he asked what was good about it, no one knew. He pointed out that there were hardly any adjectives. It took me a long time to realize that the adjective was the enemy of the noun."

After graduating, Guthrie traveled across the country looking for work: harvesting rice in Mexico, working on an assembly line in California, and finally returning to Montana in 1924 to become a census-taker for the U.S. Forest Service, followed by a brief stint as a salesman for a feed store owned by relatives in Attica, New York. He finally returned to journalism in 1926 with the *Lexington Leader* in Kentucky. "That was really a time of growing up. I figure the years from the teens to thirty-five are a period of learning where you start to gather some solidity in your convictions."

Guthrie's job at the *Lexington Leader* lasted twenty-one years as he rose from reporter to executive editor. "I was so busy as a newspaperman that I must have worked seventy hours a week. It was a daily and Sunday paper and I seemed to have to put them all out and enjoyed it. Toward the end, however, it got to be a routine and I wanted to get out."

(From the movie "The Kentuckian," starring Burt Lancaster. With screenplay by Guthrie, it was produced by Hecht-Lancaster Films, 1955.)

It was during those "growing years" that Guthrie began to question religious concepts and formulated his own values. "I'm convinced that legends, superstitions, and ceremony are the basis of religion. Heaven and Hell are the invention of man. I believe in an ethical religion of honesty, compassion, and mercy—all the good things we say are 'God-given,' which, I believe, man has developed in himself (the best part of him). After all, Christianity is only about 2000 years old, and how old is man? Fear and self-concern are the basis of religion: if you're good, you're rewarded; if you're bad, you're punished. That doesn't disturb me. I know when I'm dead, I'll be dead, and that's all right. What's wrong with oblivion? We have a period of oblivion every night in our sleep."

In 1943, Guthrie published his first book entitled, *Murders at Moon Dance*. "After reading other pulp stories I decided I could do as well. It's a trashy work of derivatives, but I'd embarked on it and decided to finish it. A man has to write his first book; he can't begin with his second.

"Journalism was no help except in the sense that it taught me something about the structure of language and increased my vocabulary. People think that because you can handle language in one medium, you can handle it in another. That's like saying that if you're a good bricklayer, you're also a good carpenter. They're separate disciplines, entirely."

That same year, Guthrie contracted encephalitis and returned to Montana. During the time of his recovery, he planned his next book, *The Big Sky*, which drew largly from his familiarity and love for the land. "I've always been interested in the West and it struck me that no honest novel had been written about the mountain men. There are novels, of course, but they idealized the mountain men, made little tin Jesuses out of them. I knew that wasn't true and decided to write an honest book about it."

Guthrie brought his idea to Harvard where he spent a year as a Nieman Fellow in 1945. "We were selected on the basis of our credentials and could study anything we wanted. I became very interested in international law and economics. I also developed *The Big Sky* through the auspices of Professor Theodore Morrison. He went over the book chapter by chapter and once I realized what he was talking about, I had no difficulty with his criticisms."

It was a country of sweeping valleys. (Jacket illustration by Arthur Shilstone from *Fair Land, Fair Land* by A. B. Guthrie, Jr.)

Two years later the book was published. It tells the story of mountain man Boone Caudill, who runs away from his abusive father only to discover that he'd been running away from himself. Guthrie's publisher pressed for another book and in six months Guthrie wrote *The Way West*, which dealt with western migration over the Oregon Trail. The book won the Pulitzer Prize for fiction in 1950.

Guthrie spent a brief period in Hollywood writing screenplays for several movies, most notably the screen adaption of Jack Schaeffer's "Shane." "I give director George Stevens full credit. 'Shane' turned out to be a landmark picture. Screenwriting is a very tiresome process because you have to use the present tense all the time. For a fiction writer, that gets to be old stuff."

Returning to Montana, he continued to write his western novels—*These Thousand Hills, Arfive, Wild Pitch,* among others—as well as an autobiography, a volume of poetry, and essays. "I work about three hours in the afternoons. That's the limit. If I make myself write more than that, the edge is off, and I have to rewrite the next day. It all depends on how the words go. It has to be right before I'll go on."

With works that have drawn heavily from his own experiences and his love for the region, Guthrie established a reputation as an American humanist, who has dealt more with the domestic and political aspects of the West than with its mythology. "I avoid that entirely because I don't believe in it. The formula western can be entertaining, but it's all myth and has caused a good deal of damage with its false impres-

sions. It's been a story of deceit on the part of the white man and tragedy on part of the Indians. I question whether the reservation system was the best answer we could have come up with, but that's only entered my work peripherally.

"Actually, I'm very interested in political affairs. I dislike the military mind set, however. I've never served, having gratefully escaped both world wars by accident of age. But I try not to be a preacher in my work, even though at times I seem to be one. I dislike preachers. The only things that I'm scared of these days are preachers and teenagers."[1]

FOOTNOTE SOURCES

[1]Based on an interview by Dieter Miller for *Something about the Author.*

FOR MORE INFORMATION SEE:

New York Times Book Review, May 4, 1947 (p. 1), October 9, 1949 (p. 5), November 18, 1956 (p. 1ff), January 17, 1971 (p. 30).
Writer, November, 1949 (p. 358ff).
College English, February, 1951 (p. 249ff).
Saturday Review, November 17, 1956, April 12, 1958 (p. 56ff), February 20, 1960 (p. 19).
Life, April, 1959 (p. 79ff).
Reporter, November, 1962 (p. 50ff).
James K. Folsom, *The American Western Novel,* College & University Press, 1966.
Thomas W. Ford, *A. B. Guthrie, Jr.,* Steck-Vaughn, 1968.
Western American Literature, summer, 1969 (p. 133ff), fall, 1971 (p. 163ff), winter, 1972 (p. 243ff).
Christian Science Monitor, December 3, 1975 (p. 39).
John R. Milton, *The Novel of the American West,* University of Nebraska Press, 1980.
Dictionary of Literary Biography, Volume VI: *American Novelists Since World War II,* Gale, 1980.
New York Times, March 3, 1983.
Contemporary Literary Criticism, Volume 23, Gale, 1983.

GUY, Rosa (Cuthbert) 1925-

PERSONAL: Surname rhymes with "me"; born September 1, 1925 (some sources say 1928), in Diego Martin, Trinidad, West Indies; came to the United States in 1932; daughter of Henry and Audrey (Gonzales) Cuthbert; married Warner Guy (deceased); children: Warner. *Education:* Attended New York University; studied with the American Negro Theater. *Residence:* New York. *Agent:* Ellen Levine Literary Agency, Inc., 432 Park Ave. S., Suite 1205, New York, N.Y. 10016.

CAREER: Writer, 1950—. Lecturer. *Member:* Harlem Writer's Guild (co-founder; president, 1967-78). *Awards, honors: The Friends* was selected one of American Library Association's Best Books for Young Adults, 1973, *Ruby,* 1976, *Edith Jackson,* 1978, *The Disappearance,* 1979, and *Mirror of Her Own,* 1981; *The Friends* was selected one of Child Study Association of America's Children's Books of the Year, 1973, and *Paris, Pee Wee, and Big Dog,* 1986; *The Friends* was selected one of *New York Times* Outstanding Books of the Year, 1973, and *The Disappearance,* 1979; *The Friends* was selected one of *School Library Journal*'s Best of the Best Books, 1979; *The Disappearance* was selected one of New York Public Library's Books for the Teen Age, 1980, and *Edith Jackson,* 1980, 1981, and 1982; Coretta Scott King Award, 1982, for *Mother Crocodile;* Parents' Choice Award for Literature from the Parents' Choice Foundation, 1983, for *New Guys around the Block;* Other Award (England), 1987, for *My Love, My Love; or, The Peasant Girl.*

WRITINGS:

NOVELS, EXCEPT AS INDICATED

Bird at My Window, Lippincott, 1966.
(Editor) *Children of Longing* (anthology), Holt, 1971.
The Friends, Holt, 1973.
Ruby: A Novel, Viking, 1976.
Edith Jackson, Viking, 1978.
The Disappearance, Delacorte, 1979.
Mirror of Her Own, Delacorte, 1981.
(Translator and adapter) Birago Diop, *Mother Crocodile: An Uncle Amadou Tale from Senegal* (ALA Notable Book; illustrated by John Steptoe), Delacorte, 1981.
A Measure of Time, Holt, 1983.
New Guys around the Block, Delacorte, 1983.
Paris, Pee Wee, and Big Dog (illustrated by Caroline Binch), Gollancz, 1984, Delacorte, 1985.
My Love, My Love; or, The Peasant Girl, Holt, 1985.
And I Heard a Bird Sing, Delacorte, 1986.
The Ups and Downs of Carl Davis III, Delacorte, 1989.

PLAYS

"Venetian Blinds" (one-act), first produced at Topical Theatre, New York, 1954.

CONTRIBUTOR

Julian Mayfield, editor, *Ten Times Black,* Bantam, 1972.
Donald R. Gallo, editor, *Sixteen: Short Stories by Outstanding Writers for Young Adults,* Delacorte, 1984.

Guy's novels have been translated into many languages including, Japanese, German, Danish, French, and Italian.

ROSA GUY

(Cover illustration by Max Ginsburg from *The Friends* by Rosa Guy.)

Contributor to periodicals, including *Cosmopolitan, New York Times Magazine, Redbook,* and *Freedomways.*

ADAPTATIONS:

"Documentary of *The Friends,*" Thames Television, 1984.

WORK IN PROGRESS: Alexander Hamilton: The Enigma; Benidine, a novel dealing with a Trinidadian family in New York; *Sun, Sea, a Touch of the Wind; Dorine Davis,* a biography of a step-mother; research in African languages.

SIDELIGHTS: Rosa Guy's novels have brought her acclaim and international recognition as one of today's most perceptive authors writing on the lives of black Americans. Best known for her award-winning young adult novels, her humble beginnings in Harlem were a motivating factor in attaining success as a writer. "Whether . . . to act or write or do something! It was a driving force in me. It was a driving force in that orphan, out there on the streets . . . who needed something through which to express herself, through which to become a full-bodied person."[1]

Specifics about Guy's early years are limited. Two dates of birth, September 1, 1925 and September 1, 1928 appear in standard biographical sources, but she declines to verify either one. She was born in the West Indies, the second of two daughters of Henry and Audrey Cuthbert. "I was born in Trinidad, a British colony at that time. How proud we were to be a part of that great empire on which the sun never set. We learned from British books and rejected as nonsense our folklore—clinging rather to the books that made for great dreams, accepting everyone's myth as our reality.

"But my peasant feet were too large ever to fit into Cinderella's glass slippers. And, where was the princess to kiss my brother and change him back into a prince and restore his meaning . . . our kingdom? And, which dashing prince would ever kiss and awaken me to my full potential after years of sleep?"[2]

Small wonder that Guy grew into a powerful storyteller; the oral tradition in Trinidad is strong. "My life in the West Indies, of course, had a profound influence on me. It made me into the type of person I imagine that I am today. The calypso, the carnival, the religion that permeated our life—the Catholic religion—superstitions, voodoo, the zombies, the djuins, all of these frightening aspects of life that combine the lack of reality with the myth coming over from Africa, had a genuine effect on me. But it was an effect that I knew nothing about, didn't realize played an important part in my life until much later when I was writing. But they made for an interesting background . . . something that I could call back on, something that I could hold onto as I went into a new life, a new environment. Something that gave me a stake, I suppose one would say. So that when I say I am West Indian, I have all of these little things—all of that broad background—that makes up the thinking, the searching of a person when art becomes relevant."[1]

Guy's parents emigrated to the United States and, when she was about eight year old, Rosa and her older sister, Ameze, joined them in Harlem. Shortly after their arrival, their mother became ill. Because of her illness, the two girls were sent to live with cousins who were followers of the charismatic Garvey. Years later, Guy attributed her activism in human rights and her love for language to those Garveyite influences. "That's where I did my first little poem at the Garvey meeting and stood up at the corner and listened to the Black Garveyites. I had an awareness of Africa that other people didn't have. I had an awareness of language because my cousin spoke so many different languages."[1]

After her mother's death, the two girls returned to their father in Harlem, but he also died a few years later. Guy and her sister were left orphans. "Being an orphan at a young age, had to affect my personality, the way I see things, the way I absorb things.

"The whole [experience] of always being on the outside looking in, in a way formed me."[1]

"I was confronted with the worst aspects of the society, without all of the sham. People take off on Black women who are writing about ideas and issues that are pertinent. But, if we really were to write about the things that happen to us the way they really happen—things that are done to us by our people just because of a lack of understanding of where we come from—then we would really run into a lot of trouble, because nobody wants to hear it!"[3]

As orphans, the two girls grew up quickly. At the age of fourteen, Guy quit school to work in a brassiere factory in New York City's garment district in order to take care of her older sister who had become ill. "Tiptoeing my way through the casualties of poverty in the ghettos—an orphan in New York, ostracized for those traits which being West Indian and Catholic had etched into my personality—wasn't easy. I shall never forget the day I walked, cringing, the length of a snowbound street and not one snowball was hurled at my head. I knew I was grown up: I believed myself immune from those influences molding the lives of the Americans among whom I lived.

"Rubbish, of course. I realized that when I looked through the galleys of my soon-to-be published first book . . . I had internalized all their pain, their resentment—to the snowballs hurled relentlessly at my head, and firecrackers at my feet—as I ducked and dodged my way through adolescence. But I never looked back in hate—but with a kind of sadness, a regret that there had been no books yet written, no guidelines from caring adults who might have made a difference, guiding us over the deep but narrow ravines dividing us."[4]

(Jacket illustration by Gehm from *The Disappearance* by Rosa Guy.)

After her marriage and after the birth of son, Warner, Jr., Guy became involved in the American Negro Theatre. "I sort of went out of my way to meet them."[1]

At the end of the war, she divided her time between night school, the study of drama, her marriage, and her job in the clothes factory. She was part of a support group of writers and actors who had formed the committee for the Negro in the Arts. "What we wanted to do was to have a group that really projected the life, the style, the dialogue, the type of writing, [the] expression that could only come from the black experience in the United States, and in my situation, of course, the U.S. and the West Indies. So together with these people we formed a workshop—a workshop called the Harlem Writers Guild."[1]

Formed in 1951, the group supported themselves, both critically and emotionally, in their common need to write. "All of us were workers, doing some other type of work. I was working in a brassiere factory making brassieres. And every evening I had to come home to write. Mornings, I had a son to get dressed and get off to school, and then I'd go to work. I did this for a period of years because at the time publishers were not necessarily interested in black writings, nor in our concept of what writing should be."[1]

During the early years with the Harlem Writers Guild, Guy tried writing short stories, but it wasn't until 1966 that her first book was published. Besides writing, the group was involved in the politics of the time. "The 1960s, for all its traumas, was one of the most beautiful periods in American history. Only yesterday? So it seems to those of us who lived through it. Television sets were in the homes but had not yet taken over the responsibility of parents. Drugs on the streets had not yet changed youth gangs, fighting over turf, into addicts, robbing everybody's turf.

"Young people, strong in their beliefs, came out in numbers to follow Martin Luther King, Jr. They marched, sang, professed unity, a dedication to justice and human dignity for all. Black and white students, understanding the dehumanizing effect of poverty, shouted slogans, 'Black Power,' 'Black is Beautiful,' into Black communities to arouse the youth to their potential.

"What an outpouring of literature—about Blacks, about Spanish, about Indians, Chinese. Americans suddenly wanted to know the kind of world they were a part of. They were eager to do something for the good of that world, help cure its ills."[4]

Besides political ideology, the sixties was also a period of violence, and Guy was not immune to the events of the period. When her former husband, Warner, was murdered in 1962, Guy left the United States for Haiti. There, "the trauma of [my] husband's death and an earlier moment of violence in the life of a childhood friend,"[1] provided the reasons to start work on her first novel.

Another event during this period—the assassination of Malcolm X in 1965—compelled her to work on her novel. She recalled being in a hospital near the scene at the time of his murder. "The hospital was right across the street from the Audubon Ballroom and I could look out of the window and see this crowd while I'm listening to the radio and hearing about his being shot down. I saw when they brought him across and I was just about out of my mind, up on the sixth floor someplace and knowing that he was downstairs, and not knowing if he was dead.

"Hey, Imamu, my man—what about letting me hold a coin?" (From *New Guys around the Block* by Rosa Guy.)

"I'd probably never be in the hospital again for the longest time in life—and there I was right on the scene at that particular moment. And I always felt very strange about it. There I am, the person looking in; I'm always there."[1]

In 1966, after years of learning her craft, *Bird at My Window* was published. "All these years I have been wondering—and grumbling—about the reasons I had chosen, and stuck to, so low-paying, so rigidly disciplined, so devastatingly lonely a profession . . . . Looking forward from my first book, *Bird at My Window*—which I dedicated to Malcolm X—to those still to be published, the one constant I lay claim to is *caring*."[4]

In his review of the book, Thomas L. Vince called it, "the most significant novel about the Harlem Negro since James Baldwin's *Go Tell It on the Mountain*.

"This is Rosa Guy's first novel, but considering the intensity and power it evokes, we can expect more from such promising talent. Her demonstrative skills in character portrayal and in the etching of crucial incidents are certain to keep the reader absorbed. Some of the language and a few of the scenes may upset the prudish, but there is none of the garish prurience or repetitious vulgarity so common in modern fiction. *Bird at My Window* may even become a commercial success; but whatever its fate, it deserves critical attention."[5]

Another assassination of an American hero led Guy to investigate what young people were thinking throughout America. When Martin Luther King, Jr. was murdered in 1968, Guy went south. "I was so affected by the death of these two leaders; I could say three, because Lumumba's death certainly had affected me. And just the fact that no sooner than you start building up heroes—they get knocked down like that.

"I felt that when Dr. King died I just had to go. So I went to my editor at that time [Greg Armstrong at Bantam], and I said 'I want to find out what the young people are thinking.'"[1]

The result of her travels was a non-fiction book, *Children of Longing.* "I especially wanted to know how these painful events had affected their lives and their ambitions. I traveled throughout the United States from coast to coast, going into Black high schools and colleges in urban and rural areas, into writers' workshops, the cotton fields and the ghettos, seeking answers from young Black people between the ages of thirteen and twenty-three.

"I have not edited their responses for spelling, grammar, or sentence structure, except when the meaning was too unclear. Their writing skills vary according to their different (and sometimes nonexistent) educations, ages, and life experiences. Yet each possesses and clearly communicates the one quality that is the undercurrent of this book—an intense desire to overcome the obstacles of a slave past that remains in the conditions of their present lives.

"In Chicago I visited the home of one girl whose mother works as a servant for a white family. The mother was upset by my request that her daughter write an essay on what she wanted to be. 'Don't put no ideas in that girl's head,' she said to me. 'She got enough crazy ideas already. Black like she is, she got big ideas. I tell her she better get some sense and study something where she gets decent pay, never mind all them high-sounding ideas.' Sitting smugly in her expensively furnished, slum, walk-up flat (she let me know her couch cost six hundred dollars), she had no idea she was part of the quickly dying past. Young people are saying, 'Black is beautiful.' They believe it.

"I visited a mother in Harlem, New York, living in a broken-down apartment building where I had to climb over dozing winos to gain entrance. The poor woman greeted me as though all her energy had been spent by the three robust children shouting and chasing each other over old, tortured furniture. She became just a bit more energetic when I asked the whereabouts of her son. 'I don't know where that damn fool is. Out there getting in some kind of trouble. Talking about he want to go to college. He ain't even finish high school.' I insisted on knowing why she thought he was getting into trouble. I had come to interview him because I had been told he was active in the strike at Queens College, aimed at getting more students from the ghetto areas. 'All that ain't nothing but some damn foolishness. Waste of time. They ain't never gonna let Black people do nothing nohow. If he knew what's good for him, he would be going downtown to get hisself a job.'

"But today's Black students are not going to be pinned down by negative parents, by white prejudice, by liberal put-offs, or the power structure. They intend to go beyond these obstacles, and to go beyond themselves. The intensity of their desire is clearly evident in the essays of 'Inner Cities.' One girl asserts, 'I want to be somebody.' A young boy wants Black people to stop hurting each other and unite for BLACK POWER. Another girl 'stands for good education.' Two young mothers, who started out in the dead-end street to which slum living leads, write about the ancient mistakes they made that have so often devastated the lives of the young—but they also fought back to a greater definition of themselves when opportunity presented itself. Hardest of all is the problem of the young addict who is trying to pull himself up from the very bottom of ghetto life."[6]

In the early 1970s, after publishing *Bird at My Window* and *Children of Longing,* Guy began traveling in the Caribbean. Her second novel, *The Friends,* was the result. It was her first novel for young adults, and the first in a trilogy about the Cathy and Jackson families. Named by the American Library Association as "one of the Best of the Best Books," it was also adopted as part of the English curriculum for high schools in Great Britain.

In a 1973 *New York Times* review, Alice Walker, described the book as a " . . . heart-slammer. [In] *The Friends,* I relive those wretched, hungry-for-heroines years and am helped to verify the existence and previous condition of myself.

"[The] struggle that is the heart of this very important book [is] the fight to gain perception of one's own real character;

"Beat you to the other side." (Jacket illustration by Conway from *Paris, Pee Wee, and Big Dog* by Rosa Guy.)

the grim struggle for self-knowledge and the almost killing internal upheaval that brings the necessary growth of compassion and humility *and courage,* so that friendship (of any kind, but especially between those of notable economic and social differences) can exist."[7]

The second novel in the Jackson-Cathy trilogy was begun while Guy was in Haiti. *Ruby* was reviewed by *Horn Book* as "a teenage novel: rich, full-bodied, and true in its portrayal of the world of the Black teenager . . . . Ruby, deeply sensitive and lonely, finds love in a secret homosexual relationship with Daphne, a beautiful, arrogant Black classmate. Their experience fills a desperate need at a crucial time in the lives of both girls, affording them an early insight into the depths and complexities of human relations and emotions. The author writes gracefully in the West Indian idiom as she analyzes perceptively the problems of young Blacks facing up to the emotional, political, social, and educational responsibilities of their own lives."[8]

Her final book in the trilogy about three young black women, *Edith Jackson,* was completed in 1978. "I took the two characters Phylissia and Edith—and I left Sylvia, who's a very interesting character—and made *The Friends.* And then *Ruby*—who was very special to me—and then the other side of Phylissia, of course, was *Edith Jackson.*"[1]

The trilogy makes a powerful statement about the failure of adults to meet the complex needs of young people. "I do believe that I'm trying to say that we live in one world and it's a damn small world and we have to care for each other. We have to be concerned about that world. The survival of one of us depends upon all of us."[1]

Young people, too, however, have responsibilities to assume. "I believe that life is before any teenager. I try to leave all my characters with the hope that they can change their future—that they have the right to change their future; that they have the right to question parents; that they have the right to make decisions based on moral values."[9]

Critic Zena Sutherland, in her 1979 review of *Edith Jackson,* said: "The characterization is excellent, the writing style smooth, and the depiction of an adolescent torn between her need for independence and achievement and her feeling of responsibility (which has pushed her into protecting the sisters who don't want protection) strong and perceptive."[10]

The Disappearance, Guy's fourth young adult novel is a suspenseful story about a streetwise Harlem teenager Imamu Jones. The mystery led to sequels. "Believing as I do that world survival rests with the young, I like to think that my contribution as a writer to their understanding of the world lies in exposing a segment of society often overlooked, ignored, or treated with contempt. It's a segment that cannot be wished away, and in the final analysis, our approach to its problems can determine the kind of people we shall ultimately be. As spokesman for that segment, I give to my readers Imamu Jones—the detective.

"'Issue oriented' books or 'required reading' can most times be a bore. But the world loves a good mystery. So do I. A good mystery can force the mind to reach just a bit further than it believes it's capable of reaching. And because I have great respect for the capabilities of the young, the possibility that I might provide stimulation, forcing minds to stretch just a bit beyond, is a great challenge. I like to imagine that in attempting to unravel a tightly woven work old prejudices

and fixed ideas may be examined and rethought. And I live in hope that with rethinking comes joy.

"In *The Disappearance* and also its sequel, *New Guys around the Block,* the challenge to the reader is two-fold: solving a mind-boggling whodunit on the one hand, and on the other, attempting to unlock secret passages of minds that have been closed to us—minds developed in the so-called underbelly of our society, where wits are sharpened by the constant struggle for survival—from criminal elements and from daily confrontation with the law.

"Thus Imamu Jones—poor, orphaned by the death of his father and chronic alcoholism of his mother—rises above the ugliness of his environment to shoulder the burden of *my* imposed responsibility. A shrewd observer of people, sensitive, with a natural intelligence, a boy who accepts as normal the fragility of his friends' morals, a high school dropout, Imamu with his street wisdom can solve crimes that baffle the police.

In *New Guys around the Block,* the second of the Imamu series, Imamu is joined in his detective pursuits by Olivette, an exceedingly brilliant youth who because of his great intelligence and broad experiences—he has lived in every inner city in the country—is able to bring a new approach to Imamu, a new insight, as they join forces in their attempt to solve the series of crimes plaguing the city.

"What a joy it is to construct a mystery! How challenging to scatter carefully thought-out clues that must fit into the novel through characters, their motives, patterns of thought, and environmental framework. Every piece must matter. Each detail must be studied. What excitement for me, the author, to imagine the alert reader attempting to unravel those events I so painstakingly knitted. Can anyone solve the crimes that took so much hard work and time to render insoluble? How nerve-splitting it is to contemplate: readers crossing ideas like swords, with the uneducated, though highly intelligent, Imamu Jones.

"My characters are drawn from life. In *The Disappearance,* Imamu Jones, Mama, and the Aimsleys are to be found within black communities. In *New Guys around the Block,* the intriguing Olivette, a rare sort, is always a phenomenon wherever he's encountered. But the Olivettes are mesmerizing, especially when found in their natural habitat of the inner cities.

"What happens to individuals like Imamu Jones and Olivette when there are no outlets to channel their active minds or to absorb their energies? Here is the double challenge confronting the reader. The question must occur to many while reading the books and searching for clues. Surely the answers to that question are as important as those leading to the solution of the crimes. But the question confounds even the experts."

About her writing Guy commented: "The arduous task of writing novels implies that one person—an author—believes that he, or she, has a conception of time, place, and events that is unique. A gift: to observe the overlapping patterns, the delicate details of relationships obscured to the sensibilities of the average, in the rush to judgment. I do not judge. I reveal—fragments of the obscure, weaving them into what is already obvious, in order to attach a total portrait to the consciousness of those reared in an ethic of religiosity.

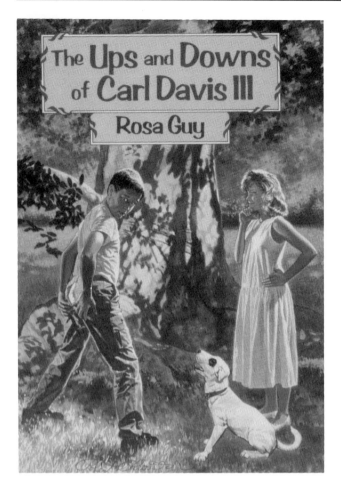

"Carl Davis," she kept repeating, "you really do some strange things." (Jacket illustration by Robert Chronister from *The Ups and Downs of Carl Davis III* by Rosa Guy.)

"Fiction is history—if you will. It is the history of emotional events, given substance in time and place. It is as true today as in the *Iliad* and the *Odyssey*, as in Dostoevski's or Flaubert's time, and has validity whether the place is China, Russia, Africa, or the United States.

"I write for people—all people, young and old, black, white, or any others whom my book might fall into the hands of. I write about ordinary people who do ordinary things, who want the ordinary—love, warmth, understanding, happiness. These things are universal. But no life is ordinary. No life is simple. Characteristics such as goodness, selfishness, kindness, wickedness, bravery, cowardice, are all cliches. They are given uniqueness when the universal becomes particular.

"Even in drug-oriented societies, events only seem to fit into the abstract. Beneath the grotesque distortion of the drug culture lies the truth of America—the capitalistic, individualistic, democratic society. My characters are products of that society. They are people continually striving for the promised, but illusory, power to shape their destinies. They are black people and they are oppressed.

"An unequal burden, a distortion, quivers beneath the abstraction of those terms: Equality. Democracy. An American dilemma: Even though much takes place in Harlem in my stories, the lives of my characters reflect all over the country.

This reflection is one that all Americans need to be cognizant of. It is our history, the emotional history of our times."

"This is the consciousness through which I write:

"I reject the notion of the innocence of youth. The television sets in our living rooms projecting the global disasters caused by wars have robbed us of innocence;

"I reject a world where the young are sheltered in innocence while the youth of other nations are condemned to perpetual misery by the greed, or wrath, of their fathers;

"I reject the innocence of children whose fathers are more interested in building jails for minority youth of this nation instead of schools;

"I reject the pampering of babies as their parents vote for bombs instead of for books;

"I reject the ignorance of the heirs of Superman and Wonderwoman, who believe themselves inherently stronger and thus immune from catastrophies created by their forefathers, their fathers;

"I reject the young of each succeeding generation who dare to say: 'I don't understand *you* people . . . .' 'I can't stand *those*

One thing he knew, for certain: He had to see this through. (Jacket illustration by Stuart Kaufman from *And I Heard a Bird Sing* by Rosa Guy.)

people. . . .' or 'Do you see the way *they* act . . . ?' They are us! Created by us for a society which suits our ignorance.

"I insist that Everychild understand this. I insist that Everychild go out into the world with this knowledge: there are no good guys. There are no bad guys. We are all good guys. We are all bad guys. And we are all responsible for each other."[2]

Guy continues to write with the conviction that art can change life. "I'm a storyteller. I write about people. I want my readers to know people, to laugh with people, to be angry with people, to despair of people, and to have hope. More than that, I want my readers to know just a little bit more, to care just a little bit more, when they put down a book of mine."[9]

"In this world growing ever smaller and more vulnerable to the holocaust that might mean its end, it is of the utmost importance that young adults break with prejudice—that value system which creates the socio-economic pressures that mangle the minds of minorities and create the dangers of world annihilation. A more profound understanding, a broader vision of those with whom we must share space between shore and sea can only make a coming together easier for the battle in which we all must engage if the world as we know it is to survive. This, I suggest, is the theme of most of my novels for young adults."[11]

FOOTNOTE SOURCES

[1]Jerrie Norris, *Presenting Rosa Guy,* Twayne, 1988.
[2]Rosa Guy, "Innocence, Betrayal, and History," *School Library Journal,* November, 1985.
[3]Judith Wilson, "Face to Face—Rosa Guy: Writing with Bold Vision," *Essence,* October, 1979.
[4]R. Guy, "All about Caring," *Top of the News,* winter, 1983.
[5]Thomas L. Vince, "Bird at My Window," *Best Sellers,* January 15, 1966.
[6]R. Guy, "Preface," *Children of Longing,* Holt, 1970.
[7]Alice Walker, "*The Friends,*" *New York Times Book Review,* November 4, 1973.
[8]"*Ruby: A Novel,*" *Horn Book,* December, 1976.
[9]R. Guy, audiotape of speech, "Children's Writing Today for Tomorrow's Adults," *Boston Globe* Book Festival, November 4, 1984.
[10]Zena Sutherland, "*Edith Jackson,*" *Bulletin of the Center for Children's Books,* March, 1979.
[11]Alleen Pace Nilsen and Kenneth Donelson, *Literature for Today's Young Adults,* second edition, Scott, Foresman, 1985.

FOR MORE INFORMATION SEE:

Washington Post, January 9, 1966, November 11, 1979 (p. 21), December 17, 1985 (p. B3).
Negro Digest, March 1, 1966 (p. 33ff).
Redbook, December, 1970 (p. 81).
New York Times Magazine, April 16, 1972 (p. 30ff).
Times Literary Supplement, September 20, 1974 (p. 1006), December 14, 1979, July 18, 1980 (p. 807), August 3, 1984.
Theressa Gunnels Rush and others, *Black American Writers Past and Present: A Biographical and Bibliographical Dictionary,* Scarecrow, 1975.
Freedomways, Volume 16, number 2, 1976 (p. 118ff).
James Page, *Selected Black American Authors: An Illustrated Bio-bibliography,* G. K. Hall, 1977.

New York Times Book Review, July 2, 1978, December 2, 1979 (p. 40), October 4, 1981 (p. 38), August 28, 1983 (p. 22), October 9, 1983, November 10, 1985 (p. 36), December 1, 1985 (p. 24).
D. L. Kirkpatrick, editor, *Twentieth-Century Children's Writers,* St. Martin's, 1978, new edition, 1983.
Washington Post Book World, November 11, 1979, November 10, 1985 (p. 17ff).
Mary Helen Washington, editor, *Midnight Birds: Stories of Contemporary Black Women Writers,* Anchor Books, 1980.
Times Educational Supplement, June 6, 1980 (p. 27), June 5, 1987.
Michael Jaye and Ann Watts, editors, *Literature and the Urban Experience,* Rutgers University Press, 1981.
Los Angeles Times, August 24, 1983.
Contemporary Literary Criticism, Volume 26, Gale, 1983.
Claudia Tate, editor, *Black Women Writers at Work,* Continuum, 1983.
Gloria Wade-Gayles, *No Crystal Stair: Visions of Race and Sex in Black Women's Fiction,* Pilgrim Press, 1984.
Dictionary of Literary Biography, Volume XXXIII: *Afro-American Fiction Writers after 1955,* Gale, 1984.
Books for Keeps, January, 1985 (p. 12ff).
Horn Book, March-April, 1985 (p. 220ff).
Sally Holmes Holtze, *Fifth Book of Junior Authors and Illustrators,* H. W. Wilson, 1985.
Geta LeSeur, "One Mother, Two Daughters: The Afro-American and the Afro-Caribbean Female Bildungsroman," *Black Scholar,* March-April, 1986.

HARRIS, Jacqueline L. 1929-

PERSONAL: Born April 6, 1929, in Columbus, Ohio; daughter of Booker W. (a dentist) and Alberta (a teacher; maiden name, Adams) Harris. *Education:* Ohio State University, B.Sc., 1951, B.A., 1966. *Religion:* Roman Catholic. *Home:* 118 Westwood Dr., Wethersfield, Conn. 06109. *Office:* Northeast Utilities, P.O. Box 270, Hartford, Conn. 06141.

CAREER: Ohio State University Medical Center, Columbus, supervisor of main chemistry laboratory, 1952-54; Providence Hospital, Detroit, Mich., medical technologist, 1954-55; Princeton Hospital, Princeton, N.J., medical technologist, 1955-57; certified medical technologist aboard the hospital ship *S.S. Hope,* 1962-64; Xerox Education Publications, Middletown, Conn., writer, 1966-78; Grolier Publishing, Danbury, Conn., science editor of *The New Book of Knowledge,* 1978-79; Purdue-Frederick Co. (pharmaceutical firm), Norwalk, Conn., medical writer, 1980-81; Northeast Utilities, Berlin, Conn., senior corporate representative, 1981—. Vice-president of Links, Farmington Valley chapter; member of board of directors, Hartford Interval House. *Member:* Women in Communications. *Awards, honors: Nine Black American Doctors* was named one of the National Science Teachers' Association's Best Science Books for Children, 1976.

WRITINGS:

JUVENILE

(With Joseph Marfuggi) *The Life of Martin Luther King, Jr.: Marching to Freedom,* Xerox Education Publications, 1968.

JACQUELINE L. HARRIS

(With Robert Hayden) *Nine Black American Doctors,* Addison-Wesley, 1976.
(With others) *Basic Science Readers,* seven volumes, McGraw, 1979.
Martin Luther King, Jr., F. Watts, 1983.
Henry Ford, F. Watts, 1984.
Science in Ancient Rome, F. Watts, 1988.

Contributor of articles to periodicals, including *Current Science.* Editor, *Scope,* Northeast Utilities employee magazine.

WORK IN PROGRESS: Crisis in Medicine; Achievements and History of NAACP.

SIDELIGHTS: "I enjoy writing for children. Much of my writing has focused on explaining science concepts in the context of science news. No one subject, however, has been more satisfying than Martin Luther King, Jr. He was, in my opinion, the greatest man the twentieth century has produced. To explain his complex philosophy to young people has been the high point of my writing career."

HOBBIES AND OTHER INTERESTS: Travel (Europe, Alaska, Hawaii, South America, the Galapagos, the Caribbean), bowling, cooking, dogs, U.S. history, leaded glass.

HASTINGS, Ian 1912-

PERSONAL: Born February 18, 1912, in Hastings, New Zealand; came to United States in 1963; son of Frederick George (an artist) and Beatrice (a housewife; maiden name, Fitzgerald) Hastings; married Eileen Mary Burns (a mail analyst), May 30, 1942; children: Warren Ian, Tanya Eileen. *Education:* Attended Wellington College, 1930-34, Wellington Technical College, and Elim University of Fine Arts, 1952-56; also studied art privately in New Zealand. *Politics:* Republican. *Religion:* Episcopalian. *Home:* 6111 North Kimball Ave., Chicago, Ill. 60659.

CAREER: Free-lance writer and illustrator, 1963—; *Success Unlimited* (magazine), Chicago, Ill., production manager, 1963-81.

WRITINGS:

Look, There Goes Pale Pink Pig, Leswing Communications, 1970.
Rufus and Christopher and the Box of Laughter, Oddo, 1972.
Rufus and Christopher in the Land of Lies, Oddo, 1972.
(With wife, Eileen Hastings) *Rufus and Christopher and the Magic Bubble,* Oddo, 1973.

Also author of *Petti-Puzzles* and *Learn with Puzzles,* published by Hayes School Publishing.

ILLUSTRATOR

Lenore H. Morgan, *Dragons and Stuff,* Oddo, 1970.

ADAPTATIONS:

"Rufus and Christopher and the Box of Laughter" (cassette), Oddo, 1972.
"Rufus and Christopher in the Land of Lies" (cassette), Oddo, 1972.
"Rufus and Christopher and the Magic Bubble" (cassette), Oddo, 1974.

IAN HASTINGS

Then the funny little man picked up the Box of Laughter Seeds. (From *Rufus and Christopher and the Box of Laughter* by Ian Hastings. Illustrated by the author.)

WORK IN PROGRESS: Journey into Yesterday, for teenagers.

SIDELIGHTS: "Born February 18, 1912 in Hastings, New Zealand, my interest in art began when I was at primary school in New Zealand. While other boys were outside playing cricket or rugby during their lunch hours, I was inside at my desk, drawing. It became a passion with me.

"As I was sneaking back into my classroom one lunch hour, another boy slammed the door neatly slicing off the tip of the middle finger of my left hand. I didn't take it quietly, and my teacher, Miss Monroe, who was rather sensitive about the sight of blood, rushed out and immediately fainted. Then another lady teacher ran out and she also passed out when she saw my bloody hand and Miss Monroe outstretched on the ground. Two down and one to carry. The third teacher walked me to my home that was close by, with one boy holding the tip of my finger in a white paper bag which he obtained from the goodie shop opposite the school, high above his head. It was the biggest and quietest procession Mt. Cook School ever had, and I was at the head of it. Not bad for a ten-year-old kid.

"The school teachers in those 'good old days,' controlled their classes very effectively by the use of one of two weapons, a heavy leather strap or a long cane. When we misbehaved or neglected to do our homework, we were ordered to hold out our hand and the teacher would strike as hard as she or he could with his or her favorite weapon. Always with these famous words: 'This hurts me more than it does you.' Six of the best was common. Three strokes on each hand. One teacher, Mr. Barry, had a three-foot cane and was a genius in its use acquired by years of dedicated practice. 'Old Smacker,' we nicknamed him.

"It was rumoured around the school that resin rubbed on a cane would cause it to split. My three friends, Kelly Howard, Peter Duncan, and Howard Elliot, and I decided it would be a good and humanitarian idea to apply some resin to Old Smacker's cane. It did not enter our silly heads that if it did split he would buy another, possibly bigger.

"I volunteered to supply the resin as my father had a supply he used for mixing with shellac for polishing furniture. I sat smugly back thinking I had done my part, the other chaps could do the dirty work. The day of retribution arrived and the unanswered question came up—'Who was going to resin Old Smacker's cane?'

"'Not me,' said Peter.

"'Not me,' said Howard.

"'Not me,' said Kelly.

"'You do it, Ian. Old Smacker won't give you the cuts even on your good hand, you're in bad shape.' The others nodded in agreement. My heart dropped, this was not what I expected. I thought I had done my share by supplying the resin. But they took off before I could state my case.

"I fingered the piece of resin in my pocket and waited for playtime to come when all the teachers would go, I knew not where, for their morning tea. 'If I'm caught, the worst I could get was a hundred lines, perhaps two, but no more,' I told myself, that's worth it. I had a secret method to write them. I always tied two pencils together which enabled me to write two lines at once, and I got away with it every time. Three pencils did not work.

"I knew where Old Smacker kept his cane, it was on a small table within easy reach of his desk. I had no difficulty in entering the classroom and finding the cane. I picked it up and rubbed it vigorously with the resin, but the resin was as hard as glass and wouldn't adhere to the smooth cane.

"'Oh the best laid schemes o' mice an' men.' I heard the door open and Old Smacker entered the room. I knew it was him by his firm determined footsteps. I was caught in the act with the evidence in my hand. We stared at one another for a few seconds, then surprise, he smiled. It was the first time he had ever looked human in my eyes. Placing his hand 'lovingly' on the back of my head he said he knew about the resin formula and it could not possibly work. I smiled back thinking he was overcome by my personality and started to leave. His smile broadened as he pulled me back, then he dropped his bomb. Oh my, what a bomb. My sentence was worse than anything I had read about in the horror stories in my weekly penny dreadfuls. It was the worst torture a ten-year-old boy in my days could have. I paled and my legs felt as if they would not hold me. I was ordered to sit with the girls in their classroom for one full day. Oh my, oh my.

"After graduating I studied fine arts at Wellington College which included amongst other subjects, sculpture and wood carving. To fill in my time at nights I studied drafting and motor body designing at Wellington Technical College. A degree in art cannot be obtained in New Zealand. 'Your portfolio is your degree,' I was told.

"It was in the middle of the great Depression when I became one of the many thousands of young men looking for employment and I was fortunate to find a position in a motor body building firm designing motor bodies of all descriptions. After a few years gathering experience, I moved to Palmerston North where I opened my own motor body building company and it was a success right from the start. Then World War II broke out. I sold my business and applied to enter the Royal New Zealand Air Force, but was assigned to Union Airways, a fledging airline where we converted their planes to bombers.

"It was at this time in 1940, I made the greatest and most successful sales pitch of my life, just what I hoped and prayed for. It was the turning point of my life and a decision I have never regretted. I asked the beautiful attractive Eileen Burns to be my wife. She did not say no. She did not say yes. She did not say maybe. All she said was 'Will you help me with the dishes?' I accepted that as a yes. We were married in 1942, and Eileen has never lost her charm and is still by my side giving me sound advice and a little push occasionally.

"After the war and the birth of our two children, Warren and Tanya, we moved to the wonderful city of Auckland where I opened my own advertising agency which, after long hours and hard work became very successful."

The couple moved to the United States to get into the children's book market. "I was required to send samples of my work to Washington when we arrived in the U.S.A. and to three independent artists in Chicago for approval, and I was not permitted to work within a radius of seven miles of another artist doing the same work.

"We arrived in San Francisco January 3, 1963 and have been here ever since. We have permanent visas and love the United States. I was art director for eighteen years on *Success* magazine, and wrote articles and five children's books in my spare time."

HOBBIES AND OTHER INTERESTS: Travel, sculpture, wood carving, furniture designing, antiques, watercolor painting.

HOBSON, Bruce 1950-
(Mwenye Hadithi)

PERSONAL: Born September 21, 1950, in Nairobi, Kenya; son of Brian Hugh (a businessman) and Joan (Knell) Hobson; married Marian Cole (a homemaker), March 24, 1979; children: Amelia. *Education:* Queen Mary College, London, B.A. (with honors), 1973. *Home and office address:* P.O. Box 34247, Nairobi, Kenya. *Agent:* Herta Ryder, 55 Great Ormond St., London WC1N 3H2, England.

CAREER: Writer. Proprietor, Concrete Jungle (horticultural business), Nairobi, Kenya. *Awards, honors: Hot Hippo* was chosen one of Child Study Association of America's Children's Books of the Year, 1987.

WRITINGS:

UNDER PSEUDONYM MWENYE HADITHI

Greedy Zebra (juvenile; illustrated by Adrienne Kennaway), Little, Brown, 1984.
Hot Hippo (juvenile; illustrated by A. Kennaway), Little, Brown, 1986.
Crafty Chameleon (juvenile; illustrated by A. Kennaway), Little, Brown, 1987 (published in England as *Crafty Chamaeleon,* Hodder & Stoughton, 1987).
Tricky Tortoise (juvenile; illustrated by A. Kennaway), Little, Brown, 1988.

Hobson's books have been translated into Danish, German, and Japanese.

ADAPTATIONS:

"Greedy Zebra" (audio recording with pictures), Revallee Studios, 1985.
"Hot Hippo" (filmstrip; cassette), Weston Woods, 1987.

WORK IN PROGRESS: A suspense novel; a romance novel about surfing.

SIDELIGHTS: "I suspect everyone who enjoys reading positively knows, with burning certainty, that they will become a great writer. This usually happens in the teenage years, when the real world is still thinly veiled. Then, as it happened to myself, the chaos of adulthood tumbles the dream. The key is perseverance, gripping the string of the dream at all costs, never letting go.

"I collect African myths and stories, traditionally spoken, not written, a great many of which are already lost to the new generations who crave pop music, fashionable clothes, and Western comics. These I present in a fashion that will please children of the Western world; they are always instinctive and somewhat moralistic, but amusing as well. It would be true to say that the majority of children's books reflect the laziness of our age—mindless entertainment en masse coupled with the worship of that which is ugly-made-cute. Children are no longer taught to see the perfect beauty of an untouched butterfly's wing. They are, rather, persuaded to love fantastically ugly adult creations, such as cute space monsters. I would like to see new authors fill this well of froth with work that is no less entertaining, but more nourishing to the spirit."

HOLABIRD, Katharine 1948-

PERSONAL: Born January 23, 1948, in Cambridge, Mass.; daughter of John Augur (an architect) and Donna (an actress; maiden name, Smith) Holabird; married Michael Haggiag (a publisher), June 15, 1974; children: Tara, Alexandra, Adam. *Education:* Bennington College, B.A., 1969. *Home:* 17 Corringham Rd., London NW11 7BS, England. *Agent:* Jane Gregory, Riverside Studios, Crisp Rd., London W6 9RL, England.

CAREER: Bennington Review (magazine), Bennington, Vt., assistant editor, 1969-70; free-lance journalist in Rome, Italy, 1970-72; nursery school teacher in London, England, 1973-76; free-lance writer, 1976—. *Member:* Women Writers Network. *Awards, honors:* Kentucky Bluegrass Award from University of Kentucky, 1985, for *Angelina Ballerina; Angelina's Christmas* was selected one of Child Study Association of America's Children's Books of the Year, 1987.

WRITINGS:

JUVENILE; ALL ILLUSTRATED BY HELEN CRAIG

The Little Mouse ABC, Simon & Schuster, 1983.
The Little Mouse One Two Three, Simon & Schuster, 1983.
Angelina Ballerina, C. N. Potter, 1983.
Angelina and the Princess (ALA Notable Book), C. N. Potter, 1984.
Angelina at the Fair (ALA Notable Book), C. N. Potter, 1985.

Angelina's Christmas (ALA Notable Book), C. N. Potter, 1985.
Angelina on Stage, C. N. Potter, 1986.
Angelina's Birthday and Address Book, C. N. Potter, 1986.
Angelina and Alice, C. N. Potter, 1987.
Alexander and the Dragon, C. N. Potter, 1988.
Angelina Book and Doll Package, C. N. Potter, 1989.
Angelina's Birthday Surprise, C. N. Potter, 1989.
Alexander and the Magic Boat, C. N. Potter, 1990.

ADAPTATIONS:

"Angelina Ballerina and Other Stories" (record; cassette), Caedmon.

Play adaptations by the author of the "Angelina" stories were performed by schoolchildren in London at American School, May, 1989.

WORK IN PROGRESS: Adapting five "Angelina" stories into play form for a book; another "Angelina" story.

SIDELIGHTS: "Most of my ideas have come from observing my children and recalling important moments in my own childhood. Certainly, I, too, passed through a very strong identification with graceful ballerinas when I was small and robust and anything but graceful.

"Sometimes, looking back on the strange obsessions of our childhood, we see that they were actually archetypal rites of passage that everyone goes through ... and it seems to me that ballerinas are an almost archetypal symbol for little girls,

KATHARINE HOLABIRD

awakening a longing to grow and change into beautiful womanhood.

"I grew up in Chicago, where the Holabirds have been architects for three generations. Our side of the family was rather unconventional. We lived in a tall wooden house, a San Francisco steamboat captain's fantasy that survived the Chicago fire and looked a bit like something Hansel and Gretel might have found in the woods, though it was squeezed between a seedy hotel and a dark rooming house by the time we lived there.

"Everyone in the family was an artist of one kind or another, and from an early age we scribbled and drew and painted with utter abandon. Our father loved painting, and once took us all down to the basement, gave us paints and brushes, and let us 'decorate' everything in sight. Later he painted his own version of Botticelli's 'Primavera' on our dining room wall. On my last birthday he sent me a painting of the backyard in Chicago, scene of so many potent childhood memories.

"My parents met while doing plays at Harvard, and when we were young they were still very involved in theater. My father was a director and set designer for a time, and made a replica of the Theater of Dionysus with me for a fifth grade Greek project. My mother recited romantic poetry and loved to dress up with us and dance to anything from Louis Armstrong to the 'Nutcracker Suite.' On Sunday mornings she accompanied an old record of 'Songs of the Auvergne' with her fluty tremolo. She was also a great peace marcher and human rights advocate. But her greatest gift was, and remains, with young children. Although she gave up a promising career on the stage when she had children, my mother knew how to make life her theater, and has always entertained us, and everyone who meets her, with her wild humour, her singing and dancing, and her very contagious 'joie de vivre.'

"I am the second of four daughters. We were born close together and were great companions through most of the adventures and scrapes of our childhood. We danced and painted together when we were small, we shared a wild passion for horses when we were old enough to ride, we quarrelled over boyfriends and makeup, but we were always loyal to each other ... and we still are.

"We all loved animals, but my sisters were generally satisfied with parakeets and kittens, while I was a mad collector of anything wild and unusual. I captured a baby skunk in the woods in Canada, and rescued an owl and a raccoon in the middle of Chicago and brought them home. Once I even adopted an infant crocodile. Thanks to my parents bemused tolerance, no one paid much attention to my menagerie. I was allowed to keep them all as pets in my bedroom for a time, and well remember the raccoon's furry little arms entwined around my head at night.

"As we grew older, my sisters gradually forsook the birds and kittens for a long series of boyfriends, but I was a loner, and chose to spend every afternoon wandering through Lincoln Park with my dog, Moppo, chasing squirrels and examining the local flora and fauna.

"When I wasn't out with my dog, I usually had my nose buried in a book, as reading is my mother's other great passion, and she was always exclaiming over her latest literary discoveries and encouraging us to do the same. I read everything I could about animals (and dogs particularly) and adored classics like *Charlotte's Web* and *My Friend Flicka*.

And then it was Angelina's turn to dance. (Illustration by Helen Craig from *Angelina and the Princess* by Katharine Holabird.)

The only mouse I remember reading about was E. B. White's *Stuart Little.* I certainly never dreamt that I would be writing about a little mouse myself when I was in my thirties.

"Angelina was created in London, where I've been living with my family for sixteen years. I knew Helen Craig as a friend before we ever worked together. We met when she was just beginning to sell her illustrations with a series of tiny accordion pull-out books called the 'Mouse House Books.' When her first books did well, Helen's publishers asked her to do a large format children's story, and she felt uncertain about writing it.

"Helen then asked me if I would like to try and write a story that she could illustrate. At the time my eldest daughter was a four-year-old prima ballerina, pink tutu, fairy wings, and all. I was delighted by Tara's balletomania, so similar to my own dreams of grandeur at her age, and knew that I wanted to write about the great passions that little hearts can have.

"I still have the earliest draft of *Angelina Ballerina,* (she was originally called Primrose) and it seems to me that I just sat down and scribbled it at the kitchen table one afternoon, as Tara and her baby sister Alexandra waltzed and pirouetted around me.

"Then Helen performed her magic: she took the story and made a detailed 'dummy,' (a handmade facsimile of a book), to show to her editor. Shortly afterwards I was invited to Aurum Press to discuss publication. It was at this first meeting that we discovered that there was already a little mouse called Primrose in another children's book. While we were searching for suitable names the editor's assistant, Angela, walked into the room. 'We could call her Angela the

Ballerina' someone joked, and suddenly we knew that she had to be Angelina Ballerina.

"Ironically, it was my own husband, Michael Haggiag, who was our first publisher. It was Michael who gave Helen her first contract, and came up with the idea for the 'Mouse House' series, when other publishers had rejected her work; and it was Michael who agreed to publish the first Angelina story (and insisted that Angelina should be drawn as a mouse, since Helen had shown such a gift in the work she'd already done).

"Michael had confidence in our collaboration from the start. He took *Angelina Ballerina* to the Bologna Book Fair, and consequently sold the series to Carol Southern at Clarkson Potter in New York.

"Although he has now left publishing, Michael is still a supportive critic at home, and is always urging me to write more.

"Every Angelina story has a slow gestation, then suddenly seems to pour out onto the page, full-blown. The process usually begins with an idea or situation, and my children's reactions are a good indication of whether the story is viable or not. Something starts it off, an incident, a child's trauma at school or home, a story I've heard somewhere. Out of this flotsam an idea gradually gathers form and content as I jot down seemingly aimless notes to myself—until one day it's there—a story.

"I always confer with Helen after I've written a first draft for myself. Then I write several drafts in long-hand before sending a word-processed story to our editor, Sue Tarsky. Chil-

Alexander and the Dragon

Story by Katharine Holabird   Illustrations by Helen Craig

Alexander began to imagine all sorts of awful things. (Illustration by Helen Craig from *Alexander and the Dragon* by Katharine Holabird.)

dren's stories look deceptively easy, but picture books are sometimes like poetry: the words must be pared down to the minimum to convey the maximum emotion.

"When Alexandra was seven she kept coming home from school in tears over fights with her best friend. Listening to Alexandra's problems brought back my own memories of early, sometimes fickle, friendships, and this formed the background for *Angelina and Alice.*

"The year that my son Adam was four years old, he loved to leap and swagger around the house with his sword and shield, battling with invisible dragons. Adam's great imagination and bravery inspired the idea for *Alexander and the Dragon,* in which the little boy befriends the dragon he fears by playing with it.

"Before I had children, I taught nursery school in London for a couple of years, and I grew to respect and admire young children's courage and imagination, and what makes them tick. I like stories that reveal the strong and difficult emotions of early childhood, as well as the small (but never inconsequential) triumphs.

"I adapted four of the Angelina stories for children's theater, and they were produced at the American School in London. Fifty third- and fourth-grade students performed in the show, and it was quite startling to see Angelina and little

cousin Henry dancing across a real stage together. At present I'm rewriting the plays in hopes that we can publish them in a paperback edition available to schools in the United States and England.

"Helen and I have collaborated recently on another Alexander story, and we'll be doing one more Angelina in the next year. I'm also thinking of writing a 'Little Henry' story, as many children have asked me for a book about Angelina's funny cousin, Henry.

"Helen still makes an elaborate dummy every time we do a book together, and I take them along when I visit schools and libraries, so I can demonstrate how a book starts from an idea and goes through quite a transformation before being published. Helen's care and attention to detail never fail to amaze me, and I think much of Angelina's success is due not only to Helen's great skill, but to her own rich recollections of her childhood in rural Buckinghamshire. Working with an illustrator like Helen Craig is an author's dream. She has a great sense of humour, and intuitively grasps the essence of the story, and makes her characters jump off the page even in the first rough sketches.

"Many writers never meet their illustrator, which seems to me a real waste of potential inspiration and collaboration. Helen and I always get together several times during the creation of a book. Sometimes our meetings are hilarious,

BANG!

The bike crashed into the rock.
Angelina flew into the air and
then fell to the ground with
a terrible bump.

(From *Angelina's Birthday Surprise* by Katharine Holabird. Illustrated by Helen Craig.)

sometimes serious, but they always bring new ideas and enliven the material we're working on.

"After many years of writing at the kitchen table, or on my desk in a corner of the bedroom, I now have my own study, and after the children leave for school I try to disentangle myself from the kitchen and the laundry room and spend most of the mornings pondering and writing as I look out on the bustling skies of north London. The afternoons are invariably busy with children and all the things I never did in the morning.

"I still love animals, but no longer keep a wild menagerie. These days I manage to limit my old passion to two Scottish sheepdogs, who now accompany me on early morning walks across Hampstead Heath, much as Moppo did in Lincoln Park thirty years ago."

HOBBIES AND OTHER INTERESTS: Nature, wildlife, hiking, walking the dogs, horseback riding, skiing.

HOPE, Christopher (David Tully) 1944-

PERSONAL: Born February 26, 1944, in Johannesburg, South Africa; son of Dudley Mitford (a banker) and Kathleen Margaret (a bookkeeper; maiden name, McKenna) Hope; married Eleanor Marilyn Margaret Klein (a music administrator), February 18, 1967; children: Jasper Antony, Daniel Clement. *Education:* University of Witwatersrand, B.A., 1965, M.A., 1971; University of Natal, B.A. (with honors), 1970. *Home:* 9 Southwood Hall, Wood Lane, Highgate, London N6 5UF, England. *Agent:* A. P. Watt Ltd., 20 John St., London WC1N 2DL, England.

CAREER: Writer, 1972—. *Military service:* South African Navy, 1962. *Member:* Authors League of America, Society of Authors, International PEN. *Awards, honors:* Pringle Award from the English Academy of Southern Africa, 1972, for creative writing; Cholmondeley Award for Poetry from the British Society of Authors, 1977; Professor Alexander Petrie Award from the Convocation of the University of Natal, 1981, for outstanding contribution to the arts and humanities; David Higham Prize for Fiction from the National Book League of Great Britain, 1981, for *A Separate Development;* International PEN Award, 1982, for *Private Parts and Other Tales;* Mother Goose Award runner-up, 1984, for *The King, the Cat, and the Fiddle;* Whitbread Book of the Year for Fiction from the Booksellers Association of Great Britain and Ireland, 1985, for *Kruger's Alp;* CNA Award from the Booksellers Association of South Africa, 1989, for *White Boy Running.*

CHRISTOPHER HOPE

WRITINGS:

JUVENILE

(With Yehudi Menuhin) *The King, the Cat, and the Fiddle* (illustrated by Angela Barrett), Benn, 1983, Holt, 1984.
The Dragon Wore Pink (illustrated by A. Barrett), A. & C. Black, 1985, Atheneum, 1986.

OTHER

(With Mike Kirkwood) *Whitewashes,* privately printed, 1971.
Cape Drives (poetry), London Magazine Editions, 1974.
A Separate Development (novel), Ravan Press, 1980, Scribner, 1981.
In the Country of the Black Pig (poetry), London Magazine Editions, 1981.
Private Parts and Other Tales (short stories), Bateleur Press, 1981.
Kruger's Alp (fiction), Heinemann, 1984, Viking Penguin, 1985.
Englishmen (poetry), Heinemann, 1985.
The Hottentot Room (fiction), Heinemann, 1986, Farrar, Straus, 1987.
Black Swan (fiction; illustrated by Gillian Barlow), Century Hutchinson, 1987, Harper, 1988.
White Boy Running (nonfiction), Farrar, Straus, 1988.
My Chocolate Redeemer (fiction), Heinemann, 1989.
Moscow! Moscow! (nonfiction), Heinemann, 1990.

PLAYS

"Ducktails," South African Television, 1976.
"Bye-Bye Booysens," South African Television, 1977.
"An Entirely New Concept in Packaging," South African Television, 1978.
"Englishmen" (a poem for voices), BBC Radio, 1986.
"Box on the Ear," BBC Radio, 1987.
"Better Halves," BBC Radio, 1988.

CONTRIBUTOR TO ANTHOLOGIES

On the Edge of the World, Donker, 1974.
A World of Their Own, Donker, 1976.
A New Book of South African Verse in English, Oxford University Press, 1979.
Modern South African Stories, Donker, 1980.
Theatre Two, Donker, 1981.
Best British Short Stories, Heinemann, 1986.
Colour of a New Day, Lawrence & Wishart, 1990.

Contributor to periodicals, including *London Magazine, Times Literary Supplement, Poetry Review, New Yorker, Transatlantic Review, Los Angeles Times, New Republic,* and *New Statesman.*

WORK IN PROGRESS: A novel dealing with British hypocrisy and German intransigence set in England of the '90s.

SIDELIGHTS: "Most of my work, I think, has been an attempt to explore the effects of discrimination, particularly racial discrimination, as exemplified by apartheid in South Africa, the injustice of it and the misery it causes are widely known; less well understood, perhaps, is the richly bizarre existence of the various population groups who must live under enforced segregation in a society obsessed with skin color. A tiny minority operate a system of racial separation everyone knows to be crazy. My novel *A Separate Development* (the official euphemism for apartheid) is a kind of joke-book, because if apartheid is cruel it is also ridiculous, and the most cheering thing about its victims is their well-nourished sense of the ridiculous. It is something the guardians of racial purity find more disconcerting than earnest moralizing. I try to convey the eerie comedy of South African life.

"I suppose, in a sense, the theme of childhood is something I return to in many of my books—from my first novel, *A Separate Development* about a boy uncertain of his colour in a country obsessed with racial classification, to my most recent memoir, *White Boy Running.* This is, among other things, an account of a childhood in South Africa. But there are also more positive reasons for exploring the theme of childhood. Not only are children less aware of the need to conform, but they possess imagination and the willingness to use it in the service of the story being told. That is why children make the best readers and why it is the child in every writer who makes for his or her best work, by urging faith in the magical power of storytelling.

"Imagination and its potential is the subject of my first book especially for children called *The King, the Cat, and the Fiddle.* It concerns a musical king, with no money, who does battle with his sensible accountants who tell the poor king that his kingdom will be saved if only he would be as sensible as they are and fire all his musicians. In *The Dragon Wore Pink,* my second picture book (both of them illustrated by Angela Barrett who shares the same beliefs in the necessity of enchantment) I relate the tale of a dragon who prefers flowers to flame-throwing, has no head for heights, and worries his friends almost as much as his enemies. *The Dragon Wore Pink* is about the pains and pleasures of being different.

(From *The Dragon Wore Pink* by Christopher Hope. Illustrated by Angela Barrett.)

"Perhaps the most extended treatment of this theme is in my novella, *Black Swan.* Despite the tendency of some critics to see it as a tragedy, I set out to write a kind of dark comedy about the power of the imagination. The teenager, Lucky, who lives in one of the large black townships in South Africa, though he has nothing else in the world, possesses a gift which no one can touch or take away from him. He is able to invent other worlds and to mentally emigrate, to live 'elsewhere.' When Lucky decides that, of all things, he wants to become a ballet dancer and take the role of Prince Siegfried in *Swan Lake,* he confirms what his friends and enemies have suspected all along—that the boy is plain crazy. Yet Lucky succeeds in a way which no one suspects. The liberating power of the imagination, especially its delight in the unexpected, unpredictable, and unconventional, is what I write about as well as the reason why I write at all."

HOBBIES AND OTHER INTERESTS: Travel, walking, cross-country skiing.

FOR MORE INFORMATION SEE:

Newsweek, December 7, 1981, June 27, 1988.
New Yorker, December 14, 1981.
New York Times Book Review, December 20, 1981, May 5, 1985 (p. 9).
Los Angeles Times Book Review, December 20, 1981.
Washington Post Book World, January 3, 1982.
South, March, 1985 (p. 94).
Wall Street Journal, May 27/28, 1988 (p. 7).

English in Africa, October, 1989 (p. 91).

HUXLEY, Elspeth (Josceline Grant) 1907-

PERSONAL: Born July 23, 1907, in London, England; daughter of Major Josceline (an army officer and farmer) and Eleanor Lillian (Grosvenor) Grant; married Gervas Huxley (a tea commissioner and writer), December 12, 1931 (died, 1971); children: Charles Grant. *Education:* Reading University, Diploma in Agriculture, 1927; attended Cornell University, 1927-28. *Politics:* "Variable, mainly disillusioned." *Religion:* "Vague." *Home and office:* Green End, Oaksey, Malmesbury, Wiltshire SN16 9TL, England. *Agent:* Heather Jeeves, 15 Campden Hill Square, London W8 7JY, England.

CAREER: Empire Marketing Board, London, England, assistant press officer, 1929-32; author, 1935—; British Broadcasting Corp. (BBC), London, England, in news department, 1941-44, member of general advisory council, 1952-59. Broadcaster for BBC, "The Critics" program, and on African matters. Justice of the Peace for Wiltshire, 1946-77; member, Monckton Advisory Commission on Central Africa, 1959-60. *Member:* National Trust, Royal Society for Protection of Birds, World Wildlife Fund, Council for the Protection of Rural England, Fauna and Flora Preservation Society, Rhino Rescue, Woodland Trust, Wiltshire Trust for Nature Conservation, Wildfowl and Wetland Trust, London Library. *Awards, honors:* Commander, Order of the British Empire, 1960; *Scott of the Antarctic* was selected one of New

York Public Library's Books for the Teen Age, 1980, 1981, and 1982.

WRITINGS:

White Man's Country: Lord Delamere and the Making of Kenya, 2 volumes, Macmillan (London), 1935, 2nd edition, Chatto & Windus, 1953, Praeger, 1968.
Murder at Government House (novel), Harper, 1937, reissued, Viking/Penguin, 1988.
Murder on Safari (novel), Harper, 1938, reissued, Perennial Library, 1982, large print edition, ABC-CLIO, 1989.
Death of an Aryan (novel), Methuen, 1939, published as *The African Poison Murders,* Harper, 1940, reissued, Viking, 1988, large print edition, ABC-CLIO, 1988.
Red Strangers (novel), Harper, 1939.
Atlantic Ordeal: The Story of Mary Cornish, Chatto & Windus, 1941, Harper, 1942.
East Africa, Collins, 1941.
The Story of Five English Farmers, Sheldon Press, 1941.
English Women, Sheldon Press, 1942.
Brave Deeds of the War, Sheldon Press, 1943.
(With Margery Perham) *Race and Politics in Kenya: A Correspondence between Elspeth Huxley and Margery Perham,* Faber, 1944, revised edition, 1956, Greenwood Press, 1975.
Colonies: A Reader's Guide, Cambridge University Press, 1947.
Settlers of Kenya, Highway Press (Nairobi), 1948, Greenwood Press, 1975.
The Sorcerer's Apprentice: A Journey through East Africa (travel), Chatto & Windus, 1948, Greenwood Press, 1975.

ELSPETH HUXLEY

You could not possibly grasp the enormous vastness of Africa. (Jacket illustration by Richard Mantel from *The Flame Trees of Thika* by Elspeth Huxley.)

African Dilemmas, Longmans, Green, 1948.
The Walled City (novel), Chatto & Windus, 1948, Lippincott, 1949.
I Don't Mind If I Do (novel), Chatto & Windus, 1950.
A Thing to Love (novel), Chatto & Windus, 1954.
Four Guineas: A Journey through West Africa (travel), Chatto & Windus, 1954, Greenwood Press, 1974.
Kenya Today, Lutterworth Press, 1954.
What Are Trustee Nations?, Batchworth Press, 1955.
No Easy Way: A History of the Kenya Farmers' Association and Unga Limited, East African Standard (Nairobi), 1957.
The Red Rock Wilderness (novel), Morrow, 1957.
The Flame Trees of Thika: Memories of an African Childhood (autobiographical fiction; first book in trilogy), Morrow, 1959, reissued, Penguin, 1974, large print edition, Ulverscroft, 1983, illustrated edition, Chatto & Windus, 1987.
A New Earth: An Experiment in Colonialism, Morrow, 1960.
On the Edge of the Rift: Memories of Kenya, (autobiographical fiction; second book in trilogy), Morrow, 1962, reissued, Penguin, 1982 (published in England as *The Mottled Lizard,* Chatto & Windus, 1962, large print edition, Ulverscroft, 1983).

A lion is about to settle down next to one of the lionesses in his pride. (Photograph by Hugo van Lawick from *Last Days in Eden* by Elspeth Huxley.)

The Merry Hippo (novel), Chatto & Windus, 1963, published as *The Incident at the Merry Hippo,* Morrow, 1964.

A Man from Nowhere (novel), Chatto & Windus, 1964, Morrow, 1965.

With Forks and Hope (illustrated by Jonathan Kingdon), Morrow, 1964 (published in England as *Forks and Hope: An African Notebook,* Chatto & Windus, 1964).

Back Street New Worlds: A Look at Immigrants in Britain, Chatto & Windus, 1964, Morrow, 1965.

Suki: A Little Tiger (illustrated with photographs by Laelia Goehr), Morrow, 1964.

Brave New Victuals: An Inquiry into Modern Food Production, Chatto & Windus, 1965.

Their Shining Eldorado: A Journey through Australia (travel), Morrow, 1967.

Love among the Daughters: Memories of the Twenties in England and America (autobiographical fiction; third book in trilogy), Morrow, 1968.

The Challenge of Africa, Aldus, 1971.

(Editor and compiler) *The Kingsleys: A Biographical Anthology,* Allen & Unwin, 1973.

Livingstone and His African Journeys, Saturday Review Press, 1974.

Florence Nightingale, Putnam, 1975.

Gallipot Eyes: A Wiltshire Diary, Weidenfeld & Nicolson, 1976.

(Editor) Mary Kingsley, *Travels in West Africa,* Folio Society, 1976.

Scott of the Antarctic, Weidenfeld & Nicolson, 1977, Atheneum, 1978, new edition, University of Nebraska Press, 1989.

Nellie: Letters from Africa, Weidenfeld & Nicolson, 1980, new edition, 1984, published as *Nellie's Story: With a Memoir by Her Daughter Elspeth Huxley,* Morrow, 1981.

(Editor with Arnold Curtis) *Pioneers' Scrapbook: Reminiscences of Kenya 1890-1968,* Evans Brothers, 1980.

(Author of introduction) Karen Blixen (pseudonym of Isak Dineson), *Out of Africa,* Folio Society, 1980.

Whipsnade: Captive Breeding for Survival, Collins, 1981.

The Prince Buys the Manor: An Extravaganza (novel), Chatto & Windus, 1982.

(With Hugo van Lawick) *Last Days in Eden* (travel), Harvill, 1984.

Out in the Midday Sun: My Kenya, Chatto & Windus, 1985, Viking, 1987.

Nine Faces of Kenya, Collins Harvill, 1990.

Contributor to periodicals, including *Daily Telegraph, Sunday Times, New York Times, Atlantic Monthly,* and *Encounter.*

ADAPTATIONS:

"The Flame Trees of Thika" (seven-part television series), "Masterpiece Theatre," PBS-TV, July 6, 1986.

(From ''Flame Trees of Thika,'' starring Hayley Mills [right]. The seven-part Masterpiece Theatre production debuted on PBS-TV, July 6, 1986.)

WORK IN PROGRESS: A biography of Sir Peter Scott, conservationist, painter, writer, and broadcaster, for Faber.

SIDELIGHTS: Elspeth Huxley, at the age of five, settled with her parents in Kenya, forty miles outside of Nairobi, to start a coffee plantation. The experience forged in her a deep love of the country, which inspired most of her work. "Writing about modern Africa is like trying to sketch a galloping horse that is out of sight before you have sharpened your pencil."[1]

"If you live long enough you find, much to your surprise, that you have lived through a part of history; people and events that you recall as if they had lived and happened yesterday vanish into a seamless past and turn into legends."[2]

"For centuries this tropical region of high mountains, vast forests, immense sun-quivering plains dotted with azure lakes and sliced through by the great Rift Valley, had lain there with its varied native peoples and its fabulous menagerie of wild beasts, beyond the range and cognizance of the people of Europe and Asia who, having eaten the forbidden fruit, had ever afterwards been chasing knowledge in whatever direction, good or ill, it might lead. Suddenly, at the turn of the century, this great hidden land had been revealed to Europeans. To them it seemed as if the Garden of Eden had never disappeared; here, Adam had not bitten into the apple, nor had angels driven him forth with flaming swords.

"There was, of course, an arrogance in this attitude not perceived at the time. This world was to become the oyster of the European, his for the opening, regardless of the feelings of the mollusc inside. But that same crustacean condoned this attitude; resentment and hostility were all to come; at the time, a strange acceptance seemed to overlay the land. The impact of the twentieth-century European was no doubt so sudden, overwhelming and incomprehensible that the African peoples were momentarily stunned. In *The Dark Eye in Africa,* Laurens van der Post suggested that 'an enormous hush fell over Africa in the wake of the coming of European man.' Africans, he wrote, were anxious to serve and to follow the European, they wanted to love and be loved."[3]

"Although I never actually lived in Africa after the age of eighteen, I continued to make frequent visits there until my mother left her farm in 1965. Over the years I visited all the countries then under British rule, as well as others which were not: I did a lot of free-lance journalism in those days, as well as broadcasting, and I suppose had a tag marked 'Africa' hung around my neck. Like actors, free-lance journalists tend to get type-cast, which can get monotonous but of course helps from the point of view of selling one's wares. I have always had to earn my living and pay my way. Luckily my husband's job involved a lot of travelling and we sometimes played a complicated game of starting off together, separating to go on our different assignments and meeting up again. Once we travelled round the world by sea, rail and automobile, and we were also among the first passengers to fly from Nairobi to London, which took six days. The Cape to Cairo service had not long been started—that took ten days. That was in 1932."

"I took to writing crime stories to pass the time on shipboard and avoid playing bridge. After the 1939-45 War I specialized on African subjects, and abandoned crime fiction, but returned to it again after serving on the Monckton Commission in central Africa, which provided a background for *The Merry Hippo.* In fact all my crime stories have an African setting. Despite Africa's immensity, diversity, and richness in crime. I don't know of any specifically African detective story writers."[4]

"Since 1939 our home was in a small village, midway between two English market towns, where in 1938 we bought a seventeenth-century farm house and a small farm—for a song in those days. There our only son spent his childhood. After my husband retired in 1967, he also took to authorship and published four fine biographies and his own autobiography before he died in 1971. I moved to a small cottage in the same village and continued writing and kept in touch with people and events in Kenya although I only made occasional and brief visits. The last of these was to watch a bit of the filming of my book *The Flame Trees of Thika,* which became a widely shown TV series in the U.S., U.K. and a number of other countries. This has been much my most successful book—it is half fiction, half true; as was its sequel called in the U.S. *On the Edge of the Rift,* but republished as *The Mottled Lizard.*"

Gallipot Eyes: A Wiltshire Diary was published in 1976 and just as Huxley had written of life in Africa she wrote of life in an English village. "This book is not intended as a village history, like several excellent village books that have lately been published. There is more about the present than the past. Nor is it meant to prove anything: that villages are good or bad, their inhabitants happy or miserable, better or worse, than they used to be. It's what its title says: a diary. I kept it for a year and then stopped.

"Why pick on Oaksey? There's nothing special about this particular village. Almost any of its ten thousand fellows would probably have done as well. It's a pleasant little village, but so are many others. It's always been, I think, a borderline case. On the border between Wiltshire and Gloucestershire, between the Cotswolds and the vale, between the midlands and the south-west; in the Middle Ages on the borders of the Forest of Braden; before that, of the kingdoms of Mercia and Wessex; almost on the borderline between the Thames flowing east and the Avon going west; if matters go on as they are doing, it will soon be on the borders of Swindon, though we haven't reached that pass yet.

"I didn't choose Oaksey, it chose me because I live there. It was only when I started on a diary that I realized how little I knew about it, and still do; how many stones remain unturned. The greatest surprise has been to discover how much can be discovered about a small and unimportant place, delving only in fits and starts, with no pre-knowledge or experience of how to go about it, all too little time, and all within a year.

"This has been possible, of course, only because a number of historians have done the serious delving and published their results, and because there is a trained, competent and, in my experience, invariably helpful and interested body of librarians, archivists and others, ready and able to tell the seeker where to look and what to look for. I am exceedingly grateful to them all."[5]

"Although I have written about ten novels, basically I have been a chronicler and observer of events, countries, people, and situations, rather than a novelist. My first book, a biography, was published [over] fifty years ago. [*Out in the Midday Sun*] which recalls memories and characters of colonial Africa, was published in 1985. At the age of seventy-eight this is quite enough and it's time that, like a willing horse, I was put out to grass.

Vultures usually settle early for the night. (Photograph by Hugo van Lawick from *Last Days in Eden* by Elspeth Huxley.)

"But another book was just published, and another has been started on."

FOOTNOTE SOURCES

[1]Elspeth Huxley, *Forks and Hope: An African Notebook,* Chatto & Windus, 1964.
[2]E. Huxley, *Out In the Midday Sun: My Kenya,* Viking, 1987.
[3]Karen Blixen, *Out of Africa,* Folio Society, 1980.
[4]John M. Reilly, *Twentieth-Century Crime and Mystery Writers,* second edition, St. Martin's, 1985.
[5]E. Huxley, *Gallipot Eyes: A Wiltshire Diary,* Weidenfeld & Nicolson, 1976.

FOR MORE INFORMATION SEE:

Nature, August 3, 1935.
Wilson Library Bulletin, January, 1961 (p. 390).
Times Literary Supplement, December 2, 1965, May 25, 1967, January 31, 1987.
Observer, May 21, 1967, September 29, 1969.
Atlantic, July, 1967.
Punch, July 19, 1967, October 9, 1968.
New York Times Book Review, September 22, 1968.
Book World, November 3, 1968.
John Wakeman, editor, *World Authors 1950-1970,* H. W. Wilson, 1975.
New York Times, March 18, 1987.
Washington Post Book World, March 22, 1987.

Dictionary of Literary Biography, Volume 77: *British Mystery Writers, 1920-1939,* Gale, 1989.

COLLECTIONS

Rhodes House Library, Oxford, England.

IMERSHEIN, Betsy 1953-

PERSONAL: Born May 23, 1953, in Long Island, N.Y.; daughter of Charles J. (a manufacturer) and Lois (a teacher; maiden name, Cohen) Imershein; married James Howe (a children's author), April 5, 1981; children: Zoe Imershein Howe. *Education:* New York University, B.A., 1975; Yeshiva University, Wurzweiler School of Social Work, M.S.W., 1977. *Religion:* Jewish. *Home and office:* 100 Burnside Dr., Hastings-on-Hudson, N.Y. 10706. *Agent:* Susan Cohen, Writers House, 21 West 26th St., New York, N.Y. 10010.

CAREER: Kingsboro Psychiatric Center, Brooklyn, N.Y., social worker and therapist in private practice, 1977-80; Jewish Repertory Theatre, New York, N.Y., managing director, 1978-80; Ensemble Studio Theatre, New York, N.Y., managing director, 1980-81; Cable Television, New York, N.Y., various positions, 1981-84; free-lance author and photographer, 1984—. Board member of Hastings Creative Arts

Council. *Member:* American Society of Magazine Photographers. *Awards, honors:* Outstanding Science Trade Book for Children from the National Science Teachers Association and the Children's Book Council, 1988, for *Animal Doctor.*

WRITINGS:

Animal Doctor: The Work People Do (self-illustrated with photographs), Simon & Schuster, 1988.
Auto Mechanic: The Work People Do (self-illustrated with photographs), Simon & Schuster, 1989.
Farmer: The Work People Do (self-illustrated with photographs), Simon & Schuster, 1990.

ILLUSTRATOR; WITH PHOTOGRAPHS

James Howe, *When You Go to Kindergarten,* Knopf, 1986.
Finding Red/Finding Yellow, (wordless picturebook), Gulliver Books, 1989.

WORK IN PROGRESS: Writing and illustrating with photographs *Chef: The Work People Do,* for Simon & Schuster.

SIDELIGHTS: "I was not born with a camera in my hands. In fact, photography didn't start to matter to me until I was an adult. As a young child I couldn't see very well and I never felt creative. Glasses and surgery corrected my vision, but I was left with the memory of what it felt like to live in an unfocused, blurry world in which I didn't have an impact. Having that impact, by teaching or helping others, has been the thrust of my life's work.

"I was born and grew up in Long Island, New York on May 23, 1953. I graduated from Valley Stream South High School in 1971, from New York University with a B.A. in psychology in 1975, and from Yeshiva University with a Masters in

BETSY IMERSHEIN

social work in 1977. Always searching for the truth about people and the world around me, I began work as a social worker/therapist only to be pulled toward the theatre.

"For quite a while the theatre felt like home to me. I was managing director of the Jewish Repertory Theatre and then Ensemble Studio Theatre for about four years. I found it exhilarating and enriching to be co-producing not-for-profit theatre in New York. Then I worked free-lance in cable television, though I did not find the satisfaction I had felt from working in the theatre.

"And along came photography. I had fooled around with a camera for some time and taken a few courses, but never seriously considered photography for my work. My husband, James Howe, whom I married in 1981, suggested that we collaborate on a book. Our book, *When You Go to Kindergarten* was published in 1986. I did more studying, became a free-lance photographer, and have since gone on to write and photograph books on my own."

JACKSON, Charlotte E. (Cobden) 1903(?)-1989

OBITUARY NOTICE: Born about 1903, in Big Oak Flat, Calif.; died June 1, 1989, in Tiburon, Calif. Children's book reviewer, editor, and author. Jackson was known for her reviews of children's books that appeared in such publications as the *New York Herald-Tribune,* the *Los Angeles Times,* the *San Francisco Chronicle* and the *Chicago Sun-Times.* She served as children's book editor for both the *Chronicle* and the *Sun-Times* beginning in 1955. She also compiled an annual collection of reviews of children's books in the *Atlantic Monthly* from 1956 to 1967. Jackson's own writings for children include *Tito, the Pig of Guatemala, Sara Deborah's Day, Roger and the Fishes, Round the Afternoon, Mercy Hicks,* and *The Story of San Francisco,* which was published in seven langauges.

FOR MORE INFORMATION SEE:

Foremost Women in Communications, Bowker, 1970.

OBITUARIES

Washington Post, June 4, 1989.

JACQUES, Brian 1939-

PERSONAL: Surname is pronounced "Jakes"; born June 15, 1939, in Liverpool, England; son of James (a truck driver) and Ellen (a housewife) Jacques; children: David, Marc. *Education:* Attended Roman Catholic school in Liverpool, England. *Politics:* "Humanitarian/socialist." *Religion:* Roman Catholic. *Office:* BBC-Radio Merseyside, 55 Paradise St., Liverpool L1 3BP, England.

CAREER: Seaman, 1954-57; railway fireman, 1957-60; longshoreman, 1960-65; long-distance truck driver, 1965-75; docks representative, 1975-80; free-lance radio broadcaster, 1980—. Radio broadcasts for BBC-Radio Merseyside include the music programs "Jakestown," and "Saturday with Brian Jacques"; six half-hour programs for junior schools, "Schools Quiz"; ten half-hour programs on cinematic knowledge, "Flixquiz"; documentaries "We All Went down

BRIAN JACQUES

the Docks," "Gangland Anthology," "The Eternal Christmas," "Centenary of Liverpool," "An Eyeful of Easter," "A Lifetime Habit" (two half-hour programs); and "The Hollywood Musicals" (a six-part series); contributor to the "Alan Jackson" show; broadcaster for BBC-Radio 1 and BBC-Radio 2; member of BBC Northwest Television Advisory Council. Presents humorous lectures at schools and universities. Patron of Royal Wavertree School for the Blind.

AWARDS, HONORS: National Light Entertainment Award for Radio from the Sony Company, 1982, for BBC-Radio Merseyside's "Jakestown"; Rediffusion Award for Best Light Entertainment Program on Local Radio, 1982, and Commendation, 1983; Parents' Choice Award Honor Book for Literature from the Parents' Choice Foundation, 1987, and Children's Book of the Year Award from Lancashire County (England) Library, 1988, both for *Redwall.*

WRITINGS:

"REDWALL" TRILOGY; JUVENILE NOVELS; ILLUSTRATED BY GARY CHALK

Redwall, Hutchinson, 1986, Philomel, 1987.
Mossflower, Philomel, 1988.

Author of numerous documentaries and plays for television, radio and stage. Columnist, *Catholic Pictorial.*

WORK IN PROGRESS: Mattimeo, the third of the "Redwall" trilogy.

SIDELIGHTS: "I did not write my first novel, *Redwall,* with publication in mind. It was mainly written as a story for the blind children's home where I am a patron. Luckily it was picked up by a reputable author and sent to Hutchinson.

"In writing children's books I feel that a 'good yarn' is essential, keeping in mind a strong moral sense of values for children. The 'Redwall' trilogy is set in the 'long ago' era

because most of the adventure and romance has gone from the world of today. Happily there are lots of children aged from nine to ninety, because I get a lot of mail from adults who enjoy both books. In Britain the books are kept in both the children's and adult fantasy departments of bookstores. Being a stage performer I love lecturing to schools, colleges, and to all ages. My lectures on writing and stories are mainly humorous, with a strong message of advice and encouragement to would-be writers."

FOR MORE INFORMATION SEE:

New York Times Book Review, August 23, 1987.
Washington Post Book World, November 6, 1988.

JAKES, John (William) 1932-
(Alan Payne, Rachel Ann Payne, Jay Scotland)

PERSONAL: Born March 31, 1932, in Chicago, Ill.; son of John Adrian (a transportation executive) and Bertha (a homemaker; maiden name, Retz) Jakes; married Rachel Ann Payne (a teacher), June 15, 1951; children: Andrea, Ellen, John Michael, Victoria. *Education:* DePauw University, A.B., 1953; Ohio State University, M.A., 1954. *Politics:* Independent. *Religion:* Protestant. *Agent:* Rembar & Curtis, 19 West 44th St., New York, N.Y. 10036. *Office:* P.O. Box 11085, Greenwich, Conn. 06831.

CAREER: Abbott Laboratories, North Chicago, Ill., 1954-60, began as copywriter, became product promotion manager; Rumrill Co. (advertising agency), Rochester, N.Y., copywriter, 1960-61; free-lance writer, 1961-65, 1971—; Kircher, Helton & Collett, Inc. (advertising agency), Dayton,

JOHN JAKES

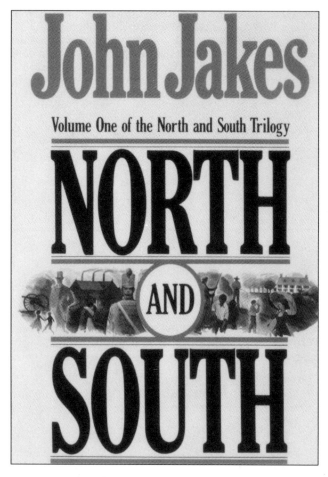

The goal wouldn't be easily reached. Too many obstacles stood in the way. (Jacket design by Paul Bacon from *North and South* by John Jakes.)

Ohio, senior copywriter, 1965-68; Oppenheim, Herminghausen, Clarke, Inc. (advertising agency), Dayton, 1968-70, began as copy chief, became vice-president; Dancer-Fitzgerald-Sample, Inc. (advertising agency), Dayton, creative director, 1970-71. Writer-in-residence, DePauw University, fall, 1979. *Member:* Authors Guild, Authors League of America, Dramatists Guild, American PEN, Mystery Writers of America, Western Writers of America, Players.

AWARDS, HONORS: LL.D., Wright State University, 1976; Litt.D., DePauw University, 1977; Porgie Award for Best Books in a Series, and Ohio Governor's Award, both 1977, and Ohioana Book Award for Fiction, 1978, all for "Kent Family Chronicles" series; Friends of the Rochester Library Literary Award, 1983; L.H.D., Winthrop College, 1985; Research Fellow, Department of History, University of South Carolina, 1988.

WRITINGS:

FOR YOUNG PEOPLE

The Texans Ride North: The Story of the Cattle Trails, Winston, 1952.
Tiros: Weather Eye in Space (nonfiction), Messner, 1966.
Great War Correspondents (nonfiction), Putnam, 1967.
Famous Firsts in Sports (nonfiction), Putnam, 1967.
Great Women Reporters (nonfiction), Putnam, 1969.

Secrets of Stardeep, Westminster, 1969, bound with *Time Gate,* New American Library, 1982.
Time Gate (Junior Literary Guild selection), Westminster, 1972.
Susanna of the Alamo: A True Story (illustrated by Paul Bacon), Harcourt, 1986.

"KENT FAMILY CHRONICLES" SERIES

The Bastard, Pyramid, 1974, Jove, 1978 (published in England in two volumes, Volume I: *Fortune's Whirlwind,* Volume II: *To an Unknown Shore,* Corgie, 1975).
The Rebels, Pyramid, 1975, Jove, 1979.
The Seekers, Pyramid, 1975, Jove, 1979.
The Furies, Pyramid, 1976, Jove, 1978.
The Titans, Pyramid, 1976, Jove, 1976.
The Patriots (contains *The Bastard* and *The Rebels*), Landfall Press, 1976.
The Pioneers (contains *The Seekers* and *The Furies*), Landfall Press, 1976.
The Warriors, Pyramid, 1977, Jove, 1977.
The Lawless, Jove, 1978.
The Americans, Jove, 1980.

"NORTH AND SOUTH" TRILOGY

North and South, Harcourt, 1982.
Love and War, Harcourt, 1984.
Heaven and Hell: The Conclusion of the North and South Trilogy, Harcourt, 1987, large print edition, G. K. Hall, 1988.

OTHER

Wear a Fast Gun, Arcadia House, 1956.
A Night for Treason, Bouregy & Curl, 1956, reissued, Pinnacle, 1982.
(Under pseudonym Alan Payne) *Murder, He Says,* Ace Books, 1958.
(Under pseudonym Alan Payne) *This'll Slay You,* Ace, 1958.
The Devil Has Four Faces, Bouregy, 1958, reissued, Pinnacle, 1981.
The Imposter, Bouregy, 1959, reissued, Pinnacle, 1981.
Johnny Havoc, Belmont Books, 1960.
Johnny Havoc Meets Zelda, Belmont Books, 1962.
Johnny Havoc and the Doll Who Had "It," Belmont Books, 1963.
G.I. Girls, Monarch, 1963.
(Under pseudonym Rachel Ann Payne) *Ghostwind,* Paperback Library, 1966.
When the Star Kings Die, Ace Books, 1967.
Making It Big, Belmont Books, 1968.
Brak the Barbarian, Avon, 1968.
The Fortunes of Brak (short stories), Dell, 1968.
Tonight We Steal the Stars (published with *The Wagered World* by Laurence M. Janifer and S. J. Treibich), Ace Books, 1969.
Brak the Barbarian Versus the Sorceress, Paperback Library, 1969, published in England as *Brak the Barbarian—The Sorceress,* Tandem, 1970.
Brak Versus the Mark of the Demons, Paperback Library, 1969, published in England as *Brak the Barbarian—The Mark of the Demons,* Tandem, 1970.
The Hybrid, Paperback Library, 1969.
The Last Magicians, Signet, 1969.
The Planet Wizard, Ace Books, 1969.
The Asylum World, Paperback Library, 1969.
Mohawk: The Life of Joseph Brant, Crowell, 1969.
Black in Time, Paperback Library, 1970.
Six-Gun Planet, Paperback Library, 1970.
Mask of Chaos (bound with *The Star Virus* by Barrington J. Bayler), Ace Books, 1970.

John Jakes (left) with Paul Bacon in front of the Alamo in San Antonio, Texas.

Monte Cristo 99, Modern Library, 1970.

Master of the Dark Gate, Lancer Books, 1970.

Conquest of the Planet of the Apes (novelization of the film), Award Books, 1972.

Witch of the Dark Gate, Lancer Books, 1972.

Mention My Name in Atlantis: Being, at Last, the True Account of the Calamitous Destruction of the Great Island Kingdom, Together with a Narrative of Its Wondrous Intercourses with a Superior Race of Other-Worldings, as Transcribed from the Ms. of a Survivor, Hopter the Vinter, for the Enlightenment of a Dubious Posterity, DAW Books, 1972.

The Best of John Jakes (short stories), DAW Books, 1972.

On Wheels, Paperback Library, 1973.

Brak: When the Idols Walked, Pocket Books, 1978.

The Bastard Photostory, Jove, 1980.

California Gold, Random House, 1989.

PLAYS

A Spell of Evil (three-act melodrama), Dramatic Publishing, 1972.

Violence (two one-act), Performance Publishing, 1972.

Stranger with Roses (one-act), Dramatic Publishing, 1972.

"Charles Dickens' A Christmas Carol: A New Version for the Stage," first produced at Hilton Head Playhouse, South Carolina, 1988.

MUSICALS; AUTHOR OF BOOK AND LYRICS, EXCEPT AS INDICATED

(Author of lyrics) *Dracula, Baby* (comedy), Dramatic Publishing, 1970.

Wind in the Willows (comedy), Performance Publishing, 1972.

Gaslight Girl, Dramatic Publishing, 1973.

Pardon Me, Is This Planet Taken?, Dramatic Publishing, 1973.

Doctor, Doctor!, McAfee Music, 1973.

Shepherd Song, McAfee Music, 1974.

UNDER PSEUDONYM JAY SCOTLAND

The Seventh Man, Mystery House, 1958, reissued under name John Jakes, Pinnacle, 1981.

I, Barbarian, Avon, 1959, reissued under name John Jakes, Pinnacle, 1979.

Strike the Black Flag, Ace Books, 1961.

Sir Scoundrel, Ace Books, 1962, reissued under name John Jakes as *King's Crusader,* Pinnacle, 1976.

The Veils of Salome, Avon, 1962.

Arena, Ace Books, 1963.

Traitors' Legion, Ace Books, 1963, reissued under name John Jakes as *The Man from Cannae,* Pinnacle, 1977.

Member of editorial board, *Writer,* 1987—. Contributor of short stories to magazines, including *Amazing Stories, Galaxy Science Fiction, Magazine of Fantasy and Science Fiction,* and *Mike Shayne's Mystery Magazine.*

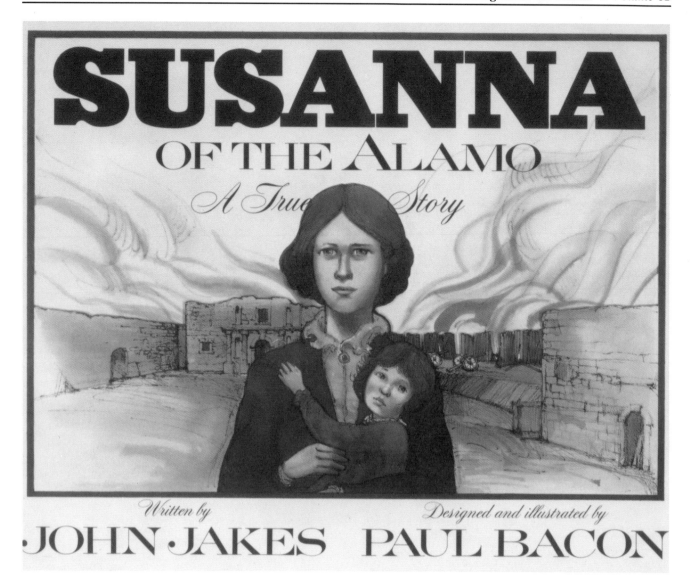

(From *Susanna of the Alamo: A True Story* by John Jakes. Jacket illustration by Paul Bacon.)

ADAPTATIONS:

TELEVISION MINI-SERIES

"The Bastard," Universal, May, 1978.
"The Rebels," Universal, May, 1979.
"The Seekers," Universal, December, 1979.
"North and South," ABC-TV, November, 1985.
"North and South: Book II" (based on *Love and War*), ABC-TV, 1986.

RECORDINGS

"Susanna of the Alamo: A True Story" (cassette with teacher's guide), Listening Library, 1986.
"Heaven and Hell" (cassette; abridged), Random Audiobooks, 1987.
"Love and War" (cassette; abridged), Random Audiobooks, 1987.
"North and South" (cassette; abridged), Random Audiobooks, 1987.
"California Gold" (cassette; abridged), Random Audiobooks, 1989.

WORK IN PROGRESS: Researching a new historical novel dealing with the history of the twentieth century.

SIDELIGHTS: John Jakes was born on **March 31, 1932,** in Chicago. "It was sometime during high school that I began sending short stories to the old science-fiction pulps, which I read avidly at the time."[1] Entertaining thoughts of becoming an actor, he also performed as part of a comedy team at dances and amateur shows.

He then attended DePauw University in Indiana to study creative writing. "I can recall that, during my sophomore year at DePauw, I moved out of the fraternity house into one of the annexes—which I really wasn't supposed to do, not being a senior—on the grounds that I was writing fiction as well as carrying on my schoolwork. I had to have some time to do this extra writing in the evening in addition to the studying, and the fraternity house was pretty noisy."[1]

His first published story about a diabolical toaster which took over its owner's body was sold for twenty-five dollars to the *Magazine of Fantasy and Science Fiction* when he was a college freshman, and published a year later.

"I became convinced that it was easier to go to the corner mailbox and make a little money than it was to go to Broadway.... When I got that twenty-five-dollar check (which I've preserved in photostat form on the wall of my office), I decided it was easier to do this than to traipse off to New York. That was when I really turned the corner. The guy with whom I had a comedy act . . . went to New York and was the leading man on the CBS soap opera 'Love of Life' for nineteen years until it was canceled. But it's a good thing I made that choice, because I've never been that good an actor. At best, I'm an adequate community theater thespian, nothing more—but that's fine."[1]

Jakes took a zoology lab course at DePauw, and fell in love with his instructor, Rachel Anne Payne, two years ahead of him. They were married at the end of his sophomore year, on **June 15, 1951.**

The next year Winston published his " . . . thirty-thousand-word children's book, *The Texans Ride North,* which I wrote on assignment from my then agent, Scott Meredith . . . . I didn't manage to sell anything else in the way of book-length fiction until four or five years later, and that first book was a mystery novel."[1]

He continued his education, earning an M.A. from Ohio State University and entering a Ph.D. program. To meet the demands of a growing family, however, he took a job with Abbott Laboratories as an advertising copywriter, followed by a stint with advertising agencies. His habit of writing several hours in the evening continued, producing many stories and books. He expressed three goals in his science fiction for young people. "Their minds are sharp, open to new ideas. And if they enjoy s-f now, they'll very likely become lifelong fans. That's good for the field as a whole. Second, I particularly wanted to tackle a time-travel book. The paradoxes involved make the time-travel story the most difficult and challenging kind of s-f to write. Third, I wanted to use the time-travel framework to voice some of my deep personal concern about the violent times in which we live—and particularly about the sick philosophy that a bullet can solve all problems. Thus the theme of presidential assassination in *Time Gate.* Regrettably, the book offers no solution to the problem. But often, writers serve a worthwhile purpose simply by refocusing attention on areas of public life that deserve serious constructive thought. Even with this intent, I still meant *Time Gate* to be entertaining. To tell an engrossing story is the writer's first, and highest, obligation."[2]

1971. Jakes left advertising and became a free-lance writer of sales meetings. His career was in a slump when he wrote a novelization of the film "Conquest of the Planet of the Apes" for a mere $1,500. "I was accepting commissions that my agent offered various writers in his stable. One of many problems that I've always had is that I like too many things. I like too many kinds of material. I enjoyed writing private-eye novels when I wrote them. I very much enjoyed science-fiction novels and really gave a couple of them everything I had, with no discernible results. So I felt when I was in my late thirties that I had spread myself too thin and that I really had no audience because I liked to do too many things; and unfortunately I think if you do too many things you never achieve any success with any one of them . . . . I was at a very low ebb in my writing career. I was thinking I probably should give it up."[3]

A couple of years later he was approached by Lyle Kenyon Engel, a packager of paperback originals, about a bicentennial series. "When I took Lyle Engel up on that offer, it happened to be a lucky combination of a good project at a time when the paperback market was just beginning to boom

. . . . All I was given by [him] was a one-sentence, back-of-the-envelope concept.

"It was basically an American family through two hundred years of American history, period. Everything else I built from the ground up . . . . Everything from the name of the family to the names of the books is my doing, and I gave it everything I had. Never imagining, of course, that what did happen would happen; but that certainly was the breakthrough, and despite the many, many differences I've had with Engel and certain things I don't like about his style of operation, I will always be grateful to him for the opportunity. I cannot deny that he gave me that and it was a very handsome one."[3]

Jakes had many reasons for accepting Engel's offer. "First of all, I think I had that basic drive that all writers have: the demand that they write. Secondly, I had a financial motive: We had four children . . . . When Rachel and I worked up a little chart of our four kids going to college, I saw that I needed a hell of a lot of money during a relatively short time—so that really was the practical spur. Virtually everything that I made from my writing went into a sinking fund for their college education.

"Like every writer I hoped one of these days it might pay off with a little of the fame, too; but it was really to make up the salary difference. I didn't want to go to work in New York in the advertising business, and that was the best compromise."[3]

Originally conceived as a five-book series, the "Kent Family Chronicles" series grew to eight books and sold forty-five million copies, with none selling less than 3.5 million. The books follow the Kent family through seven generations. Jakes attributes the tremendous success to several factors. "Number 1: To start with the simplest—I try to tell good stories. Number 2: I think we were just coming into a period when the family saga was on the brink of a rebirth. God knows, the Kent books have spawned . . . imitators. But certainly I would never claim that that was an original idea. You look at Zola and other family sagas—but those had been kind of forgotten for a while, and I think the Kents came in right at a time when there was a hunger for the genre. I had a sociology professor up North tell me a few years ago that he thought people liked to read family sagas because so many real families were deteriorating. So they liked to read about strong families succeeding. Now, I don't know if that's true or not but there might well be a grain of truth in it. So that's the second reason.

"The third, I think, is that I came into doing those books with a very strong feeling about this country. I sat through the Viet Nam-Johnson-Nixon-Watergate years—the terrible years, as we all did. I felt when I began researching American history, which I had not looked into deeply for a long time, that there was a great deal of good about this country that we had forgotten. I set out to try to state some of those positive things. I never wanted to do a Pollyanna work by any means, and if I ever did that I would throw up my hands in horror. I don't think I did. I didn't try to gloss over the slavery question or the stealing of Indian lands, for example, but nevertheless there's a good deal about this country and what it stands for that we had kind of lost sight of in that really terrible time that we went through. I think this played through strongly in the books. My mail told me that it did, and again that was a matter of sounding the right bell note—because I really believed it was the note to sound—but also of sounding it at exactly the right time by sheer accident. So those three things

(From the two-part television special "The Seekers," starring Randolph Mantooth, released for syndication, December, 1979.)

are the best factors or reasons I've been able to come up with."[3]

Research was an important aspect of this project. "I usually start with a good general work of the period, such as Allen Nevins' *Ordeal of the Union* or Margaret Leech's *Reveille in Washington.* Then I decide what events I want to zero in on and have my characters participate in. The personalities I want them to encounter. Then I begin reading biographies and social histories and anything that would be descriptive of the area in which the action took place. Then I'll read such things as diaries of the period for the little day-to-day details—not for the accurate data of what was happening, because a lot of times such works are faulty, but for details on

what people were reading in the papers or what books they were reading or what songs they were singing or how it felt to be a soldier.

"I use a lot of three by five cards and if I have books from the library, I'll make up eight-and-one-half by eleven sheets of paper—which are really just glorified file cards—listing what I can find on specific pages of the book, such as the detail of a sword, or weather on a particular day. On occasion I'll buy books and underline them very heavily. So far I haven't lost a reference note I've needed. Somehow or other I can always find a little scribbled piece of paper, or remember some book where I saw a tantalizing detail, and then I have a file and find it.

"I'm just astonished at how kind people are. If I telephone a research institution in another city for example, I introduce myself, tell them what I'm working on and the kind of thing I'm doing. If I have a specialized problem, I never ask them to look up anything. I just ask if they would steer me in the right direction. That kind of guarded inquiry usually gets them to find the material or tell you where to get it. They usually call or write in a matter of twenty-four hours."[4]

He then tries to write at least a chapter a day. "No *less* than ten pages double-spaced, often more. When I think I'm going to have to do a lot of changing on the next draft, I triple-space to leave plenty of room for correcting."[4] He now works "exclusively on a powerful computer; I have one at each of our two homes."

"I've done a good deal of self-editing on the Bicentennial books ['Kent Family Chronicles']. I think I've learned a lot that I didn't know how to do before in terms of finding out what I think is wrong with a scene. A problem I had for many years was knowing something was wrong with a scene but not being able to analyze it to figure it out. I think when you pinpoint what you wanted to achieve or what should be achieved in a given scene—once you know that for sure, then you can figure out why you didn't get there and go back and get there.

"I had an acquaintance in the writing business who wrote children's books, and he set out a few years ago to freelance. But he's the kind of guy who could only turn out a book in ten months, a children's book, and he couldn't support a family on that. I try to balance the really fast work which is useful against taking a little more time trying to improve it. That's why when I'm into my final draft for the publisher, I'll work Saturdays and Sundays, too, on it.

"I tend to be a fast writer—first draft and edit—but I think my best work has been that which has taken a long time. For example, I did a series of three novellas, back in the sixties. Science fiction that I worked and worked and worked over, deliberately, only just having come upon the idea that things might get a little better if you take time with them. And while none of them ever set the world on fire, I was very happy with the way they came out. I thought they were tighter, and made their points somewhat less melodramatically. One was published in *Orbit 3* and the other two ran in *Galaxy* and all three of them have been anthologized."[4]

Jakes has written four plays and the libretto and lyrics for six musicals. "That's really for fun. I began to write little plays for community theaters . . . —lucky enough to have some of them produced and put into catalogues. I have done some directing. I have . . . a collaboration . . . on a . . . musical with the composer who scored the Broadway musical 'Tintypes'— . . . . I think theater work has some very practical benefits for novel writing. One, it gives you a much better ear for dialogue because if you're familiar with how actors say lines you have a better and sharper ear for novelistic dialogue. Secondly: it gives you an objectivity about your work that you don't always get when you're simply sitting off writing a book. If you're standing in the back of a theater watching something you've done being performed and the audience is hating it, there is *no* excuse in the world that you can formulate other than that the material must be no damn good. You can't say the salesman didn't get out and sell it or the cover was wrong or anything like that. I do the playwriting [sic] for fun, and I would like to take it all the way to New York one of these days. I really do enjoy it and I also think it sharpens the novelistic side of the blade, too."[3]

"I'm trying to slow down a little. I now write between 3,000 and 5,000 words a day. I've been doing it for a long time.

"We took a nice anniversary vacation and traded in the old car. And, yes, I splurged on one thing I've wanted for years—a Bally pinball machine. It cost $996. I like it so much, I still keep it in the dining room."[5]

Jakes enjoys his new-found success, but still writes from 8:30 to about 2:00 every day. Relaxing doesn't come easily to someone with a prolific writing habit. "One of the publishers for whom I've written musicals wanted me to tackle the job of scaling down one of those shows for the dinner-theater market, which meant a start-to-finish revision to cut down the number of characters and simplify the scenery. So I did that; and I wrote a short concept outline for a television movie—a project I've been wanting to do for a year or more . . . . In spare minutes I think about which musical I want to direct for the local community theater, that sort of thing."[4]

Between **May, 1978** and **December, 1979,** three of his books were made into miniseries. Jakes was not involved in the scriptwriting, however, "I was on the set of each one of the three pictures for about a week. The producers were very good about sending me scripts as they came along at each stage of the rewrite. And then, of course, I did a bit part in 'The Seekers.' I had one scene, seven lines, with George Hamilton and Ross Martin, and the experience will delight me to my dying day. Both Hamilton and Martin, who regrettably is dead now, were as kind to this amateur from Podunk as they could possibly be."[1]

1982. Jakes published the first book of a new trilogy, *North and South.* The focus was the Civil War, and the experiences of two families on opposite sides: rice planters from South Carolina and ironworkers from Pennsylvania. Their sons met on their way to West Point, and found themselves enemies at the start of the war.

The new series was a sensation, eventually being made into a long mini-series by David Wolper in 1985. "I worked closely with [editor] Julian Muller to develop a final outline for each book. Julian came down to Hilton Head and we worked together, drawing the characters through history. It was almost like weaving a tapestry. In several of the Kent books, about a third of the way through, the characters went off on their own directions, but in *North and South* and *Love and War* [the second book in the trilogy], I was absolutely committed to a specific time span. I had to write much more tightly, but even with the 135-page outline for *Love and War,* there was a lot of room for invention.

"I brought in the real characters that interested me. I wanted to show Jefferson Davis's mishandling of his government. I wanted to present a little truer picture of Lincoln, who wasn't as popular then as he is now. But that's how I always write; I just hope that what's interesting to me will be of interest to readers as well. And that's why I never use a hired researcher. He or she might miss some little nugget that I would really like.

"There were many purposes moving through the book. I wanted to tell a good story, to report the war—through my own eyes and as the historical record shows it—to show the historical changes in this nation and to show them against the broader historical changes in the world. This was a much more complicated undertaking than I'd ever done before, and to be honest, I took it as a bad omen that when I was finished I was happier with this than with any other book I'd

(From the six-part mini-series "North and South," starring Patrick Swayze and Kirstie Alley. Presented on ABC-TV, November, 1985.)

written. Usually I come to the end of one and I think I didn't make it, didn't even come close. This time I was pleased."[6]

"*Love and War* was not written to demonstrate, again, that war is hell, though it is; or to show slavery, again, as our most heinous national crime, though arguably it is. Both ideas figure in the story, and not in a small way. But this is meant to be a tale about change as a universal force and constant, told in terms of a group of characters living through the greatest redefinition of America, in the shortest time, that we have ever experienced: the Civil War."[7]

1986. *Susanna of the Alamo: A True Story,* illustrated by Paul Bacon, published. "This book was not created in the typical way. By typical I mean this. The children's book author writes the manuscript and delivers it. The publisher hires an illustator, gives him or her the text, and the artwork is produced. Seldom, if ever, shall the twain of author and artist meet.

"Not so with *Susanna.* Paul and I already knew each other when we attended our first meeting to discuss the project, which we both endorsed enthusiastically.

"We planned the book page by page and spread by spread much as a film is created. We discussed the flow of the story, and how it might be handled visually. We divided scenes into 'long shots,' 'close-ups,' and the like. We are both ardent movie fans, so this process was easy and natural for us. The text was not actually written until we laid out the whole book in rough storyboard form.

"Motion picture technique solved a difficult problem for us—that of the gore when the invading soldiers slew so many in a wanton way. We needed to depict it because the excessive brutality at the Alamo helped stiffen Susanna's resolve—and that of the Texans later; we did not want to lapse into bloodthirstiness, however—especially not for young readers.

"We settled on the old movie technique of showing sinister figures or grisly happenings as oversized silhouettes; shadows on a wall. We adopted the technique happily, for it eased us through the spread in which Susanna protects Angelina from the onslaught of the attackers—now shown only as shadow-figures. But the technique is not merely the solution to a problem. It's a powerhouse of dramatic suggestion; and it worked splendidly for us, we feel.

"For this and many other reasons—not the least of them the joy of working with a friend as talented as Paul—*Susanna* was a joy to create. I think my collaborator would endorse that statement."

1987. The final book of the 'North and South' trilogy, entitled *Heaven and Hell,* was published. It dealt with the Reconstruction period. Jakes found that his readers "seem to have gained a new appreciation for American history—particularly how interesting and dramatic it truly is when removed from the embalming fluid of conventional teaching and textbooks. Time and again this has been expressed in letters, and in person, and with unashamed sentimentality I can say that no author could ask for a greater reward, or greater proof that the writer's only purpose—to reach and move a reader—was achieved."[1]

1989. *California Gold* made the *New York Times* best sellers list and was selected by the Literary Guild and *Reader's Digest* Condensed Books. One of Jakes intents as a writer is

to improve his craft. "I don't like writers who manufacture sausage. I admire people who keep going, who try to broaden themselves, like actors who play against type, for example.

"I always try to better myself and it gets harder with each book because it's like a track and field race, you're always running against yourself, trying to beat your own time, and the format doesn't change it. Oh, I'm sure there are some in the literary community who would say that there's a difference between writing a paperback and a hardcover, but to me the difference is in the practioner, not the field. When I started out with *The Bastard,* I gave it everything I had. Of course, you can't get around the apparatus of a market. Reviewers simply do give more attention to hardcovers . . . . When *The Bastard* was published there were no paperback bestseller lists in the *New York Times* or *Publishers Weekly.*

"Too many writers unwittingly play what I call Immortality Roulette. They get involved in worrying about their own reputations. How will they be remembered in a hundred years? They grow desperate, sometimes almost maniacal about it. They write nasty letters to harsh critics—or at least talk about doing it. They are happy or sad depending on a few words from a total unknown (most reviewers). The result of all this is often compensation in the form of overweening self-importance.

"The saddest cases are the most marginal . . . those very competent popular writers who probably will be largely forgotten, except by a few trivia scholars or aficionados, as time goes by. Since most of us can't answer questions about posterity—a Hemingway, acknowledged a genius in his own lifetime, is a rarity—just do the best you can. No one can ask more, and what more can you logically ask of yourself? Posterity will take care of itself, with or without you."[8]

FOOTNOTE SOURCES

[1]*Contemporary Authors New Revision Series,* Volume 10, Gale, 1983.
[2]*Junior Literary Guild,* March, 1972.
[3]*Dictionary of Literary Biography Yearbook 1983,* Gale, 1983.
[4]Kirk Polking, "John Jakes Has a Writing Fever," *Writer's Digest,* January, 1977. Amended by J. Jakes.
[5]Herbert Mitgang, "Behind the Best Sellers: John Jakes," *New York Times Book Review,* April 30, 1978.
[6]Robert Dahlin, "John Jakes," *Publishers Weekly,* November 30, 1984. Amended by J. Jakes.
[7]John Jakes, "Afterword," *Love and War,* Harcourt, 1984.
[8]J. Jakes, "To Be a Writer: What Does It Take?," *Writer,* January, 1987.

FOR MORE INFORMATION SEE:

Christian Science Monitor, November 6, 1969, April 7, 1982 (p. 17).
Washington Post Book World, March 7, 1976 (p. F10), April 3, 1977 (p. E3), October 8, 1987.
Publishers Weekly, April 5, 1976 (p. 59ff), February 14, 1977 (p. 81ff), February 27, 1978 (p. 154), December 24, 1979 (p. 56), December 18, 1981 (p. 59), October, 1985.
People Weekly, April 12, 1976 (p. 25), November 12, 1984 (p. 63ff).
New York Sunday News, August 22, 1976 (section III, p. 1).
Wall Street Journal, June 9, 1977 (p. 1ff).
New York Times Book Review, October 7, 1979 (p. 41ff), March 7, 1982 (p. 24).
Writer, November, 1979 (p. 9ff), July, 1981 (p. 9ff).

(From "North and South: Book II." The six-part mini-series, starring Parker Stevenson and James Read, was presented on ABC-TV, May, 1986.)

Robert Hawkins, *The Kent Family Chronicles Encyclopedia,* Bantam, 1979.

Washington Post, February 3, 1982, February 28, 1982 (p. L1).

Chicago Tribune Book World, February 21, 1982.

Detroit News, February 23, 1982.

Los Angeles Times Book Review, March 21, 1982.

James Vinson, editor, *Twentieth-Century Western Writers,* Macmillan, 1982.

Contemporary Literary Criticism, Volume 29, Gale, 1984.

Los Angeles Magazine, November, 1985 (p. 56).

TV Guide, November 2, 1985 (p. 12).

Charles Moritz, editor, *Current Biography Yearbook 1988,* H. W. Wilson, 1989.

Fran Woods, "From the Saga-Meister: John Jakes Writes Again, of a Young Boy Seeking Fortune," *Daily News,* September 17, 1989.

Los Angeles Times, September 18, 1989.

Donna Olendorf, editor, *Bestsellers 89: Books and Authors in the News,* Issue 4, Gale, 1990.

COLLECTIONS

Archives of Contemporary Writers, University of Wyoming Library.

Archives of DePauw University.

KASSEM, Lou(ise Morrell) 1931-

PERSONAL: Surname sounds like "*Cass*-m"; born November 10, 1931, in Elizabethton, Tenn.; daughter of Edgar Roscoe (in sales) and Dorothy (a nurse; maiden name, Graham) Morrell; married Shakeep Kassem (a financial consultant), June 17, 1951; children: Cherrie, Dottie, Lisa Kassem Kummerl, Amy-Leigh Kassem Kubicki. *Education:* Attended East Tennessee State University, 1949-51, University of Virginia, 1982, and Vassar Summer Institute of Publishing and Writing, 1984. *Politics:* Independent. *Religion:* Methodist. *Home and office:* 715 Burruss Dr. N.W., Blacksburg, Va. 24060. *Agent:* Ruth Cohen, P.O. Box 7626, Menlo Park, Calif. 94025.

CAREER: Virginia Technology, Blacksburg, Va., lab technician, 1951-52; Montgomery-Floyd Regional Library, Blacksburg, librarian, 1971-84; author; lecturer. Councilwoman, Blacksburg, Va., 1978-84. President of Armed Forces Officers Wives, 1955, Blacksburg Junior Woman's Club, 1961, and Parent-Teachers Association, Blacksburg, Va., 1965. *Member:* Society of Children's Book Writers, Writers in Virginia, Womens National Book Association. *Awards, honors: Listen for Rachel* was a Cultural Exchange Selection (Russia), 1987.

It didn't seem possible. One day you were a family. The next day you were all alone. (Jacket illustration by Linda Benson from *Listen for Rachel* by Lou Kassem.)

WRITINGS:

Dance of Death, Dell, 1984.
Middle School Blues, Houghton, 1986.
Listen for Rachel (ALA Notable Book), Margaret K. Mc-
     Elderry Books, 1986.
Secret Wishes, Avon, 1989.
A Summer for Secrets, Avon, 1989.
A Haunting in Williamsburg, Avon, 1990.

WORK IN PROGRESS: Penny Royal, about a mother/
daughter conflict; *Treasures of Witch Hat Mountain,* about a
girl who finds a real treasure in spite of her parents.

SIDELIGHTS: "I was born November 10, 1931 in Tennessee
and grew up in North Carolina, Virginia, and Tennessee. By
the time I finished high school I'd attended nine different
schools. Perhaps as a result of my transient life, I became an
avid reader. I couldn't take my friends along on each move
but I could take my books. I loved school, climbing trees,
reading, riding horses, telling stories, swimming, hiking, and
roller skating. My poor mother despaired of me ever becoming a 'proper' lady. And, being such an odd mixture of
tomboy and bookworm, often I had trouble fitting in with the
normal, stay-in-one-place crowd.

"In high school I found my niche—drama and forensics. I
represented Tennessee in oratory in 1949. My interest in

drama and public speaking continued during my college
years. I enjoyed acting and writing a feature column for my
college newspaper but becoming an author never crossed my
mind.

"In 1951 I married my high school sweetheart and moved to
Blacksburg, Virginia while he completed his degree at Virginia Tech. And in 1953 the first of our four daughters was
born. From 1953 until 1973 I was busy being a mother: PTA,
Girl Scouts, 4-H, band, forensics coach, etc. During that
period I wrote plays, skits, and monologues for my girls and
for schools, churches, and civic groups. And, as I had always
done, I told stories. In fact, long after my children were out of
grade school I was still the 'Story Lady' at an elementary
school. Sometimes I read the children books. Other times I
made up my own stories. The children loved both and it gave
the teachers a much needed break. It also was an outlet for the
ham in me that Virginia will never cure.

"It wasn't until 1973, while working part-time as an assistant
librarian in the Blacksburg Public Library, that the urge to
become an author completely overwhelmed me. I was
disenchanted with the typical view of mountain people! As a
fourth generation daughter of the Appalachian mountains, I
grew up listening to stories of my early ancestors. I knew
some of these independent mountain people. They were *not*
shiftless, ignorant, and stupid as the movies, television, and
books represented them.

"I had a story to tell and I was determined to tell it. Basing my
novel on a legend I heard when I was ten, I wrote *Listen for
Rachel.* After being rejected seventeen times and completely
rewritten seven times, *Listen for Rachel* was my *third* book
accepted for publication ... by Margaret K. McElderry.

"During the years of waiting, revising, and hoping, I wrote
other novels. My first published book was a young adult
ghost story, *Dance of Death,* published by Dell in 1984.
Regan Riley was forced to change schools just as I had done.

LOU KASSEM

Only she had to live in a house haunted by not one but three ghosts.

"Nineteen-eighty-six was a banner year. First, Houghton Mifflin published *Middle School Blues,* which is a humorous account of Cindy Cunningham's journey through the hazzards of middle school. This was a fun book to write. It's based on my experiences and those of my children and their friends. Judging from the fan mail, I seem to have touched a common nerve. When *Listen for Rachel* was published in October, my cup ran over. The ALA Notable Book in the Field of Social Studies honor filled my saucer and more.

"Avon published a paperback edition of *Middle School Blues* in 1987. And *Listen for Rachel* was chosen for the Cultural Exchange Program with Russia. In 1989 Avon published a sequel to *Middle School Blues,* entitled *Secret Wishes,* as well as *A Summer for Secrets.* After several years of delightful research, *A Haunting in Williamsburg* was completed and published by Avon also.

"With no apologies, I am a writer for young people. If I can hook one child on reading, all the rejection slips and endless waiting will have been worthwhile. Writers for children have the opportunity to make a real difference.

"A wonderful dividend of being a published author is that you are invited to schools, libraries, and writing conferences to talk with young people about writing. I've visited over seventy such groups in several states. The response is overwhelming. I heartily urge other authors to get out among their reading public. You receive much more than you give.

"I began my writing career rather late in life. Perhaps I was doing research. Whatever! It's never too late to dream."

HOBBIES AND OTHER INTERESTS: Reading, travel, golf, playing bridge.

KATZ, Welwyn Wilton 1948-

PERSONAL: Welwyn rhymes with "Ellen"; born June 7, 1948, in London, Ontario, Canada; daughter of Robert (a businessman) and Anne (a homemaker; maiden name, Taylor) Wilton; married Albert N. Katz (a professor of psychology), 1973 (separated, 1989); children: Meredith Allison. *Education:* University of Western Ontario, B.Sc., 1970. *Home and office:* 549 Ridout St. N., Unit 502, London, Ontario, Canada N6A 5N5.

CAREER: South Secondary School, London, Ontario, Canada, teacher, assistant head of mathematics, 1970-77; writer. Past refugee coordinator, Amnesty International; treasurer and member of steering committee, London Children's Literature Round Table; former researcher, Girls' Group Home of London. *Member:* Writers' Union of Canada, Canadian Society of Children's Authors, Illustrators and Performers. *Awards, honors:* Book of the Year Runner-up from the Canadian Library Association, 1985, for *Witchery Hill,* 1987, for *Sun God, Moon Witch,* 1988, for *False Face,* and 1989, for *The Third Magic;* Ruth Schwartz Award Finalist, 1987, for *False Face,* and 1988, for *The Third Magic;* International Children's Fiction Prize, Governor-General's Award Finalist, Max and Greta Ebel Award, and Trillium Award Finalist, all 1987, and selected one of *School Library Journal*'s Best Books, and a Pick of the List from the *American*

Bookseller, both 1988, all for *False Face;* Governor-General's Award, 1988, for *The Third Magic.*

WRITINGS:

The Prophecy of Tau Ridoo (juvenile; illustrated by Michelle Desbarats), Tree Frog Press, 1982.
Witchery Hill (young adult novel), Atheneum, 1984.
Sun God, Moon Witch (young adult novel), Douglas & McIntyre, 1986.
False Face (Junior Literary Guild selection), Douglas & McIntyre, 1987, Macmillan, 1988.
The Third Magic, Douglas & McIntyre, 1988, Macmillan, 1989.
Whalesinger, Douglas & McIntyre, 1990, Macmillan, 1991.

WORK IN PROGRESS: A novel set in Stratford, Ontario and Fife, Scotland.

SIDELIGHTS: **June 7, 1948.** Born in London, Canada, a fifth-generation Canadian. "My mother's ancestors were pure Highland Scots; my father's were Cornish. This may help to explain my abiding interest in Celtic mythology. I was not one of those children who are always writing. In fact, there is only one occasion that I recall actually enjoying creative writing, before I was an adult. Surprisingly, it happened in a high school final exam, a three-hour torture where we were expected to write creatively on one of five given topics. I spent two hours trying to decide which of those awful topics I would choose, and the remaining hour 'taking

WELWYN WILTON KATZ

It was only three in the morning, but Mike knew he wouldn't get back to sleep. (Jacket illustration by Steven Kuzma from *Witchery Hill* by Welwyn Wilton Katz.)

dictation' from some inspired part of my brain, the words simply flowing out of me. I got a terrific grade, but the real pleasure was the writing. It was one of the most exciting experiences I've ever had. It was years before I ever tried to repeat it."

September, 1968. "The department of mathematics at my university sent me a letter, based on my first year grades, inviting me to join honours math. Being an obliging soul, and since no one else had asked me, I did. Three years later, with a degree in mathematics, I became a high school teacher.

"My first two years of teaching were awful. Subconsciously I couldn't really believe I was going to be staying in the classroom. Every time I finished a lesson, I threw everything out—the lesson plan, the handouts, the overhead projector sheets, even the kids! Finally I settled down. Five more years passed. It was a good job, well-paid, I was pretty good at it, and I loved the students.

"But there was no—magic—in it. There was no feeling that something exciting and different might be waiting for me around the next corner. I had my ears pierced and got contact lenses and spent a fortune at Merle Norman, but it didn't seem to help. I was twenty-eight years old and I could see forty years stretching ahead, predictable and unmagical, and it gave me the creeps. And then came the double whammy. I discovered the books of J. R. R. Tolkien. With that discovery

I found that it was possible, using words alone, to create a whole world, a marvellously complex and unreal world that other people could believe in. And let me tell you, that was magical!

"I decided to write an adult fantasy novel. I spent three or four years of summers and evenings working on it before I realized that part-time writing didn't work for me. I took a year's leave of absence from teaching, and then another. After two years of writing full-time, the first draft of the book was finally finished—all 750 pages of it. By this time I knew I'd bitten off a pretty big mouthful. The book took place on a different world from Earth, a world populated by four sentient races, all of whom had to be delineated extremely carefully. Not only that, the plot required a cast of thousands, all doing different things at the same time. A tough writing job for anybody, let alone someone who had never attempted even a short story in her entire life!"

June, 1979. "I resigned teaching, then took another year and rewrote the book. Then I sent it out to a publisher. It came back. I sent it out again. When there was no one left to send it to, I cried a little—okay, a lot!—and then put the book on my top shelf. There it sits to this day. But I don't regret that book. I learned a lot about technique and style writing it. And there were some child protagonists in that book who came to life, which told me I might try writing for children the next time. I knew there *would* be a next time because by then I was hooked on writing. Even in that first book, every now and then I would have a wonderful day like that time in the exam, where words would flow out of me like a river, fast and creative and *right*. It was almost as if I were only the medium for that marvellous flow of words. I loved that feeling. It is the main reason why I'm still writing full-time, thirteen years after I began.

"In **1982**, *The Prophecy of Tau Ridoo* was published, my first book for children. Like my adult novel, this was also an 'other-world' fantasy. But this one was a lot shorter than my first fantasy, and a lot more fun to write. I got the idea by thinking about moles. They have lived in the dark so long their eyes have become incapable of seeing well in the light. So I invented a world, like Earth except that it had been completely dark for seven hundred years, whose people would be like moles in that way. Halfway through, though, I realized that the world I had invented was a physical impossibility. People lived there, and that meant they had to breathe, and that meant plants had to photosynthesize, and that meant they needed light! So I had to rework the book, allowing red light to exist on Tau Ridoo and its plants to have adapted to the red light. This worked fairly well, and the book *was* published, but the whole thing left me sweating. I vowed then and there that I would never write another 'other-world' fantasy.

"*Witchery Hill* was published in both the United States and Canada in 1984 (in 1985, Denmark, and other foreign sales followed). This story came out of a trip I made to Guernsey. Everything about that trip was chance. I went there only because the ferry that left England for Guernsey departed from the little town where I was dropping off a rental car. The hotel, picked with a pin to stay in on Guernsey, was run by someone who had made a study of the island's folklore. She made her research available to me, as soon as she heard I was a writer and interested in legends. I had always loved prehistoric stone remains, and it turned out that one of the tombs I visited on Guernsey was supposedly still being used as a site of witches' sabbats as late as 1967. After that, when I asked, people rather secretively told me that witchcraft was still being practiced on Guernsey today. Then, again by accident, I found an old copy of a *Petit Albert* in a bookshop. This was a fairly common manual of witchcraft on Guernsey and elsewhere in the late 1700s, but talking about it led to the mention of a much more 'dangerous' manual called the *Grand Albert,* which had a peculiar Guernsey legend associated with it. That made me think: what if there was an even more powerful book, say, a 'Vieux Albert,' that some modern witches on Guernsey were fighting over? All I had to do, after that, was write the book!

"Despite my earlier vow, I decided to write another 'other-world fantasy.' This one, though, would be so thoroughly prepared I just couldn't run into trouble. It would be a kind of 'prequel' to the King Arthur story, and take place on a world I would call Nwm (after Annwm, the Welsh underworld). I spent months preparing Nwm, before I even thought about writing the story. It took me, off and on, three years to write *The Third Magic,* and I loved every minute of it. Maybe I'll write some more 'other-world' fantasies, now that I've learned the trick!

"In **1986**, *Sun God, Moon Witch* came out in Canada. My interest in prehistory had taken my husband and me to many stone circles in England, and I had done a great deal of reading about them. One of the things I had read was that dowsers ('water-witchers') had often experienced powerful electric shocks touching standing stones like these. Many years before this, my father had told me a story about how an underground spring on his farm was found by a dowser, and I had been fascinated. The two things came together, along with my love of the ancient legends of the moon goddess and sun god, to make this book.

"*False Face* arose out of a visit I made to the Museum of Indian Archaeology in London, Ontario. A display case whose solitary Iroquois false face mask stared grimly out into the darkened aisles of the museum made my daughter, age three, scream out in horror. Anything that frightening to look at, I reasoned, simply had to have a book in it somewhere. So I wrote the book taking only five months from start to finish, and entered it in the International Children's Fiction contest, which I won. Part of my prize was a trip to Italy. I had thought I had never in my life heard about false face masks before the trip to the museum, but as I was getting ready for the trip, my mother gave me a present to wear in Italy. It was a tiny false face brooch accompanied by a written summary of the false face legend. I was thrilled, and wanted at once to know where she had got it. To my amazement she said that *I* had given it to *her*. Apparently I had seen the brooch in a church bazaar when I was only eight, loved the ugly little thing, and bought it for one dollar to give to her on Mother's Day! She kept it for thirty years, and all that time, unknown to me, the false face legend must have been incubating away in my mind. Now, when people ask me where I get my ideas, I am never sure I'm telling them the exact truth! *False Face* will be translated into Swedish, Norwegian, Danish, Portuguese and German, and is a Junior Literary Guild selection."

HOBBIES AND OTHER INTERESTS: Playing the flute, reading myths and legends, discovering interesting recipes to make with the herbs she grows, knitting.

FOR MORE INFORMATION SEE:

Canadian Children's Literature, number 47, 1987.

KAYE, M(ary) M(argaret) 1908-
(Mollie Hamilton, Mollie Kaye)

PERSONAL: Born August 21, 1908, in Simla, India; daughter of Sir Cecil (in India service) and Lady (Bryson) Kaye; married Godfrey John Hamilton (a major general), 1943 (died, December, 1985); children: two daughters. *Education:* Educated in England. *Religion:* Church of England. *Agent:* Harold Ober Associates, Inc., 40 East 49th St., New York, N.Y. 10017; David Higham Associates Ltd., Golden Square, London W1R 4HA, England. *Office:* c/o Penguin Books Ltd., 27 Wright's Lane, London W8 5TZ, England.

CAREER: Writer; painter. *Awards, honors:* Fellow of the Royal Society of Literature, 1980.

WRITINGS:

JUVENILE

The Ordinary Princess (self-illustrated), Kestrel, 1980, Doubleday, 1984.
Thistledown, Quartet, 1982.
(Selector) *Picking up Gold and Silver,* Macmillan, 1989.

JUVENILE; UNDER NAME MOLLIE KAYE

Potter Pinner Meadow (illustrated by Margaret Tempest), Collins, 1937.
Black Bramble Wood, Collins, 1938.
Willow Witches Brook, Collins, 1944.
Gold Corse Common, Collins, 1945.

M. M. KAYE

"Hmm!" said the Fairy Crustacea. (From *The Ordinary Princess* by M. M. Kaye. Illustrated by the author.)

FICTION

Six Bars at Seven, Hutchinson, 1938.
Strange Island, Thacker, 1944.
Death Walked in Kashmir, Staples Press, 1953, published as *Death in Kashmir,* St. Martin's, 1984.
Death Walked in Berlin, Staples Press, 1955, published as *Death in Berlin,* St. Martin's, 1985.
Death Walked in Cypress, Staples Press, 1956, published as *Death in Cyprus,* St. Martin's, 1984.
Shadow of the Moon, Messner, 1956, enlarged edition, St. Martin's, 1979.
(Under name Mollie Hamilton) *Later Than You Think,* Coward, 1958, published as *Death in Kenya,* St. Martin's, 1983.
House of Shade, Coward, 1959, published as *Death in Zanzibar,* St. Martin's, 1983.
Night on the Island, Longmans, Green, 1960, published as *Death in the Andamans,* St. Martin's, 1984, large print edition, Thorndike, 1986.
Trade Wind, Coward, 1963, revised edition, St. Martin's, 1981.
The Far Pavilions (historical novel), St. Martin's, 1978.
The Far Pavilions Picture Book, Bantam, 1979.
"Moon of Other Days": M. M. Kaye's Kipling—Favourite Verses (illustrated by M. M. Kaye and George Sharp), Hodder & Stoughton, 1988, Salem House, 1989.

NONFICTION

Share of Summer: The Sun in the Morning (autobiography), St. Martin's, 1990.

EDITOR

Emily Bayley, *The Golden Calm: An English Lady's Life in Moghul Delhi,* Viking, 1980.

ILLUSTRATOR

The Story of St. Francis, A. R. Mowbray, 1949.
Childen of Galilee, A. R. Mowbray, 1950.
Adventures in a Caravan, A. R. Mowbray, 1950.

ADAPTATIONS:

"The Ordinary Princess" (television series), produced on "Jackanory," British Broadcasting Corporation.
"Far Pavilions" (three-part television series, starring Amy Irving), HBO, April, 1984.

CASSETTES

"Death in Zanzibar," G. K. Hall, 1986.
"Death in Berlin," G. K. Hall, 1987.
"Death in Cyprus," G. K. Hall, 1987.
"Death in Kenya," G. K. Hall.
"Death in Kashmir," [England].
"Death in the Andamans," G. K. Hall, 1988.
"The Ordinary Princess," Caedmon.

WORK IN PROGRESS: Second and third volumes of her autobiography.

SIDELIGHTS: M. M. Kaye was born in India where her British father was president of the council of an Indian state in Rajputana (now Rajesthan). She spent her childhood traveling between India and schools in England. As a young adult, Kaye lived in England trying to earn a living as an illustrator. Eventually, she turned her concentration to writ-

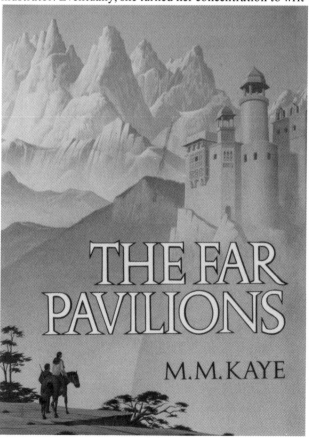

They journeyed further north. (Jacket illustration by Peter Goodfellow from *The Far Pavilions* by M. M. Kaye.)

ing and had her first children's book published in 1937. "I'm a writer entirely by mistake. My hope was to make my living as a painter, but I was a failure at it."[1]

"To my stunned surprise a children's book and my first novel, a crime story, had both been accepted for publication."[2]

When she turned her writing from children's books to thrillers, she changed her name from Mollie Kaye to M. M. Kaye. "Nobody would have taken seriously the Mollie Kaye of children's books."[3]

On a return trip to India, at age thirty-two, she met Captain Goff Hamilton, a British Army officer. "Don't ever let anyone tell you there is no such thing as love at first sight. I thought, 'That's it,' as soon as he walked through the door."[3] Although he had a wife back in Ireland, Hamilton proposed after five days and the couple was married two years later.

"In the early years of the 1950s there used to be a BBC Radio programme called 'Housewife's Choice,' which consisted of popular records—in those days, presumably 78s?—that provided a pleasant accompaniment to tedious and repetitive chores. Any tune in the Top Twenty got played fairly frequently, and one in particular caught my fancy: the first line of the refrain being 'Then I'll go sailing far—off to Zanzibar!'

"Since I myself was in the all-too-familiar position of a British Army wife—abandoned, with my two small daughters, in depressing Army quarters in a small garrison town while my husband and his regiment were on active service somewhere on the other side of the world (on this occasion, Korea!)—I would have given a great deal to go 'sailing far,' to almost anywhere. But Zanzibar is one of those names that possess a peculiar, singing magic in every syllable ... and when the radio was not playing that song I used to sing it to myself.... I read anything I could get hold of on the subject of Zanzibar: never dreaming that I would ever see it myself.

"Then, when my husband was almost due back in England, his regiment, while *en route* for home, was suddenly diverted to Kenya. And since families were allowed to go out there to join their husbands and fathers, it was not long before the children and I were setting off to Nairobi on a flight that nowadays would only take a few hours, but which in those days ... took well over twenty-four.

"It was during our time in Kenya that I got the chance to visit Zanzibar. And I fell in love with it at first sight, for it turned out to be one of those rare places that live up to everything one has hoped and dreamed that [it] would be.

"Since my husband kept being posted to all sorts of novel and entertaining places ... I made detailed notes of things I was afraid I might forget. So that when, several years later, I got around to writing [*Death in Zanzibar*], all I had to do was to hunt up my Zanzibar notebook, and there it all was. An exact description of everything I could possibly need, down to the advertisement painted on looking-glass in the Mombasa Airport, and the millipede crawling across the floor of the tiny, makeshift one on Pemba."[4]

In company with *Death in Zanzibar,* Kaye wrote several other mysteries with the same theme. But she eventually discontinued the stories, claiming that "it was getting a bit footsore."[3]

Her first agent, Paul Scott, also an Indianphile, was the author of *The Raj Quartet.* "Paul had great literary integrity. I owed him so much. When we first got to know each other I was making a small name for myself writing thrillers, but I confessed to him that I actually wanted to write a novel about the Indian mutiny. He was so practical. He said I should wait, work hard and get two thrillers ahead so that I would have time to write my novel, but not disappear from the public view."[5]

"I wanted to write about the Corps of Guides in which my husband ... served as did his father, Col. Bill Hamilton."[6]

The Far Pavilions, a fourteen-year trial of research and writing, was finally published in 1978. "I had written three chapters in 1964 when I got cancer. After I recovered I picked up the book again in 1968 when my husband retired. I spent about two years researching it—in the Indian Army Museum, the British Museum, and India Office Library, all in London. I would take the train to London in the morning and then line up at the doorstep of the British Museum. England is a wonderful place to do research—you usually find that the original documents have been saved instead of just duplicated.

"My illness was one of the reasons why the novel is so long. I never went back to redo parts. I would have if I had had the time, but I lost my grip of it and just let the book take over and write itself."[6]

"It was like trying to hold the reins of four runaway horses."[3]

Kaye "worked all day and every day, when not coping with household duties. But my brain always worked better the later it was—it was always doing fine around bed-time, and like a stone-cold engine in the morning."

"There were the usual number of interruptions—my daughters growing up, getting married, grandchildren and baby-sitting, gardening in the first home we ever had after all the Army stations.

"It never occurred to me that anyone would want to publish this big novel, but I was happy that Tom McCormack [president of St. Martin's Press] took it."[6]

After *The Far Pavilions,* McCormack reissued Kaye's *Shadow of the Moon* in full. In 1956 it had been radically cut before publication and was not well received. "I wasn't surprised, considering the cuts. I think they averaged two paragraphs for every page."[5] "It [was] about the Sepoy rebellion, and it came out when the Empire was going down the drain and feelings were very anti-colonial."[6]

"Paul Scott thought I'd written a best seller, and one English review commented that 'given a grain of luck it would be a British *Gone with the Wind*.' I gave it out for retyping, ignoring the crossings out. I read it again and realized that I'd learned a lot about writing since then. It did need *some* cutting, but not *that* much. I had a habit—I still do—of making rounded characters out of minor ones."[5]

St. Martin's Press also reissued Kaye's *Trade Wind,* another historical drama, that did not do well when published in 1963. "I can't think why it sold at all. The American edition was the same as the British, and my British publisher cut out my entire first chapter—the chapter all about the heroine and what makes her tick.

(From the three-part television series "The Far Pavilions," starring Sneh Gupta. Copyright © by Channel Four, London.)

"If [*The Far Pavilions*] hadn't been a success I don't think anybody would have taken a chance on republishing the other two."[1]

"It's a funny thing, but Americans even now can't understand the Anglo-Indian relationship. When the hardback of *The Far Pavilions* was published, *The New York Times* sent an Indian journalist to interview me, and he surprised the St. Martin's Press people by saying what a marvellous book it was. They hadn't seen that the Indians actually liked people who were born and brought up in India, even if we were British. The point was—they have disliked Britain as a nation, but not the British themselves. How else do you think we could have ruled the country for so long when the Indians outnumbered us at least 2000 to 1? When leftovers from the Raj like me go back now, they love us. I was there with my sister in 1963, and we counted up the invitations and found we had seven-and-three-quarter years' worth—many from total strangers."

"I am writing my autobiography. I want my children and my grandchildren to know what the Raj was really like."[5]

Kaye says of her fame and success: "I probably would have had a lot more fun if it had come earlier. I would have bought a mink coat, a fast car and other silly things. But when you're older, you don't want so much—you have your house, your husband and your children, and you're content. Besides, when you're older you can read all about your success and you know enough not to believe a word of it."[1]

"I've been jolly lucky and have had a marvelous life."[3]

FOOTNOTE SOURCES

[1]Edwin McDowell, "Behind the Best Sellers: M. M. Kaye," *New York Times Biographical Service,* August, 1981.
[2]M. M. Kaye, *Death in the Andamans,* St. Martin's, 1985.
[3]Fred Hauptfuhrer, "M. M. Kaye Draws on Seventy Lively Years to Create an Epic Book on Her Beloved India," *People Weekly,* November 20, 1978.
[4]M. M. Kaye, *Death in Zanzibar,* St. Martin's, 1983.
[5]Ion Trewin, "PW Interviews: M. M. Kaye," *Publishers Weekly,* June 25, 1979. Amended by M. M. Kaye.
[6]Herbert Mitgang, "Behind the Bestsellers: M. M. Kaye," *New York Times Biographical Service,* December, 1978.

FOR MORE INFORMATION SEE:

Times Literary Supplement, April 19, 1957, August 22, 1958, September 22, 1978, November 21, 1980, March 26, 1982.
New York Times, October 26, 1958, December 3, 1978.
Washington Post Book World, September 10, 1978 (p. 1ff), July 12, 1981 (p. 5).
Newsweek, September 24, 1978.
New Yorker, October 9, 1978, September 24, 1979, July 27, 1981.
Christian Science Monitor, November 13, 1978.
New York Times, March 25, 1979.
Chapter One, May-June, 1979.

Washington Post, September 11, 1979, April 21, 1984.
Maclean's, September 24, 1979.
Detroit News, October 7, 1979.
New Statesman, October 12, 1979.
Los Angeles Times, November 2, 1980, October 9, 1984, May 23, 1986.
Contemporary Literary Criticism, Volume 28, Gale, 1984.

KHALSA, Dayal Kaur 1943-1989

PERSONAL: Born April 17, 1943, in New York, N.Y.; died of breast cancer July 17, 1989, in Vancouver, British Columbia, Canada. *Education:* City College of New York, B.A., 1963. *Religion:* Sikh. *Agent:* Jane Gelfman, 250 West 57th St., New York, N.Y. 10107.

CAREER: Writer, artist, and yoga teacher. *Awards, honors:* Choice Book from the Children's Book Centre, 1984, for *Baabee Books, Series II,* and 1985, for *Merry Christmas, Baabee; Tales of a Gambling Grandma* was selected one of *New York Times* Notable Children's Books, and one of New York Public Library's Best Children's Books, both 1986, and Children's Literature Prize Honorable Mention for Illustration from the Canada Council, Ruth Schwartz Award Finalist from the Ontario Arts Council, and Amelia Frances Howard-Gibbon Award Finalist, all 1987; American Institute of Graphic Arts Show Winner's List, 1987, American Booksellers Association/Children's Book Council Children's Bestseller List, 1988, Choice Book from the Canadian Children's Book Centre, 1988-89, and one of New York Public Library's Best Children's Books, all for *I Want a Dog;* Governor General's Literary Award for Children's Illustration Finalist, and Parents' Choice Award for Book Illustration from the Parents' Choice Foundation, both 1988, both for *Sleepers; My Family Vacation* was selected one of *Booklist*'s Most Outstanding Picture Books of the Year, 1988.

WRITINGS:

Baabee Books, Series I (four books; self-illustrated), Tundra, 1983.
Baabee Books, Series II (four books; self-illustrated), Tundra, 1983.
Baabee Books, Series III (includes *Bon Voyage Baabee, Happy Birthday Baabee, Merry Christmas Baabee,* and *Welcome Twins;* all self-illustrated), Tundra, 1984.
Tales of a Gambling Grandma (ALA Notable Book; self-illustrated), C. N. Potter, 1986, published in England as *Tales of a Gambling Grannie,* MacDonald, 1988.
I Want a Dog (ALA Notable Book; self-illustrated), C. N. Potter, 1987.
Sleepers (self-illustrated), C. N. Potter, 1988.
My Family Vacation (self-illustrated), C. N. Potter, 1988.
How Pizza Came to Queens (self-illustrated), C. N. Potter, 1989.
Julian (self-illustrated), C. N. Potter, 1989.
Cowboy Dreams, C. N. Potter, 1990.

Also author of *The Snow Cat,* and editor with Bibiji Inderjit Kaur of *Taste of India,* an Indian vegetarian cookbook.

WORK IN PROGRESS: May and Her Mother.

SIDELIGHTS: Dayal Kaur Khalsa was born in 1943 in Queens, New York. Her Russian-born grandmother was a

DAYAL KAUR KHALSA

dominant figure during her formative years. "My parents worked all day, so right from the start my grandma and I were always together.

"We spent most of our time under the great weeping willow tree in our front yard. My grandma sat like a flowering mountain in her big green garden chair. All day long she knit scarfs and shawls and socks. She told me stories of her life and gave me two important pieces of advice.

"One: Never, ever go into the woods alone because the gypsies will get you or, should you escape that cruel fate, you'll fall down a hole.

"Two: Just in case the Cossacks come to Queens, learn to say 'Da' and always keep plenty of borscht in the refrigerator.

"Whenever I had a cold, Grandma let me stay in her bed. She made a tent from a sheet and an overturned chair. All day long we kept busy together polishing pennies bright copper.

"When I became bored with this, she'd slowly slide open her bedside table drawer.

"I liked that drawer.

"First there was the smell of sweet perfume and musty old pennies. Then there was a tiny dark blue bottle of Evening in Paris cologne, shaped like a seashell; a square snapshot of my grandma holding me as a baby; big, thick, wriggly legged

She could mark a card with her fingernail and hide aces in her sleeve. (From *Tales of a Gambling Grandma* by Dayal Kaur Khalsa. Illustrated by the author.)

black hairpins; and stuck in corners so I had to use the hairpins to get them out, dull brown dusty pennies.

"But most fascinating of all were my grandma's false teeth. I never saw her put them in her mouth. She always kept them in the drawer, or if she were going visiting, they stayed smiling secretly in the pocket of her dress.

"My grandma let me touch everything, even the teeth.

"And she'd promise if I would get better really fast, she'd take me somewhere."[1]

After Khalsa graduated from City College she traveled throughout the United States and Mexico. "When I was a young teenager and wanted to be a writer and couldn't wait to leave home and go on the road in search of adventure to write about my mother said, 'There are stories right in your own back yard.' Hah!, I said. So I left home, went on the road, had lots of adventures, and eventually twenty-five years later, the first book I published took place in my back yard of childhood. Hah!"[2]

In 1970 Khalsa immigrated to Canada. She first lived in Toronto, then moved to Montreal, where she became a yoga teacher and a member of the Sikh Ashram. Following her extensive observation of babies and their development, she designed the *Baabee Books,* twelve wordless board books in three series, intended for babies from birth to one year.

The multi-award-winning *Tales of a Gambling Grandma,* published in 1986, was inspired by the eccentric stories Khalsa had heard from her grandmother. "She only remembered that one night the Cossacks charged into her village, brandishing their swords and scaring all the people.

"My grandma (who was only three years old) jumped into a cart full of hay and covered herself. Somewhere she lost her shoe. And so, she escaped to America wearing only one little black shoe, hiding in a hay cart drawn by a tired white horse, all the way across the wide, slate-green Atlantic Ocean. At least, that's how she told the story to me.

"She landed in Brownsville, Brooklyn.

"There she grew up.

"When she was old enough to get married, my grandma borrowed a balalaika. She couldn't play the balalaika, but she could hum very loudly.

"Every evening she sat down with her balalaika on the front steps of her building, trying to catch a husband.

"One night, Louis the plumber, trudging home weary from work, saw her. She made such a pretty picture with her balalaika and her long golden hair and rosy cheeks that he dropped his heavy leather bag of plumbing tools—*clank*—and asked her to marry him.

"And she, actually strumming the balalaika—*plink, plank, plunk*—said, 'Yes.' ... To help make extra money, my grandma learned how to play poker.

"She was very good—sharp-eyed and quick with her hands. She could mark a card with her fingernail and hide aces in her sleeve. And, most important, she liked to win. Wherever there was a hot card game going on in Brooklyn, my grandma was there—winning money."[1]

Shortly after *Tales of a Gambling Grandma* was published, Khalsa developed cancer. However, in the three years that followed, in spite of debilitating operations and treatments, she managed to write and illustrate six more books, and wrote a seventh.

May Cutler, the president of Tundra Books, Khalsa's Canadian publisher, recalled: "In Montreal her sense of humor made her visits to our office a welcome break for everyone. She would bring in her latest illustrations and tell us the story with obvious delight. One sensed how much pleasure she had working them out. But there were poignant moments, too. Once when I asked her how she could complete so much work in such a short time, she answered: 'It's easy, May. I have a deadline.'"[3]

Khalsa died in Vancouver on July 17, 1989. Cutler remarked: "Dayal was that rarest and most precious of individuals in the children's book world. She was a total book creator and a great one, writing genuinely original stories and illustrating them in a uniquely colorful style full of fascinating details."[3]

FOOTNOTE SOURCES

[1]Dayal Kaur Khalsa, *Tales of a Gambling Grandma,* C. N. Potter, 1986.
[2]Sarah Ellis, "News from the North," *Horn Book,* May/June, 1989.
[3]*Obituary,* Tundra, July 18, 1989.

FOR MORE INFORMATION SEE:

OBITUARIES

New York Times, July 21, 1989 (p. B8).
Publishers Weekly, August 25, 1989 (p. 36).
School Library Journal, September, 1989 (p. 154).
Horn Book, November/December, 1989 (p. 822).

KIRBY, Susan E. 1949-
(Suzanne Stephens)

PERSONAL: Born August 10, 1949, in Bloomington, Ill.; daughter of Stephen F. (a farmer) and Glaida (a homemaker; maiden name, Wade) Funk; married John R. Kirby (a mechanic), June 27, 1969; children: John R. II, A. Levi. *Education:* Attended Illinois State University, 1967-68. *Religion:* Protestant-Christian. *Home:* Box 151, McLean, Ill. 61754. *Agent:* Joyce Flaherty, 816 Lynda Court, St. Louis, Mo. 63122.

CAREER: Author. *Awards, honors:* Friends of American Writers Award Second Place for Juvenile Historical Fiction, 1983, for *Ike and Porker.*

WRITINGS:

JUVENILE

Ike and Porker, Houghton, 1983.
Culligan Man Can (illustrated by Jim Spence), Abingdon, 1988.

ROMANCE NOVELS

The Maple Princess, Bouregy, 1982.
Lessons for the Heart, Bouregy, 1982.
Blizzard of the Heart, Bouregy, 1982.
Chasing a Dream, Bouregy, 1982.

Love's Welcome Home, Bouregy, 1983.
Reach for Heaven, Bouregy, 1983.
One Whispering Voice, Silhouette, 1984.
Love's Secret Game, Bouregy, 1985.
(Under pseudonym Suzanne Stephens) *The Proud Heart,*
     Bouregy, 1986.
Heart Aflame, Zondervan, 1986.
Butterscotch Moon, T. Nelson, 1986.
Cries the Wilderness Wind (historical), Zondervan, 1987.
Love, Special Delivery, Butterfield, 1987.
In Perfect Harmony, Butterfield, 1988.
Shadow Boy, F. Watts, in press.

Contributor of over 170 short stories to periodicals, including *Scholastic Scope.*

SIDELIGHTS: "My interest in writing was a natural outgrowth of my love of reading. I did not plan or prepare for a career in writing. When the urge to express myself in short stories became too strong to ignore, I was the mother of two young active boys with little spare time. I failed at balancing motherhood and all its constant yet satisfying demands, so though I'd managed to sell a few short stories, I postponed my writing ambitions until my youngest started school. The time was right! God blessed my efforts. I began to sell short stories regularly. My first children's novel knocked around a bit before it found a home with Houghton Mifflin. It was a delight to do this story of a sensitive pioneer boy who, like my own boys, was a bit timid of the dark, yet full of bright bold ideas and ambitions!

SUSAN E. KIRBY

What if the scattered wolf pack came skulking back?
(Jacket illustration by Marlies Najaka from *Ike and Porker* by Susan E. Kirby.)

"A romantic at heart, I'd published a string of light romance novels before finding an agent. And what a jewel of an agent! Joyce Flaherty has taught me much about the business as well as placing my books with major publishers. I count her not only a business 'partner,' but a dear friend.

"My children's book *Culligan Man Can* is special to me because the idea for the book was born of my son Levi's coming to terms with/and succeeding despite his learning disability. Also of importance to me is a teen work forthcoming from Franklin Watts Orchard Books. Of a more serious tone, this novel is the story of a teenage girl's gradual acceptance of the changes in her life brought about by an acccident which left her younger brother brain-injured. It is a story of strained loyalties, old and new friendships, and love tested to the limits.

"Writing is and will always be a joy to me. Yet it is also a driving force that continually looks ahead to the next challenge."

KITAMURA, Satoshi 1956-

PERSONAL: Born June 11, 1956, in Tokyo, Japan; son of Testuo (a retail consultant) and Fusae (a homemaker; maiden name, Sadanaga) Kitamura; married Yoko Sugisaki (an interior designer), December 15, 1987. *Education:* At-

He went into the kitchen and cooked himself some nice green peas. (From *When Sheep Cannot Sleep: The Counting Book* by Satoshi Kitamura. Illustrated by the author.)

tended schools in Japan. *Office:* 48A Hormead Rd., London W9 3NQ, England.

CAREER: Free-lance illustrator, 1975—. *Awards, honors:* Mother Goose Award from Books for Children Book Club, 1983, for *Angry Arthur; What's Inside* was selected one of *New York Times* Notable Books, 1985; Britain's Sixteenth Children's Science Book Award, and Children's Science Book Award from the New York Academy of Sciences, both 1987, both for *When Sheep Cannot Sleep.*

WRITINGS:

SELF-ILLUSTRATED

What's Inside: The Alphabet Book, Farrar, Straus, 1985.
Paper Jungle: A Cut-out Book, A. & C. Black, 1985.
When Sheep Cannot Sleep: The Counting Book, Farrar, Straus, 1986.
Lily Takes a Walk, Dutton, 1987.
Captain Toby, Blackie, 1987, Dutton, 1988.
UFO Diary, Andersen, 1989, Farrar, Straus, 1990.

ILLUSTRATOR

Hiawyn Oram, *Angry Arthur,* Harcourt, 1982.

H. Oram, *Ned and the Joybaloo,* Andersen, 1983, Farrar, Straus, 1988.

Roger McGough, *Sky in the Pie* (poems), Kestrel, 1983.

H. Oram, *In the Attic,* Andersen, 1984, Holt, 1985.

The Flying Trunk (anthology), Andersen, 1986.

Pat Thomson, *My Friend Mr. Morris,* Gollancz, 1987, Delacorte, 1988.

The Happy Christmas Book (anthology), Hippo Books, 1987.

Andy Soutter, *Scrapyard,* A. & C. Black, 1988.

A Children's Chorus (anthology), Dutton, 1989.

H. Oram, *Speaking for Ourselves* (poems), Methuen, 1990.

SIDELIGHTS: "I am interested in different angles of looking at things. I find great potential in picture books where visual and verbal fuse to experience and experiment these angles. Also, there is an advantage of universality of expression in this medium due to the clarity required for young readers.

"I was born and grew up in Tokyo, Japan, and since 1983 have lived and worked in London."

KLOTS, Alexander Barrett 1903-1989

OBITUARY NOTICE: Born December 12, 1903, in New York, N.Y.; died of emphysema, April 18, 1989, in Putnam, Conn. Entomologist, educator, and author. Klots was a distinguished authority on insect life. A biologist affiliated with the City College of New York (now the City University of New York) for more than three decades and a research associate of the American Museum of Natural History beginning in 1946, he specialized in lepidopterology, the branch of entomology concerned with butterflies and moths. He wrote several books for children, including *Desert Life* and *Tropical Butterflies.* His *Field Guide to the Butterflies of North America, East of the Great Plains* is considered among the definitive insect studies of the twentieth century. Klots's other writings include *The World of Butterflies and Moths,* and, with his wife Elsie B. Klots, *Living Insects of the World* and *Insects of North America.*

FOR MORE INFORMATION SEE:

American Men and Women of Science, Bowker, 1973.
Contemporary Authors, Volume 107, Gale, 1983.

OBITUARIES

New York Times, April 28, 1989 (p. B-11).

KOFF, Richard M(yram) 1926-

PERSONAL: Born January 8, 1926, in New York, N.Y.; son of Harry and Riva (Mohi) Koff; married Mary Alice Coudreaut, May 3, 1958 (divorced, February, 1969); married Hunter Duncan Campbell (a business consultant), January 29, 1977; children: (first marriage) Christopher Stephen, Kathleen Janette. *Education:* New York University, B.M.E., 1948, M.M.E., 1950. *Agent:* Jane Jordan Browne, 410 South Michigan Ave., Chicago, Ill. 60605.

CAREER: American Hydromath Corp., New York City, design engineer, 1949-55; McGraw-Hill Publishing Co., New York City, associate editor, 1955-58, senior associate editor, 1958-60, managing editor of *Product Engineering,* 1960-66;

Playboy, Chicago, Ill., administrative editor, 1966-71, manager of New Publications Division of Playboy Enterprises, 1971-74, assistant publisher, 1972-77, director of new publications, 1974-76, vice-president, 1974-77, business manager, 1976-77; management consultant in Chicago, Ill., 1977—. Member of board of directors, Oasis, 1976-79, and *Chicago Times Magazine,* 1988—. *Military service:* U.S. Army Air Forces, 1944-45. *Member:* Institute of Electrical and Electronics Engineers (associate member), Society of Midland Authors (member of board of directors, 1979-81). *Awards, honors:* Jess H. Neal Editorial Achievement Award from the American Business Press, 1959, for "Eight Steps to Better Writing," 1960, for "Design in Europe," and 1962, for "Design in Japan"; *Christopher* was selected one of Child Study Association of America's Children's Books of the Year, 1987.

WRITINGS:

(With John J. Pippinger) *Fluid-Power Controls,* McGraw, 1959.

How Does It Work?, Doubleday, 1961.

Home Computers, Harcourt, 1979.

The Home Electronics Catalog, Contemporary Books, 1979.

Christopher (fiction; illustrated by Barbara Reinertson), Celestial Arts, 1981.

It was a big, gloomy castle of a house. (Illustration by Barbara Reinertson from *Christopher* by Richard M. Koff.)

Strategic Planning for Magazine Executives, Folio, 1983, 2nd edition, 1987.
Using Small Computers to Make Your Business Strategy Work, Wiley, 1984.
Increasing Your Wealth in Good Times and Bad, Probus, 1985.

SOFTWARE

"The Magazine Budget Model," Sheridan Software, 1984.
"The Magazine Strategy Model," Sheridan Software, 1984.
"Investment Strategies," Sheridan Software, 1984.

Also author of software "New Product Diagnostic Audit," Sheridan Software. Contributor to *Cowles Complete Encyclopedia,* and to magazines, including *Playboy, Nature and Science, Folio,* and *Product Engineering.*

WORK IN PROGRESS: With Diane Tracy, *The First Book of Common Sense Management; The Silencers.*

KRONENWETTER, Michael 1943-

PERSONAL: Born February 12, 1943, in West Palm Beach, Fla.; son of Lanore Kronenwetter (founder of trucking company Foreway Express); married Catherine Patricia Patterson (a laboratory information systems supervisor), December 16, 1971; children, Catherine, Jay. *Education:* Attended Northwestern University, 1961, Senior Dramatic Workshop, 1962, and University of Wisconsin, 1963-68. *Religion:* Roman Catholic. *Home and office:* 117 Sturgeon Eddy Rd., Wausau, Wis. 54401.

CAREER: Free-lance writer. Co-owner/operator of Nonesuch Bookstore, Kingston, Ontario, Canada, early 1970s. Critic and commentator, WRIG Radio, 1982; guest critic, Wisconsin Public Radio, 1984. Member of board of directors, Central Wisconsin Children's Theater. *Member:* Children's Reading Roundtable of Chicago, Amnesty International. *Awards, honors:* Award from the National Educational Film Festival, 1983, for filmstrip "America's Power and Prestige since Vietnam"; Certificate of Merit from Wisconsin Public Radio, 1986, for unproduced radio play "A Death in Richland Center."

WRITINGS:

YOUNG ADULT

Are You a Liberal? Are You a Conservative?, F. Watts, 1984.
Capitalism Vs. Socialism: Economic Policies of the U.S. and the U.S.S.R., F. Watts, 1986.
Free Press V. Fair Trial: Television and Other Media in the Courtroom, F. Watts, 1986.
The Threat from Within: Unethical Politics and Politicans, F. Watts, 1986.
Politics and the Press, F. Watts, 1987.
Journalism Ethics, F. Watts, 1988.
The Military Power of the President, F. Watts, 1988.
The War on Terrorism, Messner, 1989.
Managing Toxic Wastes, Messner, 1989.
Taking a Stand against Human Rights Abuses, F. Watts, 1990.
Northern Ireland, F. Watts, 1990.
(Contributor) *Lincoln Homework Encyclopedia,* Harcourt, in press.

ADULT

(Contributor) *Shortcuts,* Bantam, 1981.

MICHAEL KRONENWETTER

Wisconsin Heartland, Pendell, 1984.

FILMSTRIPS

"America's Power and Prestige since Vietnam," Human Relations Media, 1982.

Also author of short story "The Indecipherable," broadcast on "Canadian Short Stories," Canadian Broadcasting Corporation Radio Network, August, 1971, and of unproduced radio play "A Death in Richland Center." Author of columns, "TV Talk," *Kingston Whig-Standard* (Canada), 1971-73, "Valley Memories," 1981-85, and "Talking about Entertainment," 1982-84, both *Valley View,* and "Talking Entertainment," *Mountain View,* 1988—.

WORK IN PROGRESS: First Kill, a detective novel for adults; *The Changing Face of Eastern Europe,* for Watts; *The Drug Wars,* for Messner; *Hate Groups,* for Walker.

SIDELIGHTS: "I was born in West Palm Beach, Florida, but raised in Wausau, Wisconsin. Between then and now, I've lived in a lot of other places, from Longueuil, Quebec to Carlsbad, New Mexico, but I find myself back in Wausau, raising my kids in the same house in which I grew up. Not many people can do that anymore.

"From as early as I can remember I had two ambitions, to write and to act. I've managed to do some of both, the writing professionally, and the acting as an amateur.

"When I was in high school, I had two wonderful teachers, Isabelle Stelmahoske and Arthur Henderson. The first one taught English and drama, and the second history. But what they did most was to help open my mind and to give me confidence in my own strivings. That's the kind of teacher every kid needs, and those of us who are lucky get at least one or two along the way. (It's interesting, though, that different teachers do that for different kids, and in different ways. The same teachers who were inspirations to me were terrors for some of my friends, and vice versa.) I was luckier than most, because I had at least three other fine teachers, too (along with a few terrible ones there's no need to talk about.)

"In high school, I won the Wisconsin state division of the 'I Speak for Democracy' contest. That got me a free trip to Washington, D.C. and a fancy dinner with my congressperson, who happened to be Mel Laird. He later became Secretary of Defense in charge of prosecuting the Vietnam War, which I opposed.

"After high school, I started college at Northwestern University in Evanston, Illinois. It has a beautiful campus, but that isn't why I went there. I went because it had (and still has, as far as I know) a top-ranked theater program. On weekends, I worked as a doorman at the Fickle Pickle coffee house, a folk song place off Rush Street in Chicago. That was educational in a whole lot of ways; but college wasn't—or didn't seem to be. So, after one quick quarter, I decided college wasn't going to make me a writer or an actor, so I quit.

(From *The War on Terrorism* by Michael Kronenwetter.)

"The next summer I went to New York, at age nineteen, to attend an acting school called the Senior Dramatic Workshop. The rumor was that the room we used for movement class had once been used as an apartment by Marlon Brando and Wally Cox. If that rumor wasn't true, I don't want to know about it.

"Eventually I found my way back to Wisconsin, and back to college at the University of Wisconsin: first in Wausau, and then in Madison. That was where I spent most of the 1960s. The University of Wisconsin and I had a love-hate thing going—at least on my part. I enjoyed the atmosphere, the companionship of the other students, and my studies in history, writing, and sociology immensely. But I hated the required work. If I went back now, I'd enjoy it all.

"The '60s was a terrible decade in many ways. It was a time of war and upheaval. But it was also an exciting time to be young. (Too exciting for many of us. It was a time when a lot of people my age were getting killed or having their souls hung out to dry in Vietnam, while others were zapping their own brains with drugs at home.) It was a time when young people mattered to the country in ways they don't matter today. We were the ones who were fighting both wars that were going on at the time—the one in Vietnam, and the one for civil rights here in the U.S., on both sides of the battle lines—so we mattered. And, just as importantly, the country mattered to us. Some of us were right, and some of us were wrong (and some of us were both), but we *cared*. We took serious things seriously.

"I took one summer off to work as a volunteer with a Community Action Project in the coal mining community of Horse Creek, Kentucky. It was a place where some of the best people were poor bootleggers, and the worst people had the most money. It taught me a lot about a side of America I hadn't seen before. In 1968, I helped to form a small, and almost completely ineffective, citizens group to support the presidential candidacy of Senator Eugene McCarthy in Wisconsin. The week Richard Nixon was elected president, I went to Canada. It was a decision I've never regretted. In the mid-70s, I moved back to the U.S. I haven't regretted that either.

"It was in Kingston, Ontario I met my wife, Pat. I had a small bookstore there for awhile, and got my first newspaper column with the (then) *Kingston Whig-Standard.* Later, we moved to Longueuil, Quebec, a suburb of Montreal. It was in Montreal that our first child, Catherine, was born. Our second child, Jay, was born in Wausau. Before the kids were born, I had no particular interest in being a father. Since they were born, I've found that it's being a father that gives real interest to everything else.

"When I was a kid, I never thought about writing for kids. I wanted to write for grownups. I thought grownups were more important than kids. I was wrong.

"At the moment, in addition to my books for young people, I'm working on a detective novel. That's a lot of fun. I've always enjoyed reading detective stories. I spent most of one teenage summer reading the complete Father Brown stories of G. K. Chesterton and the complete Sherlock Holmes stories of Arthur Conan Doyle. John Dickson Carr was my favorite at one point, Rex Stout at another. Elmore Leonard and Laurence Block are two of my favorites today.

"In some of my books (*Are You a Liberal? Are You a Conservative?, Capitalism Vs. Socialism,* and *Free Press V.*

Fair Trial, for example), I've set out to be 'objective.' That is, I've had to give a fair presentation of both (sometimes several) sides of a question about which I have strong opinions. It's an interesting challenge, and I'm proud of the fact that I've succeeded fairly well at it, at least according to reviews. It's important for people, young and old, to hear all sides of important issues. At the same time, it troubles me a little when I'm not able to say what I think myself. That's why I enjoy column-journalism, and a book like *Taking a Stand against Human Rights Abuses* where I have a chance to speak out for a cause I believe in.

"Speaking of beliefs and causes, I was raised, and am today, a Roman Catholic. Always was, I suppose. In between then and now, however, I stopped going to church for a long time. I belong to Amnesty International, and support Physicians for Social Responsibility, International Physicians for the Prevention of Nuclear War, and Right to Life. That's a combination of beliefs and causes that often surprises people, but I find them not only consistent, but logically and emotionally inevitable.

"The best piece of advice I ever heard for a writer was one word: Write!"

HOBBIES AND OTHER INTERESTS: Traveling, theater, movies, "watching the Green Bay Packers play football and my kids play anything at all."

KUSHNER, Jill Menkes 1951-

PERSONAL: Born April 25, 1951, in Teaneck, N.J.; daughter of Bradford S. (a professor) and Bette (a sales manager; maiden name, Kaplan) Menkes; married Robb Adam Kushner (a computer systems consultant), April 14, 1973; children: Matthew, Elizabeth. *Education:* Boston University, B.S. (cum laude), 1973; Fairleigh Dickinson University, M.A., 1986. *Politics:* Democrat. *Religion:* Jewish. *Home:* 540 Page Terrace, South Orange, N.J. 07079. *Office: Literary Review,* 285 Madison Ave., Madison, N.J. 07940.

CAREER: Free-lance writer, 1980-84; *Literary Review,* Madison, N.J., assistant editor, 1985—; Fairleigh Dickinson University, Madison, instructor in freshman writing, 1985-86; Associated University Presses, Cranbury, N.J., free-lance copy editor, 1986-87. *Member:* National Association for Young Writers.

WRITINGS:

The Farming Industry, F. Watts, 1984.

Contributor of articles to periodicals, including *On the Scene, Trumbull Times,* and *Connecticut Today.*

WORK IN PROGRESS: "I maintain an active interest in literature, early childhood education, language, and the fine arts."

SIDELIGHTS: "The key to writing well is twofold: you have to know what it is you're trying to say, and you have to then express that thought in an organized way. People who get 'hung up' or 'blocked' when writing are usually confused about what they want to say—as a result, they write around their subject rather than address it directly. I suggest that authors do a lot of research before they write—using inter-

views, secondary library readings, and other 'fact-finding' methods. Research makes one feel authoritative, competent, and confident.

"And when it comes to writing *style,* I suggest that authors write much the way they would speak—directly and to the point. In addition, it's a good idea to keep *Webster's Ninth* and *The Chicago Manual of Style* handy. Word spellings and usage are always in flux, and these two tools are invaluable.

"Another useful tool is to learn word processing, which is a big help for editing and revision. (And when others are editing you, don't be sensitive. Nobody's words are golden—most everything can be written better than it was the first time around.)"

HOBBIES AND OTHER INTERESTS: Synagogue activities.

LEDERER, William J(ulius) 1912-

PERSONAL: Born March 31, 1912, in New York, N.Y.; son of William Julius (a dentist) and Paula (a housewife; maiden name, Franken) Lederer; married Ethel Victoria Hackett, 1940 (divorced, 1965); married Corinne Edwards Lewis, June 24, 1965 (divorced May, 1976); children: Brian John Hackett, William Jonathan, Bruce Allen. *Education:* United States Naval Academy, B.S., 1936. *Home:* East Hill Farm, Peacham, Vt. 05862. *Agent:* Harold Ober Associates, Inc., 40 East 49th St., New York, N.Y. 10017.

CAREER: Secretary to columnist Heywood Broun, 1927-28; free-lance writer, 1928—; U.S. Navy, 1930-58, retiring as captain; wartime duty in Asia and with Atlantic Fleet; special assistant to commander-in-chief, Pacific, 1950-58; Far East correspondent for *Reader's Digest,* 1958-63. Lecturer in colleges and universities, 1949—; author-in-residence, Harvard University, 1966-67. *Member:* American Society of Magazine Photographers, Society of Magazine Writers, Sigma Delta, Lotus Club (New York), Pacific Club (Honolulu), National Press Club (Washington). *Awards, honors:* Fellowship from the Nieman Foundation for Journalism, Harvard University, 1950-51.

WRITINGS:

The Last Cruise: The Story of the Sinking of the Submarine, U.S.S. Cochino, Sloane, 1950.
All the Ships at Sea, Sloane, 1950.
Spare-Time Article Writing for Money, Norton, 1954.
Ensign O'Toole and Me, Norton, 1957.
(With Eugene Burdick) *The Ugly American,* Norton, 1958.
A Nation of Sheep, Norton, 1961.
Timothy's Song, Norton, 1965.
(With E. Burdick) *Sarkhan,* McGraw, 1965, published as *The Deceptive American,* Norton, 1977.
The Story of Pink Jade, Norton, 1966.
Our Own Worst Enemy, Norton, 1968 (published in England as *The Anguished American,* Gollancz, 1969).
(With Don D. Jackson) *The Mirages of Marriage,* Norton, 1968.
(With Joe Pete Wilson) *Complete Cross-Country Skiing and Ski Touring,* Norton, 1970, revised edition, 1972, published as *New, Complete Book of Cross-Country Skiing,* Norton, 1983.
A Happy Book of Happy Stories, Norton, 1981.

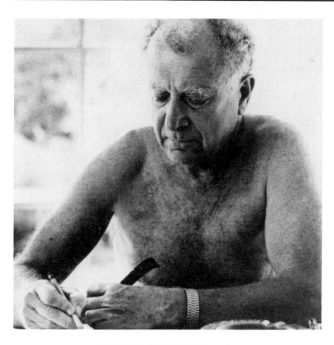

WILLIAM J. LEDERER

Marital Choices: Forecasting, Assessing and Improving a Relationship, Norton, 1981.
I, Giorghos: A Novel, Norton, 1984.
A Happy Book of Christmas Stories, Norton, 1984.
Creating a Good Relationship, Norton, 1984.

Contributor of articles and short stories to periodicals, including *Argosy, Collier's, Coronet, Esquire, Ladies' Home Journal, Reader's Digest, Saturday Evening Post,* and *This Week.*

ADAPTATIONS:

(Also author) "Ensign O'Toole and Me" (television series) starring Dean Jones, NBC-TV, September 1962-September, 1963.
"The Ugly American" (motion picture), starring Marlon Brando, Universal Pictures, 1963.

WORK IN PROGRESS: Rewriting novel *I, Giorghos;* a sequel to *Sarkhan;* a book on the topic of how to be joyful, productive, and as healthy as possible regardless of a discordant environment or if you are old.

SIDELIGHTS: "I began writing when I was sixteen because, living alone much of the time in New York, I had to earn my living. I did high school sports reporting in the *New York Times* and the New York *Evening Post.* Then I found that interviewing celebrities for the New York *World* was lucrative, five dollars for each interview. One of the celebrities was Heywood Broun who, after the interview, hired me as his secretary. Many famous authors came to his home; and I asked each the same question: 'What must I do to become an author?' Their answers were varied, however, most suggested: 1) Get an education. (I was a high school kick-out.) 2) Write, write, write. 3) The technique of writing is easily learned. The difficult part is having something about which to write, therefore, make your own life adventure-full. 4) Read! Read! Read! I recorded these interviews in speed writing (and still have them). They included many distinguished literary people."

In 1930 Lederer enlisted in the U.S. Navy and a year later entered the U.S. Naval Academy at Annapolis, Maryland. "When I was an enlisted man in the Navy, and later a midshipman at the U.S. Naval Academy, I stammered miserably. It was a peculiar type of stammering. It occurred only on informal occasions such as while talking with friends or, unfortunately, while reciting in the classroom. I never stuttered or stammered when the going got tough. In sports or during emergencies on board ship, I was a different guy, as cool as ice . . . my speech was slow and smooth.

"However, after three years my bad performance in the schoolroom caught up with me. The medical officers at Annapolis told me I would receive a medical discharge upon graduation. There was no place in the Navy for anyone with a vocal impediment, and that was that.

"But I loved the Navy and wanted to stay in. So during my next furlough I studied under two speech specialists in New York. They eliminated all traces of impediment and I returned to Annapolis so fluent and confident that I was elected president of the Naval Academy Public Speaking Society. I tried to exhibit my speaking abilities by participating in debates, plays and midshipman rallies. But I guess the Navy medical officers were not impressed; shortly after receiving my diploma I was booted out.

"As a matter of fact, I could have stayed in the navy without much trouble. A U.S. Senator who had heard me at the finals of the Naval Academy public speaking contest told me that he would bring pressure on the Navy to have me reinstated. But Cmdr. Oscar Badger, then Executive Officer of the Academy, advised me against accepting the offer.

"'If you really want a commission and have faith in yourself,' he said, 'get to work and persuade the Navy Department. If you crawl in by the political back door, you'll never be held in very high regard by your future shipmates.'

"'I suggest that you stop stuttering, go to Washington and see the Surgeon General.'

"The Surgeon General at the Navy Department wouldn't touch my case with a ten-foot boat hook. 'We can't take a chance on your speech breaking down when the going gets rugged.'

"The Surgeon General must have noticed the angry glint in my eye because he added, 'And I'll tell you this, there's no one in the Navy who can overrule me except the Chief of Naval Operations.'

"As I was walking slowly down the corridor, I saw a blue and gold sign saying, ADMIRAL STANDLEY, CHIEF OF NAVAL OPERATIONS. Some impulse gave me a quick kick in the pants and before I knew what I was doing I had walked into the anteroom of the top man in the Navy. Two people had desks here. One was a yeoman in uniform. The other was a red-headed civilian clerk. Or maybe he was the receptionist, I wasn't sure. When I told him that I'd like to see the CNO he asked in a kindly manner, 'What's the subject of your visit?'

"'I want to get back in the Navy. I was thrown out because I'm supposed to stutter.'

"The clerk drew up a chair and said, 'Sit down. Tell me

something about yourself. It would make it easier for the Admiral if I could brief him before you went in.'

"I told the clerk how I had gone to the Surgeon General, and the results. I even mentioned my decision about not accepting the Senator's help. The clerk scratched his head and said, 'Well, I believe the Surgeon General is right. You'll have to show that you're as good or better than other officers in the Navy.'

"As he said that, an idea flashed through my mind . . . . I spoke excitedly, . . . 'The only way to prove myself is by being exposed to excitement and stress and let the admiral see for himself how I react. I'll ask him to pick ten young officers, good ones, classmates of mine with the same amount of naval experience I've had—and put me in competition against them . . . . If I'm not as calm and efficient as the rest, I'll go home and shut up for good.'

"I entered a large room, heavily carpeted . . . . Admiral Standley asked brusquely, 'What do you want?'

"'I want to stay in the Navy, sir.'

"'Well, I hear that the Medical Officer at the Naval Academy and the Surgeon General recommend to the contrary. Do you know more about the Navy than they do?'

"My lips and tongue seemed plastered down but somehow the words came out smoothly, 'No, sir. I don't know more about the Navy than they do. But I do know more about *myself* than they do, sir.'

"The admiral said, 'While you were waiting outside I telephoned the Surgeon General. Do you know what he told me? He said I would be doing a disservice to the Navy if I gave you a commission. He said that if you ever got into a critical situation you'd get flustered and begin stammering. Do you agree?'

"'The Surgeon General has made a mistake, I believe, sir.'

"'All right,' said the admiral in an irritated manner, 'prove it.'

"I wiped perspiration from my face and swallowed hard. Then I told him how I'd like to compete against ten officers under emergency conditions. The Chief listened patiently. At the end of my talk he said in a hard, flat voice, 'You'd be willing to have a board of medical officers observe the test?'

"'I'd welcome it, sir.'

"Jerking his thumb toward the door, Admiral Standley said to me, 'Go out there and cool off.' Then to the red-headed clerk, 'You stay here and take notes.'

"I waited for about a half hour.

"Once more I stood at attention before Admiral Standley. He looked up and said quietly, 'Very well, it's a deal.'

"'You mean I'm to have the opportunity of being tested?'

"For the first time the Old Man smiled. 'Son,' he said, 'you've already been tested, and you've passed. Your commission and orders will be mailed you tomorrow.'

"'Gee, th-th-thank you very much, sir,' I blubbered. I didn't

know what he meant about my having been tested. But I had heard him say that I'd get a commission.

"'Don't thank me,' said the admiral. 'The first person you can thank is Oscar Badger. He tipped us off about your going to the specialists to cure your stammering and how much you wanted to stay in the Navy. Then you can thank the Surgeon General for suggesting the little run-around you've had up here. He wanted to find out if you'd have the initiative to see the CNO with a solution, and how you'd talk when you were really nervous and under stress. But more than anyone, you can thank this gentleman,' said the admiral inclining his head toward the red-headed clerk. 'He recommended to me that you get your commission. I trust his judgment.'

"'Th-th-thank you sir,' I said, edging toward the door and feeling for my handkerchief.

"The admiral offered me his hand. 'Good-by now, Lederer. I'll see you in the fleet soon.'

"I dashed into the corridor and skipped down the stairs five at a time. Then I remembered the clerk. I never even thanked him!

"I ran back to the office of the CNO, but the clerk wasn't there. I pointed to his desk and asked the yeoman . . . . 'Can I have his name and address? I want to write him.'

"'Sure,' said the yeoman. 'Just address the letter to Captain Chester Nimitz, Navy Department, Washington, D.C.'"[1]

Lederer's naval career lasted twenty-eight years. While stationed in Manila in 1940, he fell in love with " . . . Ethel Hackett, a lovely young girl who made me want to write poetry.

"In fact I wrote plenty of poetry, but I didn't have the nerve to show it to Ethel. That was the trouble. Here was the babe I had been looking for all of my life. She liked me and I loved her. I wanted to marry her; but my clumsiness and shyness blocked me from doing it.

"When I was on board ship, I made up all kinds of wonderful, romantic speeches. In my imagination I was the boldest of lovers. But when I was near Ethel and saw her gracious beauty, my dreams froze on me. I stuttered and did everything wrong.

"Two days before the *Appleby* sailed for Tokyo, Ethel and I were married in the Cathedral. It was the ding-dongiest wedding the town had had in a long while.

"Ethel looked like Venus di Milo; and me, I was reasonably handsome, too."[2]

During World War II, Lederer was stationed in Asia for three years and won a special commendation ribbon. His interest and studies of the people and culture of Asia grew when in 1951 he paid numerous visits to the Far East as a member of the staff of the commander-in-chief, Pacific.

In 1958 Lederer retired from the Navy, with the rank of captain, and became Far East correspondent for *Reader's Digest*. He was already an established writer, having published numerous magazine articles and in 1950 two books, all based on his naval experiences.

His efforts were met with critical success, and in 1954 he wrote the book *Spare-Time Article Writing for Money.* "Writing professionally sometimes rattles even the most experienced authors. If you are sensitive, an unsuccessful literary experience may bruise your ego badly.

"Every prospective author must answer this question for himself. I write for four reasons:

"1. To make money. I started because several years ago we were in a financial hole and I didn't see any other way of getting out. In a big magazine, rates for beginners start at 750 dollars for a 5,000-word article. Small publications seldom pay less than 250 dollars.

"2. I enjoy prestige. The idea of having millions of people reading my material appeals to me.

"3. I get pleasure from entertaining people. Once I wrote a book called *All the Ships at Sea.* I still receive letters from readers who tell me they got a bang from the book. I like that.

"4. Sometimes I feel I have something important to say. It is more satisfying to tell my story to a large audience than to a small group on a street corner or in the parlor.

"In 1944, when I started writing in earnest, I wrote from four to eight a.m. We had a spare room that made a good study because we were too broke to furnish it. Environment didn't influence me much then. I knew Ethel wouldn't get up until seven o'clock, and I enjoyed the knowledge that I couldn't possibly be disturbed.

"That was before we had children.

"When the youngsters came, the typing would often awaken them, or, during the summer, they'd get up on their own about five.

"Working at home, I was limited to hours very early in the morning or late at night. The beautiful long stretches of Saturday and Sunday could not be utilized because of the interruption from the children.

"But the problem was, if I didn't write at home, where could I? I had a heck of a time paying my house rent, let alone leasing an expensive office some place else. Going to my place of business was out of the question. I tried it. Office problems kept slipping into my mind and often, at six a.m., I'd find myself answering business letters instead of sticking to my manuscript.

"The easy solution came from Burke Wilkinson, the novelist. He had an office which he used from nine to five, on weekdays only. For a small payment he let me share his space. I occupied it before nine in the morning and on weekends. It was no inconvenience to him and only a small expense to me.

(Illustration from *The Ugly American* by William J. Lederer and Eugene Burdick.)

(Jacket illustration by Alan Haemer from *The Ugly American* by Lederer and Eugene Burdick.)

Marlon Brando plays a U.S. ambassador in the movie adaptation of Lederer's novel *The Ugly American*.

"Since then I have found that getting a 'part-time' office is the simplest thing in the world."[3]

Success continued with the publication of his book *Ensign O'Toole and Me,* and in 1962 was the basis for the television show "Ensign O'Toole."

Teaming up with Eugene Burdick, Lederer wrote *The Ugly American,* which proved to be his most popular book. "It [is] about Americans at work overseas in the service of the United States and freedom. Some of the people we described were doing a great job. Others were stupid, fearful or just plain incompetent and a few of these were the very people who ran our various foreign aid programs at the local level. We wrote the book hoping it would stimulate Americans to think about the mission of our country in foreign lands all over the world.

"We were hardly prepared for the explosion that resulted. Although thousands of readers understood the book and wrote us asking how they could help make America's foreign aid more effective, thousands more were outraged. Streams of angry letters poured in to Congress asking why, if the foreign aid programs were so badly run, taxpayers should support them at all. *The Ugly American* became one of the most frequently mentioned books in the . . . history of the Congressional Record. Senator William Fulbright of Arkansas, its sharpest congressional critic . . . called it 'sterile, devoid of insight, reckless and irresponsible.'"[4]

"[The book] became a *great* success after it became public knowledge that the U.S. government had taken steps to suppress the sale [of it] in foreign countries. We learned about this by chance. A bookstore owner from Manila happened to be sitting next to me on a plane, and he angrily informed me that USIS (by cutting off funds) was suppressing *The Ugly American* in the Philippines.

"Later, when George Englund and Marlon Brando were making the book into a motion picture, the government once more attempted to abort the growing popularity of the book. The Agency for International Development sent 'Asian experts' to persuade the producer that some of the things in our book were not only untrue but impossible. (For one entertaining small example, the 'experts' said it was impossible to use hollow bamboo as a pipe for water. Of course, this method has been used in Southeast Asia for thousands of years and is still being used today.)

"When the American public began asking questions regarding the ineffectiveness of our foreign policies (Burdick and I received an average of 2,000 letters a week during that time), the State Department gave evidence of concern. The Department of State had a speech prepared which was read from the legal sanctuary of the Senate floor by Senator William Fulbright. He challenged the validity of the book's premises and suggested that Burdick and I were tantamount to traitors.

"We wrote Senator Fulbright and offered to take him—at our expense—on a tour through Southeast Asia and show him what we had seen. All we requested from him was that he go incognito so that we'd have no official meddling.

"The only reply we received was a short paragraph from the senator's secretary. She said the senator was too busy."[5]

"Angry letters came to us, too, attacking us for daring to say that Americans overseas are all doing a bad job.

"We were astounded and dismayed. Astounded because the book told about a number of people—including specifically the 'ugly American' of the title—who with intelligence and devotion were bringing practical, human help to backward areas. We were dismayed because, although the book was intended to help correct the errors in America's foreign aid programs, it was now being used as a weapon to destroy foreign aid entirely. Canceling the foreign aid programs now on the ground that they contain weaknesses would be as illogical as throwing away a rifle because it sometimes jams—just when the enemy is about to attack.

"More than anything else we were depressed that so many readers should fail to appreciate the fact that thousands of 'ugly Americans' overseas are doing practical work with a no-nonsense application of elbow grease. These men and women should be supported. In a large sense we wrote our book to praise them. Thousands of these Americans are performing their good works in the line of duty, as employees of the State Department, the International Cooperation Administration and other government agencies. Still others are doing it entirely on their own—which, in a way, makes their efforts even more spectacular."[4]

In 1961 Lederer published *A Nation of Sheep,* responding to the thousands of letters he received from "average" citizens asking what they could do regarding foreign affairs: "How can the man in the street help prevent the blunders by which we have aided our enemies to turn against us in large areas of the world—areas where our influence was paramount and admiration for us high, fifteen short years ago.

"These are disturbing questions, and certainly Professor Burdick and I gave no more than hints as to their solutions in *The Ugly American.* The key to the riddle lies in the causes of the blunders; and the chief cause is ignorance—an overwhelming national ignorance of the facts about the rest of the world. A nation, or an individual, cannot function unless the truth is available and understood. Since the United States is a democracy, the broad answer to the questions asked in the thousands of *Ugly American* letters is that all of us must become informed.

"Like most simple solutions, it is a difficult one to apply. Particularly it is difficult in the United States today, when the truth is largely unavailable; when the government itself frequently is ignorant of the most obvious events occurring in other nations; when the press is so convinced that the Ameri-

can people don't want the hard facts of foreign affairs that it makes only routine efforts to report them; when lack of knowledge of international matters has made of the people of the United States a nation of sheep—uneasy, but too apathetic and uninformed to know why—endorsing any solutions which appear cheap and easy and which come from a source apparently better informed than themselves.

"This book has been written in the conviction that something can be done about it, and that it must be the average citizen who does it. It is, I hope, a useful answer to the questions implied in *The Ugly American.*"[6]

Collaborating with Burdick once again, he published *Sarkhan.* "There were many ... attempts to belittle and indirectly to suppress *The Ugly American.* But these attempts were micro-efforts compared to what happened later to our follow-up novel, *Sarkhan.*

"We published *Sarkhan* in the fall of 1965. In writing the book we had several objectives. First, we wanted to produce a book which was exciting and entertaining, the first requirement for a novel. Second, we wanted to use that narrative quality to show what was happening eight years after *The Ugly American;* and that things probably would get even worse unless the U.S. foreign relations process improved.

"However, showing the eruptions and stupidities *in the field* was not sufficient. The cause was in Washington. Among the major characters in our book were officials who made foreign relations policy and whose departments implemented these policies. The crux was that many officials were more skilled at perpetuating their own personal power and the funding of their agencies than they were knowledgeable about the true welfare and well-being of the United States.

"At publication time it seemed as if the book would be a tremendous success. There were advance orders of several tens of thousands in the bookstores. *Sarkhan* was the choice of the Literary Guild. This represented an additional 100,000 copies at least. It also was the choice of the *Reader's Digest* Book Club, which had a circulation of several hundred thousand.

"However, some strange things began happening even before books were available in the stores. First, it was reviewed in *Time* magazine several days before books were on sale. Although this sometimes happens, it seemed odd to me. My previous book, *A Nation of Sheep,* had been on the best-seller list for forty weeks before *Time* reviewed it. Now a review came *before Sarkhan's* publication. The review itself was done in a way (bearing in mind the political climate of the time) which seemed to be aimed at discrediting *Sarkhan* rather than reviewing the contents and grading the book's quality. It was so off center that I wondered whether or not the *Time* reviewer had read the book.

"I was sufficiently curious about this to mention it to an old friend, an editor of *Time.* Several days later my friend and I met at lunch in an obscure uptown restaurant (at his request) .... He ... whispered that if I ever quoted him he would deny he had spoken to me. If it became known he had supplied me with information it would cost him his job. he told me this: 'About a month ago two men came up from Washington and called on the publisher. These two men told the publisher "that it is against the interest of the United States that *Sarkhan* be a success."' This startled me, because we had written the book not only to be entertaining, but also to help the United States.

(From the movie "The Ugly American." Copyright © 1963 by Universal Pictures.)

"Shortly after publication date, I was scheduled to be on a television show in New York. On the way to the studio I stopped in at Brentano's bookstore. It pleased me to see two large stacks of *Sarkhan* in a primary display location . . . . However, when I returned to Brentano's, the two big stacks of *Sarkhan* no longer were there. I knew it was improbable that so many books would have sold so quickly. I asked the clerk for a copy of the book. She couldn't find one. She said, 'That's funny, there were a lot of them out front this morning.'

"I urged her to look about the store. She did. In a few minutes she returned and told me, 'We received a phone call and the books have been sent back.'

"Previous to this, we had been receiving vigorous interest from various Hollywood studios. Soon after publication that vigorous interest abruptly stopped. A studio executive told me that his studio had received a telephone call from Washington informing the studio that if *Sarkhan* w[as] made into a motion picture, the studio might have grave problems in obtaining their export licenses. My Hollywood informant told me he would get into much trouble if it w[as] known that he had given me information."[5]

Sarkhan was reissued in 1977 under the title *The Deceptive American.* "It seemed to me (Eugene Burdick is dead now) that in our new and current political environment the suppression of a book would be just about impossible. President Carter clearly has told us he is against that kind of business. Therefore, because *Sarkhan* is considered a good yarn by those who have read it, and because its contents are still relevant to an understanding of U.S. foreign policy effectiveness, the book is being re-issued.

"Twelve years have gone by since its initial publication. It seems proper now to give the book the title which is appropriate, *The Deceptive American.* It was the deceptiveness, the chicanery, the greed of many officials which created American failures. Changing this cultural disease, I believe, is what President Carter is attempting. If the mass circulation now of *The Deceptive American* is of any assistance—and if at the same time the story is an entertainment—it will, indeed, be a great source of satisfaction to the author and the publisher."[5]

Lederer's concern about affairs in Asia continued with his book *Our Own Worst Enemy,* written during America's military involvement in Vietnam. "I have been a professional student and observer of Asian affairs since 1940, and a professional military man even longer. I have observed wars and political turmoil in almost every Southeast Asian nation. Death, destruction, and international power struggles have been my business for the greater part of my adult life.

"I thought I had learned to control my reactions to bloodshed, havoc, ruthlessness, and national despair.

"But what I saw in Vietnam taught me better. The practices I witnessed in Vietnam violated almost everything I had learned at military schools and as a combat officer.

"American techniques in Vietnam profaned my experiences as a political activist and as a lifelong specialist in revolutionary warfare.

"I beheld the United States being beaten—not by the strength of the enemy but by its own mistakes and incompetence.

"I was embarrassed by U.S. officials who did not seem to realize that a catastrophe was exploding beneath them. Or, if the officials were conscious of America's foundering and bungling, they dissembled and spoke about the future as if success were assured. Time, they usually implied, was on our side, mistakes were being corrected, progress was certain, victory inevitable.

"We have botched up almost everything we have attempted in Vietnam. We haven't even been able to spend our billions efficiently or with dignity. The Vietnamese leaders we have supported were . . . held in contempt by the people. And when we shook our steel fists and started military campaigns, we couldn't even find the enemy. On the average, out of every 1,000 'search and destroy missions' the U.S. Army has fired at the enemy less than twenty times.

"One of the reasons we have been so impotent in Vietnam is that we have allowed two additional deadly enemies to enter the war. These two additional enemies give tremendous support to the North Vietnamese and to the Vietcong. These two enemies of the United States supply North Vietnam and the Vietcong with war material and food. They help maintain high morale. They assist in recruitment. They stimulate the determination to resist and defeat the United States.

"Even though these two allies of our enemy are among America's most dangerous foes, we have been helpless against them. We are afraid to take action to thwart their deadly actions. We do not have the courage or integrity to confront them.

"The two countries who are giving this support to North Vietnam and to the Vietcong are not Russia and Red China.

"*They are South Vietnam and the United States. We are our own worst enemy.*"[7]

Lederer's other stories and books have dealt with a wide variety of subjects; ranging from children's books, cross-country skiing, and marriage (Lederer has been married and divorced twice).

FOOTNOTE SOURCES

[1]W. J. Lederer, "The B-B-B-Best Friend I Ever Had in the Navy," *Reader's Digest,* December, 1957.
[2]W. J. Lederer, *Ensign O'Toole and Me,* Norton, 1957.
[3]W. J. Lederer, *Spare-Time Article Writing for Money,* Norton, 1954.

[4]W. J. Lederer and Eugene Burdick, "Salute to Deeds of Non-Ugly Americans," *Life,* December 7, 1959.
[5]W. J. Lederer, Preface to *The Deceptive American,* Norton, 1977.
[6]W. J. Lederer, *A Nation of Sheep,* Norton, 1961. Amended by W. J. Lederer.
[7]W. J. Lederer, *Our Own Worst Enemy,* Norton, 1968.

FOR MORE INFORMATION SEE:

"Keeping Posted," *Saturday Evening Post,* January 14, 1950.
Nation, October 4, 1958.
Spectator, February 13, 1959, October 27, 1961.
Yale Review, March, 1959.
Wilson Library Bulletin, April, 1961 (p. 659).
Christian Science Monitor, April 26, 1961.
Saturday Review, April 29, 1961, November 9, 1968.
New Republic, May 1, 1961.
Atlantic, June, 1961.
Times Literary Supplement, October 20, 1961.
Reader's Digest, March, 1962 (p. 207ff), January, 1963 (p. 99ff).
New York Times Book Review, June 30, 1968.
John Wakeman, editor, *World Authors 1950-1970,* H. W. Wilson, 1975.

LIEBERMAN, E(dwin) James 1934-

PERSONAL: Born November 21, 1934, in Milwaukee, Wis., son of Benjamin (a physician) and Ruth (a musician; maiden name, Perssion) Lieberman; married Susan Brown, 1959 (divorced); married Carol Silverman Hall, 1988; children: Karen, Daniel. *Education:* University of California, Berkeley, A.B., 1955; University of California, San Francisco, M.D., 1958; Harvard University, M.P.H., 1963. *Politics:* "Gandhian." *Religion:* Jewish. *Home and office:* 3900 Northampton St. N.W., Washington, D.C. 20015. *Agent:* Gail Ross, 1666 Connecticut Ave. N.W., Washington, D.C. 20009.

CAREER: National Institute of Mental Health, Center for Studies of Child and Family Mental Health, Bethesda, Md., psychiatrist and chief of staff, 1963-70; Howard University, Washington, D.C., clinical assistant professor of psychiatry, 1968-77; Hillcrest Children's Center, Washington, D.C., director of family therapy, 1971-74; American Public Health Association, Washington, D.C., mental health project director, 1972-75, director of family planning project, 1975-77; George Washington University, Washington, D.C., clinical associate professor of psychiatry, 1977-86; University of Maryland, College Park, adjunct professor of family and community development, 1987—. Visiting lecturer at Harvard School of Public Health, 1969-73. Member of board of directors, Sex Information and Education Council, 1966-69, 1973-76.

MEMBER: Esperanto League for North America (president, 1972-75), American Psychiatric Association (fellow), American Association of Marriage and Family Therapists (fellow), American Public Health Association (fellow), National Council on Family Relations (member of board, 1970-73). *Awards, honors: Sex and Birth Control* was selected one of American Library Association's Best Books for Young Adults, 1973; *Acts of Will* was selected one of American Library Association's Best Science Books, 1985.

E. JAMES LIEBERMAN

WRITINGS:

(With Ellen Peck) *Sex and Birth Control: A Guide for the Young,* Crowell, 1973, revised edition, Schocken, 1981.

(Editor) *Mental Health: The Public Health Challenge,* American Public Health Association, 1975.

(With Marcella Brenner) *Interview Art and Skill,* Irvington, 1980.

Acts of Will: The Life and Work of Otto Rank, Free Press, 1985.

Contributor to periodicals and professional journals, including *New Republic, New York Times Magazine,* and *Washington Post.*

WORK IN PROGRESS: Translating from Esperanto a novel by J. H. Rosbach; *Seven Deadly Sins of Marriage.*

SIDELIGHTS: "I grew up surrounded by books. My father, a doctor, collected anything related to the history of medicine, in addition to a wide range of general science and literary classics. Early favorites of mine were Grimm, Dr. Doolittle, Mary Poppins, Captain Hornblower and other adventure, and sports books by Howard Pease. As a teenager I snuck into Dad's set of Havelock Ellis for some sex education.

"This was before television. On Saturdays I'd go to the movie theater for cartoons, news, adventure serials, and World War II dramas. Dad had volunteered for the Army, and we moved a lot—five different elementary schools for me. So I wrote a lot of letters, and learned to manage as an outsider in school and neighborhood settings. Cello lessons and learning to play chess helped give me a focus. I didn't like to practice cello, but enjoyed orchestra and chamber music playing.

"I took a correspondence course in creative writing when I was about eighteen; never finished it, but learned some things. In college, at Berkeley, I was concerned with getting good grades in pre-med classes but also wanted a good general education. Thanks to two great professors in the English department, Sears Jayne and Mark Schorer, the flame of interest in literature lit up in me, and has never died down since. I took a mini-course in Chinese literature from Peter Boodberg, who told us to read *Ivanhoe* before venturing too far afield: it's important to know your own roots before going exotic. He was right—I finally read Scott's marvelous novel in 1970, when I was thirty-six!

"By then through medical school, psychiatric, and public health specialization, and a seven-year stint at the National Institute of Mental Health in Washington (my adopted home), I had developed a strong interest in prevention of disease and health promotion. Having trained in child psychiatry too, I was convinced that parenting was so demanding that the best thing to do for the next generation was to see to it that people were really prepared for child rearing before they became parents. Parent education, sex education, and family planning seemed the logical way to go; in those days they were quite controversial. Ellen Peck, a writer and former junior high school teacher, suggested we collaborate on a book, and *Sex and Birth Control* appeared in 1973, a revision in 1981 (paperback editions in each case, and a Spanish translation of the original, also). For several years she and I wrote a teen advice column syndicated in about forty papers.

"About 1976 a study group was started in Washington consisting of psychotherapists (social workers, psychologists, psychiatrists) interested in the writings of one of Freud's most brilliant but little-known disciples, Otto Rank (1884-1939). I liked what I read, though it was slow going. There was a short biography (by Jessie Taft, 1958) which aroused more interest, and I decided to write a fuller one, since more information had come out, and the centenary of his birth was around the corner. I had to resurrect my rusty German from college days, learn to use a word processor, get up my nerve to contact Rank's daughter, his widow, and the few former students and patients who were still living. I found about twenty-five, all past seventy; even Anna Freud answered a few questions by mail shortly before her death. I learned a tremendous amount doing this book, was relieved to have it over, and am glad to be playing a part in restoring an unsung pioneer of modern psychology to his rightful place in history.

"When I was about twenty, traveling to Europe for the first time, I found out that Esperanto, the international language, was still alive, growing, and working. A third of a century later, having learned to read, write, and even speak it fairly well with relatively little practice (compared with the time I spent on Latin and German), I am translating a novel by a Norwegian author from the original Esperanto into Engish. Why would anyone write a book in Esperanto? It's the best way to reach a small but special audience of internationally-minded readers: The novel, about teenagers growing up in pre-World War II Norway, gripped me when I read it ten years ago while visiting that country. Unfortunately I haven't met the author, Johan Hammond Rosbach, but he knows English well and we exchange comments by mail. This is a labor of love in every sense; Esperanto has taught me a great deal about language in general, including my native tongue. If the translation is published it will help show skeptics that Esperanto is a complete language fully capable of transmitting literature of real consequence. I wrote a small syllabus on sex education for a course I gave in Esperanto in Belgium, and I've lectured at World Esperanto Congresses in Iceland and China."

HOBBIES AND OTHER INTERESTS: Cello playing, Esperanto, swimming.

FOR MORE INFORMATION SEE:

Library Journal, March 1, 1985.
New York Times Book Review, March 24, 1985.
Psychology Today, April, 1985.
New Republic, May 20, 1985.
Globe & Mail (Toronto), June 24, 1985.
Times Literary Supplement, January 3, 1986.

LOZANSKY, Edward D. 1941-

PERSONAL: Born February 10, 1941, in Kiev, U.S.S.R.; came to the United States, 1977; became U.S. citizen, 1982; son of Dmitry R. (a clerk) and Dina (a homemaker; maiden name, Chizhik) Lozinsky; married Tatiana Yershova (a chemist), February 27, 1971; children: Tania. *Education:*

Moscow Institute of Physical Engineering, M.S., 1966; Moscow Institute of Atomic Energy, Ph.D., 1969. *Politics:* Republican. *Religion:* Jewish. *Home and office:* 3001 Veazey Terrace Ave., Washington, D.C. 20008.

CAREER: Moscow Institute of Atomic Energy, Moscow, U.S.S.R., senior scientist, 1970-76; University of Rochester, Rochester, N.Y., professor of physics, 1977-80; American University, Washington, D.C., professor of mathematics, 1980-83; Long Island University, Brooklyn, N.Y., professor of mathematics and physics, 1984-88; International Educational Network, Washington, D.C., president, 1988—. Executive director of Andrei Sakharov Institute Independent University, 1980—.

WRITINGS:

Mathematics, University Press, 1976.
Theory of the Spark, Atomizdat, 1976.
Andrei Sakharov and Peace, Avon, 1985.
For Tatiana: When Love Triumphed over the Kremlin, Holt, 1986.
Introduction to Mathematics Competition, NCEE, 1988.
(With Cecil Reutheau) *Winning Solutions,* Springer, 1990.

Contributor of articles to newspapers and magazines, including *Kontinent* (Russian magazine).

WORK IN PROGRESS: Five-volume mathematics textbook.

SIDELIGHTS: "My major professional interest is the improvement of the quality of American education in the areas of mathematics and science, and the establishment of a full-scale American university in the Soviet Union.

"My major public interest is to work for the promotion of democratic changes in the U.S.S.R."

HOBBIES AND OTHER INTERESTS: Skiing, music.

MacLACHLAN, Patricia 1938-

PERSONAL: Born March 3, 1938, in Cheyenne, Wyo.; daughter of Philo (a teacher) and Madonna (a teacher; maiden name, Moss) Pritzkau; married Robert MacLachlan (a clinical psychologist), April 14, 1962; children: John, Jamie, Emily. *Education:* University of Connecticut, B.A., 1962. *Home:* Williamsburg, Mass.

CAREER: Bennett Junior High School, Manchester, Conn., English teacher, 1963-79; author of children's books; Smith College, Northampton, Mass., visiting lecturer, 1986—. Lecturer; teacher of creative writing workshops for both adults and children. Board member, Children's Aid Family Service Agency, 1970-1980.

AWARDS, HONORS: Golden Kite Award for Fiction from the Society of Children's Book Writers, 1980, for *Arthur, for the Very First Time;* Notable Children's Trade Book in the Field of Social Studies from the National Council for Social Studies and the Children's Book Council, 1980, for *Through Grandpa's Eyes,* 1982, for *Mama One, Mama Two,* and 1985, for *Sarah, Plain and Tall; Boston Globe-Horn Book* Award

Honor Book for Fiction, 1984, for *Unclaimed Treasures;* Golden Kite Award for Fiction, one of *School Library Journal*'s Best Books of the Year, and one of *New York Times* Notable Children's Books of the Year, all 1985, Newbery Medal from the American Library Association, Scott O'Dell Historical Fiction Award from the Scott O'Dell Foundation, Christopher Award, Jefferson Cup Award from the Virginia Library Association, and one of Child Study Association of America's Children's Books of the Year, all 1986, Garden State Children's Book Award for Younger Fiction from the New Jersey Library Association, and International Board on Books for Young People Honor List, both 1988, all for *Sarah, Plain and Tall;* Parents' Choice Award from the Parents' Choice Foundation, 1988, for *The Facts and Fictions of Minna Pratt.*

WRITINGS:

The Sick Day (illustrated by William Pene Du Bois), Pantheon, 1979.
Through Grandpa's Eyes ("Reading Rainbow" selection; illustrated by Deborah Ray), Harper, 1980.
Moon, Stars, Frogs, and Friends (illustrated by Tomie de Paola), Pantheon, 1980.
Arthur, for the Very First Time (ALA Notable Book; Junior Literary Guild selection; illustrated by Lloyd Bloom), Harper, 1980.
Cassie Binegar (Junior Literary Guild selection), Harper, 1982.
Mama One, Mama Two (illustrated by Ruth Lercher Bornstein), Harper, 1982.

PATRICIA MacLACHLAN

"It's morning," she called through the door. "It's time for divided grapefruit with a cherry in the middle." (Illustration by Maria Pia Marrella from *Seven Kisses in a Row* by Patricia MacLachlan.)

Tomorrow's Wizard (illustrated by Kathy Jacobi), Harper, 1982.
Seven Kisses in a Row (Junior Literary Guild selection; illustrated by Maria Pia Marrella), Harper, 1983.
Unclaimed Treasures (ALA Notable Book), Harper, 1984.
Sarah, Plain and Tall (ALA Notable Book; *Horn Book* honor list; Junior Literary Guild selection; illustrated by Marcia Sewall), Harper, 1985, large print edition, ABC-CLIO, 1988.
The Facts and Fictions of Minna Pratt (ALA Notable Book), Harper, 1988.
Three Names (illustrated by Alexander Pertzoff), Harper, in press.

ADAPTATIONS:

"Arthur, for the Very First Time" (filmstrip with cassette), Pied Piper, 1984.
"Sarah, Plain and Tall" (filmstrip and cassette), Random House, 1986, (cassette), Caedmon, 1986.
"Mama One, Mama Two," "Through Grandpa's Eyes," and "The Sick Day," (cassette), Caedmon, 1987.

WORK IN PROGRESS: A novel about a boy living in a special place with a brook and a waterfall, and a picture book in the same setting. "After twenty-four years of living in one home, I'm about to move to a house with a brook and a waterfall on the property. So images of place are very much with me these days, and my characters and their stories are grounded there.

"I am also finishing the screenplay for *Sarah, Plain and Tall*—a whole new craft which took the better part of a year to accomplish. Because we have a two-hour television slot, I had to add and develop characters, which meant substantially rewriting the story. I told the producers from the outset that I'd never written for movies, but they wanted me to do the script. When I turned in the first draft they responded much as my editors do. They asked questions which opened up new vistas and allowed me to proceed with a sense of adventure rather than with the feeling that I was being scolded for not having 'gotten it right.' I've come to realize how much actors shape the material they're given. Glenn Close, who did the cassette of the book for Caedmon, is playing Sarah. Glenn is quite literary, and I'm gratified that the film is not being 'Hollywoodized.' The quiet tone of the book, which is derived from the sparseness of the land, carries over into the film.

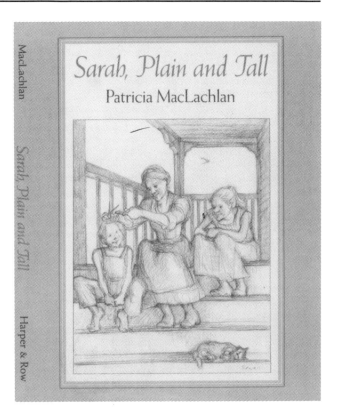

At dusk Sarah cut Caleb's hair on the front steps. (Illustration by Marcia Sewall from *Sarah, Plain and Tall* by Patricia MacLachlan.)

"I look forward to the production—a 'sentimental journey' into my family history. I am also aware of and welcome the changes that come with film. The book was mine, but for it to be a good film, I must give it away, so to speak, so that the director, actors, and crew can do their job."[1]

SIDELIGHTS: "Born in Wyoming and raised in Minnesota, the western landscape has always been a powerful force in my life, fueling my mind and imagination and giving me a sense of belonging to a particular place. As an only child, I spent a lot of time with my parents. My father at age nineteen began teaching in a one-room schoolhouse on the prairie. He was often amused in later years when he read about some 'progressive' teaching method. Usually it was something he'd been doing for decades out in what some people call the 'hinterlands.' There was no such thing as an 'unsuitable' or a 'banned' book in our household. My parents were very liberal and very literate. I measured my life in terms of when I read a particular book. *Little Women* marked a very specific period of my growing up. The same with *Charlotte's Web* and scores of other classics.

"Music, too, was a big part of our lives. I studied piano from a young age and then played the cello. I also spent a great deal of time eavesdropping on my parents conversations with their friends. Much of what I overheard has found its way into my books."[1]

"The only story I remember writing in school was part of a school assignment. 'Write a story for tomorrow,' said my teacher. 'It must have a beginning, a middle, and an end, and it must be about your pets.' I wrote a story on a three by five card. I still have it: 'My cats have names and seem happy. Often they play. The end.' My teacher was not impressed. I

Moira pushed her feet down into the mud of the pond bottom. (Illustration by Lloyd Bloom from *Arthur, for the Very First Time* by Patricia MacLachlan.)

was discouraged, and I wrote in my diary: 'I shall try not to be a writer.' I was very fond of *shall* at age eight. I find the word *try* interesting. It did not occur to me then that everything in my diary was fiction, carefully orchestrated and embroidered tales of an exciting life—an unreal life. Or was it? The question of what was real and what was not fascinated me, and I spent lots of time asking people, becoming a general annoyance.

"I surrounded myself with invented characters: kings and queens, brave men and cowards lived in my closet. I slipped into their skins, practicing, rehearsing to be the person I wished to be, the person I could be, the person I am. I invented an imaginary friend named Mary who was real enough for me to insist that my parents set a place for her at the table. Mary was a free spirit. She talked me into drawing a snail on the living room wall, larger and larger, so that the room had to be repainted. She invited me to run away on a hot summer day to find a white horse. She lured me to the lake, unsupervised, to feed the ducks. My parents tolerated Mary with good humor, though I'm sure it was trying. Mary was ever present. 'Don't sit there,' I'd cry with alarm. 'Mary's there!' One of my early memories is of my father, negotiating with Mary for the couch after dinner. Then I went one step further. I invented Mary's mother, a freewheeling, permissive woman who, in my words, 'wanted Mary to be creative on the

It had thrown a shoe and was lame with a burden of vegetable sacks and a fat squire on its back. (Illustration by Kathy Jacobi from *Tomorrow's Wizard* by Patricia MacLachlan.)

wall.' Years later, when Mary and her mother were only at the edges of my memory, I had a fantasy that my mother had Mary's mother done away with."[2]

"What I really became was an educator, following in my father's footsteps. While my children were small I was very involved in the Children's Aid Family Service Agency, doing publicity and interviewing foster mothers. And as my parents had done with me, I spent a lot of time reading with my kids. When they became more independent, I felt a need to do something else-go to graduate school or go back to teaching, perhaps. It dawned on me that what I really wanted to do was to write. How would I ever have the courage, I wondered. It was very scary to find myself in the role of student again, trying to learn something entirely new. I gave myself a few years to publish with a promise that if I didn't get there within that time, I'd devote myself to another kind of work. But in the space of a year I had a couple of books accepted and an agent took me on.

"Living in the western Berkshires among other writers was a great help. I found a writing class taught by Jane Yolen. Her honest opinions of my work were invaluable. She suggested I send my manuscripts to publishers on her recommendation and introduced me to an agent. Writers need advocates, someone to help them along. Jane's help changed my life, and I try to do the same for my students.

"My books derive chiefly from my family life, both as a child with my own parents as well as with my husband and kids. *The Sick Day*, my first book, could happen in almost any family. *Mama One, Mama Two* comes from my experiences with foster mothers and the children they cared for."[1]

"One of the characters [in *Arthur, for the Very First Time*] . . . is Aunt Mag, who was a mail-order bride. I had a distant relative who was a mail-order bride. I can remember my mother telling me that fact when I was a very small child. What I didn't remember was how she brought a prism with her that sent colors everywhere in the house when the sun touched it. That appeared in the story, though.

"'I can't believe you remembered!' my mother exclaimed when she first read the story. 'You were so young!' I was amazed. I hadn't remembered. I thought I had created that part of the story. Then I realized that this is the magic. When you write you reach back somewhere in your mind or your heart and pull out things that you never even knew were there. This part of writing, my sons would agree, is like fishing for bait and catching a rainbow trout instead.

"When I first wrote *Arthur, for the Very First Time*, it had many more characters. One of the hardest things I had to do was to put some of these characters aside. My children, who had read this first version, were upset. 'You're killing them off!' one of my sons said. 'I like them.' I assured them I could not kill them off. They are waiting until I find the right story for them.

"I didn't begin writing stories as a child, as many writers did. Probably it was because I was afraid of putting my own feelings and thoughts on a page for everyone to read. This still is a scary part of writing. What I did do, was to have all sorts of conversations with myself and with characters that I made up. I still do this. I talk with characters in the car, over a sink full of dishes, in the garden. And when I get to know them well enough, I begin writing about them."[3]

"Wait!" I cry. I am still on one, two when Grandpa is on three, four. (Illustration by Deborah Ray from *Through Grandpa's Eyes* by Patricia MacLachlan.)

"Sometimes I find that characters come to me in the 'wrong' book. For example, the characters I removed from *Arthur* really belonged in *Cassie Binegar* and *Seven Kisses in a Row*. This isn't as strange as it might seem at first. There are subtle and sometimes not so subtle interrelationships in the stories. All my books are about families and relationships. My characters feel like brothers, sisters, aunts, and uncles. With each book, I extend my family a little further.

"I start my books with a character. Plot was always my downfall until I learned that basically character and plot amount to the same thing. One grows from the other. As I get to know my characters they let me know what they need. This means that I do a lot of 'head work' before I set a single word on paper. It isn't that I'm plotting things out beforehand, but that I need a fairly long period to live with my characters. It's a fluid, organic, and even a little mysterious process. By the time I sit down to write I have a general idea of what the book is about, but much like the reader, I learn the details as I go along. I never work from an outline, and often I don't know how the story will end.

"I'm asked if I have 'favorite characters.' I don't think so, although I'm awfully fond of my older characters, which may be unusual for a writer of books for young people. Perhaps Pepper from *Unclaimed Treasures* is a favorite. Older people have achieved an admirable tranquility and tend to be more tolerant and open than the rest of us. They also seem more willing to explore beyond their own thinking, which is why the kids in my books will often have 'soulmates' who are in their sixties, seventies, and eighties.

"When I talked to students about writing, I stressed the importance of working every day. It helps hone your craft. But as I get older, I follow this advice less and less. My writing rhythm has 'peaks and valleys.' Sometimes we aren't meant to write and have to let our minds roam, instead. I find that much of my work comes to me when I'm 'not looking.' But I can always tell when I'm getting ready to write. I start rereading books I love—often something by Natalie Babbitt or William Steig who put words together in such intriguing ways.

"Reading is absolutely crucial for a writer. Like children, we all learn by imitation. Not that writers copy each other; in fact, we try to be 'original.' But books provide us with models, possibilities, inspiration, and courage. Reading is not a passive activity. Each time we read a book, we go on a journey. And as with all journeys, books change us and bring us back to our deeper selves.

"I also derive a lot of sustenance in the company of other writers. I have been part of the same writers group for over ten years, which includes Jane Yolen, Ann Turner, and Shulamith Oppenheim. We meet once a week to read our work in progress to each other. It's a very honest, keenly critical and supportive group. As writers we differ quite a bit. Jane is probably one of the most prolific writers in the country (I write little compared to her). Some in the group tend to do a whole draft before they begin revisions. I can't move on until Chapter One is tight and well-written. I do countless drafts of the opening pages. Funny things have happened. One day Jane telephoned to read me a passage about a dragon laying eggs. After she finished I said, 'I didn't realize that dragons laid eggs, I thought they had live young.' Jane was bowled over by my response. 'Patty, dragons are mythic creatures!' Well, the writing was so good I never doubted for a second. I was totally taken in by the truth inherent in the beauty of the storytelling."[1]

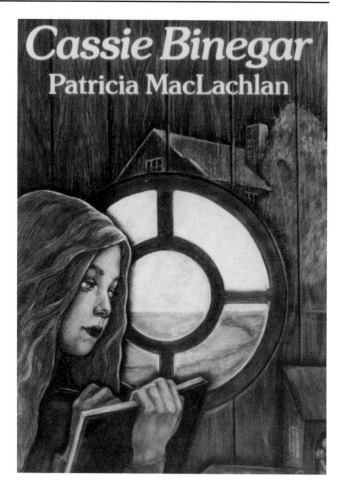

She carried a ... list of complaints and angers, now numbering twenty-two. (Jacket illustration by Arieh Zeldich from *Cassie Binegar* by Patricia MacLachlan.)

As a writer of both novels and picture books, MacLachlan has given thoughtful consideration to the demands of these genres. "It is more difficult to write a picture book than a novel. A good picture book is much like a poem: concise, rich, bare-boned, and multi-leveled. And the rhythm of image and text must create a sort of music. When I want to stretch into greater self-indulgence, I write a novel. When I'm in need of a bracing sort of discipline, I do a picture book. You've got thirty-two pages in which to tell a story, create a form and provide inspiration for an illustrator. Often this means cutting back on descriptive language. I do, however, have a keen visual sense of my characters walking through scenes. I'm very good at letting the illustrator have a free hand. If the text is my province, so to speak, then the pictures must belong to the artist.

"Very often, I'm astonished at what an illustrator has come up with. It is a great pleasure to realize that something I've created and seen in one way is rich enough to spawn a myriad of visions. In the past the illustrator and I have always worked separately. However, for my last picture book—about a North Dakota farm and a one-room schoolhouse on the prairie—I asked a friend of mine who is a wonderful landscape painter to do the illustrations. It's fun but frightening, too, because I don't want to impose my view on him."[1]

MacLachlan is perhaps best known for *Sarah, Plain and Tall*, which won the Newbery Medal, the Christopher Award, the Golden Kite Award for Fiction, the Scott O'Dell Award for Historical Fiction, the Jefferson Cup Award and a place on the Notable Children's Books of the Year lists in the *New York Times, Christian Science Monitor, School Library Journal* and other prestigious newspapers and magazines. "I have to admit, writing was very hard after the attention garnered by *Sarah, Plain and Tall*. Not that it's ever easy. But before I had the comfort—luxury, really—of feeling anonymous. Now I was 'famous.' Now people had all kinds of intimidating expectations of me. It's hard not to fall into that trap of thinking, 'The next book has to be even better.' It's almost impossible to work well and enjoy yourself with that kind of pressure.

"The Newbery has changed my life in some ways that were very welcome, however. Many more people know about my other books, in addition to *Sarah, Plain and Tall*. It's hugely gratifying to know that kids all over read what I write. My earnings certainly increased, and the many invitations I receive put me in touch with my readers in a very personal way. I believe in going around to schools, talking with students, doing writing workshops.

"In my experience, children believe that writers are like movie stars. I am often asked if I arrived in a limousine. I admit that sometimes I'm a little flattered at the exalted idea kids have

PATRICIA MacLACHLAN

The Facts and Fictions of Minna Pratt

There were small frogs, large frogs, some jumping in the water. (Jacket illustration by Ruth Sanderson from *The Facts and Fictions of Minna Pratt* by Patricia MacLachlan.)

about writers. But more importantly, I feel it's crucial that kids who aspire to write understand that I have to rewrite and revise as they do. Ours is such a perfectionistic society—I see too many kids who believe that if they don't get it right the first time, they aren't writers. Whenever I do school appearances, I bring in several drafts to illustrate how at certain stages things don't work and need to be changed. I let them know how awful I feel when the writing isn't going well and when I haven't the slightest idea how to proceed. On a number of levels, writing is about finding your way, discovering where you want to go, what you think, and who you are. I try to show them that they have a wealth of material right at their fingertips. Their mothers, fathers, grandparents, aunts, uncles are all full of stories. 'Themes' and 'messages' come by the wayside. A writer shouldn't worry about 'instructing' or 'enlightening' his readers. If I had that weight on my shoulders, I would probably find it impossible to write.

"I am continually impressed by the sophistication of children. One child observed, 'In *Sarah, Plain and Tall* the characters were never seen going to church even though religion was important at that time. Why is that?' An interesting point, and one I hadn't pondered. It seems to me that with the media onslaught, children are given a lot of information. And even with all the truncated narrative inherent to video and the generally visual thrust of our culture, I think many kids are writing better than ever.

"I find the whole 'boom' in literature for young readers very interesting. Books are not being ignored. More important, children gain access to adulthood through literature, books offering them a way to begin to understand their own lives and where they fit in a world that is not always good to children. For my part I think it's important to have vigorous yet thoughtful literature for kids. Children have many of the same fears and feelings as adults, yet they articulate differently, and therefore, need those problems dealt with in a congenial idiom. A book about divorce, for example, has to be written differently for them.

"The idea that writers of children's books aren't 'good enough' to write for adults is disappointing. As Jane Yolen has pointed out, we don't ask pediatricians if they hope one day to look at adult sore throats. Yet this attitude is reflected in a myriad of ways. The major review media often devote very little space to children's books. This is particularly grating because the revenues from children's books support other, less lucrative, genres. It's misleading to present children's books as a small subset of the publishing industry when in fact they are a very strong part of the foundation. Some of the best painting being done in this country today is for picture books. And similarly, some of our boldest, most original writers—Jane Yolen, William Steig, Robert Cormier, Natalie Babbitt, to cite just a few—write for children and adolescents."[1]

MacLachlan concedes that she considers herself a wife and mother first and a writer second. "It sounds very 'unliberated,' doesn't it? But I grew up in a liberal family where gender roles, however, were not rigid. So I married a man who is very much at ease with cooking and cleaning, where I am not. In fact my husband has been instrumental in my becoming a writer. My decision to become a writer meant that we became a single-salary family with some lean years while I was learning my craft. More than once I said to my husband, 'Look, I think I should go out and get a real job,' but he never agreed. I'm not at all sure I would be at this point in my career if I hadn't had the time and space in which to

Unclaimed Treasures

by Patricia MacLachlan

"Hi," he called. His hair was fair and hadn't been brushed. (Jacket illustration by Ruth Sanderson from *Unclaimed Treasures* by Patricia MacLachlan.)

develop. I also feel like a wife and mother first because my literature grows out of my family life.

"When I'm not writing I love to read. Both my husband and I read voraciously. There are books in every nook and cranny of our house, and whenever we go anywhere, we pack the car full of books. I also love to travel, particularly through the west and the plains. I need to see and touch the prairie every so often. My husband and I also play chamber music with friends who live nearby. He plays the viola, I the cello. And living in western Massachusetts where there are so many colleges, we don't lack for concerts, lectures, films, and theatre. It's important to have things to do besides writing."[1]

FOOTNOTE SOURCES

[1]Based on an interview by Marguerite Feitlowitz for *Something about the Author.*
[2]Patricia MacLachlan, "Facts and Fiction," *Horn Book,* January/February, 1986.
[3]"*Arthur, for the Very First Time,*" *Junior Literary Guild,* September, 1980.

FOR MORE INFORMATION SEE:

School Library Journal, March, 1986 (p. 84).
Publishers Weekly, April 25, 1986 (p. 36).
New York Times Book Review, June 29, 1986 (p. 31), January 8, 1989.

Horn Book, July/August, 1986 (p. 407ff), November/December, 1989 (p. 736ff).
Children's Literature Review, Volume 14, Gale, 1988.

McCULLOUGH, David (Gaub) 1933-

PERSONAL: Born July 7, 1933, in Pittsburgh, Pa.; son of Christian Hax (a businessman) and Ruth (a housewife; maiden name, Rankin) McCullough; married Rosalee Barnes (a housewife), December 18, 1954; children: Melissa, David, Jr., William, Geoffrey, Doreen. *Education:* Yale University, B.A., 1955. *Home and office:* Music Street, West Tisbury, Mass. 02575. *Agent:* Janklow & Nesbit Associates, 598 Madison Ave., New York, N.Y. 10022.

CAREER: Writer, 1956—; editor and writer for Time, Inc., New York, N.Y., 1956-61, U. S. Information Agency, Washington, D.C., 1961-64, and American Heritage Publishing Co., New York, N.Y., 1964-70. Host of PBS series "Smithsonian World," 1983-88, "A Man, a Plan, a Canal, Panama" on "Nova," 1987, and "The American Experience," 1988—. Narrator of documentaries including "Huey Long," "The Statue of Liberty," "The Shakers," and "Brooklyn Bridge." *Member:* Society of American Historians.

AWARDS, HONORS: Special Citation for Excellence from the Society of American Historians, and Diamond Jubilee Medal for Excellence from the City of New York, both 1973, and Certificate of Merit from the Municipal Art Society of New York, 1974, all for *The Great Bridge;* National Book Award for History from the American Publishers Association, Francis Parkman Award from the Society of American Historians, Samuel Eliot Morison Award, and Cornelius Ryan Award, all 1978, all for *The Path between the Seas;* New

DAVID McCULLOUGH

"An extraordinary and fascinating picture of the family, home life and background that created the endlessly interesting man and President." —Barbara Tuchman

MORNINGS ON HORSEBACK
◆BY◆
DAVID McCULLOUGH
AUTHOR OF THE PATH BETWEEN THE SEAS
WINNER OF THE NATIONAL BOOK AWARD

THE STORY OF AN EXTRAORDINARY FAMILY, A VANISHED WAY OF LIFE, AND THE UNIQUE CHILD WHO BECAME THEODORE ROOSEVELT

(From *Mornings on Horseback* by David McCullough.)

York Public Library's Literary Lion Award, 1981; Los Angeles *Times* Biography Prize, 1981, and American Book Award for Biography from the American Publishers Association, and selected one of New York Public Library's Books for the Teen Age, both 1982, all for *Mornings on Horseback;* Emmy Award from the National Academy of Television Arts and Sciences, for interview of Anne Morrow Lindburgh aired on "Smithsonian World"; Guggenheim Fellowship, 1987; honorary degrees in the humanities and engineering.

WRITINGS:

(Editor) C. L. Sulzberger, *The American Heritage Picture History of World War II,* American Heritage Press, 1966.
(Editor) *Smithsonian Library,* six volumes, Smithsonian Institution Press and American Heritage Press, 1968-70.
The Johnstown Flood, Simon & Schuster, 1968.
The Great Bridge, Simon & Schuster, 1972, revised edition, Avon, 1982.
The Path between the Seas: The Creation of the Panama Canal, 1870-1914, Simon & Schuster, 1977.
Mornings on Horseback (ALA Notable Book), Simon & Schuster, 1981.
(Author of introduction) David Plowden, *An American Chronicle,* Viking, 1982.

(Author of introduction) Herman J. Viola, *The National Archives of the United States,* Abrams, 1984.
(Author of introduction) Christian Blanchet and Bertrand Dard, *Statue of Liberty: The First Hundred Years,* American Heritage, 1985.
(With Robert A. Caro and others) *Extraordinary Lives,* American Heritage, 1986.
(Author of introduction) Paul Horgan, *A Writer's Eye,* Abrams, 1988.
(Contributor) Michael E. Shapiro and Peter H. Hassrick, *Frederick Remington, the Masterworks,* Abrams, 1988.

Contributor to periodicals, including *Audubon, Architectural Forum, Geo, Smithsonian, New York Times, Life, Psychology Today, New Republic, Country Journal, TV Guide, New York Times Magazine, New York Times Book Review, Parade, New Republic, Book World, Chicago Sun-Times Book Week,* and *Washington Post.* Contributing editor, *American Heritage,* 1979—.

WORK IN PROGRESS: A biography of Harry Truman.

HOBBIES AND OTHER INTERESTS: Painting, travel, photography.

FOR MORE INFORMATION SEE:

Book World, April 7, 1968.
Best Sellers, May 1, 1968, November 1, 1972.
Vineyard Gazette, September 29, 1972.
Saturday Review, September 30, 1972, June 11, 1977.
New York Times Book Review, October 15, 1972, June 19, 1977.
New York Times, May 24, 1977.
Time, June 6, 1977.
Smithsonian, February, 1984.
Cornell Alumni News, January, 1990.

MILOTTE, Alfred G(eorge) 1904-1989

OBITUARY NOTICE—See sketch in *SATA* Volume 11: Born November 24, 1904, in Appleton, Wis.; died April 24, 1989. Film producer, cinematographer, photographer, graphic artist, illustrator, lecturer, and author. Milotte and his wife Elma, who died five days before Alfred, will be remembered for their award-winning nature films and photography. Early in their marriage in the mid-1930s the couple owned and operated a photographic studio in Ketchikan, Alaska. Milotte worked as a commercial artist and lecturer in Alaska and produced war and educational films during the late 1930s and early 1940s before commencing an eleven-year association with Walt Disney. Working with his wife, the acclaimed filmmaker shot footage for Disney from locations in the Alaska wilderness, Florida, Africa, and Australia. The couple won six Academy Awards for documentary and short subject nature films, including "Seal Island," and "Alaskan Eskimo." In addition, Milotte illustrated a number of Disney nature books and wrote several children's books, including *The Story of the Platypus, The Story of a Hippopotamus,* and, with his wife, *The Story of an Alaskan Grizzly Bear.*

FOR MORE INFORMATION SEE:

Contemporary Authors Permanent Series, Volume 1, Gale, 1975.

Who's Who in the West, 16th edition, Marquis, 1978.
The Writers Directory: 1988-1990, St. James Press, 1988.

OBITUARIES

Chicago Tribune, April 27, 1989.
New York Times, April 27, 1989 (p. B-16).
Los Angeles Times, April 28, 1989.
Washington Post, April 28, 1989.

NARAYAN, R(asipuram) K(rishnaswami) 1906-

PERSONAL: Born October 10, 1906, in Madras, India; son of Krishnaswami Iyer (a headmaster in the government education service) and Gnanambal Narayan; married Rajam (died, 1939); children: Hema. *Education:* Maharaja College (now University of Mysore), B.A., 1930. *Home:* 15 Vivekananda Rd., Yadavagiri, Mysore 570002, India. *Agent:* David Higham Associates, 5-8 Lower John St., Golden Square, London W1R 4HA, England. *Office:* c/o Wallace & Sheil Agency, Inc., 177 East 70th St., New York, N.Y. 10021; Anthony Sheil Associates, 2 Morwell St., London WC1B 3AR, England.

CAREER: Writer. Indian Thought Publications, Mysore, India, owner. *Awards, honors:* National Prize of the Indian Literary Academy, 1958; Padma Bhushan (India), 1964, for distinguished service; National Association of Independent Schools Award, 1965; D.Litt. from the University of Leeds, 1967; English-Speaking Union Book Award, 1975, for *My*

R. K. NARAYAN

He posed me constantly against the flowers in the garden, in the company of my pets. (Cover illustration by Christopher Brown from *My Days: A Memoir* by R. K. Narayan.)

Days; The Ramayana was selected one of New York Public Library's Books for the Teen Age, 1980, 1981, and 1982.

WRITINGS:

Swami and Friends: A Novel of Malgudi, Hamish Hamilton, 1935, Fawcett, 1970, published with *The Bachelor of Arts: A Novel,* Michigan State College Press, 1954.
The Bachelor of Arts: A Novel, T. Nelson, 1937.
The Dark Room: A Novel, Macmillan, 1938.
Malgudi Days (short stories), Indian Thought Publications, 1941, Viking, 1982.
Dodu and Other Stories, Indian Thought Publications, 1943.
Cyclone and Other Stories, Indian Thought Publications, 1944.
The English Teacher (novel), Eyre & Spottiswoode, 1945, published as *Grateful to Life and Death,* Michigan State College Press, 1953.
An Astrologer's Day and Other Stories, Eyre & Spottiswoode, 1947.
Mr. Sampath (novel), Eyre & Spottiswoode, 1949, published as *The Printer of Malgudi,* Michigan State College Press, 1957.
The Financial Expert: A Novel, Methuen, 1952, Michigan State College Press, 1953.

Waiting for the Mahatma: A Novel, Michigan State College Press, 1955.

Lawley Road: Thirty-Two Short Stories, Indian Thought Publications, 1956.

The Guide (novel), Viking, 1958.

Next Sunday: Sketches and Essays, Pearl Publications, 1960.

My Dateless Diary (essays), Indian Thought Publications, 1960.

The Man-Eater of Malgudi (novel), Viking, 1961.

Gods, Demons and Others (short stories), Viking, 1965.

The Vendor of Sweets (novel), Viking, 1967 (published in England as *The Sweet-Vendor,* Bodley Head, 1967).

A Horse and Two Goats and Other Stories, Viking, 1970.

(Translator) *The Ramayana: A Shortened Modern Prose Version of the Indian Epic,* Viking, 1972.

My Days: A Memoir, Viking, 1974.

The Reluctant Guru (essays), Hind Pocket Books, 1974.

The Painter of Signs, Viking, 1976.

The Emerald Route, Government of Karnataka, 1977.

(Translator) *The Mahabharata: A Shortened Prose Version of the Indian Epic,* Viking, 1978.

A Tiger for Malgudi, Viking, 1983.

Under the Banyan Tree and Other Stories, Viking, 1985.

Talkative Man, Viking, 1987.

A Writer's Nightmare: Selected Essays 1958-1988, Penguin, 1988.

The World of Nagaraj, Viking, 1990.

(From *Under the Banyan Tree* by R. K. Narayan. Cover illustration by Christopher Brown.)

Also author of *Mysore,* 1944, and of *Malgudi Days II.* Contributor to *Fiction and the Reading Public in India,* edited by C. D. Narashimhaiah, 1967. Also contributor of short stories to *New Yorker.*

ADAPTATIONS:

"The Guide" (play), adapted by Harvey Breit and Patricia Rinehart, produced Off-Broadway in New York City at the Hudson Theatre, March 6, 1968.

SIDELIGHTS: R. K. Narayan is one of India's best-known and highly-respected writers. Born into the Hindu Brahmin caste and educated in English schools, Narayan has always written in English, even though his mother tongue is Tamil. He is steeped in the Indian classics and has done a contemporary version of *The Ramayana.* "'Indian English' is often mentioned with some amount of contempt and patronage, but is a legitimate development and needs no apology. We have fostered the language for over a century and we are entitled to bring it in line with our own habits of thought and idiom."[1] "India will, I think, evolve an English of its own, an English different from the original, like that of Australia or even America. A new language will come, and fiction will be written in the new language."[2]

In Narayan's view, this new English, and the literary works it spawns, will have ancient roots: "Our tradition is more 'Aural,' that means a story-teller is in greater demand than the story-writer. The story-teller who has studied the epics, the Ramayana and the Mahabharata, may take up any of the thousand episodes in them, create a narrative with his individual stamp on it, and hold the attention of an audience, numbering thousands, for hours, while the same man if he sat down to write his stories would hardly make a living out of his work. Being ideal listeners by tradition, our public are not ideal readers."[3]

Graham Greene, who was responsible for the publication of Narayan's first novel, *Swami and Friends,* has always championed Narayan's work. "There are writers—Tolstoy and Henry James to name two—whom we hold in awe, writers—Turgenev and Chekhov—for whom we feel a personal affection, other writers whom we respect—Conrad for example—but who hold us at a long arm's length with their courtly 'foreign grace.' Narayan (whom I don't hesitate to name in such a context) more than any of them wakes in me a spring of gratitude, for he has offered me a second home. Without him I could never have known what it is like to be Indian. Kipling's India is the romantic playground of the Raj . . . . E. M. Forster was funny and tender about his friend the Maharajah of Dewas and severely ironic about the English in India, but India escaped him all the same . . . . No one could find a second home in Kipling's India or Forster's India."[4]

Narayan is indeed a master at describing his life in India as a child, student, struggling writer, and cultural elder. During the school year Narayan lived with his grandmother, as his father, a schoolteacher, had been posted to a remote area. "The house was built around an enormous Indian-style courtyard . . . Its doors were thick teakwood slabs four feet wide and six or seven feet high, covered with studs and ornaments, and flanking the doors were matching smooth pillars crowned with little brass figures of monkeys, elephants, eagles, and pigeons. I would climb up the columns, jump from door to door, raise myself to another tier by the balustrade, and wander from one empty room to another.

Ammani [meaning Madam, by which he referred to his grandmother] could never find me."[5]

"Most afternoons, when I was tired of the sand dump, I moved to the threshold of the door opening on Purasawalkam High Road and watched the traffic, which consisted of cyclists and horse-or bullock-drawn carriages. A caravan of corporation carts passed along, stuffed to the brim with garbage, with the top layer blowing off in the high wind coming from the sea at this hour. The last few carriages forming the rear of the caravan were wagons, tar-painted and sealed, filled with night-soil; the entire column moved westward and was soon lost in the dusty glare of the evening sun, but it left an odorous trail which made me jump up and rush in crying, 'Rubbish carts are passing.' This announcement was directed at Grandmother, who would thereby understand that it was time to begin her evening operations, namely, the watering of over fifty flower beds and pots. (She knew a potter who made special giant-sized pots for her, a size I have never seen anywhere before or since, each one being capable of bearing a tree.) She reared in her garden over twenty hibiscus families, blue, grey, purple, double-row petals, and several kinds of jasmine, each scattering its special fragrance into the night air—numerous exotic flowers in all shapes and sizes. A corner of her garden was reserved for nurturing certain delicate plants which gasped for breath. She acquired geronia, geranium, lavender, and violet, which could flourish only at an altitude of three thousand feet in Bangalore, and stubbornly tried to cultivate them in the salty air of Madras. When the plants wilted she shed tears and cursed the Madras climate. Even after the plants had perished in their boxes, she tended them hopefully for a few days before throwing them over the wall, to be ultimately gathered into the corporation caravan going westward.

"Filling up a bronze water-pot, a bucket, and a watering can by turns, my grandmother transported water from a tap at the back yard impartially to all her plants, and finally through a brass syringe shot into the air a grand column of water which would descend like a gift from the heavens on the whole garden, dampening down the mud and stirring up an earthy smell (which tempted one to taste the mud), the foliage glittering in the sun like finely cut diamonds as water dripped off their edges. The peacock kept pace with us as we moved up and down bearing the water-pots. When a shower of water descended, the peacock fanned out its tail, parading its colors."[6]

Narayan intensely disliked going to school. "Ours was a Lutheran Mission School—mostly for boarders who were Christian converts. The teachers were all converts, and, towards the few non-Christian students like me, they displayed a lot of hatred. Most of the Christian students also detested us. The scripture classes were mostly devoted to attacking and lampooning the Hindu gods, and violent abuses were heaped on idol-worshippers as a prelude to glorifying Jesus. Among the non-Christians in our class I was the only Brahmin boy, and received special attention; the whole class would turn in my direction when the teacher said that Brahmins claiming to be vegetarians ate fish and meat in secret, in a sneaky way, and were responsible for the soaring price of those commodities. In spite of the uneasy time during the lessons, the Biblical stories themselves enchanted me. Especially the Old Testament seemed to me full of fascinating characters—I loved the Rebeccas and Ruths one came across. When one or the other filled her pitcher from the well and poured water into the mouth of Lazarus or someone racked with thirst, I became thirsty too and longed for a draught of that chrystal-clear, icy water. I stood up to be permitted to go out for a drink of water at the back-yard tap. When Jesus said, 'I shall make you fishers of men,' I felt embarrassed lest they should be reminded of fish and Brahmins again. I bowed my head apprehensively at such moments.

"The teacher did not seem to mind how I wrote or what I produced, so long as I remained within the classroom without making myself a nuisance in any way. All that he objected to, in me or anyone, was sticking out one's tongue while writing, which most children are apt to do. He kept a sharp lookout for tongues-out in the classroom, and tapped his desk violently with the cane and shouted, 'Hey, you brats, pull your tongues back,' and all of us obeyed him with a simultaneous clicking of our tongues—one golden chance, not to be missed, for making a little noise in that otherwise gloomy and silent atmosphere.

"My grandmother examined my slate when I returned home, and remarked, 'They don't seem to teach you anything in your school.' Every day she commented thus and then ordered, 'Wash your feet and hands under the tap and come into the kitchen.' When I had accomplished these difficult tasks, she would have coffee and tiffin for me in the kitchen. She would have interrupted her gardening to attend to me, and resuming it, go on until late in the evening. From her gardening, after changing into dry clothes, and chewing betel-nut and leaf, she came straight for me. She would place an easy chair in the garden for herself and a stool beside it for me, fix up a lamp, and attempt to supplement with her coaching the inadequate education I got in the school. She taught me multiplication; I had to recite the tables up to twelve every day and then all the thirty letters of the Tamil alphabet, followed by Avvaiyar's [an ancient Tamil poetess] sayings. She also made me repeat a few Sanskrit sloakas praising Saraswathi, the Goddess of Learning. And she softly rendered a few classical melodies, whose Raga were to be quickly identified by me. If I fumbled she scolded me unreservedly but rewarded me with a coin if I proved diligent. She was methodical, noting in a small diary my daily lessons to be gone through. The schedule was inflexible and she would rise to give me my dinner only after I had completed it. I felt sleepy within a few minutes of starting my lessons; but she met the situation by keeping at hand a bowl of water and dabbing my eyes with cold water to keep me awake—very much like torturers reviving and refreshing their victims in order to continue the third degree. Grandmotherhood was a wrong vocation for her; she ought to have been a school inspectress. She had an absolute passion to teach and mould a young mind.

"In later years, after my uncle was married and had children, as they came of a teachable age she took charge of them one by one. She became more aggressive, too, as at teaching time she always kept beside her long broomsticks of coconut leaf-ribs, and whacked her pupils during the lesson; she made them sit at a measured distance from her, so that they might not be beyond her reach. Her brightest pupil was my cousin Janaki, now a grandmother, who at ten years of age was commended at all family gatherings for her recitations, songs, and prayers, but who had had to learn it all the hard way; she was a conscientious pupil and always picked up a choice of broomsticks along with her books whenever she went up for her lessons (an extension of the non-violence philosophy, by which you not only love your enemy but lend your active cooperation by arming him or her with the right stick.)"[6]

I possess a soul within this forbidding exterior. (Cover illustration by Christopher Brown from *A Tiger for Malgudi* by R. K. Narayan.)

Even after serving as Distinguished Visiting Professor at a number of universities, Narayan remains an academic maverick. "My educational outlook had always differed from those of my elders and well-wishers. And after five or more decades, my views on education remain unchanged, although in several other matters my philosophy of life has undergone modification. If a classification is called for I may be labelled 'anti-educational.' I am not averse to enlightenment, but I feel convinced that the entire organization, system, outlook and aims of education are hopelessly wrong from beginning to end; from primary first year to Ph.D., it is just a continuation of an original mistake. Educational theories have become progressively high-sounding, sophisticated and jargon-ridden (like many other subjects aspiring to the status of a science), but in practice the process of learning remains primitive. In the field of education, the educator and the educatee seemed to be arrayed in opposite camps, each planning how best to overwhelm the other."[1]

Narayan has said that his disinclination toward formal schooling actually enhanced his learning. "After failing in the university entrance examination, I had a lot of time, since I could appear for the next year's examination without attending classes. That left me free for a whole year to read

what I pleased, and ramble where I pleased. Every morning I left for a walk around Kukanahalli Tank, with a book in my pocket. It could be Palgrave's *Golden Treasury*, or Tagore's *Gitanjali*, or Keats in the World Classics. After a walk around the tank, I sat down under a lone tree on a rise of the ground, opened the book, and partially read and partially observed the water birds diving in. Of course cows and goats, ubiquitous in Mysore, grazed around. But everything fitted into the scheme beautifully.

"I felt I was inducted into the secrets of Nature's Glory. So did much of Palgrave, Keats, Shelley, Byron, and Browning. They spoke of an experience that was real and immediate in my surroundings, and stirred in me a deep response. Perhaps I was in an extremely raw state of mind. My failure at the examination, and seeing my classmates marching ahead, induced a mood of pessimism and martyrdom which, in some strange manner, seemed to have deepened my sensibilities."[6]

Narayan finally graduated from the university in 1930. After a taxing and unfruitful round of job interviews arranged through his father, he settled down to his vocation, working on a monstrous typewriter. "It looked like a computer. It had separate keys for capital and lower cases; and its carriage moved with a big boom. All afternoon I sat on the landing and typed a play called *Prince Yazid*, the story of an independent-minded Mughal prince who was tortured and tormented by his father .... The entire staircase rocked and boomed when I was at work, and my father sometimes protested against the noise, whereupon I would have to haul the machine over to the roof of the house and type there .... My father occasionally enquired of me, 'What are you attempting on that road-roller?' (my typewriter). He gently suggested that I should not be wasting my time thus.

"On a certain day in September, selected by my grandmother for its auspiciousness, I bought an exercise book and wrote the first line of a novel; as I sat in a room nibbling my pen and wondering what to write, Malgudi with its little railway station swam into view, all ready-made, with a character called Swaminathan running down the platform peering into the faces of passengers, and grimacing at a bearded face; this seemed to take me on the right track of writing, as day by day pages grew out of it linked to each other. (In the final draft the only change was that the Malgudi Station came at the end of the story.) This was a satisfactory beginning for me, and I regularly wrote a few pages each day."[6]

This routine was briefly interrupted by a teaching job procured for Narayan by his father. Boarding with a young couple in their tiny, two-room home without sanitation and teaching in a militaristic school in the hinterlands was not for Narayan. He soon returned home to face his family's disappointment and concern over his decision to devote himself to writing. "Unwisdom! Unwisdom!" one of father's friends repeatedly admonished him, but the young man had taken his stand. "I did not encourage anyone to comment on my deed or involve myself in any discussion. I sensed that I was respected for it. At least there was an appreciation of the fact that I knew my mind. I went through my day in a businesslike manner, with a serious face. Soon after my morning coffee and bath I took my umbrella and started out for a walk. I needed the umbrella to protect my head from the sun. Sometimes I carried a pen and pad and sat down under the shade of a tree at the foot of Chamundi Hill and wrote. Some days I took out a cycle and rode ten miles along the Karapur Forest Road, sat on a wayside culvert, and wrote or brooded over life and literature, watching some peasant ploughing his field, with a canal flowing glitteringly in the sun .... I returned home at noon in time for lunch, read something inconsequential for an hour or two. I took care not to read too much or anything that might influence my writing at the moment.

"Day by day *Swami* was developing. The pure delight of watching a novel grow can never be duplicated by any other experience. I cannot recollect how much I wrote each day, perhaps a few hundred words, or a thousand. Swami, my first character, grew up and kept himself alive and active; the novel was episodic, but that was how it naturally shaped itself; a series of episodes, escapades, and adventures of Swami and his companions. Each day as I sat down to write, I had no notion of what would be coming. All that I could be certain of was the central character. I reread the first draft at night to make out how it was shaping and undertook, until far into the night, corrections, revisions, and tightening up of sentences."[6]

Swami and Friends came out in London in October 1935. After the book had been rejected at several publishers, Graham Greene recommended it to Hamish Hamilton who accepted it immediately. Reviews were generally favorable, but sales were disappointing and Hamilton declined Narayan's second book. Still, *The Bachelor of Arts* found a publisher in Thomas Nelson and appeared in 1937. The next year Macmillan published *The Dark Room: A Novel*. With the mythical town of Malgudi, Narayan had found a rich well of inspiration. The sales from these books could not support the author, but the reviews encouraged him. The first two novels fall into the genre of the *bildungsroman*; the third deals with the marriage between a submissive wife and her strong-willed mate.

Narayan, who by this time had married and was helping to raise a daughter, relied on newspaper and magazine work for the bulk of his income. "I left home at about nine in the morning and went out news-hunting through the bazaar and market-place—all on foot. I hung about law courts, police stations, and the municipal building, and tried to make up at least ten inches of news each day before lunchtime. I returned home at one o'clock, bolted down a lunch, sat down at my typewriter, and typed the news items with appropriate headings. I now had an old Remington portable (the double-barrelled one having been given away for twenty rupees, off-setting the bill for cigarettes and sweets at a shop), which was a present from my younger sister. It took me an hour or more to type the items, and then I signed and sealed the report in the envelope, and rushed it to the Chamarajapuram post office before the postal clearance at 2:20 p.m. If my youngest brother (Laxman, now a famous cartoonist) was available, he would be ready, with one foot on the pedal of his bicycle, to ride off to the post office for a tiny fee of a copper for each trip; but when he wasn't there, I practically sprinted along with my press copy.

"Murders were my stand-by. From Nanjangud or Chamaranjnagar, at the extreme south of Mysore District, the police brought in a steady stream of murder cases. On such occasions, I let myself go. I hung about the mortuary for the post-mortem verdict and the first police report. As long as I used the expression 'alleged' liberally, there was no danger of being hauled up for false reporting or contempt of court. I knew a lot of police officers, plainclothes-men, and informers—apart from presidents and secretaries of various public bodies (including the Pinjarapole, a home for aged or disabled animals) who craved publicity and sought my favour."[6]

The sudden death of Narayan's beloved wife was a turning point in the author's life. He has said that if he and his wife hadn't had a child, he would have thrown himself on her funeral pyre. He was profoundly depressed for several years and believed he would never again be able to write. Only after he was able to commune with his deceased wife through the agency of a spiritualist was he able to resume his normal patterns of activity. Narayan has professed to repeated communications with his wife, out-of-body meditations and telepathic abilities.

Narayan's return to well-being was marked by *The English Teacher* (published in the U.S. as *Grateful to Life and Death*). "More than any other book, [this one] is autobiographical in content, very little part of it being fiction."[6] The English teacher, who lives in Malgudi, loses his wife and comes to grips with her death in the same way as had the author. "That book falls into two parts—one is domestic life and the other half is 'spiritual.' Many readers have gone through the first half with interest and the second with bewilderment and even resentment, perhaps feeling that they have been baited with the domestic picture into tragedy, death, and nebulous, impossible speculations."[6]

Narayan has come to favor the short story over the novel. "At the end of every novel I have vowed never to write another one—a propitious moment to attempt a short story

I have earned this title, I suppose, because I cannot contain myself. (Cover illustration by Christopher Brown from *Talkative Man* by R. K. Narayan.)

or two. I enjoy writing a short story. Unlike the novel, which emerges from relevant, minutely worked-out detail, the short story can be brought into existence through a mere suggestion of detail, the focus being kept on a central idea or climax.

"Speaking for myself, I discover a story when a personality passes through a crisis of spirit or circumstances . . . . Almost invariably the central character faces some kind of crisis and either resolves it or lives with it. But some stories may prove to be nothing more than a special or significant moment in someone's life or a pattern of existence brought to view.

"I can detect Malgudi characters even in New York: for instance, West Twenty-Third Street, where I have lived for months at a time off and on since 1959, possesses every element of Malgudi, with its landmarks and humanity remaining unchanged—the drunk lolling on the steps of the synagogue, the shop sign announcing in blazing letters EVERYTHING IN THIS STORE MUST GO WITHIN A WEEK. FIFTY PER CENT OFF ON ALL ITEMS, the barber, the dentist, the lawyer and the specialist in fishing hooks, tackle and rods, the five-and-ten and the delicatessen—all are there as they were, with an air of unshaken permanence and familiarity. Above all, the Chelsea Hotel, where I revisited after many years and was received with a whoop of joy by the manager, who hugged me and summoned all his staff (or those who were still alive) to meet me, including the old gentleman in a wheelchair, now one hundred and sixteen years old, a permanent resident who must have been in his early nineties when I last stayed in that hotel."[7]

Narayan stresses that he works intuitively. "I, for one, am prepared to assert that all theories of writing are bogus. Every writer develops his own method or lack of method and a story comes into being for some unknown reason and anyhow . . . . If asked, I cannot explain how a story comes to be written. All that I can say is that at one time I found material for my stories in the open air, market-place, and streets of Mysore . . . . The first story I wrote was about a one-armed beggar who stood in the middle of a narrow street in front of a coffeehouse . . . . 'A Breath of Lucifer' was dictated by me into a cassette when I had to spend ten days in bed with eyes bandaged following a cataract operation, and was attended on by a crazy male nurse. 'Annamalai' is almost a documentary of a strange personality who served as a watchman in my bungalow for fifteen years; 'A Horse and Two Goats' was suggested by an American friend's visit to my house one evening in a station wagon, crammed with an enormous clay horse which he had picked up at a wayside village. 'The Shelter' developed out of a whispered conversation between a couple, overheard during a bus journey."[8]

"I like a work of art that has a life of its own independent of its creator. When I write, I write for myself. While writing, I don't think of readers' reactions. A book, a piece of writing, even a paragraph, has an organic life of its own, and people are free to view it in any manner they like. I would like to be free of the responsibility for my fictional characters."[9]

Critics, academics, and interviewers are frequently lampooned in Narayan's work. "'Are you still writing?' I am sometimes questioned. It may be no more than an attempt on the part of a visitor to make polite conversation but, alas, I do not like it. The question seems to be in the category of 'Have you stopped beating your wife?' . . . [The] man who really puts me off is the academician who cannot read a book for the pleasure (if any) or the pain (in which case he is free to throw it out of the window) . . . . A certain English professor

has managed to draw an intricate map of Malgudi with its landmarks laboriously culled out of the pages of all my novels. To see an imaginary place so solidly presented with its streets and rivers and temples, did not appeal to me; it seemed to me rather a petrification or fossilization of light wish-like things floating across one's vision while one is writing.

"Another scholar sought the following clarification: 'In one of your novels you mention that the distance between Trichy and Malgudi is 150 miles but you have placed Malgudi midway between Trichy and Madras while Trichy is only a night's journey from Madras. Also in a certain novel you have put the distance from Malgudi railway station to Albert Mission as three miles while in another . . . .' He was offended when I replied, 'If you are obliged to calculate such distances you should employ not an ordinary measuring tape but a special one made of India rubber, since distances in fiction are likely to be according to Einstein's theory.'

"The man who really charmed me was a slightly drunken stranger who was introduced to me as one of my admirers at a friend's house. The man looked me up and down skeptically and said, 'You are the novelist? No you can't be.'

"'Why not?' I asked.

"'All the time I had pictured in my mind the author of my favorite novels such as *The Guide,* etc., so differently. Now you look like this. You must be an impostor.'

"'Absolutely right,' I cried. 'You are the first sane person I have come across. So difficult to convince others that I'm not myself.'"[1]

FOOTNOTE SOURCES

[1]R. K. Narayan, *A Writer's Nightmare,* Penguin, 1988.
[2]Lois Hartley, "In 'Malgudi' with R. K. Narayan," *Literature East and West,* winter, 1965.
[3]Harsharan S. Ahluwalia, "Narayan's Sense of Audience," *Ariel,* January, 1984.
[4]Graham Greene, "Introduction," *The Bachelor of Arts* by R. K. Narayan, Heinemann, 1978.
[5]Ved Mehta, "The Train Had Just Arrived at Malgudi Station," *John Is Easy to Please: Encounters with the Written and the Spoken Word,* Farrar, Straus, 1971.
[6]R. K. Narayan, *My Days,* Penguin, 1989.
[7]R. K. Narayan, "Introduction," *Malgudi Days,* Penguin, 1984.
[8]R. K. Narrayan, "Introduction," *Under the Banyan Tree and Other Stories,* Penguin, 1987.
[9]Stephen R. Graubard, "An Interview with R. K. Narayan," *Daedalus,* fall, 1989.

FOR MORE INFORMATION SEE:

New York Times, March 23, 1958 (p. 5ff), August 1, 1965, June 20, 1976, August 8, 1983, March 14, 1987 (p. 14).
Writers Workshop (Calcutta), March-April, 1961 (p. 21ff), September-October, 1961 (p. 50).
Listener, March 1, 1962.
New Yorker, September 15, 1962 (p. 51ff), October 14, 1967, March 16, 1968, July 5, 1976 (p. 82), August 2, 1982 (p. 84ff).
Encounter, October, 1964.
Harper's, April, 1965.
Books Abroad, summer, 1965 (p. 290ff), spring, 1971, spring, 1976.
Journal of Commonwealth Literature, December, 1966.

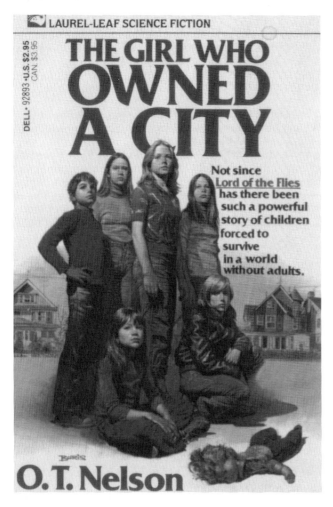

A writer feels gratified when a stranger nods knowingly at the mention of his name. (Cover illustration by Subrata Chowdhury from *A Writer's Nightmare: Selected Essays 1958-1988* by R. K. Narayan.)

New Republic, May 13, 1967, April 28, 1981 (p. 24ff), March 31, 1982 (p. 45ff).

New York Times Book Review, May 14, 1967, June 20, 1976 (p. 6ff), September 4, 1983 (p. 4), July 21, 1985.

Times Literary Supplement, May 18, 1967, October 18, 1985 (p. 1168), October 3, 1986 (p. 1113).

New Statesman, June 2, 1967.

New York Review of Books, June 29, 1967.

Season of Promise: Spring Fiction, University of Missouri, 1967.

Literary Criterion, winter, 1968.

Banasthali Patrika, January 12, 1969, July 13, 1969.

Osmania Journal of English Studies, Volume VII, number 1, 1970.

Christian Science Monitor, February 19, 1970.

Washington Post, April 14, 1970, July 11, 1976 (p. E8), September 4, 1983 (p. 3ff), July 28, 1985 (p. 7ff), April 5, 1987 (p. 7).

London, September, 1970.

William Walsh, *R. K. Narayan: A Critical Appreciation,* Longman, 1971, University of Chicago Press, 1982.

Illustrated Weekly of India, January 23, 1972 (p. 34ff).

Lakshmi Holmstrom, *The Novels of R. K. Narayan,* Writers Workshop (Calcutta), 1973.

Nation, June 28, 1975.

Sewanee Review, winter, 1975.

Newsweek, July 4, 1976.

Book World, July 11, 1976, December 5, 1976.

Contemporary Literary Criticism, Gale, Volume 7, 1977, Volume 28, 1984, Volume 47, 1988.

Washington Post Book World, March 7, 1982 (p. 3ff).

Wall Street Journal, August 22, 1983 (p. 14).

Hilda Pontes, *R. K. Narayan,* Concept Publishers (New Delhi), 1983.

Village Voice, November 5, 1985 (p. 55).

NELSON, O. Terry 1941-

PERSONAL: Born June 30, 1941, in Minneapolis, Minn.; son of Leslie B. (a Boy Scout executive) and Ellen (a homemaker; maiden name, Boraas) Nelson; married Karen Kosek, December 19, 1960 (divorced, 1975); married Judith (a homemaker), January 29, 1983; children: (first marriage) Lisa Ann, Owen Todd. *Education:* Attended University of Iowa, 1961-63. *Politics:* "Libertarian at heart." *Religion:* Christian. *Home and office:* 501 West 53rd St., Minneapolis, Minn. 55419.

CAREER: Painter, contractor. College Craft Ent. Ltd., Wheaton, Ill., founder, 1959—; Room Painters, Inc., Minneapolis, Minn., founder, 1983—.

(Cover illustration by Boris Vallejo from *The Girl Who Owned a City* by O. T. Nelson.)

WRITINGS:

The Girl Who Owned a City, Lerner, 1975.

Also author of handbooks, trade manuals, advertising copy and various unpublished writings.

WORK IN PROGRESS: Revelation at Castle Danger; The Greyhound Cowboys, a journal of father/daughter's five-year adventure; *The Storm Before the Calm,* a fictionalized autobiography.

SIDELIGHTS: "I have a very active mind. I go to bed at night eager to rise early *every* morning for my 'quiet time' of Bible study and writing. I exist more to find meaning in daily life than for money or material things. This has been my conscious motive since I was about fifteen.

"In 1973, as a humanist-libertarian, I wrote *The Girl Who Owned a City* primarily to share with my children Ayn Rand's philosophy about the fullest extent of value and meaning possible to human beings in this world . . . during a lifetime. In 1987, as a Christian-libertarian, I finished the sequel book: *Revelation at Castle Danger* to share my faith about the incalculably greater value and meaning available to Christians in the universe . . . forever.

"In 1988, as our first grandson, Justin, learned to walk, I resolved to be a godly influence in his life. Knowing that anyone who claims to be a Christian must 'walk' as Jesus did (I John 2:6), I suspended most of my writing projects indefinitely, determined to live out my faith more in actions, than just mere words. We both took significant first steps in the spring of that year. I began the long process of re-arranging my priorities, of 're-investing' my hours and dollars and expectations *as if the invincible government* of God was, in fact, *soon coming* (Matthew 4:17, 24:13; Mark 13:33).

"I'm still learning to live like a loyal and faithful subject of the invisible God. Like my childhood hero, Robin Hood, I am clinging to the hope that my rightful King will soon return victoriously. And in the meantime, my work is to trade in the trivial pursuits of this world (the self-promoting, self-reliant, self-indulgent busy-ness) for the Christlike pursuits of eternity (faith, love, joy, patience, peace, goodness, kindness, gentleness, and self-control as in Galatians 5, Matthew 5, Romans 12, etc.).

"I am now disposing of all my personal possessions except what I can carry in my backpack and two suitcases. I try to work and walk and shop and worship in my immediate neighborhood. My purpose in such simplified living is to liberate the first half of each day for kingdom business (Bible study, contemplative prayer, worship, discipleship, and outreach) in order to more authentically serve God during the rest of the day (Matthew 6:33-Luke 10:27). 'The Kingdom of God is not a matter of talk, but of power' (I Corinthians 4:20). 'The only thing that really matters is faith expressing itself through love' (Galatians 5:7).

"The delight of my free time is what I call 'life-style-engineering.' I love to invent or rediscover ways to live a simpler kingdom—efficient life in the midst of the computer age. I've been called a kind of 'backwards pioneer,' replacing high tech luxuries with low to no tech alternatives (walking, not driving; meeting, not phoning; sharing, not buying; reading aloud, not watching television; washing by hand, not machine; daylight, not lamplight, etc.).

"Currently my project is to substantially increase my daily hours of solitude in natural settings. I take prayer and meditation walks in search of nearby solitary places where I can experience more of what God has made than of what man has re-arranged. In such settings I practice being still and close to God for long periods of time (Psalm 46:10).

"The consequence of these past few years of simpler living is the gradual return to a more childlike happiness, a noticeably deeper sense of peace and joy and purpose which had been missing during the four decades I'd been striving to amount to something on my own. 'Freedom's just another word for knowing who you are . . . and living like it.'

"'Amazing grace.'"

FOR MORE INFORMATION SEE:

"Enterprise," *Newsweek,* September 11, 1972.

NICKLAUS, Carol

PERSONAL: Education: Ohio State, B.F.A., 1965.

CAREER: Author and illustrator of children's books. Has worked for *Mademoiselle,* New York, N.Y. *Awards, honors: Hosea Globe and the Fantastical Peg-Legged Chu* and *Taffy Finds a Halloween Witch* were each chosen one of Child Study Association of America's Children's Books of the Year, both 1975, and *So What If It's Raining!,* 1976; Christopher Award, 1978, for *Where's Your Head? Psychology for Teenagers;* Mildred L. Batchelder Award, 1979, for *Konrad.*

WRITINGS:

That's Not Chester (self-illustrated), Platt & Munk, 1975.
Katy Rose Is Mad, Platt & Munk, 1975.
Mabel and the Rainbow, Platt & Munk, 1975.
What's That Noise?, Platt & Munk, 1975.
Harry the Hider (self-illustrated), F. Watts, 1979.
Drawing Pets (self-illustrated), F. Watts, 1980.
Drawing Your Family and Friends (self-illustrated), F. Watts, 1980.
Flying, Gliding, and Whirling: Making Things That Fly, F. Watts, 1981.
Making Dolls (self-illustrated), F. Watts, 1981.
The Picture Life of Cyndi Lauper, F. Watts, 1985.

ALL WITH HARRIET MARGOLIN

Moving Day, Golden Press, 1987.
Shopping Day, Golden Press, 1987.
Swimming Day, Golden Press, 1987.
Tooth Day, Golden Press, 1987.

ILLUSTRATOR

Florence Parry Heide, *Look! Look! A Story Book,* McCall, 1971.
Vicki Cobb, *Sense of Direction: Up and Down and All Around,* Parents Magazine Press, 1972.
Bronson Potter and Rala Ashworth, *Shadow, the Cigar-Smoking Cat,* Atheneum, 1972.
V. Cobb, *The Long and Short of Measurement,* Parents Magazine Press, 1973.
Barbara Fields and Lorelle Phillips, *Instant Needlepoint Designs,* Grosset, 1973.

"I wonder where he is?" (From *Harry the Hider* by Carol Nicklaus. Illustrated by the author.)

Dale Bick Carlson, *Girls Are Equal, Too: The Women's Movement for Teenagers* (Junior Literary Guild selection), Atheneum, 1973.

Linda Hayward, *Letters, Sounds, and Words: A Phonic Dictionary*, Platt & Munk, 1973.

Can You Find What's Missing? (pop-up book), Random House, 1974.

Peter Goodspeed, *Hugh and Fitzhugh*, Platt & Munk, 1974.

Graydon Beeks, *Hosea Globe and the Fantastical Peg-Legged Chu*, Atheneum, 1975.

Donna Lugg Pape, *Taffy Finds a Halloween Witch*, Garrard, 1975.

Martha Shapp and Charles Shapp, *Let's Find Out about Water*, F. Watts, 1975.

M. Shapp and C. Shapp, *Let's Find Out What's Big and What's Small*, F. Watts, 1975.

E. Richard Churchill, compiler, *The Six-Million-Dollar Cucumber: Riddles and Fun for Children*, F. Watts, 1976.

Patricia Thackray, *Raggedy Ann's Sweet and Dandy, Sugar Candy Scratch and Sniff Book*, Golden Press, 1976.

(With others) Pappy Klima, compiler, *The Almost Anything You Might Ask Almanac*, Platt & Munk, 1976.

Miriam Burt Young, *So What if It's Raining!*, Parents Magazine Press, 1976.

Christine Nostlinger, *Konrad*, translated by Anthea Bell, F. Watts, 1977.

David Strong, *The Magic Book*, Platt & Munk, 1977.

D. B. Carlson, *Where's Your Head? Psychology for Teenagers*, Atheneum, 1977.

Rita Golden Gelman, *Hey Kid!*, F. Watts, 1977.

Jovial Bob Stine, *How to Be Funny: An Extremely Silly Guidebook*, Dutton, 1978.

Mike Thaler, *Madge's Magic Show*, F. Watts, 1978.

P. Thackray, *Big Bird Gets Lost*, Golden Press, 1978.

Isabel Langis Cusack, *Ivan the Great*, Crowell, 1978.

E. R. Churchill and Linda R. Churchill, *The Bionic Banana*, F. Watts, 1979.

Connie Klayer and Joanna Kuhn, *Circus Time!: How to Put On Your Own Show*, Lothrop, 1979.

Floyd Black, *Alphabet Cat*, Gingerbread House, 1979.

Holiday Hullabaloo!, F. Watts, 1979.

Annie Ingle, *Alph and Ralph*, Gingerbread House, 1980.

A. Ingle, *Brenda the Brat*, Gingerbread House, 1980.

Paul Glickman, *Magic Tricks*, F. Watts, 1980.

Joan M. Lexau, reteller, *Jack and the Beanstalk*, Random House, 1980.

J. B. Stine and Jane Stine, *The Sick of Being Sick Book*, Dutton, 1980.

D. B. Carlson, *Boys Have Feelings Too: Growing Up Male for Boys*, Atheneum, 1980.

Michaela Muntean, *If I Lived Alone: Featuring Jim Henson's Sesame Street Muppets*, Western, 1980.

L. Hayward, *A Phonic Dictionary*, Platt & Munk, 1981.

Caroline Arnold, *My Friend from Outer Space*, F. Watts, 1981.

Jonathan Reed, *Do Armadillos Come in Houses?*, Atheneum, 1981.

J. B. Stine, *Don't Stand in the Soup: The World's Funniest Guide to Manners*, Bantam, 1982.

Gina Ingoglia, adapter, *Aurora Presents Don Bluth Productions' The Secret of Nimh: Mrs. Brisby and the Magic Stone*, Golden Press, 1982.

Selma Boyd and Pauline Boyd, *Footprints in the Refrigerator*, F. Watts, 1982.

Jane F. Gerver, *Raggedy Ann and Andy and the Haunted Dollhouse*, Bobbs-Merrill, 1982.

Barbara Williams, *The Horrible, Impossible Bad Witch Child*, Avon, 1982.

Stephanie Spinner, *Raggedy Ann and Andy and How Raggedy Ann Was Born*, Bobbs-Merrill, 1982.

Jeffrey Moss, *People in My Family*, Golden Press, 1983.

Anna H. Dickson, *I Can Dress Myself*, Golden Press, 1983.

Madeline Sunshine, *Puppy Love: Featuring Jim Henson's Sesame Street Muppets*, Golden Press, 1983.

L. Hayward, *The City Worm and the Country Worm: Featuring Henson's Sesame Street Muppets*, Golden Press, 1983.

Winsome Smith, *Elephant in the Kitchen*, Scholastic, 1983.

L. Hayward, *The Simon and Schuster Picture Dictionary of Phonics from A to ZH*, Simon & Schuster, 1984.

L. Hayward, *The Julian Messner Picture Dictionary of Phonics: From A to ZH*, Messner, 1984.

A. H. Dickson, *"Where's My Blankie?": Featuring Jim Henson's Sesame Street Muppets*, Golden Press, 1984.

M. Muntean, *Grover's Book of Cute Little Words*, Golden Press, 1985.

H. Margolin, *Busy Bear's Closet*, Grosset, 1985.

H. Margolin, *Busy Bear's Cupboard*, Grosset, 1985.

H. Margolin, *Busy Bear's Refrigerator*, Grosset, 1985.

H. Margolin, *Busy Bear's Room*, Grosset, 1985.

Harriet Ziefert, *A Dozen Dogs: A Read-and-Count Story*, Random House, 1985.

H. Ziefert, *So Sick!*, Random House, 1985.

L. Hayward, *Sounds and Letters*, Random House, 1986.

Bonnie L. Lukes, *How to Be a Reasonably Thin Teenage Girl (Without Starving, Losing Your Friends, or Running Away from Home)*, Atheneum, 1986.

Felice Haus, *Happy Birthday, Cookie Monster*, Random House, 1986.

H. Ziefert, *Lewis the Fire Fighter*, Random House, 1986.

H. Ziefert, *Good Night, Lewis*, Random House, 1986.

H. Ziefert, *Lewis Said, Lewis Did*, Random House, 1987.

H. Ziefert, *So Hungry!*, Random House, 1987.

Marcella sat up. "Who are you?" she asked. "Are you really talking?"

"We are Raggedy Ann and Andy," said the dolls. "We're awfully glad you found us up in the attic. We haven't had anyone to talk to or play with for such a long time."

"We were getting restless," said Raggedy Ann.

(From *Raggedy Ann and Andy and How Raggedy Ann Was Born* by Stephanie Spinner. Illustrated by Carol Nicklaus.)

H. Margolin, *The Good-Day Bunnies in the Great Spring Cookie Hunt,* Golden Press, 1988.

L. Hayward, *Sail Away! A Phonic Reader with Learning Cards: Blue Ladder Books for Kids through Six Years,* Random House, 1988.

Bobbi Katz, *Tick Tock, Let's Read the Clock: Green Ladder Books for Kids through Six Years,* Random House, 1988.

H. Ziefert, *The Best Castle Ever,* Random House, 1989.

Gail Herman, *The Haunted House: Book and Puzzle Set,* Random House, 1989.

Work has appeared in *Good Housekeeping, Playbill,* and *Bravo.*

ADAPTATIONS:

"Let's Find Out What's Big and What's Small" (filmstrip), Doubleday Multimedia.

SIDELIGHTS: Carol Nicklaus grew up in Columbus, Ohio, where she attended Ohio State and earned a B.F.A. in fine arts in 1965. While still at the university she was a guest editor for *Mademoiselle,* and after graduation she moved to New York and worked for the magazine for three years before leaving to freelance.

FOR MORE INFORMATION SEE:

Dorothy A. Marquardt and Martha E. Ward, *Illustrators of Books for Young People,* Scarecrow, 1975.

PARKS, Van Dyke 1943-

PERSONAL: Born January 3, 1943, in Hattiesburg, Miss.; son of Richard Hill (a doctor) and Mary Joy (a homemaker; maiden name, Alter) Parks; married Durrie Craig (divorced); married Sara Rightor (a homemaker), September 15, 1978; children: Zoenda Joy, Elizabeth Taylor, Richard Hill III. *Education:* Attended Carnegie Mellon. *Politics:* Democrat. *Religion:* Episcopalian. *Home:* P.O. Box 207, Studio City, Calif. 90029.

CAREER: Composer of film music. Warner Brothers' Records, artist, 1966—. Arranger, conductor, and composer for Paramount Pictures; composer for Warner Bros. and Universal Pictures; soundtracks for "National Geographic," and "Wonderworks"; has written lyrics for the Beach Boys and done many recording projects as producer and arranger, including Harper's Bizarre's "Anything Goes," Mojo Men's "Sit Down I Think I Love You," Beach Boys' album "Smile," and Arlo Guthrie's album "Running down the Road." *Member:* Audubon Society, Green Peace, Broadcast Music. *Awards, honors:* Association for Library Service to Children Notable Children's Book, 1986, for *Jump: The Adventures of Brer Rabbit.*

WRITINGS:

(Adapter with Malcolm Jones) Joel Chandler Harris, *Jump: The Adventures of Brer Rabbit* (illustrated by Barry Moser), Harcourt, 1986.

(Adapter) J. C. Harris, *Jump Again! More Adventures of Brer Rabbit* (illustrated by B. Moser), Harcourt, 1987.

WORK IN PROGRESS: Two musicals, "Jump" and "Prince and Pauper"; a third book on Southern folklore, *Tales of Peter Rabbit;* musical on Commodore Perry's opening trade with Japan.

SIDELIGHTS: Best known for his songwriting and production work, especially with Beach Boy Brian Wilson's "Surf's Up" and "Heroes and Villains," Parks began his career as a child actor and eventually became a songwriter for Walt Disney Productions. He drifted from his own work into production, including such mid-1960s groups as Harper's Bizarre and the Mojo Men and then more ambitious tasks, such as the "Smile" album with Beach Boy Brian Wilson in the late 1960s. Throughout the 1970s he has worked on a variety of projects in a variety of positions, from producer to sessions piano work.

"My incursion into children's books came via *Jump* and Harcourt's interest in popular music writers with an interest in authoring children's books. Harcourt had heard my record on Warner Brothers and thought it would make a great reissue. I modified the vernacular—less codified in these editions—at my daughter's request, 'Poppa, read it in English.' With the preeminence of Barry Moser's brilliant illustrations, these books represent great reality to be the genius of these folkloric tales, which have been viewed to 'racially irreproachable.' I agree."

VAN DYKE PARKS

PECK, Robert Newton 1928-

PERSONAL: Born February 17, 1928, in Vermont; son of F. Haven (a farmer) and Lucile Peck; married Dorothy Houston (a librarian and painter), 1958; children: Christopher Haven, Anne Houston. *Education:* Rollins College, A.B., 1953; attended Cornell University. *Religion:* Protestant. *Home:* 500 Sweetwater Club Circle, Longwood, Fla. 32779.

CAREER: Author. Director of Rollins College Writers Conference, 1978—. *Military service:* U.S. Army, Infantry, 1945-47; served with 88th Division in Italy, Germany, and France.

AWARDS, HONORS: Book World's Children's Spring Book Festival Award Honor Book, 1973, *Media & Methods* Award (paperback), and one of American Library Association's Best Books for Young Adults, both 1975, Colorado Children's Book Award from the University of Colorado, 1977, and one of New York Public Library's Books for the Teen Age, 1980 and 1981, all for *A Day No Pigs Would Die; Millie's Boy* was selected one of *New York Times* Outstanding Books, 1973; *Millie's Boy* was selected one of Child Study Association of America's Children's Books of the Year, 1973, *Bee Tree and Other Stuff,* 1975, *Hamilton,* 1976, and *Soup on Ice,* 1987.

Hang for Treason was selected one of New York Public Library's Books for the Teen Age, 1980, 1981, and 1982, and *Clunie,* 1980 and 1982; Mark Twain Award, 1981, for *Soup for President; Justice Lion* was selected a Notable Children's Trade Book in the Field of Social Studies by the National Council for Social Studies and the Children's Book Council, 1982, and *Spanish Hoof,* 1986; Michigan Young Readers Award from the Michigan Council of Teachers, 1984, for *Soup; Spanish Hoof* was exhibited at the Bologna International Children's Book Fair, 1985.

WRITINGS:

A Day No Pigs Would Die (ALA Notable Book), Knopf, 1972, large print edition, ABC-CLIO, 1987.
Millie's Boy, Knopf, 1973.
Soup (illustrated by Charles Gehm), Knopf, 1974.
Fawn, Little, Brown, 1975.
Wild Cat (illustrated by Hal Frenck), Holiday House, 1975.
Bee Tree and Other Stuff (poems; illustrated by Laura Lydecker), Walker, 1975.
Soup and Me (illustrated by Charles Lilly), Knopf, 1975, large print edition, Cornerstone Books, 1990.
Hamilton (illustrated by L. Lydecker), Little, Brown, 1976.
Hang for Treason, Doubleday, 1976.
Rabbits and Redcoats (illustrated by L. Lydecker), Walker, 1976.
King of Kazoo (musical; illustrated by William Bryan Park), Knopf, 1976.
Trig (illustrated by Pamela Johnson), Little, Brown, 1977.
Last Sunday (illustrated by Ben Stahl), Doubleday, 1977.
The King's Iron, Little, Brown, 1977.
Patooie (illustrated by Ted Lewin), Knopf, 1977.
Soup for President (illustrated by T. Lewin), Knopf, 1978.
Eagle Fur, Knopf, 1978.
Trig Sees Red (illustrated by P. Johnson), Little, Brown, 1978.
Basket Case, Doubleday, 1979.
Hub (illustrated by T. Lewin), Knopf, 1979.
Mr. Little (illustrated by B. Stahl), Doubleday, 1979.
Clunie, Knopf, 1979.

ROBERT NEWTON PECK

Soup's Drum (illustrated by Charles Robinson), Knopf, 1980.

Trig Goes Ape (illustrated by P. Johnson), Little, Brown, 1980.

Kirk's Law, Doubleday, 1981.

Justice Lion, Little, Brown, 1981.

Soup on Wheels (illustrated by C. Robinson), Knopf, 1981.

Banjo (illustrated by Andrew Glass), Knopf, 1982.

Trig or Treat (illustrated by P. Johnson), Little, Brown, 1982.

The Seminole Seed, Pineapple Press, 1983.

Soup in the Saddle (illustrated by C. Robinson), Knopf, 1983.

Dukes, Pineapple Press, 1984.

Soup's Goat (illustrated by C. Robinson), Knopf, 1984.

Spanish Hoof, Knopf, 1985.

Jo Silver, Pineapple Press, 1985.

Soup on Ice (illustrated by C. Robinson), Knopf, 1985.

Soup on Fire (illustrated by C. Robinson), Delacorte, 1987.

Soup's Uncle (illustrated by C. Robinson), Delacorte, 1988.

The Horse Hunters, Random House, 1988, large print edition, Thorndike Press, 1989.

Hallapoosa, Walker, 1988.

Arly, Walker, 1989.

Soup's Hoop, Delacorte, 1990.

NONFICTION

Path of Hunters: Animal Struggle in a Meadow (illustrated by Betty Fraser), Knopf, 1973.

Secrets of Successful Fiction, Writer's Digest, 1980.

Fiction Is Folks: How to Create Unforgettable Characters, Writer's Digest, 1983.

My Vermont, Peck Press, 1985.

My Vermont II, Peck Press, 1988.

ADAPTATIONS:

"Soup" (teleplay), ABC-TV, 1978.

"Soup and Me" (Afterschool Special), ABC-TV, February 4, 1978.

"Soup for President" (Afterschool Special), November 18, 1978.

"A Day No Pigs Would Die" (cassette), Listening Library.

SIDELIGHTS: "I am tall, and awkward, and [a] stubborn Vermonter who wears mule-ear boots, a ten-gallon hat and what I like to think of as a country-boy grin.

"My favorite sport is curling; I play piano honky-tonk style; I'm a rotten dancer and I'm allergic to English walnuts. My speaking voice is about as melodic as a train wreck, but I do sing in a barbershop quartet."[1]

"Not surprising, as so many of my books feature a simple song or two which I've composed. I play self-taught ragtime piano, by ear, sometimes by fingers. To get raised as an uproader country boy means you've been treated to a spate of toe-tapping tunes.

All I saw was a big orange blast of powder. (From *Millie's Boy* by Robert Newton Peck.)

"Music enters a child's *soul,* not his mind. It enters through an ear, not an eye. Even today, a sheet of music looks to me about as easy to savvy as a page in the Tokyo phonebook.

"Some of the most spiritual and rewarding moments of my fun-packed life occurred when I sang *lead* in three barbershop quartets. A lead singer has to snarl out the most authoritative part, and he's also usually the best looking. *Names* of barbershop quartets are always fun. We were the Humbugs, the Deep Throats, and the Broadjumpers.

"We were beer, cigars, outrageous macho jokes, and best of all, *buddies.*"[2]

"Socially, I'm about as sophisticated as a turnip."[3]

"I love our USA. I'm the corniest flag-waving patriot ever to skip along the pike. If you can't find scores of things, and folks, to admire in these United States, then perhaps loving is beyond your reach and grasp.

"My three morning rules are these: Up at 6:00, breakfast at 6:15, and at 6:30 . . . back to bed. But come to think about it, my life has been mostly work. I was a mite too busy for hopes, prayers, or dreams. So here's my personal motto.

"Wish not for apples. Grow strong trees."[2]

Robert Newton Peck, son of F. Haven and Lucile Peck, was born in Vermont on **February 17, 1928.** As Peck's father was a farmer who earned his living butchering hogs, Peck's childhood memories of his encounters with nature figure prominently in his writing. "Farmers are the hardest-working people I know. Also the healthiest and happiest. Maybe there's a connection.

"Most of my wisdom (what little I have) was given to me by a mother, a father, an aunt and a grandmother . . . none of whom could read or write."[2]

"I have only to examine the ghosts of my boyhood, again to hear the scoldings and the wisdom, and my heart is moved by memory. My parents were Plain People, quiet farmer folk who led almost silent lives. However, when they spoke, we youngsters listened up proper. Perhaps because Papa and Mama spoke only when their thinking deserved words.

"Growing up on a farm, as I did, a kid doesn't really have to ask a bunch of dumb questions about Right or Wrong. Luckily, it's all there to see, to feel, and to tend.

"Unnecessary chatter was considered frivolity. Still, I asked pesky questions, as kids do; and was told by Mama, Papa, Aunt Carrie, or my grandmother, to open my eyes and look.

"They promised I'd understand.

"Natural Law exists, and *acts,* so powerfully that it makes civil or canon law appear, by comparison, a tad flimsy. 'Obey!' our governments and churches warn, or you'll land in Hell or Sing Sing.

"Nature's Law does not threaten. Instead, it *acts.*

"Furthermore, it acts unencumbered by human whim or will. It merely behaves, without morality. The strong seagull snatches a fish from the beak of a weaker gull. A tall oak will spread her branches upward, her roots below, taking sunlight and water and nourishment from lesser trees.

"Until a tempest topples her.

"My grandmother, when I was a tadpole, led me to a pine. Reaching upward, she pulled a normal clump of five needles in order to place it upon the five fingers of my small hand. Grandmother pointed to the tree, then to me, so I would forever know that we are brothers."[4]

Coming from an uneducated family, Peck was the first to learn to read and write. "Miss Kelly . . . taught first, second, third, fourth, fifth, and sixth in a tumble-down, one-room, dirt-road school in rural Vermont.

"She believed in scholarship, manners, and soap.

"But more, she believed in *me.* In all of us, telling us that in America you don't have to be what you're born . . . . My father . . . [did] . . . hard work, but he was a harder man. Like all hard men, he was kind, quiet, and gentle. I wanted to be like Papa, yet I wasn't sure I'd grow up only to kill hogs.

"'Robert,' said Miss Kelly, 'perhaps you'll surprise us all, and amount to something.'

"It was years later when somebody pointed to a large building and said, 'That's a library.'

"I didn't believe it, because in Miss Kelly's little one-room school, we all knew what a library was. Not a building. It was a *board!* A three-foot-long shelf in the corner, a plank, upon which sat our few precious worn-out books. According to custom, we washed our hands before touching them.

"So there we sat in her school, soldier straight, learning about people like Mark Twain and Calvin Coolidge, and Ty Cobb and Charles Lindbergh and Booker T. Washington.

"We were the sons and daughters of illiterate farmers, millworkers, and lumberjacks. Some of the folks, in town, called us uproaders. And we called *them* downhillers. But I knew they could do what I had me an itch to do.

"They could *read.*

"Sometimes, at home, a learned scholar would stop by, and he was always asked, following supper, to read to our family. There was only one book in our mountain home. It was black and large, yet we never referred to it as our *Bible.* It was known only as The Book.

"Then, after I'd fetched it, the clerk of the local feed store in town (if he happened to be our guest) would read to us. Mama's usual favorite was Isaiah, especially the part about swords into plowshares and spears into pruning hooks.

LAUREL-LEAF HISTORICAL FICTION

A Day No Pigs Would Die

by Robert Newton Peck

DELL·92083-3·U.S. $2.95
CAN. $3.95

I should of been in school that April day. (From *A Day No Pigs Would Die* by Robert Newton Peck.)

"We listened.

"The grown-up people nodded their heads, as if absorbing and agreeing with whatever verses were being read.

"At school . . . Miss Kelly read to us by the hour. She gave us *Tom Sawyer* and *The Wind in the Willows* and *Ivanhoe,* in an effort to lead us from the bondage of ignorance and poverty.

"She earned her thirteen dollars a week.

"I was the youngest of seven children, yet the first to attend any school. Papa and Mama had opposed my going. Yet when I finally introduced Papa to Miss Kelly, initially he said nothing. But he took off his hat.

"'Thank you,' Miss Kelly told my father, 'for giving me Robert. I shall try to be deserving of your trust.'

"'We hope he's got manners,' Papa told her with a straight face. 'And whatever he breaks, we'll pay for.'"[2]

"Every child hikes to a fork in the trail.

"Is it a wee eating fork, made of white plastic, and discarded by a littering picnicker? Oddly enough, no.

"As I see it, the fork is a choice between books or no books. I was lucky [that] Miss Kelly . . . was my . . . teacher.

"The most noble job in the world is being a teacher. A good one has to believe in himself, get kids to believe in him, then to believe in themselves.

"Miss Kelly once told us . . . that teachers are akin to farmers. Because a farmer gets up and goes to his garden; but she then added, she was more fortunate, as her garden came to her."[5]

"She died at age ninety-seven. For me, this was difficult to believe, because when we were her pupils . . . [we] suspected that Miss Kelly was at least 144. I am most thankful that she lived to share in my success as a writer. I've dedicated more than one book to her, and she became almost as proud of me as I will ever be of her."[2]

"As I see it, an author turns his furrow and sows his seed somewhere between a farm and a school. A lot of my characters are teachers—all of whom are strong, fair, and respected.

"Perhaps my books shall, if worthy enough, become [Miss Kelly's] monument."[5]

Peck's first successful story, *A Day No Pigs Would Die,* is a semi-autobiographical tale of his family and his childhood on the farm. "I wrote *A Day No Pigs Would Die* in twenty-one days. I had always wanted to write about my father but needed a way to bring the story-line into focus. I finally realized that 'the pig' was it; it allowed me to bring out his honor and decency and special kind of sophistication. He was so knowledgeable about relationships in the natural order and he accepted life for what it is—understanding its violence and its beauty. If I had to describe what PIGS mean to me I guess I think of it as the Bar Mitzvah of a gentile boy—and it also seems to be a little core of truth about living things."[1]

"You have only to read *A Day No Pigs Would Die* to know that my father's ghost will follow me forever. No, that's

I'll say this for Soup. He almous always had some rope. (Illustration by Charles C. Gehm from *Soup* by Robert Newton Peck.)

wrong. He will lead me. Haven Peck, like an honestly sweating Vermont plow, was worth following. His share still swims like quicksilver and knifes through a mud of trouble.

"My father . . . once told me this: 'It matters not what a man's religion is unless his dog and cat are the better for it.'

"As a writer, I believe that a professional way to show a character in a book is to allow the reader a look at, for example, a farmer tending his stock. It's my guess that a great deal of the success of my first novel, *A Day No Pigs Would Die,* stems from its intimate human-animal contact."[4]

"Basically, I am still a Vermont farmer.

"I can't con readers that bacon is made by duPont out of soybeans. Killing hogs is honest work. My father did it. So did I. One time, at a cocktail party, I watched people ram goose liver into their maws and then announce how opposed they all were to violence. My, how Papa would have darn near smiled."[5]

In **1958,** Peck married a woman equally interested in books. "I wed my favorite librarian. Dorrie (MLS, Columbia University). Who was my best man? Fred Rogers, better known as the famous 'Mister Rogers' on TV. He's a super guy and we disagree about everything. We will always be pals.

"Dorrie and I have two children.

"Christopher Haven Peck . . . and Anne Houston Peck . . . . I hope they both grow up to have a tough gut and a gentle heart. Because I don't want to sire a world of macho men or feminist women, but rather a less strident society of ladies and gentlemen."[5]

1973. Peck's second book, *Path of Hunters: Animal Struggle in a Meadow,* published. "Respect for living creatures led to *Path of Hunters,* which examines the poetic yet brutal life and death struggle for survival among small animals in a meadow."[3]

"I'm sometimes frightened by a feeling that we're raising whole generations of kids who lack . . . awareness . . . . They don't seem sensitive to the life all around them; their eyes don't seem to see what goes on within nature. Most of them seem to think that pork chops are made out of soybeans behind the counter at the supermarket. This feeling, more than any other, led me to *Path of Hunters.* In examining the excitement of the life and death struggles for survival among small animals I hoped that some readers' eyes would be opened to the brutal truths of nature and all of its beauty."[1]

Peck has become known for the realism he employs when describing the often-brutal relationships between animals in the wild. Reviewer Edith C. Howley said of *Path of Hunters,* "Children accustomed to the charm of puppies and kittens and with the general concept of animals as furry, if not cuddly, friends going gently about their quaint business in the calm and peace of the country landscape will be jolted into

Mr. McGinley sat behind the wheel, waiting, as you're supposed to do whenever you "flood it." (Illustration by Ted Lewin from *Soup for President* by Robert Newton Peck.)

another world if they read *Path of Hunters.* Here, in all its savage violence, is the bloodstained tapestry of life and death as the hunter in turn becomes the hunted.

"Birth, hunger and death are the main threads woven inexorably into that pattern called, euphemistically, the balance of nature. The writing is direct and compelling. The visit to the pet shop will never be quite the same again, and the awareness of the harsh reality beneath the quiet of the meadow will not easily be lost."[6]

A critic for the *Christian Science Monitor* said of *A Day No Pigs Would Die:* "In showing just how earthy farm life is and how stoic a farmer and his children must be Mr. Peck spares

us nothing. Vivid animal mating scenes, butcherings, a cruel economy that forces a boy to help slaughter his beloved pig and his father to insist that he does—we get the lot."[7]

In response to the sometimes negative criticism of his realistic descriptions, Peck commented, "As a Vermont redneck author, I get tired of urbane reviewers . . . . We farmers lead a physical life . . . . Yet we performed our work without hatred or vitriol."[7]

Nature figures prominently in much of his work, and his concern for the animal kingdom is as pronounced as his belief in the necessity of working the land with your hands. "*Work* is a solid thing to believe in. Vermonters usually do. Granite folk on granite land. Much like their statues in village squares, they are the granite sentries of liberty, standing free.

"Sure, I remember the guys I played on teams with, and drank beer with, and sang with ... but I don't guess I remember them any more fondly than the men I *worked* alongside. Farmers, lumberjacks, old woodhooks at a paper mill, men I helped slaughter hogs, and fellow soldiers when I was a seventeen-year-old private overseas in the U.S. Army.

"These special people, so many of them unschooled, sit upon an honored throne in my heart.

"In later years, I worked as an advertising executive in New York City, with people whose hands were always clean. Yet sometimes, their mouths, deeds, and souls were so filthy. They frittered away their hours in bars and fancy restaurants, and frittered their money on an analyst's couch. Why? Because they somehow suspected that what they did for a living served no righful purpose. Their work built nothing. Fed no one."[2]

Peck's advice to future writers is this: "Before you try to become a *novelist,* become a *naturalist.*

"Mother God has something to teach us all; and, like so many precious and holy things on our green and blue marble, Her lessons are entirely free. No tuition. No tepid textbooks, like the one you're now holding, written by the hand of some arrogant author who thinks *he* gave himself all of his gifts.

"Make a meadow your classroom. Go at night, because the darkness is Nature's dramatic stage. Most animal life is nocturnal. Watch and learn; and cast aside the limp lessons given to you by fools like me.

"Why study Nature? To create characters who behave, in your pages, as real human beings, and only by the fervent study of stream and forest, and sky, will you discover exactly who you are. An analyst's couch won't point the way. Yet a child's arm, which points upward at a rainbow, will.

"Humankind looked into a starlit sky long before it saw a library reference room or a computer printout. Empty yourself of thought, to be filled by soul. And, as your neck begins to ache from stargazing, if you feel like it, cry."[4]

1979. *Clunie,* story of a retarded girl, published. "I dedicated the book to kids who can never read it, hoping that the kids who can will care."[5]

"It was a difficult book to write because I had to attempt to be not only a female but also a retarded teenage girl. I took several trips to a home for retarded children and observed them, day after day, as they tried to work or play or feed themselves.

"One particular young lady looked at me and smiled a chubby smile. Her shoe was untied. So I approached her very slowly, quietly, and then did a strange thing. Bending down, I untied my own shoe. I let her watch me as I retied it. Then I retied hers.

"That's all it took. She followed me everywhere I went as my shadow. And cried when I, out of necessity, went to the men's room.

"One day I brought a camera and took her picture.

Mayor Swagg fainted into the arms of Miss Beekin. (Illustration by Pamela Johnson from *Trig Sees Red* by Robert Newton Peck.)

"What she liked best was when I played the home's beat-up piano. As I played, she sang. Not in words. Only noises. But whenever I'd stop playing to listen to her, she would stop. Then we would both laugh at each other. It became a game. It was one of the few areas in which this pathetic and wonderful girl manifested any intelligence.

"She talked but made no sense.

"I liked her, even though it would be hard to explain exactly why. It was somehow more than pity. Perhaps we all tend to warm to people who like us. She liked me. It was truly an honor, like when I won the Mark Twain Award. It was a genuine thrill.

"At night, after coming home from visiting her, I would lie awake and pretend that I was a retarded girl who had a very tall friend named Rob who played a piano for me.

"I did one other thing.

"Wearing a pair of heavy ski mittens, I tried to dress myself, eat, and play the piano. Not in front of her. These acts I performed in my own home, when alone. Our maid, who caught me at it, probably thought I was nuts. She was correct. Because, mittens and all, I was actually acting retarded.

"The female part was hardest. I tried wearing a long wig and brushed my false hair. It didn't help much.

"What helped was giving that special child a hug, a song, and a laugh. Merely allowing her simple and female thoughts to touch me as though I were not her special gentleman caller, but rather her sister, who cared. I decided that what I really wanted, and finally discovered, was the little girl inside me who wanted to please another child.

"To conclude, I believe that all humans are, inside, half male and half female. You are a product of a mother and a father, so it makes sense. God's plan.

"If you are a big strapper of a man, and you deeply love a woman, you can perhaps best show your love by being, in quiet and private moments, the *sister* that she always wished she had.

"Therefore, it is not surprising that both male and female characters, and characteristics, lie dormant inside you, waiting to be released upon your pages. This is my philosophy on the matter; and if you disagree, beware.

"I'll hit you with my purse."[4]

Critic Emily C. Farnsworth recommended the book with hopes that " . . . it might raise some consciousness about the sensitivities and needs of retarded teenagers."[6]

The reviewer feels that Peck, however, may be resting on his laurels. "Characterization is really shallow . . . . Clunie's oppressions are almost too bad to be true . . . . The book is much too short for any real character development; thus, the conclusion loses much impact. This simply does not measure [up to] his previous works."[6]

However, reviewer Patricia Lee Gauch said, "Robert Newton Peck has never been more the consummate storyteller than in [*Clunie*]."[6]

1983. *Fiction Is Folks,* a writer's textbook composed for aspiring writers, published. "*Fiction Is Folks* will show you, chapter by chapter, how to flip over a rock and find folks for your fiction. How to recognize a character when you see him, or her, and then how to examine, calibrate, and hone a passel of personalities. After all, life is rife with people. They are your basic raw material.

"This is my second book on writing.

"My first, *Secrets of Successful Fiction,* was also published, in 1980, by *Writer's Digest.* Although that tiny text is chiefly a book on *style,* several of its chapters touch on characters and how they roll up their sleeves and work for you.

"It's true.

"My characters write my books.

"People, not authors, determine a plot. Because authors aren't *in* books. Characters are.

"Humor is the best tool of teaching. Too many textbooks are dull. Result? Teachers who use them can become dull. Since I like and respect teachers, this book's purpose is to help profs, as well as emerging authors, discover the fun of writing.

"Education needs a face *lift.* A grin!

"Readers are people.

"Ergo, what interests people (and editors) most is other people, the ones that live in your pages.

"*Fiction Is Folks* is not only a guide to characterization for an emerging writer. It's also a text for teachers. My purpose is not to bore but rather to excite, to agitate, and to goose. Writing is fun. If you don't agree, then perhaps you're in the wrong business. Writing is work, for sure. You must make it your hobby, your dreams, and your secret love.

"Rapture in it.

"The easiest way for this to happen is when you, the author, fall in love with a character and share him or her with a neighbor. A gift to a reader. Forget the royalties. Because, you see, it isn't your greed that creates your novel.

"I am all my heroes.

"Most times, I get away with it. Yet, on occasion, my editor's eye will pop and his pencil itch, when he detects an obvious Peckian pronouncement. I expect this. When this occurs, an editor is merely performing his job, and well.

"These deletions, which willy-nilly always follow, don't always upset me. I'll fight to keep some of them in the story and even win a round or two.

"Again, I repeat: It's easier for an editor to delete than it is for him to add or to suggest additions for you to make. Therefore, I am not in the least shy about Pecking up my people. I dump more Peck into my characters than water into Jell-O.

"Why do I do this?

"The answer is pig simple. Because I've got so much of *me* to give. Like you, I am abrim with likes, dislikes, talents, cumbersome inabilities, joys, triumphs, and failures . . . so why should I even consider wasting such a storehouse?"[4]

"Compared to the work of so many talented authors, my novels aren't really so doggone great. Yet secretly, I truly believe that I am the best teacher of creative writing in the entire galaxy."[2]

"I didn't start out to write for any particular age group. If my books turn out to be right for teenagers, as well as adults and/ or kids, it just happens that way. I can only write about what I know and I've never been shy about telling people what I know. As a matter of fact, when I told my mother, who is eighty-two, that three of my books were about to be published by a very important publishing house, she thought for a minute, looked up at me and said, 'Son, you always did have a lot to say.'"[1]

Peck spends much of his time lecturing young adults at schools with hopes of having an impact on the teachers as well as the students. "My first hurdle, whenever I lecture (do a gig) at a college or university, is to open up minds. Not the minds of students, because theirs are already open. I try, and often fail, to open the minds of the *faculty.* They resent me, because I represent success in the off-campus world. Colleges persist in evaluating someone by what degree he holds, or what title. At lunch, bank presidents never ask me. On a campus, there are so many *doctors* I feel like I'm watching television's 'General Hospital.'

"Life is fun. It's a hoot and a holler.

Let's play "Indian Love Call." (Illustration by Charles Robinson from *Soup's Drum* by Robert Newton Peck.)

"I doubt I'll go to Heaven, that is, if I have a choice. So many of my closest buddies will probabl[y] go somewhere further south, where there's a red piano, a red poker table, and a red pool table with corner pockets that are eight inches wide. And I'll be there, filling inside straights with bourbon, and making old Hades a Heaven for the ladies."[2]

FOOTNOTE SOURCES

[1]"Reflections: A Profile of Robert Newton Peck," publicity from Random House.
[2]*Something about the Author Autobiography Series,* Volume 1, Gale, 1984.
[3]Anne Commire, editor, *Something about the Author,* Volume 21, Gale, 1980.
[4]Robert Newton Peck, *Fiction Is Folks,* Writer's Digest, 1983.
[5]"From the Inside Out—The Author Speaks," publicity from Knopf.
[6]*Contemporary Literary Criticism,* Volume 17, Gale, 1981.
[7]*Contemporary Authors,* Volumes 81-84, Gale, 1979.

PETERSEN, David 1946-

PERSONAL: Born May 18, 1946, in Oklahoma City, Okla.; son of Archie L. and Frances (Harper) Petersen; married Gwendolyn Odom, February 14, 1965 (divorced, 1978); married Carolyn Sturges (a homemaker), October 30, 1981; children: (first marriage) Christine Anne. *Education:* Chapman College, B.A., 1976; Fort Lewis College, B.A., 1982. *Politics:* Independent. *Religion:* "Deep Ecology."

CAREER: Road Rider, Laguna Beach, Calif., editor, 1976-80; free-lance writer, 1980-83; *Mother Earth News,* Hendersonville, N.C., editor, 1983-90. Part-time English and writing instructor at Fort Lewis College, Durango, Colo. *Military service:* U.S. Marine Corps, achieved rank of captain, 1968-74. *Member:* Outdoor Writers Association of America.

WRITINGS:

Airports, Childrens Press, 1981.
Airplanes, Childrens Press, 1981.
Helicopters, Childrens Press, 1982.
Submarines, Childrens Press, 1983.
Newspapers, Childrens Press, 1984.
Solar Energy at Work, Childrens Press, 1985.
(With Mark Coburn) *Meriwether Lewis and William Clark: Soldiers, Explorers, and Partners in History,* Childrens Press, 1988.
(Editor) *Big Sky, Fair Land: The Environmental Essays of A. B. Guthrie, Jr.,* Northland Publishing, 1988.
Among the Elk: Wilderness Images (photographs by Alan Carey), Northland Publishing, 1988.
Apatosaurus, Childrens Press, 1989.
Tyrannosaurus Rex, Childrens Press, 1989.
Wind, Water and Sand: The Natural Bridges Story, Canyonlands Natural History Association, 1990.
Among the Aspen, Northland Publishing, in press.

Also contributor of hundreds of articles to magazines.

WORK IN PROGRESS: Racks: The Natural Histories of Antlers and the Animals That Wear Them.

SIDELIGHTS: "My primary interests are natural history and environmentalism. I am primarily an outdoor writer. My primary exemplars and mentors have been Edward Abbey and A. B. Guthrie, Jr."

This was man's country onc't. (From *Big Sky, Fair Land: The Environmental Essays of A. B. Guthrie, Jr.,* edited by David Petersen.)

HOBBIES AND OTHER INTERESTS: Whitewater boating, nature observation, bow hunting, fly fishing, camping.

DAVID PETERSEN

PEYTON, Kathleen (Wendy) 1929-
(Kathleen Herald; K. M. Peyton)

PERSONAL: Born August 2, 1929, in Birmingham, England; daughter of William Joseph (an engineer) and Ivy Kathleen Herald; married Michael Peyton (a commercial artist and cartoonist), 1950; children: Hilary, Veronica. *Education:* Attended Kingston School of Art, 1947; Manchester Art School, Art Teacher's Diploma, 1952. *Home:* Rookery Cottage, North Fambridge, Essex, England.

CAREER: Northampton High School, Northampton, England, art teacher, 1952-56; writer, 1956—. *Member:* Society of Authors. *Awards, honors:* Carnegie Medal Commendation from the British Library Association, 1962, for *Windfall,* 1964, for *The Maplin Bird,* 1965, for *The Plan for Birdsmarsh,* 1966, for *Thunder in the Sky,* 1967, for *Flambards,* 1969, for *Flambirds in Summer,* and 1977, for *The Team; New York Herald Tribune* Spring Book Festival Award Honor Book,

"You will breathe, you little bundle! I'll do it for you." (Illustration by Victor G. Ambrus from *The Maplin Bird* by K. M. Peyton.)

1965, for *The Maplin Bird;* Carnegie Medal, 1969, for *The Edge of the Cloud; Boston Globe-Horn Book* Award Honor

KATHLEEN PEYTON

Book for Text, 1969, for *Flambards; Guardian* Award, 1970, for the "Flambards" trilogy; *Fly-by-Night* was selected one of Child Study Association of America's Children's Books of the Year, 1969, *Pennington's Last Term,* 1971, *Pennington's Heir,* 1974, and *The Team,* 1976; *Prove Yourself a Hero* was selected one of the American Library Association's Best Books for Young Adults, 1979; *A Midsummer Night's Death* was selected one of *School Library Journal*'s Best Books for Spring, 1979.

WRITINGS:

JUVENILE; UNDER NAME KATHLEEN HERALD

Sabre, the Horse from the Sea (illustrated by Lionel Edwards), A. & C. Black, 1947, Macmillan, 1963.
The Mandrake (illustrated by L. Edwards), A. & C. Black, 1949.
Crab the Roan (illustrated by Peter Biegel), A. & C. Black, 1953.

JUVENILE; UNDER NAME K. M. PEYTON

North to Adventure, Collins, 1959, Platt & Munk, 1965.
Stormcock Meets Trouble, Collins, 1961.
The Hard Way Home (illustrated by R. A. Branton), Collins, 1962, published as *Sing a Song of Ambush,* Platt & Munk, 1964.
Windfall (illustrated by Victor Ambrus), Oxford University Press, 1962, published as *Sea Fever* (ALA Notable Book), World Publishing, 1963.
Brownsea Silver, Collins, 1964.
The Maplin Bird (*Horn Book* honor list; illustrated by V. Ambrus), Oxford University Press, 1964, World Publishing, 1965.
The Plan for Birdsmarsh (*Horn Book* honor list; illustrated by V. Ambrus), Oxford University Press, 1965, World Publishing, 1966.
Thunder in the Sky (illustrated by V. Ambrus), Oxford University Press, 1966, World Publishing, 1967.
Flambards (trilogy; ALA Notable Book; illustrated by V. Ambrus), Oxford University Press, 1967, World Publishing, 1968.
Fly-by-Night (self-illustrated), Oxford University Press, 1968, World Publishing, 1969.
The Edge of the Cloud (illustrated by V. Ambrus), World Publishing, 1969.
Flambards in Summer (ALA Notable Book; illustrated by V. Ambrus), Oxford University Press, 1969, World Publishing, 1970.
Pennington's Seventeenth Summer (self-illustrated), Oxford University Press, 1970, ABC-CLIO, 1989, published as *Pennington's Last Term* (ALA Notable Book), Crowell, 1971.
The Beethoven Medal (ALA Notable Book; self-illustrated), Oxford University Press, 1971, Crowell, 1972.
A Pattern of Roses (ALA Notable Book; self-illustrated), Oxford University Press, 1972, Crowell, 1973.
Pennington's Heir (ALA Notable Book; *Horn Book* honor list; self-illustrated), Oxford University Press, 1973, Crowell, 1974.
The Team (*Horn Book* honor list; self-illustrated), Oxford University Press, 1975, Crowell, 1976.
The Right-Hand Man (illustrated by V. Ambrus), Oxford University Press, 1977.
Prove Yourself a Hero (*Horn Book* honor list), Oxford University Press, 1977, Collins, 1978.
A Midsummer Night's Death (*Horn Book* honor list), Oxford University Press, 1978, Collins, 1979.

Marion's Angels (illustrated by Robert Micklewright), Oxford University Press, 1979.

Flambards Divided, Oxford University Press, 1981, Philomel, 1982.

Dear Fred, Bodley Head, 1981.

Going Home (illustrated by Chris Molan), Oxford University Press, 1982, U.S. edition (illustrated by Huck Scarry), Philomel, 1982.

Free Rein, Philomel, 1983.

Who, Sir? Me, Sir?, Oxford University Press, 1983, large print edition, ABC-CLIO, 1989.

The Last Ditch, Oxford University Press, 1984.

Froggett's Revenge, Oxford University Press, 1985.

Downhill All the Way, Oxford University Press, 1988.

Plain Jack, Hamish Hamilton, 1988.

Skylark, Oxford University Press, 1989.

Darkling, Delacorte, 1989.

Poor Badger, Doubleday, 1990.

ADULT

The Sound of Distant Cheering, Bodley Head, 1985.

No Roses Round the Door, Methuen, 1990.

(Cover illustration by Robert Barrett from *The Edge of the Cloud* by K. M. Peyton.)

"Fetch me a basin of pease pudding at the shop." (Illustration by Victor G. Ambrus from *Flambards in Summer* by K. M. Peyton.)

ADAPTATIONS:

"Flambards" (television series), ITV (Yorkshire, England), 1976.

"Going Home" (cassette), G. K. Hall, 1986.

WORK IN PROGRESS: An adult novel; two filmscripts.

SIDELIGHTS: K. M. Peyton was born on August 2, 1929 in Birmingham, England, but grew up in the suburbs of London. "When I was small, I was always writing. I think I was nine when I started my first story which was long enough to call a book. It was all written in longhand, of course, and was called, I remember, 'Gray Star, the Story of a Race Horse.' It was in the first person. *I* was the race horse. After that I always had a book going . . . . As soon as I finished one, I started another. Once when I was at school, a teacher asked me to do some illustrations for a book. I said I'd do the illustrations for my own book. She was interested, so she read it. She thought it was good and told me to get it typed. I sent it to a publisher, and it was accepted for publication . . . I was fifteen."[1] The book was *Sabre, the Horse from the Sea.* "I was very horsey, crazy about horses—and the first three books were about ponies and riding."[1]

Peyton did not intend to become a writer. Instead she received her degree from art school at Kingston-on-Thames. "I don't myself even subscribe to the idea that one sets out to be a writer; one writes, and if the work sells and eventually enables one to make a living from it, one presumably is a writer . . . . I set out to be a painter, and became a teacher, which I liked very much; but I was a writer all the time, and eventually this became my profession."[2]

At twenty-one she married fellow art student Michael Peyton. They traveled through Europe and North America on a frugal budget before settling down not far from London, on the Essex coast, where they pursued their interest in sailing which provided early subject matter.

Peyton began writing full time with the birth of her daughter. "I . . . needed the money desperately, so I wrote boys adventure stories; *North to Adventure, The Hard Way Home, Stormcock Meets Trouble;* Michael, my husband, thought up all the plots and I wrote them down. I didn't know what was going on half the time. Then there was *Brownsea Silver,* which was written for the centenary of the Scout movement; that was a commission. The Scouts were founded on Brownsea Island, and that was lovely. We went there before it was open to the public, and it was all very wild . . . . We went there in our boat, and anchored off it, and clambered all over it thinking up this plot.

"The *Scout* magazine published all my early work, and they just said 'How about writing a story that would do for the centenary?' They didn't say what, so I never thought of it as a commission so to speak."[3]

With *Windfall* (published in the United States as *Sea Fever*) Peyton for the first time moved beyond mere adventure. An ALA Notable Book, *Windfall* was the last book Peyton wrote with her husband. "I've sailed all that area . . . . My own experiences definitely went into *Sea Fever.* Everything in the background . . . is . . . authentic, the way these old fishermen lived."[1]

Set in the Thames estuary in the 1870s, *The Maplin Bird* recounts the tribulations of two orphans, Toby and Emily. The book was a *New York Herald Tribune* Children's Spring Book Festival Award Honor Book in 1965. "Everything Emily suffered in the smack 'My Alice' in *The Maplin Bird* I had suffered in my own sailing experience at this time."[4]

The Plan for Birdsmarsh was published in 1965, Paul, who expected to carry on the family farm, was disappointed to see it sold for a marina. "*The Plan for Birdsmarsh* had more or less a ready-made plot, in that the survival-suit idea was real and we had been helping the inventor, a friend of ours, to test it from our own boat. Michael, who did and still does the drawings for the *New Scientist,* had all the information on industrial spies, and the marina plan was being splashed in the local newspaper, so I put it all together, the various themes getting rather out of control at times, I feel."[4]

The following year Peyton published *Thunder in the Sky,* set during World War I. "In *Thunder in the Sky,* the actual plot of the spying I made up, although it was going on all the time during the war. But all the part of the barges going across the Channel and how the war affected them is . . . authentic."[1]

"*Thunder in the Sky* took more work than any of my other books, a great deal of research being required. Where we live is still the home of the remaining sailing barges, and there are quite a lot of the old skippers still around to talk about their experiences. I knew absolutely nothing about the 1914-18 war when I started this book. I think seeing Joan Littlewood's production of 'Oh, What a Lovely War!' probably started me off on this subject; I don't think I have been so moved by anything as by that play. Books that also opened my eyes were Robert Graves's *Goodbye to All That,* Frank Richards's *Old Soldiers Never Die,* and, most of all, Siegfried Sassoon's books. (I think *Memoirs of a Fox-Hunting Man* is my idea of a perfect book.) I knew what the general theme of

Thunder in the Sky was going to be, and had the setpiece of sailing out the burning ammunition barge in my mind in all its detail before I worked out the plot. I like Gil one of the best of all my characters. I remember I wrote all that part in a great frenzy and blew him up on Christmas Eve, and then had to do the sprouts and mince pies and fill the children's stockings, and I was in a complete daze all the time."[4]

In 1967 Peyton published *Flambards,* the first volume in what was to become a trilogy. Flambards is a decaying estate where orphaned Christina experiences the changes in social patterns prior to World War I. *The Edge of the Cloud* and *Flambards in Summer* completed the trilogy. The books have won numerous awards and were dramatized as a British television series. "When I came to *Flambards,* I was tired of writing about sailing and decided to have a complete change. I enjoyed writing this book, and particularly its successor, more than any I have written. I have always loved aeroplanes, and during the Second World War could recognize them all, so I thoroughly enjoyed all the reading-up involved. I did not write *Flambards* with the intention of having a sequel, but the idea developed and I could see two more books eventually."[4]

What was going to happen afterwards he neither knew nor cared. (Jacket illustration by Tony Morris from *Pennington's Seventeenth Summer* by K. M. Peyton.)

"At the end of the first *Flambards* book [Christina] goes off with Will, and I was prepared to leave it there, though as I was writing the book I realized that it could well go on from there. And because I had got so interested in them as I was writing, I wanted to go on, very badly, and the next one then carried on directly. But after that there was a bit of a gap, before I wrote the third one; ... I could see how it would all work out, but it meant killing off Will, which I thought was such a bad thing to do that I couldn't do it. I discussed this with my editor before I started the book; ... she wasn't all that sure that I ought to do it either. She didn't mind about killing Will, she thought that was all right. I thought it was all right statistically, it was correct, because I don't think a single pilot who joined up in 1914 survived until 1918, but I didn't want to do it just for the sake of writing another book."[3]

"I think that getting help from other people is very necessary because you can't know all these points that arise. For example, I needed medical advice in *Flambards* for the problem of Will breaking his leg. I wanted him to be injured in such a way that he would be fairly active for other things but would not actually be able to ride a horse again. It was very difficult to work something out which would just cover this point, but I did manage it with some medical advice. Then I had some more trouble afterwards when I wanted to write a sequel. It was necessary then that William should be able to fly an airplane, which wasn't easy when he had a stiff leg. I had to have medical advice to see how this leg could be fixed again, which at that period apparently was not a very easy thing to do. But I was assured it was all right, that it could be done in Switzerland. This dictated a part of the plot, really, because it meant he had to go to Switzerland."[1]

Published in 1970, *Pennington's Seventeenth Summer* (published in the U.S. as *Pennington's Last Term*) tells about Patrick Pennington, a defiant yet musically gifted teenager. Peyton followed him in two sequels: *The Beethoven Medal* and *Pennington's Heir*. Pennington becomes a promising pianist and falls in love with the heroine of *Fly-by-Night* and *The Team*. "[Pennington] was modeled on a boy—I don't usually do this with characters consciously, but this one was particularly modeled on a boy who used to go on the train ... and he used to come home from school with his friends; they were real louts, they used to play cards and swear and talk about girls .... I thought it was quite fascinating .... This particular boy was an enormous great thug, and he wore a little school cap—of course they don't wear caps any more. The book's dated anyway, because of the hair thing and everything .... That's how the book started, and I must admit I got rather involved, I enjoyed it."

"[Pennington] calms down, gets far more responsible—but whether it's successful as a piece of character drawing, as a picture of growing up, I wouldn't like to say—perhaps not entirely."[3]

"I [didn't] realize that a dabbling in music which started with the children's recorder lessons in the village school would lead me to the complexities of following Pennington in his virtuoso career—and I shall be eternally grateful to that particular hero for driving me to learn to play the piano, which ironically has made more inroads into my 'writing-time' than any of my other commitments."[2]

"I liked the music side of it, listening to records for hours and hours and saying I was working. I didn't know a lot about music when I started, but that was the driving force of the books really. I learned to play the piano! I took it very seriously, and had it vetted by some musical people; they were all very helpful."[3]

An ALA Notable Book, *A Pattern of Roses* was published in 1972. "I got the idea because we actually moved house ourselves; in my mind I see their place in the book as quite different from our place, but there's a little churchyard like that, where we've moved to—they've ruined it a bit, all the elm trees are dying of elm disease and it's all been cleared out by a very keen man new to the village—but before he started messing about with it it was lovely. I got the idea of the two stories running together, and the parallel between the old couple and the modern couple; now this was an ambitious book, and I found it very difficult to write. I think I probably worked harder at this book than at any I've ever written. It was technically very difficult, to have the two stories running, without jarring when you went from one to the other, and what to leave out and what to put in. But I think if you were to ask me which is my best book, I'd say that one. It wasn't so enjoyable to write, though; the others rather rush[ed] along. This one didn't ... —perhaps that's what I ought to do more often."[3]

Asked whether she means to influence her readers, Peyton replied: "When a writer knows he has a juvenile audience, a certain responsibility is inevitably felt, but to think that he can 'con' his audience into what might be called correct attitudes must be doomed to failure. The writer's own attitudes probably show through, but whether these are uplifting or depressing depends on who is the judge. I feel that the only possible limitation in writing in this sphere is the necessity to write within the framework of the reader's understanding, but as this is as wide or as narrow as the writer cares to make it (as wide, for example, as set by Alan Garner in *The Owl Service* or as narrow as the view of Enid Blyton in the 'Famous Five' or 'Secret Seven' series), it is scarcely to be thought of as limiting. I have not yet found this a difficulty, and when I do I suppose the time will have come to write 'a proper book.' Until then I shall continue as I am."[2]

By 1974, following the acclaim some of her books had received, Peyton was not worried about their success. "But you wonder whether you're going to repeat yourself, and how much there is to say and whether you want to say it. But I'm sure this must happen, and in fact I'm amazed it hasn't happened before.

"I think writers are apt to put this sort of thing into books too often—their own predicaments—and when you think about it, most of the readers aren't writers anyway. There's a bit of a preponderance of this sort of thing in modern fiction. I don't think children are particularly interested in the worries of a middle-aged writer, are they?"[3]

"I have no strongly held theories on 'writing for children.' An honest writer writes first and finds the appropriate market, if it exists. His bad luck if it doesn't .... I became a children's writer because I started writing as a child and naturally wrote children's books. Since then I must have suffered some sort of mental retardment, for I still write, as I did then, the sort of stories I like writing best and my audience is still young .... My mother ask[ed] me, 'When are you going to write a proper book?' 'They *are* proper books,' I repl[ied] stiffly."[2]

Peyton doesn't have a conscious grasp of character development before she sits down to write a book. "But I realize myself that the interest to me in writing books is always in the characters of the people. I find that I use the plots to follow my own interest in the people, so to speak, and I find that the

(From *Flambards* by K. M. Peyton. Illustrated by Victor G. Ambrus.)

plots grow from the way the people interact one on the other. I don't sit down and write a book and say this is going to be about the growth of this character. But I've heard this said so often about my writings. It must be something about the way I work, the way I like to make out my plots.

"My characters are never anybody I know very well. I sometimes start off on a character perhaps by using somebody I've met once. Winnington, in *The Plan for Birdsmarsh,* was somebody I met on vacation, and I used him. Of course, I didn't really know him. It was only his appearance, really, and his superficial character that came over to me that I used . . . . I think my female characters always seem to come out the same, which isn't very satisfactory. Emily in *The Maplin Bird* and Christina in *Flambards* are rather the same character, which annoys me a bit. But on the whole, I don't think I base my characters on real people."[1]

"I don't feel [my characters] too young for what happens, but I think there is always a technical problem in children's books. If you want anything to happen, and problems to arise, to make a story, if they have understanding parents the problems are ironed out for them. This is why I—and not only I, but many people—tend either to have them as orphans, which is the easiest thing, as in *The Maplin Bird*—which was all right in Victorian times because that happened so often, but now it's pretty rare—or get rid of their parents abroad, or make them horrible parents like in the *Pennington* books. So that these children really have got problems. But there again, back to William Mayne, he writes beautiful books, and nearly always with very understanding parents. But perhaps I need this, I need to have in my books the sort of problems that parents might be able to solve."[3]

"When I get frustrated by the demands of . . . other commitments deflecting me from the writing, I console myself that they are the lifeblood of what I am writing about, and that the ivory tower, attractive as it may appear at times, would not suit. The male writer, quiet in his room with coffee and lunch served, the interruptions deflected by a devoted wife, is at times my great envy; but at other times I feel that the very frustrations are somehow a part of my driving force.

"I have no help at home, and consider myself fairly fully occupied with the normal ferrying of schoolchildren, housework and look after five horses (since, in desperation, cut down to two)—the horses, like the piano, are time-consumers, but necessary . . . . One of the horses, lent by a farmer from the village three miles away, used to get out of the field and go home, sometimes taking the other four with her, at a flat gallop. When this happened in the middle of the night my husband used to turn over in bed and remind me, as we listened to the departing clatter of hooves down the lane, that the horses were my department; his was the boat. But out of these calamities, nice cameos remain: creeping through someone's back garden with headcollar in hand, dressed in long nightdress, amarak and gum-boots, and being speared by torchlight from the bedroom window, or returning home in the car with my daughter riding the mare ahead in the light from the headlamps, cantering fast along the verge with only a halter for tack, and me thinking, 'Oh, God, if she falls off the mare will go all the way back again.'"[4]

"I think now that if I only had a book to write, and nothing else to do, I would just sit and stare into space. To know that on Tuesday, for instance, Fred will call for coffee and chat at half-past ten, the butcher will interrupt at eleven fifteen and

Midnight . . . was pulling madly for the wood. (Jacket illustration by Joy Barling from *Who, Sir? Me, Sir?* by K. M. Peyton)

want to know what I shall want next Friday, and that I've got to get to the nearest shop, three miles away, to buy a loaf before it shuts at one, concentrates the mind wonderfully. My mother needs to talk to me at length twice a week at least, a pony needs shoeing (five miles there and five miles back and an hour in the middle), and in the summer the garden and the field are a full-time job (mine). It is no good at all pleading my vocation, for my only local claim to fame is not in writing but as secretary of the Pony Club, and when this keeps me almost fully occupied throughout the summer months I console myself by the richness of the material I am building up in this direction. The fact that pony books are now out of fashion, a relic of the nineteen thirties and forties, will not deter me from embarking on this saga before long, so eagerly does the spring bubble up. Where would I be without my interruptions? Still staring at a blank sheet in the typewriter."[2]

"I used to consider 700 words an average day and 1,000 pretty good, but now write more quickly than I did, and do 3,000 on a really good day. I wrote *The Edge of the Cloud* in three months, but took over a year with *Windfall*. I like to do the research for a book, and read books relevant to the period all the time. I enjoy this part of it, even going to Beckton gasworks for *Thunder in the Sky* and the Admiralty's hydrographical centre for the buoyage of the Thames estuary for *The Maplin Bird*. Often research on one book will set me off on the next—for example, researching the tiny bit in *Thunder in the Sky* about the aeroplane that rescued the barge when it was being fired on by the Frenchman set me off on the flying theme in *Flambards*."[4]

"I know fairly well what's going to happen when I start a book. I always know the theme, obviously, and what the whole point of the book is, what the main story line is, where I want to finish. Generally I know that, but sometimes I'm not always clear about how I'm going to develop the middle."[1]

"The fact is, I like writing very much, better than anything else. I write to entertain, but whether I'm entertaining them or myself I've never quite decided. Sometimes I think it is more for them, sometimes for me. This is not to say that I don't find writing hard work; the concentration required in the actual doing is considerable, and the hours of just thinking about it are very long, if perfectly pleasant. I do most of this in bed, on trains and on long sailing holidays, and when gardening, peeling potatoes, cleaning the windows, washing the kitchen floor, etc. Not when driving the car, which I've proved is dangerous. What it is all for, entertainment apart, I could not say. Does it have to be justified? Whether it cleanses one of one's hang-ups, a personal therapy disguised as art, or whether one is trying to wield an influence in the wide world, I could not say. I certainly do not feel it this way, but these motives are put.

"Books reveal all. It is the occupational hazard one learns to accept, only hoping that the reader is too interested in the story to wonder about what prompted it to be written. When I was small my books were locked away and no one was ever allowed to read them, except the one favoured publisher's editor on whom I conferred the honour. When he had returned it I locked it away again. But when I eventually got published, the agony of realizing that anyone could read what I had written was considerable, and for years I wrote with a certain caution, not always putting down exactly what I would have liked for fear of appearing a bit soppy. Later, with more confidence, I wrote it all down and got labelled a 'romantic' writer. This is a highly dangerous label which I am scrupulously conscious of. And yet, should anyone tax me to defend myself, I could quote such actual, factual incidents

that have happened to me that my critic would (I hope) be quite confounded. I wrote an article once for the *Guardian* (which at that time accepted most of what I sent them) about what had happened to me on my first 'exchange' visit to France at the age of sixteen, and Mrs. Stott sent it back saying how much she had enjoyed it, but of course could not publish it as it obviously wasn't true. Every word of it was true, in fact, but I didn't stoop to defend myself."[2]

"I don't really have a favorite among my books. I always like the one I'm writing now better than any of the others. Once they are written, I sort of forget about them, really."[1]

FOOTNOTE SOURCES

[1]Cornelia Jones and Olivia R. Way, *British Children's Authors: Interviews at Home,* American Library Association, 1976.

[2]K. M. Peyton, "On Not Writing a Proper Book," *The Thorny Paradise: Writers on Writing for Children,* edited by Edward Blishen, Kestrel, 1975.

[3]Justin Wintle and Emma Fisher, *The Pied Pipers: Interviews with the Influential Creators of Children's Literature,* Paddington Press, 1974. Amended by K. M. Peyton.

[4]John Rowe Townsend, *A Sense of Story: Essays on Contemporary Writing for Children,* Lippincott, 1971.

FOR MORE INFORMATION SEE:

Horn Book, August, 1969 (p. 418ff), December, 1969, February, 1971 (p. 390ff), August, 1971, October, 1972, October, 1973, April, 1975, October, 1976, November, 1976.

Doris de Montreville and Donna Hill, editors, *Third Book of Junior Authors,* H. W. Wilson, 1972.

Children's Literature in Education, July, 1972 (p. 5ff), November, 1972 (p. 5ff), summer, 1982.

Junior Bookshelf, October, 1977, April, 1980, August, 1986.

Times Literary Supplement, December 2, 1977, September 29, 1978, July 23, 1982, September 17, 1982.

D. L. Kirkpatrick, editor, *Twentieth-Century Children's Writers,* St. Martin's, 1978, 2nd edition, 1983.

John Rowe Townsend, *A Sounding of Storytellers,* Lippincott, 1979.

Bulletin of the Center for Children's Books, February, 1979, October, 1979, December, 1979, March, 1980, March, 1982, January, 1983, January, 1984, February, 1984.

Publishers Weekly, November 12, 1982.

Children's Literature Review, Volume 3, Gale, 1984.

Growing Point, January, 1986, January, 1987.

PLAIN, Belva 1919-

PERSONAL: Born October 9, 1919, in New York, N.Y.; daughter of Oscar (a contractor) and Eleanor Offenberg; married Irving Plain (a physician), June 14, 1941 (died December, 1982); children: three. *Education:* Attended Barnard College. *Residence:* New Jersey. *Agent:* Dorothy Olding, Harold Ober Associates, 40 East 49th St., New York, N.Y. 10017.

CAREER: Writer.

WRITINGS:

NOVELS

Evergreen, Delacorte, 1978, large print edition, 1981.
Random Winds, Delacorte, 1980, large print edition, 1981.

BELVA PLAIN

Eden Burning, Delacorte, 1982, large print edition, G. K. Hall, 1983.
Crescent City, Delacorte, 1984, large print edition, G. K. Hall, 1984.
The Golden Cup, Delacorte, 1986, large print edition, G. K. Hall, 1987.
Tapestry, Delacorte, 1988, large print edition, Doubleday, 1988.
Blessings, Delacorte, 1989, large print edition, Doubleday, 1989.
Harvest, Delacorte, 1990, large print edition, Doubleday, 1990.

Contributor to periodicals, including *McCall's, Good House-keeping, Redbook,* and *Cosmopolitan.* Plain's books have been published in French, German, Spanish, Hebrew, Portuguese, Italian, Dutch, Swedish, Danish, Finnish, Norwegian, Turkish, Slovene, and Greek.

ADAPTATIONS:

"Evergreen" (cassette), Cassette Books, 1984, (miniseries), NBC-TV, June 12, 1988.
"Random Winds" (cassette), Books on Tape, 1985.
"Eden Burning" (cassette), Books on Tape, 1986.
"Blessings" (cassette), Brilliance.

WORK IN PROGRESS: Another novel.

SIDELIGHTS: The daughter of a prosperous contractor, Belva Plain was born **October 9, 1919,** in New York City and grew up on Park Avenue. While attending Barnard College, majoring in history, a creative writing teacher told her: "'You have no feeling for words.'

"The professor shall go nameless. Needless to say, I wasn't discouraged."[1]

1941. Married Irving Plain, an opthomologist, on June 14, after a romantic courtship. "In my case it had been not roses, but gardenias. I met him in the spring. Gardenias weren't as expensive then as they are now and he brought me one every Sunday afternoon. I pinned it on the lapel of my navy-blue coat—Heaven forbid that you should wear anything but navy in the spring or brown in the fall! I had a yellow hat that year, wide-brimmed, like a sombrero. Thirty years afterward he still talked about that beautiful hat, and thirty years afterward the scent of a gardenia, even as it dies with the faded edge curling over the cream, is enough to bring it all back to me: the March wind hurling itself through the cold street, a book he gave me, his first present, a certain music, and most of all his face, the face of the handsomest young man I had ever seen."[2]

Plain published a few short stories before the birth of her children, but soon she was caught up in the life of a doctor's wife and mother to three children: "I had always wanted to write a novel. I was about to say that I didn't *have* the time, but the truth is I didn't *make* the time. You see, in the years that I was rearing a family, you were not supposed to do anything *but* rear a family. Nowadays we know that it is sometimes better if a woman doesn't spend all her time with the children and does do something else. In those years, I would have felt a great deal of guilt if I had just shut myself away to do it. But I always wanted to."[3]

"I . . . became a suburban dweller. With millions of other women who had waited, during the war and afterward when our husbands went back for futher education, for the day when we might hang curtains in a home that would be permanent, I had clipped pictures from home and garden magazines and drawn plans in my head. The house and the children were to be our whole world; we never thought otherwise.

"'Togetherness' was the theme. We gave backyard barbecues for family and friends. The husband, in chef's hat and apron, broiled the Sunday steak; we hadn't heard about cholesterol, we thought red meat was 'strengthening,' and we filled our baked potatoes with sour cream. In the evenings we sat in the new 'family room' and watched television. My family bought its first one in 1950. The screen was tiny compared with what people have today, but it was a marvel nevertheless, and there were plenty of families right on our street who still owned no television, although very soon it would become a necessity.

"The next necessity was the second car. Mine was a Jeep station wagon that could seat nine, not counting a dog or two. It was often filled to capacity; the era of the car pool had begun. And car pools or no, we needed large cars for our own children. I had the minimal three, but many of my friends had more.

"We were informed through learned and popular articles alike that we, as educated women, had an obligation to society to produce children. For, if we did not, who would build that brave new world? Since there was almost no inflation during the 50s, and our incomes—or, rather, our husbands' incomes—were rising in a steady, modest way, we saw no reason not to have large families.

"Our husbands were also willing and took great pride in fatherhood. I remember, though, that this pride was never extended to changing diapers! My own husband, who was a loving father and a good companion to older children, left such details to me. This was the natural order of things.

"There was a defined division of labor between woman and man. I was responsible for the care of the children, for mending and tending to my husband's clothes, for the meals

For a long time the days and the years were all the same. (Jacket illustration by Craig Nelson from *Evergreen* by Belva Plain.)

and the interior of the house. Exterior repairs or any mechanical interior repairs were the man's area; it was he who negotiated with plumbers and electricians.

"There was never any question about who was the head of the family. The husband supported us all, so he was entitled to have the final word. I cannot, of course, know how this assumption worked in other households, but I can say it worked well in mine. My husband was very kind and giving; we talked over our problems and usually reached agreement, but whenever we were unable to arrive at the same conclusion, I *wanted* the final decision to be his. This, too, was the natural order of things. Had not my mother deferred, when the need arose, to my father? But let me make this clear: This deference never made me feel weak or inferior. It was simply a question of normal function. The male had his function and the female had hers. There even seemed to be something rather romantic about the superior strength of the male, about reliance on his judgment.

"What about the woman who possessed special talents? Well, most of us put them aside while the children were growing up. A friend who is a lawyer gave up practicing until her children left home for college, well after the 50s were over. I myself published nothing for years, although I had published many short stories before my family arrived.

"My life was too full of other things to allow me the personal time one needs for writing, the hours I now have when, driving alone in the car, I can let my thoughts flow or pull the

car to the side of the road while I make hasty notes. My life in the 50s was filled with school—where I was president of the PTA—with scouting, piano lessons and trips to the shoe store, the barber, the orthodontist, the skating rink, birthday parties and religious school. It was all a question of priorities. One knew one's obligations.

"It was a far more constricted way of life, and yet simpler. I look at old snapshots to let the feel of the time come back. A thin young self looks up at me from under her flower-wreathed straw hat; on her way to a ladies' luncheon to raise money for the hospital, she is dressed in a new spring suit and white gloves. (Now I have a small drawer full of white gloves, not worn in thirty years, and I do not own any hats except a knitted cap for snowy weather.) She is smiling; she likes her life. Even though she has had to postpone her ambition as a writer, she likes her life.

"Oh, life was easier, no doubt of that! My husband and I used to take long evening walks, coming back through the dark streets without fear. No speakers came to warn the fourth grade about drugs, and no drug peddlers hung about the schoolyard. You could take a child to the movies without wincing over barnyard language and sex scenes. You could turn on the television or open a magazine without seeing more of the same.

"I know it is often said that the 50s were dull and self-centered. But after the sorrowful upheaval of the war, wasn't it natural to want to have the safe house and the tight little

(From the six-hour miniseries "Evergreen," starring Lesley Ann Warren, first broadcast on NBC-TV June 12, 1988. Photograph courtesy of the National Broadcasting Company, Inc.)

family that had been postponed for so long? One didn't want to think about what was happening in the larger world, far from America. Yes, the Cold War had begun and there was bad trouble in Korea, but if one didn't have a soldier there, it was easy not to think about it too much.

"In the smaller world, though, we made our contribution. Along with most of the women I knew, I worked with the village government, the library committee, the League of Women Voters and the hospital. The 50s was the golden age of the volunteer. And the results of our efforts can still be seen and felt.

"So, it wasn't entirely a selfish time. But it wasn't paradise either. I understand now how unjust it was for a woman to struggle for a place in a medical school that a man with lesser credentials could easily achieve. I know that blacks still rode at the back of the bus. I know that children still died of polio every summer. I know and I rejoice that these evils and others have been overcome. Yes, we have climbed a long way upward during these last thirty years.

"But don't blame me for seeing the 50s with some nostalgic affection. After all, I spent the best of my youth then. There's the photo album again: I'm standing next to my husband who has his arm around me. I have a page-boy hairdo, I'm wearing a waist-cincher and a crinoline under my wide taffeta skirt. We are at his aunt's and uncle's golden wedding celebration. How many of those do you go to anymore?"[4]

After Plain's children had grown, she returned to her dream of writing a novel. She had written a number of stories for *Redbook, McCall's, Good Housekeeping* and *Cosmopolitan.* "I had written a number of short stories that were all published. I have been very, very fortunate and haven't had any rejections and I'm most grateful. I feel very lucky."[3]

March, 1974. Plain began working on an idea for a long novel about Anna Friedman, a Jewish immigrant at the turn of the century who rose from poverty to wealth. "I called my agent, Dorothy Olding, who had worked with me for years with my short stories. She told me to come into the city to discuss it, so we had lunch in one of those little French places on the East Side. We talked, and she told me she thought the idea was excellent."[1]

1978. At the age of fifty-nine, Plain published her first novel, *Evergreen,* which was an instant best seller. Delacorte bought it for an $87,000 advance. "It was small because it was a first novel. I was very, very pleased that they took it at all. When you realize how many thousands of novels publishers receive, and how few ever get published."[1]

"The seed [for *Evergreen*] was planted when my own nice suburban middle-class children first thought of asking who their forebears were. But it was not until my children began presenting me with grandchildren that their questions merged in my mind with the whole mystique of the past and finally took shape in this, my first novel.

"I had always been curious about my own grandmother, who came here from Europe alone at the age of sixteen. Such courage! I think of her still saying a final goodbye and sailing toward an unknown world so long ago. She never saw her people again.

"Of course, all that is a common American adventure: the loneliness, the struggles and failures—and sometimes, the rise to shining affluence. In such ways *Evergreen* is every-

body's story whether he be of Irish, Italian, Polish, or any other stock. Yet there is a special Jewish aspect to the book, too. I was and am weary of reading the same old story, told by Jewish writers, of the same old stereotypes: the possessive mothers, the worn-out fathers and all the rest of the neurotic, rebellious, unhappy, self-hating tribe. I admit that I wanted to write a *different* novel about Jews, and a truer one."[5]

Two years later, Plain published her second novel, *Random Winds.* "I got a $100,000 advance on my second novel."[1]

1982. *Eden Burning,* about a Caribbean paradise, was published. In December of that year, her husband died. "After he died, I found a note in a desk drawer; in it he told me what I meant to him, that he wasn't afraid to die, but didn't want to leave me. And I stood there reading it, and remembering. The clumsy sandwich he brought upstairs for my lunch when I was working at my desk. His fright when he thought I was sick. (He was a doctor, responsible, caring and calm with his patients, but absolutely terrified when I was the patient.) His trust in me when he left for the army and put everything he owned in my name.

"I feel a chill when I read about prenupital financial agreements. Just prudence, they tell me, in case things don't turn out. Well, maybe so. But is there no more conviction and are there no more starry eyes? I feel a chill when I think of a life without a permanent love, loving and being loved alike, a life without lasting trust.

(From *Eden Burning* by Belva Plain. Jacket illustration by Craig Nelson.)

"Oh, we had our differences, of course we did! He was sloppy and I obsessively neat, the kind of person who won't go to sleep until the pictures all hang straight on the walls. He could be irritable and I am critical. We quarreled. As the wry joke goes, we sometimes could have killed each other. But we could never have left each other. I knew he would be there for me always. He knew I would be there for him, and I was until the end. We were *friends.* A lover, a husband, a wife is a *friend.*"[2]

"I try not to let it influence my life because I realize that death is a part of life. You can mourn inside, but you musn't let it show too much because people don't want to hear it. We all know, each of us, that death affects us, and we don't want to be reminded of it. You don't want to see a sad widow around. You don't want to read about it either. So I don't think it has been reflected in my work at all."[3]

1989. In August, Delacorte published *Blessings,* about an adopted child who appears in her natural mother's life just as she is about to remarry. "We live in this world that is rapidly changing. Every morning's newspaper has ten ideas for a novel. I've been reading so much about adoption that it seemed to me that this is a problem with enormous potential for emotional conflict. How would people react? I heard a story recently about a woman who heard the doorbell, answered the door, and found a woman there who said, 'I am the mother of the child you adopted fifteen years ago, and I would like to see her.' Now how's that for a bomb dropping in your lap? So that's the kind of thing that made me think about writing this novel."[3]

Plain works in a second-story room in her family home in Short Hills, New Jersey. She writes from Monday through Thursday, and visits friends and family on other days. "Then I go out and take a three-mile walk. I try to do that every day, because writing is so sedentary."[1]

On certain days she doesn't feel like writing, however. "On a day like that, obviously, I'm not creative, but there are other things I can do. I write three drafts, so if I don't feel like pushing ahead, I can go back and polish and do the final touches. In other words, I don't waste the day."[3]

She uses a typewriter to compose. "A funny thing—one of my grandsons said the other day, 'Are you still working on that antique, it's not even electric!' And lo and behold, I picked up the *New York Times* and in the Home section saw an article about people who will not part with their old typewriters. It listed places where they can get them cleaned and repaired. It also mentioned authors who use typewriters, of which they are very fond, that are thirty or forty years old. That's how I am. I would have to take a course to learn how to use a computer. By that time, I could have half of another book finished!"[3]

Most of Plain's books have positive endings. "I don't really sit down and say, 'Well, now I'm going to write a cheerful book.' So they must reflect something of myself; I feel that this is a marvelous world. There's a lot of suffering in it, but who would say 'I'm sorry I was born.' Sometimes when people are in terrible, terrible straits, they have moments when they say it, but they don't mean it for long. Everything that lives wants to live. Maybe I'm talking from the point of view of somebody who isn't starving in Africa. I can't know how that feels. I can only speak from my point of view and I do take a cheerful, optimistic point of view."[3]

Plain admits that she writes to entertain. "When I say entertainment, I don't mean something, I hope, that slips past the eye and through the ear and is forgotten in an hour. Not that I'm comparing myself with the greats, but even the greatest novelists are entertainers—Dickens or any great novelist. So even in my modest way I feel I can say that I want to entertain without disparaging myself, because, I think that storytelling is a fundamental need. People love stories. They like to see what happens to other human beings, what situations they get themselves into and how they handle them. It's a kind of curiosity.

"I do enjoy it . . . . Someone was telling me about something that happened to an acquaintance, not telling it in a malicious way—maybe you could just call it harmless gossip—and I said, 'Tell me more.' I like to know what happens, because that's where ideas come from. Also, you gain an understanding of people, in the way they handle things that happen to them.

"I have a very good relationship with my publishing company and editor; they are most thoughtful, most considerate, and actually, the things they ask me to do, I find kind of fun.

"There is that savings bank of notes and ideas that I speak of. None of them has been developed yet. But I'm sure something will develop. I'll pick up some notes, perhaps from years ago, and I'll think, 'This is what I want to write about now.'"[3]

FOOTNOTE SOURCES

[1]Judy Klemesrud, "Behind the Best Sellers: Belva Plain," *New York Times Book Review,* July 30, 1978.
[2]Belva Plain, "A Valentine to Love," *Woman's Day,* February 16, 1988.
[3]"A Chat with Belva Plain," Delacorte Press publicity.
[4]B. Plain, "The Fifties," *Woman's Day,* November 27, 1987.
[5]*Contemporary Authors New Revision Series,* Volume 14, Gale, 1985.

FOR MORE INFORMATION SEE:

New York Times Book Review, July 30, 1978, August 22, 1982, October 7, 1984.
People Weekly, August 7, 1978 (p. 85).
McCall's, December, 1980 (p. 20).
Chicago Tribune, October 12, 1984.
Woman's Day, November 4, 1988 (p. 90).

ROSS, Ramon R(oyal) 1930-

PERSONAL: Born November 1, 1930, in Walla Walla, Wash.; son of Royal Chester (a farmer) and Wanda Josephine (a homemaker; maiden name, McCarty) Ross; married Lorna Ann Burgess, June 10, 1951 (divorced, 1975); married Pamela Joyce Tuck, June 21, 1980; children: (first marriage) Jane Marie, Susan Gaye Ross Kewar, Michelle Annette; (second marriage) Lauren Alexandra. *Education:* Central Washington University, B.A., 1951; University of Idaho, M.Ed., 1959; University of Oregon, Ed.D., 1961. *Politics:* Democrat/Independent. *Religion:* Protestant. *Home:* 9227 Virginian Lane, La Mesa, Calif. 92041. *Agent:* Jane Jordan Browne, 410 S. Michigan Ave., Chicago, Ill. 60605. *Office:* San Diego State University, San Diego, Calif. 92182.

RAMON R. ROSS

CAREER: San Diego State University, San Diego, Calif., professor of education, 1961 —. Visiting lecturer at University of Oregon, University of Wisconsin, University of Colorado, State University of New York at Buffalo, and McGill University (Montreal). *Military service:* U.S. Army, 1952-54. *Member:* National Council of Teachers of English, National Conference Research in English, International Reading Association, National Association for the Preservation and Perpetuation of Storytelling (member of editorial board, 1980-84). *Awards, honors:* Notable Work of Fiction from the Southern California Council of Literature for Children and Young People, 1985, for *Prune.*

WRITINGS:

(With Leo Charles Fay and Margaret LaPray) *Young American Basic Reading Program: Levels 1-10,* Lyons & Carnahan, 1968 —.
Storyteller, Charles Merrill, 1978, second edition, 1981.
(With Jacqueline Chaparro and Pamela Ross) *Readers Theater Kit,* Economy, 1982.
Prune (illustrated by Susan Sarabasha), Atheneum, 1984.

Prune has been translated into Danish. Contributor to educational texts.

WORK IN PROGRESS: Harper, a novel set in the Walla Walla Valley in 1940; *Why Tables Have Legs,* a picture book; *The Blue Gate,* a Chinese fairytale.

SIDELIGHTS: "I grew up on a small fruit ranch in the Walla Walla Valley in the state of Washington, half a mile from the Oregon state line. My father raised apples and prunes. (Blue Mountain Italian prunes are not to be confused with plums, which are rounder and usually not free stoned. The prunes we grew were eaten fresh and plump and golden and are delicious. They are never dried. Cooked, or canned, their juice is a beautiful rich purple.)

"The Walla Walla Valley is dry country, but tiny springs bubbled out of the ground in unlikely places, and my sister and I would search for them, and clear the undergrowth away and build miniature cities in these little oases, with roadways and canals and castles, the clear water making its way over boulders the size of a pea and losing itself among the horsetail weeds and lamb's-quarters.

"A small creek ran behind the house, and we spent summer days there, building dams, heaping up boards and gunny sacks filled with dirt, trying to create a vast lake. Each night the dam would wash out, helped, probably, by my father, and the next morning we'd start over again, patient as beavers. We sailed down stream in copper boiler tubs, and built rafts, and scouted the creek banks for evidence of weasels and muskrats, which my Uncle Shorty trapped during the winter months.

"The orchard was a magical place, as well, with the long aisles of trees in blossom in the spring, and the dark purple fruit ripening during the summer months. In August the prune pickers would arrive, hiking along the railroad tracks with their bedrolls, or driving up from California or Florida or Georgia in their old trucks and cars. They'd pitch tents or set up camp down by the creek, or under the black walnut trees, and in the evenings, after supper, we'd sit by their camp fires and listen to their stories.

"Springdale School, which I attended, had two teachers and twenty-seven children in the entire eight grades. There was no kindergarten. I was the only child in the first grade, and my teacher, perhaps to save herself trouble, soon promoted me to second grade, where there were more children. That school, incidentally, had no indoor plumbing, and the library consisted of a dozen or so tattered books, including Nathaniel Hawthorne's *Tanglewood Tales.* During recess we played tag in the branches of giant cottonwoods that grew behind the school. Ah, Tarzan!

"My mother and father were determined that we get 'educated.' Every Saturday morning included a trip to Walla Walla, for our piano lessons and a visit to the city library, where we selected our week's supply of books. I grew up loving to read, majored in English when I went to college, and after college bought a small farm in the valley, (raising prunes, naturally) and taught school.

"I soon realized that I wasn't going to be able to support a family and a farm on a teacher's salary, and started back to graduate school at the University of Oregon, where I had the good fortune to take a class in children's literature from Winifred Ladley, who rather tartly reminded me how little I knew about children's books, and urged me to learn more. I owe Professor Ladley a big debt.

"Presently I teach classes in children's literature and storytelling at San Diego State University, and train teachers and clinicians to work with children with reading and learning difficulties.

"My first writing for publication (other than scholarly articles) was a basal reader series, published by Lyons & Carnahan. About that same time, I wrote a book called *Storyteller*, no doubt harkening back to those early memories of stories the prune pickers told around the camp fire.

"*Prune* had its start one summer afternoon, when my wife and I were in Montreal, where I was teaching at McGill University. It was one of those blue Sunday afternoons, and we were both a little homesick, and she asked me to 'tell her a story.' I hesitated for a moment, and then said, 'Well, once upon a time there was Prune.' She laughed. '. . . And one day he got picked and started his long journey, to see the world, and on the way he fell in love with a . . . Raspberry.' She laughed again. I told her the rest of the story, and she said I should write it down.

"I thought the story would be ten or fifteen pages in length, but as it turned out, there was much more there than I had originally known. I was fascinated in *Prune* by the idea of a central character who had no means of getting about on his own, and yet who seemed whole. But getting that down took a long time, and for a year or more the book sat in limbo. It was only during a sabbatical, and a few months living in a small town in Mexico that I was able to move into the second—and it seems to me, most satisfying—half of the story.

"There were tags and bits and pieces of other 'human' stories in *Prune*. I'm working on those, and also on a novel about Harper, the boy in *Prune*. That, story, too, has friendship as one of its central themes, but the story is also one of adventure and mystery.

"Writing, though, moves slowly for me. In part, perhaps, because I have what a friend calls 'clever paws,' probably left over from those days on the creek. Given a choice of sitting at a typewriter, or building a house or a pond or a garden, I'll choose the latter any day."

HOBBIES AND OTHER INTERESTS: Cooking, gardening, restoring old houses, playing the piano, reading, riding my mountain bike, walking, camping.

FOR MORE INFORMATION SEE:

Karen Kenyon, "Award Winning *Prune:* Children's Book with a Wrinkle," *Los Angeles Times*, February 12, 1986.
"Interview with Ramon Ross," *Writing Teacher*, April-May, 1989.

RUBLOWSKY, John M(artin) 1928-

PERSONAL: Born March 5, 1928, in Evansville, Pa; son of Peter (a crane operator) and Frances (Ryska) Rublowsky; married Ruth Kulin (a guidance counselor), March 19, 1949; children: Mia Rublowsky Simmons, Stefan. *Education:* Attended Columbia University, 1946-49; studied violin with J. Thibaud, Paris, France, 1949-50; attended Manhattan School of Music, 1950-51. *Home:* 452 Fifth St., Brooklyn, N.Y. 11215.

CAREER: Violinist with St. Louis Symphony, 1951-55; *Brooklyn Heights Press*, Brooklyn, N.Y., and *Village Voice*, New York, N.Y., columnist-writer, 1955-59; *Space World* (magazine), New York, N.Y., editor, 1959, 1963; full-time free-lance writer, 1963—. *Military service:* U.S. Navy, 1944-46. *Member:* Authors Guild, Anonymous Arts Recovery Society (co-founder), New York Cactus and Succulent Society (co-founder).

WRITINGS:

Is Anybody Out There?, Walker & Co., 1962 (published in England as *Life on Other Worlds*, Constable, 1964).
Life and Death of the Sun, Basic Books, 1964.
Light: Our Bridge to the Stars, Basic Books, 1964.
Pop Art, Basic Books, 1965.
Nature in the City, Basic Books, 1967.
Popular Music, Basic Books, 1967.
Music in America, Macmillan, 1967.
After the Crash: America in the Great Depression, Crowell-Collier, 1970.
Black Music in America, Basic Books, 1971.
The Stoned Age: A History of Drugs in America, Putnam, 1974.
Born in Fire: A Geologic History of Hawaii, Harper, 1981.

WORK IN PROGRESS: A fairy tale for children, for Harper; research for a book on work attitudes in America from the earliest European settlements to the present.

RUNYON, Catherine 1947-

PERSONAL: Born April 2, 1947, in Reed City, Mich.; daughter of James Henry (a laborer) and Blanche Irene (a laborer; maiden name, Joslin) Hatfield; married Randall Ray Runyon (in hospital maintenance), November 23, 1967; children: Nathan Randall, David Ray, Edward Joseph. *Education:* Attended Moody Bible Institute, diploma, 1971. *Politics:* Independent. *Religion:* "Conservative evangelical." *Home:* 3918 Bradford N.E., Grand Rapids, Mich. 49506.

CAREER: Moody Bible Institute, Chicago, Ill., secretary, retail bookstore clerk, and editorial assistant, 1969-71; free-lance writer and speaker for church groups, 1971—. *Member:* Mid-Michigan Romance Writers Association, Society of Children's Book Writers.

WRITINGS:

JUVENILE; ALL SELF-ILLUSTRATED

All Wrong Mrs. Bear, Moody, 1972.
The Trouble with Jud, Moody, 1973.
Mrs. Oodle's Noodles, Moody, 1973.
The Missionary Mouse, Moody, 1973.
A Trace of Blackmail, Moody, 1974.
Too Soon, Mr. Bear, Moody, 1979.

Contributor to religious periodicals.

WORK IN PROGRESS: Young adult career/romance set in Gatlinburg, Tennessee.

SIDELIGHTS: "I really believe that a person cannot attain his true potential as an artist until he is in a right relationship to God. Of course, my writing reflects that relationship. I believe that a writer cannot help but convey his own philosophy in his writing, and I don't try to conceal it. Jesus Christ is a motivating force in my life, and I try to create tasteful, beautiful writing that portrays Him as the Person He is."

RYBOLT, Thomas R(oy) 1954-

PERSONAL: Born March 13, 1954, in Orlando, Fla.; son of Howard Roy (an engineer) and Peggy (a housewife; maiden name, Helms) Rybolt; married Ann Harris (a physician), May 30, 1976; children: Leah Marie, Megan Joan, Ben Thomas. *Education:* Furman University, B.S., 1976; Georgia Institute of Technology, M.S., 1979, Ph.D., 1981. *Politics:* Independent. *Religion:* Methodist. *Home:* 4715 Murray Hills Dr., Chattanooga, Tenn. 37416. *Office:* Chemistry Department, University of Tennessee, Chattanooga, Tenn. 37403.

CAREER: University of Tennessee, Chattanooga, assistant professor, 1981-86, associate professor, 1986—. Co-inventor with R. A. Pierotti of "Method for Utilizing Gas-Solid Dispersions in Thermodynamic Cycles for Power Generation and Refrigeration," 1982. *Member:* American Chemical Society, Tennessee Academy of Science, Phi Beta Kappa, Sigma Xi Research Society. *Awards, honors: Adventures with Atoms and Molecules* was selected one of New York Public Library's Books for the Teen Age, 1986.

WRITINGS:

(With Robert C. Mebane) *Adventures with Atoms and Molecules: Chemistry Experiments for Young People,* Enslow, 1985.
(With R. C. Mebane) *Adventures with Atoms and Molecules Book II: More Chemistry Experiments for Young People,* Enslow, 1987.
(With R. C. Mebane) *Adventures with Atoms and Molecules Book III,* Enslow, 1990.

Contributor of scientific articles to research journals, including *Journal of Chemical Physics, Journal of Colloid and Interface Science, Journal of Chemical Education, Industrial Chemical News, Journal of the American Institute of Chemical Engineers, Langmuir, Journal of Physical Chemistry, Journal of Tennessee Academy of Science,* and *Journal of Pharmaceutical Sciences.*

WORK IN PROGRESS: Five Friends and the Tiger Gang, a preschool children's story; *Bakerman and Friends,* a series of four-line rhymes describing various occupations; *Entropy: The Principle Governing Change in Our World,* a science book for teenagers describing the tendency toward disorder in our universe.

SIDELIGHTS: "As a professional scientist, teacher, father of three children, and uncle to eighteen nephews and nieces, writing science for young people seems to combine my natural interests. Bringing these interests into focus and creating a useful science book was made possible by teaming up with my friend and professional colleague, Rob Mebane. We both realize that science is a process and not just a body of knowledge. Too often science is taught as a collection of facts to be memorized. We want to help increase the awareness among teachers, parents, and young people that science is an activity, a mental process, a way of looking at the world, and a way to have fun.

"We have written three books in what we expect to be a continuing series of 'Adventures with Atoms and Molecules' chemistry experiment books for elementary school age children. Each book contains thirty experiments and suggestions for about seventy additional activities and experiments. Each experiment begins with a question and follows a similar format. The question is followed by sections that include: materials—what you need, procedure—what you do, observations—what you might expect to see, discussion—an explanation based on the behavior of atoms and molecules, and other things to try—suggestions for additional related activities. All the experiments are designed so they can be done at home with simple grocery store supplies and materials. Although designed for upper elementary school, these activities are of interest to older students and adults.

"This type of book is well suited for a team approach. We begin not by writing, but by independently doing experiments in our kitchens. Through trial and error we gradually develop a set of reasonable questions and workable experiments. We write our experiments and then exchange them. Through constructive criticism and revision the final versions are developed.

"I am continually impressed by the extent to which young children are delighted and interested in simple experimental activities—add a drop of food coloring to water and watch it spread, mix vinegar and baking soda and trap the bubbles of gas in a balloon, bend a stream of water with a charged comb, make butter from whipping cream, etc. Adults are easily caught up in this excitement and with the help of children can learn to see the world as fresh and full of surprises.

"Apart from my interest in science writing, I am interested in writing books for preschool children. Since I found myself creating stories to entertain my own young children, after a time it seemed only natural to put them in writing.

"As time goes on, certain stories and poems seem to naturally grow and improve. If a story or poem is repeatedly requested by my children, then I know it must be good. Only after I've told a story many times do I put it in writing. By the time I've reached this stage my children can usually tell the story better than I."

HOBBIES AND OTHER INTERESTS: Scientific research, reading, writing, racquetball, raising children.

SAYERS, Frances Clarke 1897-1989

OBITUARY NOTICE—See sketch in *SATA* Volume 3: Born September 4, 1897, in Topeka, Kan.; died after a stroke, July 24, 1989, at her home in Ojai, Calif. Librarian, educator, editor, and author. Nationally known for promoting literature for children, Sayers spent a large part of her career at the New York Public Library, first as assistant in the children's room from 1918-1923 and later as superintendent of work with children from 1941-1952. After her marriage to Alfred Sayers she moved to California, where she taught children's literature in the English department and at the School of Library Service, both at University of California, Los Angeles. She was sponsored by *Compton's Picture Encyclopedia* as a "Prestige Service" lecturer, visiting other colleges to promote children's literature. Known to be outspoken, she criticized Walt Disney for commercializing children's stories.

Among her writings are children's books such as *Bluebonnets for Lucinda, Mr. Tidy-Paws, Tag-Along Tooloo, Sally Tait, Ginny and Custard,* and *Oscar Lincoln Busby Stokes.* Sayers also co-edited two editions of *The Anthology of Children's Literature,* and published a collection of her essays and speeches, *Summoned by Books.* In addition, she wrote a biography of her friend and mentor at the New York Public Library, Anne Carroll Moore.

Sayers served as a consultant to the Library of Congress and was instrumental in establishing their Children's Book Section. Among the many honors and awards she won were the Joseph W. Lippincott Award for Distinguished Service in the Profession of Librarianship (1965), the Clarence Day Award for *Summoned by Books* (1966), the Southern California Council on Literature for Children and Young People's Award (1969), and the Catholic Library Association's Regina Medal (1973).

FOR MORE INFORMATION SEE:

Stanley J. Kunitz and Howard Haycraft, *Junior Book of Authors,* H. W. Wilson, 1951.
Horn Book, June, 1970.
Martha E. Ward and Dorothy A. Marquardt, *Authors of Books for Young People,* Scarecrow, 1971.
Contemporary Authors, Volume 19-20R, Gale, 1976.
ALA World Encyclopedia of Library and Information Services, 2nd edition, American Library Association, 1986.

OBITUARIES

New York Times, July 27, 1989.
Los Angeles Times, July 28, 1989.
Times (London), August 17, 1989.
School Library Journal, September, 1989 (p. 145ff).
Horn Book, December, 1989 (p. 822).

SCHUBERT, Dieter 1947-

PERSONAL: Born July 15, 1947, in Oschersleben, West Germany; son of Erich (a locksmith) and Elfriede (a housewife; maiden name, Boettcher) Schubert; married Ingrid Gabrys (an illustrator), November 5, 1976; children: Hannah. *Education:* Muenster Academy of Design, Designer, 1975; graduate study at Duesseldorf Academy of Art, 1975-76, University of Muenster, 1975-77, and Gerrit Rietveld Academy (Amsterdam), 1977-80. *Home and office:* Reigerweg 12, 1027 HC Amsterdam, Netherlands. *Agent:* Lemniscaat, Vijverlaan, Rotterdam, Netherlands.

CAREER: Tengelmann Wholesale Trade, Hamm, West Germany, merchant, 1963-71; Academy of Restoration, Amsterdam, Netherlands, teacher, 1980—; author and illustrator, 1980—. Teacher of art expression workshop, Amsterdam, 1982—. *Awards, honors:* Golden Brush Award for Best Illustrated Picture Book of the Year (Holland), 1987, and International Board on Books Honor List, 1988, both for *Where's My Monkey?*

WRITINGS:

JUVENILE; SELF-ILLUSTRATED

Jack in the Boat, Lemniscaat, 1982, Kestrel, 1982.
Where's My Monkey?, Dial, 1987.

JUVENILE; AUTHOR AND ILLUSTRATOR WITH WIFE, INGRID SCHUBERT-GABRYS

There's a Crocodile under My Bed, Lemniscaat, 1980, McGraw, 1981.
The Magic Bubble Trip, Lemniscaat, 1981, Kane Miller, 1985.
Who's a Sissy, Lemniscaat, 1983.

Funny Reading, Schroedelverlag, 1984.
Little Bigfeet, Lemniscaat, 1985.
Look at My Letter, Jacob Dijkstra, 1988.
The Monsterbook, Lemniscaat, 1989.
Santa Claus/Father Christmas, Lemniscaat, 1989.
The Inventor, Lemniscaat, 1989.

TELEPLAYS; WITH I. SCHUBERT-GABRYS

"Look at Me," Dutch School Television, 1982.
"Who's Coming to My Little House?," Dutch School Television, 1982.
"Father Christmas/Santa Claus," Dutch School Television, 1989.

WORK IN PROGRESS: Funny Reading, a schoolbook for young children with I. Schubert-Gabrys, for Schroedel Schulbuchverlag (West Germany).

SIDELIGHTS: "While in Germany and Holland I studied painting, drawing, and 'free' graphics. At the start of my studies I had been preoccupied with illustrating stories. During my study at the Gerrit Rietveld Academy, I was inspired by Piet Klaasse, a very famous illustrator in Holland, who at that time was a teacher there. I then started to spend more time on illustration.

"Although I started illustrating adult literature (Kafka), I soon began illustrating for children. I later preferred illustrating for very small children because I find them very fascinating in their thoughts and adventures. What is more, by making up stories and illustrating them, one's own feelings from childhood come back again, and I take pleasure in that.

"My wife Ingrid (an illustrator as well) and I started to write and illustrate our own stories. In 1979 we contacted the publishing firm Lemniscaat who liked our first idea for a book. They made our first international contact at the Frankfurt Book Fair. In 1980 that first book, *There's a Crocodile under My Bed,* was translated into eleven languages and published in fourteen countries. In 1981 reprints appeared in three countries. Since then, a new book of ours has been published internationally each year."

HOBBIES AND OTHER INTERESTS: Playing guitar, listening to good music.

SCHUBERT-GABRYS, Ingrid 1953-

PERSONAL: Born March 29, 1953, in Essen, West Germany; daughter of Oswald (a landlord) and Maria (a landlady; maiden name, Smeets) Gabrys; married Dieter Schubert (an illustrator), November 5, 1976; children: Hannah. *Education:* Received degree from Muenster Academy of Design, 1976; graduate study at Duesseldorf Academy of Art, 1976-77, University of Muenster, 1976-77, and Gerrit Rietveld Academy (Amsterdam), 1977-80. *Home and office:* Reigerweg 12, 1027 HC Amsterdam, The Netherlands. *Agent:* Lemniscaat, Vijverlaan, Rotterdam, The Netherlands.

CAREER: Gabrys, Borken, West Germany, merchant, 1968-70; worked as a potter in Stadtlohn, West Germany, 1970-71; teacher in educational play-group for children, Muenster, West Germany, 1976-77; teacher at art expression workshop, Amsterdam, The Netherlands, 1981—.

Dieter and Ingrid Schubert

Exhibitions: International Exhibition of Children's Books, Bratislava, Czechoslovakia, 1981, 1983, 1985, 1987, 1989; Premi Catalonia d'Illustracio, Barcelona, Spain, 1984; Twenty-second Exhibition of International Children's Books, Tokyo, Japan, 1987.

WRITINGS:

JUVENILE; AUTHOR AND ILLUSTRATOR WITH HUSBAND, DIETER SCHUBERT

There's a Crocodile under My Bed, Lemniscaat, 1980, McGraw, 1981.
The Magic Bubble Trip, Lemniscaat, 1981, Kane Miller, 1985.
Who's a Sissy, Lemniscaat, 1983.
Funny Reading, Schroedelverlag, 1984.
Little Bigfeet, Lemniscaat, 1985.
Look at My Letter, Jacob Dijkstra, 1988.
The Monsterbook, Lemniscaat, 1989.
Santa Claus/Father Christmas, Lemniscaat, 1989.
The Inventor, Lemniscaat, 1989.

TELEPLAYS; ALL WITH D. SCHUBERT

"Look at Me," Dutch School Television, 1982.
"Who's Coming to My Little House?," Dutch School Television, 1982.
"Father Christmas/Santa Claus," Dutch School Television, 1989.

SIDELIGHTS: "In 1978 my teacher at Gerrit Rietveld Academy inspired and encouraged me to illustrate children's books. My first commission was for illustrating a children's book by author Roald Dahl. From that moment my interest in children's literature grew. My husband, Dieter Schubert, also an illustrator, and I started to write and illustrate our own stories. In 1979 we contacted the publisher Lemniscaat, and they liked our first idea for a book. *There's a Crocodile under My Bed,* was later translated into eleven languages and published in fourteen countries. We still enjoy working together making books for children."

SCOFIELD, Penrod 1933-

PERSONAL: Born June 18, 1933, in Stamford, Conn.; son of Harold N. (an engraver) and Evelyne K. (a writer and journalist; maiden name, Kenefic) Scofield. *Education:* Attended Parsons School of Design, 1952, and Art Students League, 1953-56. *Home and office:* 1 David Lane, Yonkers, N.Y. 10701. *Agent:* Jo-An Pictures Ltd., 41 Union Square, Suite 1036, New York, N.Y. 10003.

CAREER: Illustrator and artist. Muralist, 1960—; filmstrip illustrator for Miller Brody Productions, Spoken Arts, and Listening Library, 1960s-1980s; Walt Disney Studios, Hollywood, Calif., animator, 1976. Has designed sets and costumes for off-Broadway shows. *Exhibitions:* Coeval Gallery,

New York, N.Y., 1953; State Capitol, Albany, N.Y., 1957; Reis Gallery, St. Thomas, Virgin Islands, 1963. *Awards, honors:* Audiovisual Award for Best Filmstrip of the Year from *Learning,* 1965-66, for "Meet the Newbery Author," and 1976-77; Best Filmstrip of the Year Award from *School Library Journal,* 1966, for "Children of Courage;" Best Filmstrip of the Year from *Learning,* 1977, for "The Magic Fishbone"; New York City Public Library Award, 1984, for *Isaac Bashevis Singer.*

ILLUSTRATOR:

Derek Tangye, *Monty: The Biography of a Marmalade Cat,* Coward, 1962.
The American Judaism Reader, Abelard, 1967.
Your Own Word, Spoken Arts, 1974.
Paul Kresh, *Isaac Bashevis Singer: The Story of a Storyteller,* Lodestar, 1984.

ILLUSTRATOR; FILMSTRIPS

"Children's Fairy Tales: The Ass, the Stick, and the Table," Spoken Arts, 1976.
"Children of Courage: Pancho's Puppets," Spoken Arts, 1976.

The time is the year 1904, and the country is Poland. (Illustration by Penrod Scofield from *Isaac Bashevis Singer: The Story of a Storyteller* by Paul Kresh.)

"The Magic Fish Bone," Listening Library, 1977.
"Zlateh the Goat," Miller Brody, 1978.
"Meet the Newbery Author: Isaac B. Singer," Miller Brody, 1980.
"Holidays around the World: Christmas in Mexico," Spoken Arts, 1980.
"Mexican Folk Tales: How Tepotzan Killed the Giant," Spoken Arts, 1980.

Contributor of illustrations to periodicals.

WORK IN PROGRESS: "Designing and engineering a toy for preschool children based on an alphabet book that I have written and illustrated, incorporating design and color; designs for a new series of beach wear; 'Sun Jewels by Penrod' for the '91 Market."

SIDELIGHTS: "I grew up in a small town in Northern Westchester County in New York State about fifty miles from New York City. On my sixth birthday I announced that I was going to be a fireman. One month later I said, 'I want to draw and paint.' My mother cringed, my father looked puzzled. But they said, if that was what I wanted, it was all right with them. I started drawing and painting, and I guess you could say that I have never stopped.

"One of the best things about living in the country is that at a very early age you become aware of nature. You see its forms and shapes and colors. Seasons truly change. One summer evening when I was seven or eight, I remember seeing the Northern Lights. They are still vivid in my mind.

"My father was an engraver at Conde Nast Publications. He brought home proof sheets of an art book he was working on called *A Treasury of Art Masterpieces.* That was my first introduction to art. I would study those proof sheets over and over. I still have some of them.

"In school everyone would be drawing a rabbit based on the circle theory, but I would start with the ears and work down—upsetting my teacher because I wasn't drawing the rabbit the way everybody else did.

"In high school I became aware of design and shape and form under the guidance of my art teacher Kay Couragess. I entered the Scholastic Art Awards contest and won third prize.

"After graduating from high school I spent a year at the Parsons School of Design. I wasn't a good student. I wasn't really ready yet for art school. I spent most of that year drawing street people all over the city. (Many years later I was to do the same thing with the homeless of the city again, turning the results into a theatrical event in collaboration with the poet Owen Dodson for the 'Poet at the Public' series produced by Joseph Papp under a grant from the New York State Council on the Arts in 1982.)

"Following my year at Parsons I attended the Art Students League. There I found myself, and the beginning of a language of art in which I could communicate what I wanted to say. I spent a year there full time. After that, for the next two years, I had to take on a full-time job to support myself, and continued my studies at the League part-time.

"I have done paintings, drawings, book illustrations, filmstrips, and murals. My largest mural was thirty-five feet long by ten feet wide. It depicted a wedding in the Punjab. I have done murals for private homes, for a veterinary hospital, for children's nurseries, for apartment house lobbies, for restaurants, and for a pool house. I find murals fun although they take a huge amount of time. What is fascinating about them is that you are dealing with big-scale proportions. That is challenging and exciting.

"Working as an illustrator of stories, books, and filmstrips is exciting and challenging too. You are taking someone's words and adding the illusion of life. With filmstrips you also have to think in terms of camera angles—close-ups, overhead shots, long shots, and so forth.

"Painting calls for entirely different approaches to subject matter. Yet all the forms of art require me to speak in the language of my own personal style as an artist.

"I enjoy being an artist. I cannot imagine life—my life, at least—without creating art."

HOBBIES AND OTHER INTERESTS: Gardening, cooking, classical music, swimming.

SENDER, Ruth M(insky) 1926-

PERSONAL: Born May 3, 1926, in Lodz, Poland; came to the United States, 1950; naturalized citizen; daughter of Avrom and Nacha (Grundman) Minski; married Morris Sender, July 7, 1945; children: Louis, Allen, Harvey, Nancy. *Education:* Attended Jewish Teachers Seminary. *Religion:* Jewish. *Home:* 18 Karen Place, Commack, N.Y. 11725.

CAREER: Writer. Sholem Aleichem-Peretz School of the Workmens Circle, N.Y., teacher of Yiddish, Jewish history and culture, and the Holocaust, 1973—. Lecturer on the Holocaust. *Awards, honors:* Notable Children's Trade Book in the Field of Social Studies from the National Council of Social Studies and the Children's Book Council, 1986, and Merit of Distinction Citation from the International Center for Holocaust Studies of the Anti-Defamation League of B'nai B'rith, and selected one of New York Public Library's Books for the Teen Age, both 1987, all for *The Cage;* Notable Children's Trade Book in the Field of Social Studies, Notable Trade Book for Language Arts, and selected one of New York Public Library's Books for the Teen Age, all 1988, all for *To Life.* Major Joseph H. Lief J.W.V. Brotherhood Award, 1989, for "her efforts in teaching and in her books to further understanding between all people."

WRITINGS:

The Cage, Macmillan, 1986.
To Life, Macmillan, 1988.

Sender's works have been published in Dutch and Danish. Contributor to *World Over, New York Times, Newsday, Forward,* and *Hadassah.*

WORK IN PROGRESS: "*A Home at Last,* about my life as a Holocaust survivor in America. The struggle to build a future without forgetting the past."

SIDELIGHTS: "I love to teach. I love to write. I wrote my first story in Yiddish, when I was ten years old in Lodz, Poland. It was an essay we had to write as a homework assignment and got to choose our own topic.

RUTH M. SENDER

"My mother, who made little girls' coats, had made me a rag doll from scraps of fabric. I called my story, 'What My Doll

The nightmares fill most of my nights and stay with me through most days. (From *The Cage* by Ruth Minsky Sender.)

Tells.' The doll told of a widow with seven children to support, involved in her children's education, active in the women's labor movement who still finds time to make her child a rag doll. (She could not buy the fancy dolls.) The story was about my mother. The teachers loved my story and I had to read it to all the students. I felt scared but proud.

"Even as a child I always wanted to teach and write. I wrote poems even in the Nazi death camps. They helped me to hold on to hope, to life.

"*The Cage* and *To Life* are my life story and the story of the millions who perished during the Holocaust. A million and a half children perished, their crime, they were born Jewish. I am a Jew. I was a child during the Holocaust, yet I survived. I feel, as one who did survive, it is my duty to write, speak, and teach about it. I hope the world will learn what hate, prejudice, and indifference lead to. I feel I must tell of the human spirit that can still hope when all is hopeless. I must tell of the courage to hold on to dignity, surrounded by moral decay.

"'As long as there is life there is hope.' Those were my mother's words that helped me survive. I believe that we must never lose hope. Never give up.

"I wrote a short story in 1968 in *Hadassah* magazine called 'The Cage.' I told of the struggle of four children, my three little brothers and I, then sixteen, clinging to each other with love and devotion after the Nazis surrounded the ghetto and took our mother from us. I wrote more stories for *World Over*, a children's magazine and received many letters from kids wanting to know more. I started working on a book. Even when I read the touching letters of the magazine readers I wondered if I was wasting my time, the emotional strength, the tears it took to write *The Cage*. Would people want to read a book about us, caged into a ghetto, sick, hungry, alone, surrounded by death, yet still capable of loving, of caring for one another. I would stop, then start again.

"When I finally submitted the manuscript, it was rejected by several publishers because they do not accept unsolicited material. I tried getting an agent and was told there is no chance of publishing a book on this topic.

"In 1983, at the gathering of Holocaust survivors in Washington, I spoke to a publisher about the manuscript I had at home. He shook his head and said, 'Dear lady, do you have children, grandchildren?'

"'Yes,' I answered, not understanding his question.

"'Well, listen to me. Make copies of the manuscript for them and forget about publishing. No one wants to read Holocaust books.'

"I did not give up, and kept on sending the manuscript to publishers. In 1985 I received a letter from Macmillan telling me they would be honored to publish *The Cage*. The sequel, *To Life*, was published by Macmillan in 1988. *The Cage* is used for social studies in schools and is recommended by the *English Journal* as a companion to *The Diary of Anne Frank*.

"I had a letter from someone who read the galley proofs for *To Life* asking for a sequel about my life in America. I receive many letters and phone calls from all over the country, that are warm, moving, and sensitive. I am overwhelmed by it.

"Had I given up in the Nazi death camps I would not have survived to tell my story. Had I given up when told there was no chance to publish my story, many, many people, young and old, would never have learned of the spiritual resistance against evil and those who perished would have been forgotten. I am glad I did not give up. As long as there is life, there is hope."

HOBBIES AND OTHER INTERESTS: Reading, needlepoint.

FOR MORE INFORMATION SEE:

Commack News, May 12, 1983 (p. 3), March 27, 1986 (p.9), May 19, 1988 (p. 6), November 24, 1988 (p. 2).
Western Student Press, November 23, 1983 (p.4).
Smithtown Messenger, October 16, 1986 (p. 3).
Jewish Week, February 13, 1987 (p. 2ff).
Forward, February 12, 1988 (p. 17).
Commack Courier, June, 1988 (p. 9).
Stimson Stylus, June, 1988 (p. 4).
East Northport Voice, November 18, 1988 (p. 3).
Smithtown News, November 24, 1988 (p. 1).
Commack Weekender, November 26, 1988 (p. 3).
Long Islander, December 15, 1988 (p. 5).
Spotlight, January, 1989 (p. 81).
Jewish World, May 5, 1989 (p. 26).
Long Island Catholic, November 22, 1989 (p. 5).
Tablet, January 27, 1990 (p. 7).

SOMERLOTT, Robert 1928-
(Robert Carson)

PERSONAL: Born September 17, 1928, in Huntington, Ind.; son of Vera Somerlott. *Education:* Attended Northwestern University, 1946, Michigan State University, 1947, and University of Michigan, 1948. *Home:* Apdo. 288, San Miguel de Allende, Mexico. *Agent:* McIntosh & Otis, Inc., 475 Fifth Ave., New York, N.Y. 10017.

CAREER: Professional actor and stage director, 1948-63; free-lance writer in San Miguel de Allende, Mexico, 1963—. Lecturer on Mexican studies. *Member:* International PEN. *Awards, honors:* Short story prize from *Atlantic Monthly,* 1964, for "Eskimo Pies."

WRITINGS:

The Flamingos (fiction), Little, Brown, 1967.
The Inquisitor's House (fiction), Viking, 1968.
Here, Mr. Splitfoot (nonfiction), Viking, 1971.
The Writings of Modern Fiction (essays), Writer, 1972.
Introduction to the Maya Epic (nonfiction), University of Wisconsin Press, 1974.
Blaze (fiction), Viking, 1981.
Death of the Fifth Sun (fiction), Viking, 1987.
(Under pseudonym, Robert Carson) *Mississippi* (nonfiction), Childrens Press, 1988.
The Penguin Guide to Mexico (nonfiction), Penguin, 1989.

Work represented in anthologies, including *Best American Short Stories,* 1965, *Stories That Scared Even Me,* edited by Alfred Hitchcock, 1972, and *The Twelve Crimes of Christmas,* edited by Isaac Asimov, 1981. Contributor to magazines, including *Cosmopolitan, Ms., Mademoiselle, American Heri-*

ROBERT SOMERLOTT

tage, Ellery Queen's Mystery Magazine, Good Housekeeping, and *Atlantic.*

SIDELIGHTS: "I moved to Mexico in hope of a career as a free-lance writer. Almost immediately I began to publish short stories, then novels and other works. Most of my work is set in Mexico and I draw heavily from Mexican archaeology and history."

Somerlott's books have been translated into most European languages.

HOBBIES AND OTHER INTERESTS: Mexican archaelology, German shepherd dogs.

SPEARE, Elizabeth George 1908-

PERSONAL: Born November 21, 1908, in Melrose, Mass.; daughter of Harry Allan (an engineer) and Demetria (Simmons) George; married Alden Speare (an industrial engineer), September 26, 1936; children: Alden, Jr., Mary Elizabeth. *Education:* Attended Smith College, 1926-27; Boston University, A.B., 1930, M.A., 1932. *Home:* 48 Bibbins Rd., Easton, Conn. 06612.

CAREER: Rockland High School, Rockland, Mass., teacher of English, 1932-35; Auburn High School, Auburn, Mass., teacher of English, 1935-36; writer, 1955—. *Member:* Authors Guild.

AWARDS, HONORS: Society of Colonial Wars Award from the State of New York, and Newbery Medal from the American Library Association, both 1959, International

Board on Books for Young People (IBBY) Honor List, and selected one of American Institute of Graphic Arts Children's Books, both 1960, and New England Round Table of Children's Librarians Award, 1976, all for *The Witch of Blackbird Pond;* Newbery Medal, 1962, and IBBY Honor List, 1964, both for *The Bronze Bow;* Child Study Children's Book Award from the Child Study Children's Book Committee at Bank Street College of Education, one of American Library Association's Best Young Adult Books, Teachers' Choice from the National Council of Teachers of English, one of Child Study Association of America's Children's Book of the Year, one of *School Library Journal's* Best Books of the Year, a *Booklist* Children's Reviewers' Choice, and one of *New York Times* Outstanding Books, all 1983, and Newbery Medal Honor Book, Scott O'Dell Award for Historical Fiction, and Christopher Award, all 1984, all for *The Sign of the Beaver;* Laura Ingalls Wilder Award, 1989, for a distinguished and enduring contribution to children's literature.

WRITINGS:

Calico Captive (juvenile; ALA Notable Book; illustrated by W. T. Mars), Houghton, 1957.
The Witch of Blackbird Pond (juvenile; ALA Notable Book; illustrated by Nicholas Angelo), Houghton, 1958, large print edition, Cornerstone Books, 1989.
The Bronze Bow (juvenile; ALA Notable Book; *Horn Book* honor list), Houghton, 1961.
Child Life in New England, 1790-1840, Old Sturbridge Village (Mass.), 1961.
Life in Colonial America (nonfiction), Random House, 1963.
The Prospering (adult novel), Houghton, 1967.

ELIZABETH GEORGE SPEARE

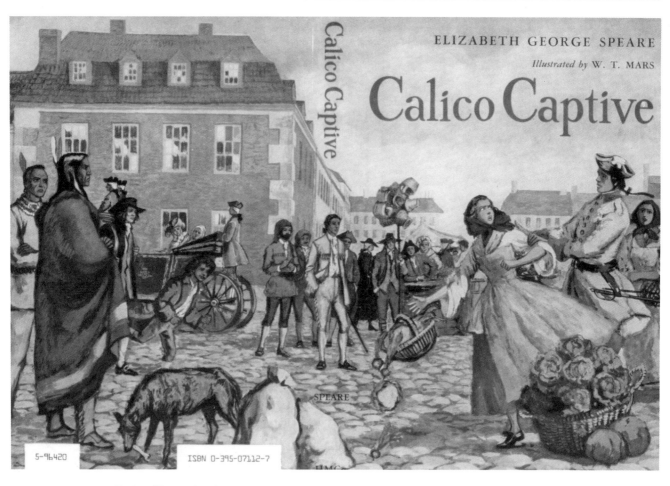

(Jacket illustration by W. T. Mars from *Calico Captive* by Elizabeth George Speare.)

The Sign of the Beaver (ALA Notable Book; *Horn Book* honor list; illustrated by Robert Andrew Parker), Houghton, 1983, large print edition, Cornerstone Books, 1988.

Contributor of articles to periodicals, including *Better Homes and Gardens, Woman's Day, Parents, American Heritage, Today's Health,* and *Horn Book.*

ADAPTATIONS:

"Abby, Julia and the Cows" (television play; based on an
    article for *American Heritage*), Southern New England
    Telephone Company, January 7, 1958.
"The Bronze Bow" (record; cassette; filmstrip with cassette),
    Random House.
"The Witch of Blackbird Pond" (cassette), Random House.
"The Sign of the Beaver" (cassette; filmstrip with cassette),
    Random House.

SIDELIGHTS: "I was born in Melrose, Massachusetts . . . have lived all my life in New England, and though I love to travel I can't imagine ever calling any other place on earth home. It is easy for me to feel right at home in colonial times, because in some ways the countryside and the New Englanders themselves have not changed very much in three hundred years.

"I had one brother, and I remember my childhood as an exceptionally happy one. I am sorry for children—like my own—who have not grown up surrounded as I was by a large clan of aunts and uncles and cousins. They made my growing-up immeasurably richer. Looking back on so many totally different personalities and talents and interests, I can see with gratitude how each one of them helped to stretch my mind and heart. Some of my best memories are of family reunions—big Christmas dinners and summer picnics under the trees.

"Whenever one branch of our family met, a favorite cousin just my own age and I, with barely a greeting to anyone else, used to rush into a corner clutching fat brown notebooks and breathlessly read out loud to each other the latest stories we had written. One summer day an aged uncle invaded our corner and to our dismay asked permission to listen. He sat for some time very gravely, and then got up and walked away shaking his head in bewilderment. But nothing ever discouraged us. Years later when we were in college we still never visited each other without tucking into our suitcases, along with the new formal and the daring new lipstick, a few dog-eared manuscripts.

"Since I can't remember a time when I didn't intend to write, it is hard to explain why I took so long getting around to it in earnest. But the years seemed to go by very quickly. After I graduated from Boston University I divided my time between teaching in a small private school in Boston and studying in Graduate School, running three blocks back and forth between classes. At the end of two years I had acquired a Master's Degree and the illusion that I could teach. Then, still shy and naive, in the midst of the Depression, I ventured into

They were pushing forward next morning in a chill fog and drizzle. (Illustration by W. T. Mars from *Calico Captive* by Elizabeth George Speare.)

a high school and offered my Shakespeare and Browning to a volcanic classroom crowded to bursting with boys who were only biding their time till the closed factories would reopen. I don't suppose any of them has ever remembered a word of what I tried to teach them, but I have never fogotten what they taught me. Surprisingly, in that first toughening year I discovered that I really *liked* teaching.

"In 1936 I married Alden Speare and came to Connecticut, where he . . . worked as an Industrial Engineer. Any family can fill in the record for the next fifteen years, crowded with piano practice and dancing school and camping and orthodontists and PTA and Cub Scouts and Brownies—those familiar things which never seem dull and conven-

tional when they happen to *you* and which leave little time for writing. Not till both children were in junior high school did I find time at last to sit down quietly with pencil and paper.

"At first I followed the advice of those who insist that one must write about what he knows best. I turned naturally to the things which had filled my days and thoughts and began to write magazine articles about family living. My first success came with an article about skiing with children. My husband was . . . an ardent skier, and by their fifth birthdays our two children were schussing down the most terrifying hills with mother snowplowing behind. Family memories and practical experience proved to be a happy combination. Reading out loud, making Christmas presents, learning to

From the moment in the meadow Kit ceased to plan at all. (From *The Witch of Blackbird Pond* by Elizabeth George Speare.)

get along with each other—much of our fun and some of our problems went into what the family called 'mother's sermons.' They went out hopefully and came back and went out again and eventually found a home, though sometimes in a magazine no one had ever heard of. Occasionally my imagination took a short flight into a story or a one-act play."[1]

Speare's first published piece, on skiing, appeared in *Better Homes and Gardens.* She also wrote for *Woman's Day, Parents* and *American Heritage* magazines. She soon discovered her vocation in history and historical fiction. In 1958, an article she wrote on the celebrated Smith sisters of colonial Glastonbury, Connecticut was adapted and shown on television. The Smiths had refused to pay taxes and as a consequence the town confiscated their land and cows. Eventually, the sisters got their land back but in exchange for their right to vote.

While reading a history of Connecticut, she came upon the diary of Susanna Johnson (*Narrative of Captivity of Mrs. Johnson*), first published in 1807. The journey recounts a family's kidnapping by Indians who later bartered them to French captors. Speare was particularly fascinated with Susanna's sister Miriam, who was to become the heroine of *Calico Captive.* "For a long time this girl haunted my imagination, and finally I began to write down her adventures, filling in the outlines of the actual events with new characters and scenes of my own creation. It was like living a double life, stepping every day from my busy world into another time and place and into a family that came to seem as familiar as my own. In the evenings, as breathlessly as I had once read those brown notebooks, I read the latest chapters to my patient daughter. Her encouragement kept me writing and her frank comments kept me strictly down to earth. When *Calico*

Captive finally was published [in 1957] it was dedicated to her."[1]

The following year Speare published *The Witch of Blackbird Pond,* the book for which she is best known. Critical response was glowing, and her selection as recipient of the Newbery Medal was determined by unanimous vote, a very rare occurrence. "All writers must feel, like Tennyson's Ulysses, that 'life piled on life were all too little,' and in a very real way the hours spent in creating a book are hours crowded with encounters. It has been noted that all our conscious impressions, even the vicarious adventures of reading or the unsubstantial but vivid excursions of our dreams—even of our daydreams—pass into our memory and become one with our experience. I am sure it must be true of all writers, that in the months in which they live closely with the people they have created, these fictitious lives become entangled with their own, and on looking back they find that the imagined experiences have merged with the actual past and that the past is infinitely richer because of them.

"Where these imaginary people come from is one of the intriguing mysteries of this solitary profession, just as I presume the gift of a lovely melody can never be explained. One of the most common questions asked any writer is, 'How do you begin your stories? Do they start with an idea, or an

At eighteen Daniel bar Jamin was unmistakably a Galilean. (From *The Bronze Bow* by Elizabeth George Speare.)

incident, or a character?' Looking back, I can answer that for me they begin with people."[2]

Speare won a second Newbery Medal for *The Bronze Bow.* The book centers on Daniel, a young Israelite in Biblical Palestine, consumed with hatred for the Romans who had captured his land. Eventually the teachings, and ways, of Jesus change Daniel's thinking, infuse his consciousness with love and faith for the man from Nazareth. "I made the mistake of trying to begin this story with a theme. I knew what I wanted to do. I was teaching a Sunday School class at the time, and I longed to lift the personality of Jesus off the flat and lifeless pages of our textbook. I wanted to give my pupils, and others like them, a glimpse of the divided and turbulent society of Palestine, an occupied country with many parallels in our own day. And I wanted to stir in them some personal sharing of what must have been the response of boys and girls who actually saw and heard the carpenter from Nazareth.

"But how could I portray Jesus, when many years of searching to understand his life and his teachings left me still facing a mystery? I read countless versions of the life of Jesus, most of them written with reverence and deep faith, some with skepticism, a few even with venom, each one differing from the others. The personality of the Man from Nazareth has been at the mercy of hundreds of interpreters. There is no definitive biography. The quest for the historical Jesus has never yielded the surety for which the scholars hoped. The incontestable facts of history barely establish his having lived at all. Yet he stands like a mountain peak, which, however high we climb, looms forever higher, rising into the mist, its full dimension hidden from our sight.

"In the end I realized that in this case research was defeating my purpose and only clouding my vision. The sum of my search is contained in one line which I put into the mouth of Simon the disciple, 'We are forced to choose, not knowing.' In my portrait of Jesus I failed. I know that failure was intrinsic in the attempt, but I wish that I could have climbed higher. I knew before I had gone far on this road that I was not big enough to do what I had hoped. But I set myself to do, to the best of my ability, one small thing. I would show the change wrought in just one boy who came to know the teacher in Galilee. This is the story of *The Bronze Bow.*"[3]

In her Newbery acceptance speech, Speare articulated her writer's creed. "I believe that all of us who are concerned with children are committed to the salvaging of Love and Honor and Duty. Not only our own faith, but the children themselves compel us. Young people do not want to accept meaninglessness. They look urgently to the adult world for evidence that we have proved our values to be enduring. Yet perhaps never before have they looked so clearly, so despairingly, at the evidence we offer. They demand an honest answer. Those of us who have found Love and Honor and Duty to be a sure foundation must somehow find words which have the ring of truth."[3]

She then wrote the nonfiction classic, *Life in Colonial America.* Speare pondered her interest in the past. "Every book begins with questions. How must it have seemed to the people who lived through this experience? What choices would I have made in their place? I must find the answers by going back in the past, by living side by side with them until the world they lived in becomes as real to me as the room in which I am working. This is an enormously satisfying experience. I find that I always come back to my own problems with renewed perspective and a sort of reinforcement of the spirit.

It is exactly these gifts from the past that I think a young person—a person of any age, but especially a young person—can gain from the reading of historical fiction.

"When I read Bruno Bettelheim's persuasive book, *The Uses of Enchantment,* I was delighted to find my own tenuous philosophy articulated with a skill that I could never approach. It is his thesis, and I do not quote him exactly, that children need heroes with whom they can identify, heroes who face terrifying and seemingly insurmountable odds and, armed with courage and truth, win out against them—that in reading of such heroes children are strengthened and given courage to face the very real dangers and difficulties of their own lives. Bettelheim was writing of fairy tales and fantasy. But I thought, as I read his words, that very much the same function is fulfilled by the historical novel. Historical fiction, too, gives young people heroes who have faced the testing of courage and endurance, and it offers the heartening assurance that in every age there have been men and women who have stood bravely against danger and injustice and tyranny.

"But history, unlike fairy tales, cannot promise a happy-ever-after ending. History itself is a record of injustice. And children learn very early that life is not fair and that dangers have not always been overcome. Even to walk through the living room when the evening news is coming from the television can be a shattering experience for a child. I do not believe that a historical novel should gloss over the pain and ugliness. But I do believe that the hero with whom a young reader identifies should on the last page not be left in despair but should still be standing, with the strength to go on to whatever the future may hold."[4]

FOOTNOTE SOURCES

[1]Publicity from Houghton.
[2]Elizabeth George Speare, "Newbery Award Acceptance," *Horn Book,* August, 1959.
[3]E. G. Speare, "Report of a Journey: Newbery Award Acceptance," *Horn Book,* August, 1962.
[4]E. G. Speare, "Laura Ingalls Wilder Award Acceptance," *Horn Book,* July/August, 1989.

FOR MORE INFORMATION SEE:

Publishers Weekly, March 23, 1959 (p. 21ff), March 19, 1962 (p. 28ff).
Wilson Library Bulletin, April, 1959 (p. 542).
ALA Bulletin, April, 1959 (p. 309ff).
Library Journal, April 15, 1959 (p. 1291ff), March 15, 1962 (p. 1254).
Current Biography 1959, H. W. Wilson, 1960.
Junior Bookshelf, November, 1962 (p. 269), November, 1963 (p. 304).
Commentary, February, 1963 (p. 112ff).
Muriel Fuller, editor, *More Junior Authors,* H. W. Wilson, 1963.
Lee Kingman, editor, *Newbery and Caldecott Medal Books 1956-1965,* Horn Book, 1965.
Young Reader's Review, October, 1966.
Best Sellers, June 1, 1967.
Times Literary Supplement, September 7, 1967.
Martha E. Ward and Dorothy A. Marquardt, *Authors of Books for Young People,* 2nd edition, Scarecrow, 1971.
"Profiles in Literature" (videotape), Temple University.
Lee Bennett Hopkins, *More Books by More People,* Citation, 1974.
D. L. Kirkpatrick, *Twentieth-Century Children's Writers,* St. Martin's, 1978, 2nd edition, 1983.

As punishment, the boy in front is being made to wear a wooden gag and sign. (Illustration by Charles Walker from *Life in Colonial America* by Elizabeth George Speare.)

"A Visit with Elizabeth George Speare" (videotape), Houghton.
Horn Book, March/April, 1988 (p. 163ff).

COLLECTIONS

Mugar Memorial Library, Boston University.

STEINER, George 1929-

PERSONAL: Born April 23, 1929, in Paris, France; came to the United States in 1940, naturalized citizen, 1944; son of Frederick George and Elsie (Franzos) Steiner; married Zara Alice Shakow (a diplomatic historian), July 7, 1955; children: David Milton, Deborah Tarn. *Education:* University of Chicago, B.A., 1948; Harvard University, M.A., 1950; Oxford University, Ph.D., 1955. *Home:* 32 Barrow Rd., Cambridge, England.

CAREER: Economist, London, England, member of editorial staff, 1952-56; Institute for Advanced Study, Princeton, N.J., fellow, 1956-58; Princeton University, Princeton, Gauss Lecturer, 1959-60; Cambridge University, Cambridge, England, fellow of Churchill College, 1961—. Visiting professor at New York University, 1966-67; University of California, Regents Lecturer, 1973, Massey Lecturer, 1974; University of Geneva, Geneva, Switzerland, professor of English and comparative literature, 1974. *Member:* Royal Society of Literature (fellow), Athenaeum Club (London), Savile Club (London) Harvard Club (New York City). *Awards, honors:* Bell Prize, 1950; Rhodes Scholar, 1955; Fullbright Professorship, 1958-59; O'Henry Short Story Prize, 1959; Zabel Award from the National Institute of Arts and Letters (United States), 1970; Guggenheim Fellowship, 1971-72; Cortina Ulisse Prize, 1972; D.Litt from the University of East Anglia, 1976; *The Portage to San Cristobal of A. H.* was named one of *School Library Journal*'s Best Books for Young Adults, 1982.

WRITINGS:

Tolstoy or Dostoevsky: An Essay in the Old Criticism, Penguin, 1958, Dutton, 1971.
The Death of Tragedy, Hill & Wang, 1960.
(Editor with R. Fagles) *Homer: A Collection of Critical Essays,* Prentice-Hall, 1962.
Anno Domini: Three Stories, Atheneum, 1964.
(Editor) *The Penguin Book of Modern Verse Translation,* Penguin, 1966, reissued as *Poem into Poem: World Poetry in Modern Verse Translation,* Penguin, 1970.
Language and Silence: Essays on Language, Literature, and the Inhuman, Atheneum, 1967.
Extraterritorial: Literature and the Language Revolution, Atheneum, 1971.

In Bluebeard's Castle: Some Notes toward the Redefinition of Culture, Yale University Press, 1971.
Fields of Force: Fischer and Spassky at Reykjavik, Viking, 1974.
Nostalgia for the Absolute, CBC Enterprises, 1974.
After Babel: Aspects of Language and Translation, Oxford University Press, 1975.
Martin Heidegger, Viking, 1978 (published in England as *Heidegger,* Fontana, 1978).
On Difficulty and Other Essays, Oxford University Press, 1978.
The Portage to San Cristobal of A. H., Simon & Schuster, 1981.
George Steiner: A Reader, Oxford University Press, 1984.
Antigones, Oxford University Press, 1984.
Real Presence: Is There Anything in What We Say?, University of Chicago Press, 1989.

Contributor of numerous reviews, stories, and articles to periodicals and journals, including *Commentary, Harper's, Nation,* and *New Yorker.*

RECORDINGS

"A Necessary Treason: The Poet and the Translator" (cassette), J. Norton, 1970.
"The Poet as Translator: To Traduce or Transfigure," J. Norton, 1970.

HOBBIES AND OTHER INTERESTS: Music, chess, mountain walking.

GEORGE STEINER

FOR MORE INFORMATION SEE:

Times Literary Supplement, September 28, 1967.
New Statesman, October 20, 1967, January 31, 1975.
Yale Review, autumn, 1967.
Commonweal, October 27, 1967.
London, December, 1967.
Commentary, October, 1968, November, 1975.
Time, July 26, 1971.
New Yorker, May 5, 1975.
Christian Science Monitor, May 25, 1975.
New York Times Book Review, June 9, 1975.
New York Review of Books, October 30, 1975.
Contemporary Literary Criticism, Volume 24, Gale, 1983.
Dictionary of Literary Biography, Volume 67, Gale, 1988.

TAMAR, Erika 1934-

PERSONAL: Accent is on last syllable of surname; born June 10, 1934, in Vienna, Austria; came to the United States, 1939; daughter of Julius (a physician) and Pauline (a housewife; maiden name, Huterer) Tamar; divorced; children: Ray, Monica, Michael. *Education:* New York University—Washington Square College, B.A., 1955. *Politics:* "Sometimes Democrat, often eclectic." *Religion:* Jewish. *Home:* New York, N.Y. *Agent:* Joanna Cole, Elaine Markson Agency, 44 Greenwich Ave., New York, N.Y. 10011.

CAREER: Leo Burnett Co., Inc., New York, N.Y., production assistant/casting director for "Search for Tomorrow" television serial, 1959-64; free-lance writer, 1982—. Play Troupe of Port Washington (community theater), actress and director. *Member:* Authors Guild, Society of Children's Book Writers. *Awards, honors: Blues for Silk Garcia* was selected one of New York Public Library's Books for the Teen Age, 1983, and *Good-bye, Glamour Girl,* 1984; *It Happened at Cecilia's* was selected one of American Library Association's Young Adult Books for Reluctant Readers, 1990.

WRITINGS:

Blues for Silk Garcia, Crown, 1983.
Good-bye, Glamour Girl, Lippincott, 1984.
It Happened at Cecilia's, Atheneum, 1989.
High Cheekbones, Viking, 1990.
Out of Control, Atheneum, in press.

WORK IN PROGRESS: The Summer of Susan, for Atheneum; a sequel to *It Happened at Cecilia's;* a sports series for young readers; picture books; an adult novel.

SIDELIGHTS: "I was born in Vienna, Austria and came to the United States in 1939, just before my fifth birthday. My older brother and I were refugees from the Nazis and we came to the United States with a B'nai B'rith rescue action of fifty children. We lived with a foster family in Houston, Texas. My parents were able to come over several months later after the war had already broken out, and we joined them in New York City where I grew up.

Good-bye, Glamour Girl picks up my story from the time I arrived in New York. It is fiction, of course, but it includes my father's efforts to start all over again as a physician and my

'Americanization' via the movies. *Blues for Silk Garcia,* takes place in a facsimile of Port Washington, where I lived for many years, and my love for jazz, my daughter's virtuosity in classical guitar became the basis of a fictional story. We had a parakeet when I was writing it, so even parakeets flew into the novel. *It Happened at Cecilia's* takes place in Greenwich Village, an area that I've loved since my New York University undergraduate days. The story concerns the ups and downs of a Cajun-Hungarian restaurant, and a cat named Katie is an important character. My older children sometimes worked in restaurants during their college days and I used their often zany stories. My beloved cat Katie had a very similar adventure, and I'm sure you can guess my favorite cuisine. *High Cheekbones* tells the story of a young girl who is suddenly catapulted into the world of high-fashion modeling, a world for which she is totally unprepared. It is loosely based on a model I knew during my television days. My experiences and feelings, people I've known, things that move me or make me laugh, go into my novels in big fictionalized chunks—and that's what makes writing so much fun.

"I've loved reading as long as I can remember and I've always liked telling a story. I think I always wanted to be a writer—except for the period when I wanted to be a movie star. (I took that as far as being a child actress in an off-Broadway play—a terrific experience that I might write about someday.) I majored in English with emphasis on creative writing at New York University; I was sidetracked by a class in screenwriting and then classes in film production, and by graduation, I really wanted to direct television or film—another way of telling a story. It was probably a rather unrealistic dream in that pre-feminist era. I was production assistant and casting director for a television serial for five

I didn't believe in talent scouts all that much, not deep in my heart, but you never knew. (Jacket illustration by John Quirk from *Good-bye, Glamour Girl* by Erika Tamar.)

years, when television was live and less compartmentalized—and someday I'll write about that crazy and exciting time, too. When my first child was born, I moved to Long Island. I was a full-time mother and satisfied my creative urge by getting involved with community theater. It was the young adult novels that my children brought home that spurred me—the 'I can do that' syndrome. A writing workshop at the New School taught by Margaret Gabel was very helpful. So now I'm a writer at last and absolutely delighted to be."

TEGNER, Bruce 1928-1985

PERSONAL: Born October 28, 1928, in Chicago, Ill.; died in 1985; married Alice McGrath. *Education:* LaVerne College, B.A., 1975. *Residence:* Ventura, Calif.

CAREER: Specialist in self-defense and sport forms of weaponless fighting; has trained actors and devised fight scenes for films and television; operator of Bruce Tegner School, Hollywood, Calif., 1952-67; Moorpark College, Moorpark, Calif., instructor in defense tactics, beginning 1970; taught in Physical Education Division, Ventura College, Ventura, Calif. *Military service:* U.S. Army, 1950-52; trained instructors to teach weaponless fighting, taught military police tactics, and coached sport judo teams.

ERIKA TAMAR

BRUCE TEGNER

WRITINGS:

Karate, Thor, Volume I: *The Open Hand and Foot Fighting,* 1959, 3rd edition, 1965, Volume II: *Traditional Forms for Sport,* 1959, 3rd edition, 1963.

Bruce Tegner Method of Self-Defense: The Best of Judo, Jiu-Jitsu, Karate, Savate, Yawara, Aikido, Ate-waza, Thor, 1960, 3rd edition, 1971.

Savate: French Foot Fighting, Self-Defense, Sport, Thor, 1960, 3rd revised edition, 1982.

Aikido Self-Defense: Holds and Locks for Modern Use, Thor, 1961.

Judo for Fun: Sport Techniques Made Easy, Thor, 1961.

Self-Defense for Women: A Simple Method, Thor, 1961, 2nd edition (with wife, Alice McGrath), 1969.

Stick Fighting for Self-Defense: Yawara, Police Club, Aikido, Cane, Quarter-Staff, Thor, 1961, 3rd edition, 1972.

Teach Your Boy Self-Defense and Self-Confidence, Thor, 1961.

Judo-Karate for Police Officers: Defense and Control, a Simple Method, Thor, 1962.

Bruce Tegner's Complete Book of Self-Defense, Stein & Day, 1963, revised edition, Thor, 1975.

Judo and Karate Belt Degrees: Requirements, Rules, Regulations, Thor, 1963, revised edition, 1967.

Judo and Karate Exercises: Physical Conditioning for the Un-Armed Fighting Arts, Thor, 1963, revised edition published as *Karate and Judo Exercises,* 1981.

Karate: Self Defense and Sport, Dell, 1963.

Isometric Power Exercises, Dell, 1964.

Instant Self-Defense, Grosset, 1965.

Bruce Tegner's Complete Book of Karate, Bantam, 1966, 3rd edition, Thor, 1970.

Black Belt Judo, Karate, and Jukado: Advanced Techniques for Experts, Thor, 1967.

Complete Book of Judo, Thor, 1967, revised edition published as *Bruce Tegner's Complete Book of Judo,* 1975.

Complete Book of Karate, Thor, 1967, 3rd edition, 1970.

(With A. McGrath) *Self-Defense for Girls: A Secondary School and College Manual,* Thor, 1967, revised edition, Grosset, 1969.

Complete Book of Jukado Self-Defense: Judo, Karate, Aikido (Jiu-Jitsu Modernized), Thor, 1968.

Kung Fu and Tai Chi: Chinese Karate and Classical Exercises, Thor, 1968, revised edition, 1981.

Self-Defense: Nerve Centers and Pressure Points for Atewaza, Jukado, and Karate, Thor, 1968, revised edition, 1978.

Self-Defense for Boys and Men: A Secondary School and College Manual, Thor, 1968, revised edition, 1969.

Aikido and Jiu-Jitsu Holds and Locks, Thor, 1969.

Bruce Tegner's Complete Book of Aikido and Holds and Locks, Grosset, 1970.

Judo for Fun: Sport Techniques, Thor, 1970.

Self-Defense You Can Teach Your Boy: A Confidence-Building Course, Thor, 1970.

Defense Tactics for Law Enforcement: Weaponless Defense and Control, Thor, 1972, revised edition, 1978.

Stick Fighting: Sport Forms, Thor, 1973.

Judo: Sport Techniques for Physical Fitness and Tournament, Thor, 1976.

(With A. McGrath) *Self-Defense for Your Child,* Thor, 1976.

Bruce Tegner's Complete Book of Jiu-Jitsu, Thor, 1977.

(With A. McGrath) *Self-Defense and Assault Prevention for Girls and Women,* Thor, 1977.

Self-Defense: A Basic Course, Thor, 1979.

(With A. McGrath) *Solo Forms of Karate, Tai Chi, Aikido, and Kung Fu,* Thor, 1981.

Judo: Beginner to Black Belt, Thor, 1982.

Karate: Beginner to Black Belt, Thor, 1982.

(From *Karate: Beginner to Black Belt* by Bruce Tegner.)

(From *Aikido and Bokata* by Bruce Tegner.)

(With A. McGrath) *The Survival Book,* Thor, 1982.
Aikido and Bokata, Thor, 1983.

SIDELIGHTS: Bruce Tegner was born in Chicago, Illinois, where his training in martial arts started at the age of two. His mother and father, both professional teachers in Judo and Jiu-Jitsu, instructed him until he was eight when he began studying with Asian and European experts. After he won the California State judo championship at twenty-one, Tegner gave up competition to further his education in the field, and teach. "Karate is the generic term for many styles of the martial arts which use hand and foot blows as their primary techniques. It is thought that a form of karate originated in Tibet, was introduced to China, and from there spread to the other Asian countries. In each country adaptations occurred and stylistic differences developed.

"Some specialties of the martial arts are practices for recreation and fitness, some for self-defense, and others are tournament sports. Today's adaptations of the martial arts include the lovely, gentle movements of tai chi, the heavy power punching of some styles of karate, formalized *sumo* wrestling, the stylized routines of aikido, practical self-defense based on jiu-jitsu, and sport judo as it is played in the Olympic Games.

"The Zen Buddhist influence is important in some of the martial arts. Others are concerned only with fighting skill or fitness exercises. Concepts range from glorification of feudal attitudes (identifying with samurai warriors) to an appreciation of the health and safety concerns of modern physical education.

"If 'martial arts' included boxing and Western styles of archery and fencing, it would be more accurate. These and other Western sports also derive from ancient battle skills and have been modified for present-day recreation and competition."[1]

His broad knowledge, in all forms of the martial arts, earned Tegner a world-wide reputation as an authority on the subject. "Today there are about a dozen main styles of karate, with many substyles and hundreds of sub-substyles. Each teacher believes that his style is best. If there is, in fact, a 'best' style, we must ask why there is no consensus and why there are still so many variations in karate styles. The answer suggests itself: There is no 'best' karate. There are personal preferences for different schools, teachers, and styles.

"Kung fu, or gung fu, wu shue and pa kua are among the Chinese styles of karate. Tai kwan do and hapkido are Korean styles. Okinawa-te is practiced in Okinawa. Tai boxing, or Siamese boxing, is another style, and is thought to have influenced savate, French fist-and-foot fighting.

"But no matter what name is used, the many styles of karate have this in common: they all use a relatively small group of hand blows and kicking techniques. An open hand slashing blow is, after all, an open hand slashing blow whether it is used in kenpo karate, shito-ryu, or called by a Japanese, Korean, Chinese or English name.

"Some karate styles emphasize hand blows more than kicking techniques. Some styles emphasize foot blows. Some styles train to develop power and strength (the hard schools), while others train for speed and precision (the soft schools)."[1]

Over the years Tegner developed a system of karate which he presented in his book *Karate: Beginner to Black Belt,* in 1982.

"It is a system based on several styles . . . . I have selected the techniques and arranged the material in what I believe to be the most useful for individuals studying alone and have divided it into sections that are characteristic of proficiency ranking found in many styles of karate."[1]

From 1952 through 1967 Tegner operated a school in Hollywood, California, where he taught men, women, children, and blind and disabled people. He trained actors, including Rick Nelson, James Coburn, and Joan Crawford for film, and he choreographed fight scenes for movies and television. "Self-defense does not begin with the act of striking back; it starts with concepts of self-respect, self-reliance and autonomy. Self-respect is the feeling that your individual self is worth defending from assault; self-reliance is the conviction that you are competent to take care of yourself; autonomy implies that you are able to make decisions for yourself and take responsibility for your health and well being."[2]

"In my view, the basis for a rational, ethical, practical method of self-defense is the recognition that there is a wide range of aggressive actions from mildly hostile to very serious. Defense actions should be appropriate to the situation. Treating all aggressive actions as though they were vicious assault is counterproductive. Individuals who are taught to defend themselves against a serious assault but do not know how to cope with demeaning horseplay have the choice of overreacting or not reacting at all. Overreacting means using more force than is appropriate. Passive submission may result in persistent feelings of powerlessness, rage, frustration and humiliation. Such feelings lead to a loss of self-respect and self-control.

"On televison and in movie theaters there is constant reinforcement of the myth that manly men are violent. The message coming from the screens is that there are only two kinds of men— the dominating, violent, punishing, vigilante male who is admired, and the passive, helpless, incompetent victim who is despised or pitied.

"Since neither of these stereotypes offers a satisfying model for self-actualization in the real world it appears that there are two intolerable alternatives and no acceptable choices.

"There is another choice but it is seldom portrayed on the screen and not often discussed. The rational alternative to aggression is not submission, but assertion. The rational choice is to refuse to play the game of abused-or-abuser. The life-enhancing choice is to become self-reliant, able to cope with the threat of assault using the least possible force and knowing the procedures which minimize the possibility of having to use physical defense actions."[3]

FOOTNOTE SOURCES

[1]Bruce Tegner, *Karate: Beginner to Black Belt,* Thor, 1982.
[2]B. Tegner and Alice McGrath, *Self-Defense and Assault Prevention for Girls and Women,* Thor, 1977.
[3]B. Tegner, *Self-Defense: A Basic Course,* Thor, 1979.

TILLY, Nancy 1935-

PERSONAL: Born June 8, 1935, in Atlanta, Ga.; daughter of Bradford (a publisher) and Sarah (a housewife; maiden name, Davis) McFadden; married Eben Fletcher Tilly, Jr. (a group travel coordinator), July 27, 1963; children: John Eben Bradford. *Education:* University of North Carolina at Chapel Hill, B.A. (with honors), 1957, M.A., 1958; Univer-

NANCY TILLY

sity of Chicago, M.A., 1960. *Politics:* Democrat. *Religion:* Episcopalian. *Home and office:* 628 Kensington Dr., Chapel Hill, N.C. 27514. *Agent:* Jean V. Naggar, Jean V. Naggar Literary Agency, 216 East 75th St., New York, N.Y. 10021.

CAREER: City Colleges of Chicago, Chicago, Ill., instructor in English, 1961-63, assistant professor of humanities, 1964-68, associate professor of humanities, 1968-73; writer, 1973—. Teacher of creative writing to elementary school students, 1977-82. *Member:* Society of Children's Book Writers, National Book Critics Circle (board member), North Carolina Writers' Network, Phi Beta Kappa. *Awards, honors:* Second Prize from the *Carolina Quarterly* Fiction Contest, 1979, for short story "Belle of the Ball," and 1986, for "Marina Grande"; First Prize in North Carolina Writers Contest, 1979, for "Two Women"; Fellow, Bread Loaf Writers' Conference, 1985; North Carolina Division of the American Association of University Women Award in Juvenile Literature, 1986, for *Golden Girl.*

WRITINGS:

Golden Girl (young adult novel), Farrar, Straus, 1985.

Contributor of articles, reviews, interviews, and stories to magazines and newspapers, including *Writer's Digest* and *North Carolina Homes and Gardens.* Book reviewer, *Newspaper* (Chapel Hill, N.C.), late 1970s—, *News and Observer* (Raleigh, N.C.), 1986—, *Morning Herald* (Durham, N.C.), and *Journal* (Winston-Salem, N.C.).

WORK IN PROGRESS: All American Love, an adult novel; *Winter Fireworks,* a young adult novel about the Thornton family's Christmas holiday visit to their grandmother's in Austria.

SIDELIGHTS: "I have wanted to be a writer since I was nine years old and in love with Judy Bolton and Nancy Drew, girl detectives. My fifth grade essay on the vice-president of the Confederacy won a prize. I dreamed of glorious places and idyllic families, but only wrote an unromantic high school gossip column called 'The Foghorn.' I, too, was called 'Foghorn' because damp weather and yelling at football games made me hoarse. My first published short story came out in the school magazine. Classmates from those days remember me as a cheerleader. I confess the truth: I was an alternate.

"I graduated with honors in creative writing from the University of North Carolina in Chapel Hill. Jesse Rehder and Max Steele asked what I had learned from the course. I replied, 'That I don't want to be a writer.' This was untrue: It was criticism I was terrified of. To write was my deepest wish. Instead, I did graduate study at the University of North Carolina and the University of Chicago.

"After two Masters' degrees, I fulfilled a dream with a seven-month tour of Europe. Back in the real world, I taught in the Chicago City Colleges and married Eben Tilly, who promotes international travel. We honeymooned in Greece. I published two articles about Europe. An insomniac, I filled notebook after notebook with existential anguish. I wrote long letters and the occasional short story, but couldn't finish my stories or revise and send them out. We roamed Scandinavia, Mexico, and the south of France. We spent Christmas in Austria, twice, but something was missing. Russia left us depressed. We went to London and Curacao. I quit teaching, had a longed-for baby, and we moved to Chapel Hill.

"When our son Jeb went to kindergarten, I missed him so that I searched for a consuming activity. 'Get a Ph.D. and go back to teaching,' my friends urged. I needed more than that. A writing course made me feel better right away. I entered writers' contests and had good luck.

"Our family bought a Queen Anne Victorian cottage in Beaufort, behind North Carolina's Outer Banks. I fell in love with our house, our neighbors, the town. I yearned for people to recognize good mothers in all their guises and to take children as seriously as adults. To get all those feelings onto paper was my passion and the origin of *Golden Girl.* A well-known writer at the Bread Loaf Writers' Conference told me to throw that manuscript 'into the fire.' Later, I discovered those were the immortal words of Goethe which were the making of Schiller as an artist. It would have helped to know this earlier. Jean Naggar, a literary agent I met at Bread Loaf, took *Golden Girl* on. I thought she'd sell the book in a month. It took five years.

"I wrote a second book, an adult novel, *All American Love.* Our family travelled to Austria, and I fell in love with its winter beauty. At the rate my stories were selling, I figured I could write and sell a novel more quickly. That turned out to be true.

"My first contract gave me half the money for *Golden Girl* 'up front,' the other half to be paid if the publisher accepted my revisions. My editor and I had rapport. In six months, I received the balance of the money. Then came copy-editing.

Maybe Jack finally took some notice of me, Penny thought. (Jacket illustration by William Low from *Golden Girl* by Nancy Tilly.)

Day after day, my editor and I went over every sentence, page, chapter, striking through words, phrases, clauses, whole paragraphs. Always she asked, 'Is this necessary?' This was the forging of my craft. *Golden Girl* won a juvenile literature prize, had a second printing and a paperback sale.

"I began *Winter Fireworks* to explore the good of a visit to grandmother in Austria for all seven members of the Thornton family, especially fourteen-year-old Cassie. My husband took us to Kitzbuehel to do research. Eighty-two pages of notes later, I had learned enough to finish the book. My publisher turned the manuscript down. My agent sent it to another house.

"My stories often receive encouraging letters from the respected literary magazines that reject them. Occasionally I win a prize or see my work in print. I teach workshops, read and speak when asked. One day, I believe, someone will publish *Winter Fireworks* and *All American Love.* I have several novels and short stories in mind, and am currently writing stories as well as articles and reviews for newspapers and magazines. Last year I made less than 1,500 dollars. Why do I keep writing?

"I suspect that in following my characters, I am working out something for myself. No other vocation would allow me to sit down at 8:30 in the morning, look up five minutes later and find it's three in the afternoon. My half-formed, almost never-admitted wish is to write something so deeply felt that

someone somewhere will read it and cry, 'Yes, that's the way it is. That's the truth!'"

HOBBIES AND OTHER INTERESTS: Swimming, fishing, waterskiing, surfing, biking, skateboarding, cooking, gardening, playing scrabble, Word Yahtzee, gin rummy.

FOR MORE INFORMATION SEE:

News-Times (Carteret County, N.C.), June 3, 1985.
Herald (Durham, N.C.), October 27, 1985.

TUNNICLIFFE, C(harles) F(rederick) 1901-1979

PERSONAL: Born December 1, 1901, in Langley, East Cheshire, England; died in 1979; son of William (a farmer) and Margaret Tunnicliffe; married Winifred Wonnacott (an artist), 1929 (died, 1969). *Education:* Attended Macclesfield School of Art and Manchester School of Art; Royal College of Art, Diploma in Painting, 1923, and A.R.C.A.

CAREER: Painter, engraver, and illustrator. *Member:* Royal Academy (associate). *Awards, honors:* Gold Medal from the Royal Society for the Protection of Birds, 1975; Officer of the Order of the British Empire, 1978.

WRITINGS:

SELF-ILLUSTRATED

My Country Book, Studio, 1942.
Bird Portraiture, Studio, 1945.
How to Draw Farm Animals, Studio, 1947.
(With Sidney Rogerson) *Our Bird Book,* Collins, 1947.
Mereside Chronicle: With a Short Interlude of Lochs and Lochans, Scribner, 1948.
(With S. Rogerson) *Both Sides of the Road,* Collins, 1949.
Birds of the Estuary, Penguin, 1952.
Shorelands Summer Diary, Collins, 1952.
Wild Birds in Britain, Happy House, 1974.
A Sketchbook of Birds, Holt, 1979.
Tunnicliffe's Birds, Gollancz, 1983.

ILLUSTRATOR

Henry Williamson, *Tarka the Otter* (juvenile), Putnam, 1932, reissued, 1949.
H. Williamson, *The Lone Swallows,* Putnam, 1933.
H. Williamson, *The Old Stag,* Putnam, 1933.
H. Williamson, *The Star Born,* Faber, 1933.
Kit Higson, *The Dull House,* Putnam, 1934.
Richard Patrick Russ, *Beast Royal,* Putnam, 1934.
Harcourt Williams, *Tales from Ebony,* Putnam, 1934, new edition, Nattali & Maurice, 1947.
H. Williamson *The Peregrine's Saga,* Putnam, 1934.

(From "The Three Sillies," in *Tales from Ebony* by Harcourt Williams. Illustrated by C. F. Tunnicliffe.)

H. Williamson, *Salar the Salmon,* Faber, 1936, new edition, 1948.
Mary Priestley, *A Book of Birds,* Gollancz, 1937.
Kenneth Williamson, *The Sky's Their Highway,* Putnam, 1937.
E. L. Grant Watson, editor, *Nature Abounding,* Faber, 1941, new edition, 1951.
H. E. Bates, *In the Heart of the Country,* Country Life, 1942.
Negley Farson, *Going Fishing,* Country Life, 1942.
H. E. Bates, *O More Than Happy Countryman,* Country Life, 1943.
Mary O'Hara, *My Friend Flicka,* Eyre & Spottiswoode, 1943.
Alison Uttley, *Country Hoard,* Faber, 1943.
E. L. Grant Watson, *Walking with Fancy,* Country Life, 1943.
Charles S. Bayne, *Exploring England,* Collins, 1944.
D. H. Chapman, *Farmer Jim,* Harrap, 1944.
F. F. Darling, *The Care of Farm Animals,* Oxford University Press and National Federation of Young Farmers' Clubs, 1944.
Charles S. Bayne, *The Call of the Birds,* Collins, 1944.
R. T. Gould, *Communications Old and New,* R. A. Publishing, n.d.
Richard Church, *Green Tide,* Country Life, 1945.
A. Uttley, *The Country Child,* Faber, 1945.
R. I. Pocock and others, *The Wonders of Nature,* Odhams, n.d., reissued, 1946.

Charles Tunnicliffe at the Royal College of Art, about 1921. (From *Portrait of a Country Artist* by Ian Niall.)

Norman Ellison, *Wandering with Nomad,* University of London Press, 1946.

A. Uttley, *Country Things,* Faber, 1946.

C. Henry Warren, *Happy Countryman,* Eyre & Spottiswoode, 1946.

Robert Forman, *The Art of Scraperboard,* Clifford Milburn, 1946.

N. Ellison, *Out of Doors with Nomad,* University of London Press, 1947.

Terence Horsley, *Fishing and Flying,* Eyre & Spottiswoode, 1947.

T. Horsley, *The Long Flight,* Country Life, 1947.

Ronald M. Lockley, *Letters from Skokholm,* Dent, 1947.

Crichton Porteous, *Farmer's Creed,* Harrap, 1947.

W. F. R. Reynolds, *Angling Conclusions,* Faber, 1947.

E. L. Grant Watson, *The Leaves Return,* Country Life, 1947.

The Children's Wonder Book in Colour, Odhams, c. 1948.

N. Ellison, *Over the Hills with Nomad,* University of London Press, 1948.

R. M. Lockley, *The Cinnamon Bird,* Staples Press, 1948.

A. Uttley, *Carts and Candlesticks,* Faber, 1948.

Percy V. Bradshaw, *Come Sketching,* Studio, 1949.

N. Ellison, *Roving with Nomad,* University of London Press, 1949.

(Frontispiece from *Salar the Salmon* by Henry Williamson. Illustrated by C. F. Tunnicliffe.)

Richard Jefferies, *Wild Life in a Southern County,* Lutterworth, 1949, Moonraker Press, 1978.

A. Uttley, *The Farm on the Hill,* Faber, 1949.

Brian Vesey-Fitzgerald, *Rivermouth,* Eyre & Spottiswoode, 1949.

E. L. Grant Watson, *Profitable Wonders,* Country Life, 1949.

Nature through the Seasons in Colour, Odhams, n.d.

N. Ellison, *Adventuring with Nomad,* University of London Press, 1950.

C. D. Dimsdale, *Come Out of Doors,* Hutchinson, 1951.

N. Ellison, *Northwards with Nomad,* University of London Press, 1951.

Monica Edwards, *Punchbowl Midnight,* Collins, 1951.

A. Uttley, *Ambush of Young Days,* Faber, 1951.

Rachel L. Carson, *Under the Sea-Wind,* Staples Press, 1952.

(Contributor) *Oxford Union Encyclopaedia,* Oxford University Press, 1952.

A. Uttley, *Plowmen's Clocks,* Faber, 1952.

Ernest Hemingway, *The Old Man and the Sea,* J. Cape, 1953.

J. C. W. Houghton, *Rural Studies Book 4,* Dent, 1953.

A. Uttley, *Here's a New Day,* Faber, 1956.

A. Uttley, *A Year in the Country,* Faber, 1957.

M. E. Gragg, *The Farm,* Wills & Hepworth, 1958.

R. Meinertzhagen, *Pirates and Predators,* Oliver & Boyd, 1959.

A. Uttley, *The Swans Fly Over,* Faber, 1959.

E. L. Grant Watson, *What to Look for in Winter,* Wills & Hepworth, 1959.

A. Uttley, *Something for Nothing,* Faber, 1960.

E. L. Grant Watson, *What to Look for in Summer,* Wills & Hepworth, 1960.

E. L. Grant Watson, *What to Look for in Autumn,* Wills & Hepworth, 1960.

J. Wentworth Day, *British Birds of the Wild Places,* Blandford Press, 1961.

Drawing for "Radio Times," forward by R. D. Usherwood, Bodley Head, 1961.

E. L. Grant Watson, *What to Look for in Spring,* Wills & Hepworth, 1961.

A. J. Huxley, *Wild Flowers of the Countryside,* Blandford Press, 1962.

A. Uttley, *Wild Honey,* Faber, 1962.

(Contributor) A. Landsborough Thomson, editor, *A New Dictionary of Birds,* T. Nelson, 1964.

A. Uttley, *Cuckoo in June,* Faber, 1964.

Ian Niall, *The Way of a Countryman,* Country Life, 1965.

Arthur Cadman, *Dawn, Dusk and Deer,* Country Life, 1966.

(Contributor) James Fisher, *The Shell Bird Book,* Ebury Press, 1966.

A. Uttley, *A Pack of Gold,* Faber, 1966.

George Ewart Evans, *The Horse in the Furrow,* Faber, 1967.

I. Niall, *A Galloway Childhood,* Heinemann, 1967.

I. Niall, *A Fowler's World,* Heinemann, 1968.

A. Uttley, *The Button Box and Other Essays,* Faber, 1968.

R. M. Lockley, *The Island,* Deutsch, 1969.

R. M. Lockley, *The Naturalist in Wales,* David & Charles, 1970.

A. Uttley, *A Ten O'Clock Scholar,* Faber, 1970.

C. L. Coles, editor, *The Complete Book of Game Conservation,* Barrie & Jenkins, 1971.

A. Uttley, *Secret Places,* Faber, 1972.

R. M. Lockley, *Orielton,* Deutsch, 1977.

I. Niall, *To Speed the Plough,* Heinemann, 1977.

Linda Bennett, *The Royal Society for the Protection of Birds Book of British Birds,* Hamlyn, 1978.

Nellie W. Brocklehurst, *Up with the Country Lark,* Arthur H. Stockwell, 1978.

A. Uttley, *Country World: Memories of Childhood,* selected by Lucy Meredith, Faber, 1984.

Tunnicliffe's wood-engravings for Bob Martin's dog food ads.

SIDELIGHTS: C. F. Tunnicliffe was born on **December 1, 1901,** in Langley, East Cheshire, England, the only son of William and Margaret Tunnicliffe. His early life was spent drawing. "What urged me to draw and paint in the first place I cannot say; what is it which compels one man to be a farmer, another a wheelwright, and another a driver of trains?"

"When I was very young I scribbled shapes and marks which were supposed to be horses and cows. One of my earliest memories is of the occasion when my father erected a shed to house a cart and some implements. One side of the shed was made of wood, and was constructed of oblong-shaped panels framed up with thicker timber. The panels were most inviting, for had I not been given a fine, brand-new stick of chalk! The shed was duly creosoted and the panels dried out a nice dark brown colour, lovely! Chalk drawings would look grand on them! One day, on returning home, father found the whole side of the shed embellished with chalk drawings of

horses, cows, pigs, hens, ducks, pigeons and heaven knows what else. In spite of the fact that my drawings were now recognisable as particular animals and birds, he was not at all impressed—at least, not in the way I had hoped. What made matters worse was the fact that my wooden art gallery was in full view of the road which ran past the farm gate. It required weeks of rain before the drawings were obliterated, and, in the meantime, threats and ominous warnings had been uttered concerning chalk and any reappearance of it. So for a long time the chalk lay low and, when I had exhausted all the available clean paper in the house, I had to content myself with pencil scribbles on the white-washed walls of the shippons and stables.

"As I continued to deface the walls of the house and farm buildings, my Christmas presents became boxes of paints, drawing books and sketch blocks. I shall never forget my first sketch block—I thought it was a great invention: so flat and rigid, and with a beautiful clean sheet under each one I tore

(Scraperboard illustration from *Letters from Skokholm* by Ronald M. Lockley. Illustration by C. F. Tunnicliffe.)

off. Alas, the sketch block did not last for ever, and after I had drawn portraits of the cows which gave the most milk, the big sow and the glowing Rhode Island Red cock, not to mention various dogs, cats, and a neighbour's bull which persistently broke through into our pastures, I came at last to the cardboard back of the block."[1]

Tunnicliffe attended the Macclesfield School of Art and the Manchester School of Art. "And so to school, where the drawing lessons were the bright spots in a less bright routine of reading, writing, arithmetic, history and geography. Drawing lessons were held three times per week on Mondays, Wednesdays and Fridays. On Mondays we drew from white painted wooden models of cubes, prisms and cones. I cannot remember of what the Wednesday lesson consisted, but Friday was the day, for then we had memory drawing and could do just whatever we pleased. So the drawing books became filled with all sorts of things; savage beasts, cowboys and Indians, and, of course, the inevitable farm animals.

"As I grew older and stronger, more and more work on the farm fell to my lot. By the time I was ten years old I was up in the morning with the earliest, milking the cows. I also learnt to ride a horse and, although it was all bareback riding at first, I could never get enough of it."[1]

Tunnicliffe lived and worked on the farm until he was nineteen years old. Those early years influenced his work which was invariably steeped in nature and in the expression of the natural world surrounding him.

He also did a series of pencil drawings of his neighbors. "The parishioners of my native village were organising a garden fete, and someone suggested a way in which I might help in raising money. I agreed, on condition that at least forty of the parishioners sat for pencil portraits, the drawings to remain my property. In return I would exhibit the drawings at the fete and the parish would have whatever money was raised as admission to the exhibition. Round the countryside I went, drawing churchwardens, choirmen, farmers, members of the Mothers' Union and Girls' Friendly Society, the village blacksmith and the lads of the village, and a 'fine time was had by all' but especially the artist! One farmer's wife threatened to tear down the whole exhibition if I exhibited the drawing I had made of her husband. Another lady of the parish thought I was no artist as I had drawn *all* of her chins; yet another, who was not quite clear as to why I was doing the drawings, posed for me in her curling pins, and was frantic when she heard the news that she was to be exhibited locally. One farmer who had promised to sit for me must suddenly have changed his mind, for when I arrived in the farmyard all ready to draw him, he almost foamed at the mouth and threatened to shoot me with his twelve-bore. I beat a hasty retreat from the farm precincts and subsequent events showed that I had been wise in doing so. The exhibition was eventually held without mishap and I greatly prize those drawings for they are a very intimate link with my boyhood."[1]

1919-1923. After four years in London, Tunnicliffe received his diploma in 1923 from the Royal College of Art. "Smells of petrol and tar were everywhere, and I had not been in London more than an hour when I was wishing myself well out of it. What a fool to leave those fresh fields and lovely hills, the familiar faces and friendly animals! I would have given anything to be astride the black mare which I had helped to break in and which I was so fond of riding. That first month in London was a bad one: I was terribly homesick, and, to make matters worse, I was living in a tiny bed-sitting room, in Earls Court which was anything but homely and, emphatically, not my country.

"In time, however, the awful nostalgia wore off as I gradually became absorbed in college work. During that first term I discovered the Zoo and the Natural History Museum, and any opportunity found me at one or the other of those delectable places. My sketch book soon became full of animal and bird studies from both stuffed and live specimens, but before long I became critical of the art of the taxidermist, and concentrated more on the living animal, using the museum only as reference for plumage or anatomical details. In the college itself, the painting school was dominated by the study of the human figure and the compositions demanded were figure compositions. So I studiously drew and painted from the life, but for my compositions I always made use of my farmers and farming scenes. If a composition was required with 'Summer' as its subject, I could think of nothing but the mowing and carting of hay. 'Winter' meant the hungry cattle and the big knife cutting into the hay stacks, a pig-killing scene, or a group of rough-coated colts with their tails to the weather. And while those students who talked much rolled out the names of Cezanne, Picasso, Gauguin and Matisse, I was more interested in the works of certain other masters—Piero della Francesca, Pieter Breughel, Hans Memlinc, Albrecht Duerer and, nearer to our own time, John Constable, Thomas Girtin, and John Sell Cotman. We all had our gods.

"Every vacation from college I spent at home on the farm, and much of the spare time from the work of the farm was utilised in making studies of landscape, animals, and people to be employed in compositions on my return to college. 'Absence makes the heart grow fonder' so it is said; and I was quite sure, on my several returns to the farm, that there was no country like my own corner of east Cheshire. On a summer Sunday evening I often saddled the black mare and rode into the hills to sit for hours gazing over the forty miles of Cheshire Plain where, away to the west, the mountains of Wales rose in dim blue ridges, one behind the other, while the mare cropped the roadside grass and the sound of the church bells came faintly from the village below.

"During my fourth year in London I joined the College engraving school, and soon became absorbed in the art of etching. The first exercise was to copy a head by one of the masters of etching. I chose a small self-portrait by Rembrandt, but my second etching portrayed four farmers and two horses leaving the hayfield. Subsequent plates also reeked of the farm and the farming life. Rembrandt, Duerer, Paul Potter and Millet were now my masters. For seven years I lived in London, etching many plates and, during the latter part of my stay, publishing some."[1]

In **1929,** Tunnicliffe married fellow artist, Winifred Wonnacott.

1932. After illustrating *Tarka, the Otter,* a book for children by Henry Williamson, he collaborated with Williamson on several other books, among them the *The Peregrine's Saga.* To research peregrines he worked with some falconers. "I followed the young falconers into the paddock behind the inn . . . . In the shade of the lime trees was a line of perching birds, some of which greeted the return of the young falconers with shrill calls. Absorbedly I watched the unhooding of the falcons; with a deft pull of teeth and fingers the hoods were slackened and slipped off the birds' heads to reveal pairs of wonderful dark eyes which gazed round haughtily . . . . All these peregrine falcons were young birds, which, only a few

Tunnicliffe at work, April, 1974. (Photograph by Sean Hagerty from *Portrait of a Country Artist* by Ian Niall.)

weeks before, had been nestlings in cliff-side eyries. They were beautiful in their first plumage of grey, brown-laced backs, dark crowns, and striped breasts. I made many studies of them, but this meet of falconers had brought other birds to the paddock. At the end of the line was a fine adult goshawk, a bird greater in size and fierceness than any peregrine. It sat upright and still, its cruel yellow feet grasping the leather padding of the bow-perch. But the feet were not so cruel as the yellow-ringed eyes, which glared at every moving thing, and did not miss the smallest bird which passed over. I was fascinated by this hawk and could not resist the chance to draw it. A front view of the bird's head was one of the most devilish things I had ever beheld. But, in spite of this, it was beautiful, and irresistible, and stole some of the time which had been intended for the drawing of peregrines."[1]

In addition to other juvenile titles for authors like Derek Henry Chapman and Alison Uttley, Tunnicliffe published his own work, much of it on birds. *Bird Portraiture* tells aspiring painters how he worked. "For some years, I have been in the habit of making careful measured drawings, in colour, of any dead bird which has come into my hands, providing it has been in fresh condition. Whenever possible I have drawn the birds exactly life size. I try to arrange them so that the upper surfaces, including that of the fully-opened wing, are shown: the under surfaces with wings in the same position: a side view with the wings closed, and any other details, such as a front view of the head, accurate studies of legs and feet, and drawings of single feathers,—in fact, anything which I think may be of use.

"It is in this matter of settings that so many bird pictures fail. Often the bird is painted skilfully, but its surroundings 'fizzle out' into a doubtful and uncertain hotch-potch of unstudied details which ruin the picture.

"If you would see fine examples of bird-painting in which the settings have been given the same meticulous care as the birds themselves, you have but to study the work of the Chinese painters ... the exquisite drawing of flower and branch,

tussock, reed and bamboo, an exquisiteness which does not detract one jot from the importance of the bird, but which does give a precious and lovely quality to the work. You might also spare some time to look at the work of John James Audubon, who did such admirable work in drawing and painting the birds of America. His attitude towards birds was not purely an artistic one, as he was a fine ornithologist for his time. His work was scientific in intention. Nevertheless, it was also artistically excellent, a combination of qualities which is woefully lacking in many modern text-books on birds."[2]

Tunnicliffe and his wife eventually moved to "Shorelands" in Anglesey, Wales. "We were no strangers to this fair country, but our journey to-day was different from all previous ones for, at the end of it, in a little grey village at the head of an estuary, there was an empty house which we hoped to call home as soon as we could get our belongings into it. Our other visits had been short holidays, spent chiefly in watching and drawing birds and landscape of which there was great variety. Several sketchbooks had been filled with studies of Anglesey and its birds, and we had been specially delighted to find that the island in spring and autumn was a calling place for many migratory birds, while summer and winter had their own particular and different species. Occasionally, to add to the excitement, a rarity would appear. Whatever the season there were always birds and this fact had greatly influenced us in our choice of a new home.

"Our intention to establish ourselves in this Celtic land was not to be accomplished without opposition however, for Anglesey, the Mother of Whales, had built a little church on one side of our lane, and the stone wall of a cottage garden on the other. The furniture vans were monstrous and stuck fast between church and garden wall and could proceed no farther. After we had scratched our heads in perplexity, and listened to suggestions from interested observers, Mon Mam Cymru relented and sent a coal lorry to our aid. The sun shone, the furniture went into the house via the coal lorry, and the Shelducks on the sands laughed and cackled all day."[3]

(From *Tarka the Otter* by Henry Williamson. Illustration by C. F. Tunnicliffe.)

Years later Tunnicliffe was awarded a Gold Medal from the Royal Society for the Protection of Birds.

In **1978,** he received the Order of the British Empire. "I am not a man for parading in medals. It gives me great satisfaction to have my work recognised, to have it appreciated. I wouldn't be human if it didn't. Just the same, I must say that I find something incongruous in being honoured for doing what I love doing, or for earning my living, as I have done, by cultivating what talent I have."[3]

1979. Tunnicliffe died of a heart attack, at the age of seventy-eight.

FOOTNOTE SOURCES

[1]C. S. Tunnicliffe, *My Country Book,* Studio, 1942.
[2]C. S. Tunnicliffe, *Bird Portraiture,* Studio, 1945.
[3]Ian Niall, *Portrait of a Country Artist: C. F. Tunnicliffe, R.A., 1901-1979,* Gollancz, 1985.

FOR MORE INFORMATION SEE:

B. M. Miller and others, compilers, *Illustrators of Children's Books 1946-1956,* Horn Book, 1958.
Martha E. Ward and Dorothy A. Marquardt, *Illustrators of Children's Books,* Scarecrow, 1975.

VANDE VELDE, Vivian 1951-

PERSONAL: Born June 18, 1951, in New York, N.Y.; daughter of Pasquale (a linotype operator) and Marcelle (Giglio) Brucato; married Jim Vande Velde (a computer analyst), April 20, 1974; children: Elizabeth. *Education:* Attended State University of New York at Brockport, 1969-70, and Rochester Business Institute, 1970-71. *Religion:* Catholic.

CAREER: Writer. *Member:* Society of Children's Book Writers, Science Fiction Writers of America. *Awards, honors: A Hidden Magic* was selected one of Child Study Association of America's Children's Books of the Year, 1986; *Writer's Digest* Honorable Mention, 1987, for short story "Forever Yours"; *Highlights for Children* Author of the Month Award, 1988.

WRITINGS:

Once Upon a Test: Three Light Tales of Love (illustrated by Diane Dawson Hearn), A. Whitman, 1984.
A Hidden Magic (illustrated by Trina Schart Hyman), Crown, 1985.
A Well-Timed Enchantment, Crown, 1990.

Contributor of short stories to *Cricket, Opus Two, Softalk, Sunday Digest, Dash, Upstate, Living with Children, Buffalo Spree, Highlights for Children, Electric Company, Kid City, School, Young American,* and *Aboriginal Science Fiction.*

WORK IN PROGRESS: User Friendly, a young adult novel about "a group of friends (and one tag-along mother) playing a fantasy role-playing game on a computer which makes them feel as though they're really experiencing their adventure. But there's something wrong with the program, and they can't get out, and then Mom gets sick . . . . "

SIDELIGHTS: "I can't remember a time when I wasn't making up stories. As a child, I would invent an adventure for my stuffed animals and help them act it out—not a play, not for the rest of the family—but just for my own pleasure. This isn't to say I was a creative genius; most of my stories were a mish-mash: I might take part of the Cinderella story here, part of the legend of Ivanhoe there, throw in a dash of Superman, add a couple of dinosaurs stomping around—elements meant to please me.

"I still find myself most excited, most stimulated to write, after hearing a good story. I've known writers who will read something, hate it, declare 'I could do better than that,' and be inspired to write. With me it works the opposite way. Reading a book (or watching a movie) that bores me, or which seems predictable or implausible, or in which the characters bear no relationship to anybody I have ever known, makes me more sad and annoyed than anything else. I feel no need to prove that I can do better. However, when I come in contact with a story that carries me away, that makes me forget it's only a story, whose characters are so real I have to believe that somewhere— somehow—they really do exist: then I say: 'I want to be able to do that.'

"My stories aren't usually based on things that really happened, but I try to base them on real feelings. Although I don't write autobiographically, to a certain extent my characters are like me. Often the people in my stories are uncomfortable with the way they look, or they feel clumsy, or they find themselves having to take charge in a situation for which they are totally unprepared. I can't imagine myself writing convincingly about someone without any self-doubts, who is the best at what she (or he) does and only has to prove herself to others. Most of my characters are quite surprised to find—by the story's end—that they can cope after all."

HOBBIES AND OTHER INTERESTS: Reading, needlecrafts, quiet family things.

VESEY, A(manda) 1939-

PERSONAL: Surname is pronounced *Vee*-sy; born May 24, 1939, in England; daughter of George Douglas (a military general) and Patricia (Marsh) Heyman; married Thomas Vesey (a chartered surveyor), December 2, 1967; children: Emily, Sarah. *Education:* Attended Salisbury College of Art; Chelsea College of Art, N.D.D., 1960. *Religion:* Church of England. *Home:* Lulham House, Madley, Hereford HR2 9JL, England.

CAREER: Teacher at Gunnersbury Grammar School, London, England, La Retraite, Salisbury, England, and Convent of the Sacred Heart, Woldingham, England; tutor at Salisbury College of Art, Salisbury, England; free-lance author and artist. *Awards, honors:* Mother Good Award Runner-up from Books for Children Book Club (England), 1981, for *Cousin Blodwyn's Visit;* Smarties Prize Runner-up, 1985.

WRITINGS:

FOR CHILDREN; ALL SELF-ILLUSTRATED

Cousin Blodwyn's Visit, Methuen, 1980.
Gloria, Methuen, 1983.
(Reteller) *The Princess and the Frog,* Atlantic Monthly, 1985.

Merry Christmas, Thomas!, Atlantic Monthly, 1986 (published in England as *Thomas and the Christmas Present*, Methuen, 1986).

WORK IN PROGRESS: Children's books.

SIDELIGHTS: "I am rather reclusive. I live in a large country house and look after sheep, horses, dogs, cats, and so on. I like children: their minds, their imaginations, and their paintings. My only real ambition is to write a book which will give children pleasure, feed their imagination, and stimulate their minds."

WALSH, Ann 1942-

PERSONAL: Born September 20, 1942, in Jasper, Ala.; Canadian citizen; daughter of Alan Barrett (a speech therapist) and Margaret Elaine (a speech therapist; maiden name, Slaughter) Clemons; married John F. D. Walsh (a French teacher), January 3, 1964; children: Katherine Margaret Ann, Megan Elizabeth Alva. *Education:* University of British Columbia, B.Ed., 1968. *Home:* 411 Winger Rd., Williams Lake, British Columbia, Canada V2G 3S6. *Office:* Canadian Children's Book Centre, 229 College St., 5th floor, Toronto, Ontario, Canada M5T 1RA.

CAREER: Elementary school teacher in Vancouver, Williams Lake, 1964-78; community college instructor, 1979-89; full-time writer, 1990—. Holds workshops and does readings in schools. Adjudicator, Creative Writing Division of Cariboo Music Festival, 1988. Has held various executive positions for the Williams Lake Player's Club. *Member:* Federation of British Columbia Writers (regional representative, 1986—), Writers' Union of Canada, Childrens' Literature Roundtable, Canadian Children's Book Centre. *Awards, honors:* Canada-wide Young Adult Award runner-up, and selected one of *Emergency Librarian's* top Canadian Children's Books, both 1984, and selected one of Our Choice/ Your Choice Canadian Children's Books, 1985-86, all for *Your Time, My Time; Moses, Me and Murder!* was short-listed for the Geoffrey Bilson Award for Excellence in Historical Fiction for Young People, 1990.

WRITINGS:

Your Time, My Time, Press Porcepic, 1984.
(Contributor) *Skelton at Sixty* (anthology), Porcupine's Quill, 1986.
(Contributor) *Hungry Poet's Cookbook,* Applezeba Press, 1987.
Moses, Me and Murder! (illustrated by C. Allen), Pacific Education Press, 1988.
(Contributor) *The Skin of the Soul* (anthology), Paper Back Books, 1990.
The Ghost of Soda Creek, Press Porcepic, 1990.

UNPUBLISHED PLAYS

"The Making of a Hero" (juvenile), performed by Williams Lake Player's Club, 1979.
"The First of Sixty" (playlet), 1989.
"Banana Who?" (juvenile), performed by Williams Lake Player's Club, 1980.

Contributor of short stories and poetry to magazines, including *Jack and Jill, Canadian Short Stories, Hornby Collection,*

ANN WALSH

Woman to Woman, Quarry, Prairie Journal of Canadian Literature, and *Woman's World.*

WORK IN PROGRESS: Shabash!, a juvenile about a Sikh boy and his problems with prejudice in minor hockey; a story of a cowboy who dies at a stampede in 1932 and his love for a real princess from Europe, based on events that occurred in British Columbia in the 1930s.

SIDELIGHTS: "My childhood was spent in many different countries and eleven different schools by the time I reached grade six. Arriving in Kansas with a broad South African accent, then returning to Africa with my accent now Americanized and holding traces of my visits back to the deep South where I was born, made me an oddity among my classmates, and some of my best friends as a child were the characters in the books I read voraciously. Although I remember little about the politics or geography of the various areas where I grew up, I remember the long ocean voyages, the cross-state travel in an old truck pulling a decrepit trailer, and I remember reading wherever we went and whatever we did. The constancy of my fictional friends, to whom I never had to bid goodbye, is perhaps, one of the main reasons that today I am a writer, even if a rather late-blooming one!

"As a burnt-out classroom teacher I finally had time to turn to writing almost full-time, a long-held wish. A good instructor during a short summer course in 1981 gave me the impetus to actually try a full length novel, which was finished that year, much to my surprise! I enjoy children and young people, which is probably why my novels are for them, and have access to a rich historical area here. The ghosts of the Gold Rush still linger in my Cariboo area.

"I am thoroughly enjoying being a 'writer,' and am doing a lot of workshops for young writers as well as plugging away at the new book and have recently given up my job at the local community college to write full time."

HOBBIES AND OTHER INTERESTS: Amateur theatre, reading, the outdoors, literacy volunteer, travel.

FOR MORE INFORMATION SEE:

Writers in the Classroom Directory, Federation of British Columbia Writers, 1988.

WARREN, Cathy 1951-

PERSONAL: Born January 24, 1951, in Larned, Kans.; daughter of Robert E. (an optometrist) and Margaret (an artist and teacher; maiden name, Bellinger) Bair; married Russell Warren (an artist), January 2, 1970; children: Tasha, Tanya. *Education:* University of St. Thomas, B.A. (cum laude) 1975; graduate work at University of North Carolina at Charlotte, 1979-80. *Politics:* Unaffiliated. *Religion:* Roman Catholic. *Home and office:* P.O. Box 991, Davidson, N.C. 28036.

CATHY WARREN

CAREER: Methodist Hospital, Houston, Tex., assistant psychiatric counselor, 1973-75; Mother Earth Early Child Development Center, San Antonio, Tex., director, 1976-77; Beacon Hill Elementary School, Lakeland, Fla., teacher, 1977-78; Children's Schoolhouse, Davidson, N.C., director, 1980-85; free-lance writer, 1983—; Queens College, Charlotte, N.C., instructor in continuing education, 1988—. Acting president of local 4-H chapter, 1981. *Member:* Authors Guild, Society of Children's Book Writers, North Carolina Writers Network. *Awards, honors: The Ten-Alarm Camp-Out* was selected a Parents' Choice Remarkable Book by the Parents' Choice Foundation, 1983; *Roxanne Bookman, Live at Five* was selected for inclusion in *Children's Books of the Year* at Bank Street College, 1988.

WRITINGS:

The Ten-Alarm Camp-Out (Junior Literary Guild selection; illustrated by Steven Kellogg), Lothrop, 1983.
Victoria's ABC Adventure (illustrated by Patience Brewster), Lothrop, 1984.
Fred's First Day (illustrated by Pat Cummings), Lothrop, 1984.
Springtime Bears (illustrated by P. Cummings), Lothrop, 1987.
Saturday Belongs to Sara (illustrated by DyAnne DiSalvo-Ryan), Bradbury, 1988.
Roxanne Bookman: Live at Five, Bradbury, 1988.

Author of weekly column "Art and Artists," *Charlotte Observer,* 1981-82.

WORK IN PROGRESS: Picture book about life on the farm.

SIDELIGHTS: Cathy Warren was born in Larned, Kansas. "It was a real 'Leave It to Beaver' kind of place. I had my own little island in the middle of the creek, and I had plenty of trees to curl up in and read, read, read, all summer long. But best of all, I had the kind of freedom every child needs.

"I've been interested in writing ever since I can remember. I used to make up songs and write poems and then perform them for various clubs and organizations. In college, my main area of interest was developmental psychology, but I was equally interested in children's literature. On weekends, while other students were busy crawling around in the stacks of the library, I would be squeezed into those tiny chairs in the children's section, giggling over the latest children's books.

"Writing children's books wasn't a conscious decision on my part, but rather, something that grew out of my fascination with the language and my love of children. These two elements seemed to combine and I realized that I could speak to children's concerns, tickle their funny bones and share that love through the written word.

"When I write, I never think, 'I'm going to write this for a child.' Instead, I think, 'I will write this for the child in me.' When I approach writing in this way, I know I will reach my audience.

"I have lived in Kansas, Texas, New Mexico, Colorado, Montana, Florida, and North Carolina. As a result of all that moving around I think I have learned to observe people and be a good listener. This, in turn, has helped me be a better writer.

She pretended she didn't hear me and went on practicing her flute. (Illustration by DyAnne DiSalvo-Ryan from *Saturday Belongs to Sara* by Cathy Warren.)

"It's funny, in a way, that I became a writer, because I always made bad grades in creative writing classes in college. I majored in psychology in college and thought I would become a psychiatrist. I wrote poetry for relaxation and my own enjoyment. Somewhere along the way, my desire to write turned into a need and I have never regretted my decision. Also, I've discovered that what I learned in psychology has helped me immensely in my writing."

Warren worked as director of an early childhood development center in Houston, Texas, her first position as a college graduate. "It was there that I was introduced to armadillos. They ran along the hills and bumped into rocks and were so disarmingly sweet. I felt an immediate affection for them. It was also in San Antonio, at our summer camp, that I began writing children's stories. Every afternoon, the children and I would gather around an old mesquite tree and make up stories.

"The idea for *The Ten-Alarm Camp-Out* grew out of my love for armadillos and a personal compulsion for neatness. I'm really a neat freak! I thought it would be funny for animals to create some kind of havoc, just because their sense of order might not always jibe with our sense of order. Armadillos seemed the perfect animals for this situation because they are such awkward yet benevolent little creatures. As I worked on it, the words seemed to fall with a definite rhythm, and before

I knew it, I had a whole family of armadillos rolling along, just as neat as you please.

"Next to writing, music is my passion. I love to write music and have recorded some of my songs with my friends. We have a band called 'The Part-Time Miracle Singers.' I'm the lead singer and play acoustical guitar.

"I also enjoy traveling and have traveled all over the United States, Mexico, and Spain. I prefer traveling by train, whenever possible. It's unhurried and a wonderful way to meet people from all walks of life.

"When I'm not writing, singing or traveling, I am busy raising two daughters with my husband, artist Russ Warren. We live on a small farm in North Carolina. We have three horses, three dogs, two cats and a hampster!"

HOBBIES AND OTHER INTERESTS: Music, traveling.

WATSON, Richard Jesse 1951-

PERSONAL: Born January 15, 1951, in Ridgecrest, Calif.; son of Jesse Robert (a physicist) and Elsie M. (an artist and homemaker; maiden name, MacLeod) Watson; married Rebecca Sue Davis (an artist and homemaker), December 27,

RICHARD JESSE WATSON

1970; children: Jesse Joshua, Faith Christina, Benjamin James. *Education:* Attended Pasadena City College, and Art Center College of Design, Pasadena. *Politics:* Democrat. *Religion:* Christian. *Home and office:* P.O. Box 1470, 4137 Northwood Dr., Murphys, Calif. 95247. *Agent:* Jim Heacock, 1523 6th St., Suite 14, Santa Monica, Calif. 90401.

CAREER: U.S. Post Office, Pasadena, Calif., letter carrier, 1971-75; World Vision International, Monrovia, Calif., assistant art director, 1975-79; Hallmark Cards, Inc., Kansas City, Mo., artist, 1979-82; free-lance graphic designer and illustrator, 1982—. Volunteer art teacher at Albert Michelson Elementary School; leader of workshops in drawing and painting for children in public schools, and of art workshops for elementary teachers and librarians. *Exhibitions:* American Institute of Graphic Arts, New York, N.Y., 1987; Master Eagle Gallery, New York, N.Y., 1987; Society of Illustrators, New York, N.Y., 1987, 1989; Springfield Art

Association, Springfield, Ill., 1989; "Every Picture Tells a Story," Gallery of Fine Art, Los Angeles, Calif., 1989; American Booksellers Convention Exhibit, New York, N.Y., 1989; Santa Barbara Arts Festival, Santa Barbara, Calif., 1989. *Military service:* Performed alternate service to the draft during the Vietnam War as a conscientious objector.

AWARDS, HONORS: Best Book Design from the American Institute of Graphic Arts, 1986, and Parent's Choice Award for Illustration from the Parent's Choice Foundation, 1987, both for *Bronwen, the Traw, and the Shape-Shifter;* Ezra Jack Keats Fellow from the Kerlan Collection at the University of Minnesota, 1987; Graphic Arts Award for Best Printed Children's Book from the Printing Industries of America, and one of *Booklist*'s Editor's Choices, both 1989, and Golden Kite Award from the Society of Children's Book Writers, 1990, all for *Tom Thumb.*

WRITINGS:

(Reteller) *Tom Thumb* (self-illustrated), Harcourt, 1989.

ILLUSTRATOR

James Dickey, *Bronwen, the Traw, and the Shape-Shifter: A Poem in Four Parts,* Harcourt, 1986.
Betsy James, *The Dream Stair,* Harper, 1989.
Nancy Willard, *The High Rise Glorious Skittle Scat Roarious Sky Pie Angle Food Cake,* Harcourt, 1990.

WORK IN PROGRESS: George MacDonald's *The Fairy Fleet;* a Christmas book by Ruth Bell Graham, wife of evangelist Billy Graham. "This book promises to be an extremely challenging project. It calls for historical accuracy in tracing major developments in the Old Testament leading to the birth of Christ. It will be difficult to capture the complexities and feelings of that astounding epoch. The Graham Foundation sent me to Israel, Egypt, and Jordan to research—a humbling experience in the face of so much history, so much tradition, so much beauty, so much struggle among different peoples."

SIDELIGHTS: "I can't remember a time when I wasn't doing art of one kind or another. My mother, an artist as well, encouraged my efforts and provided me with all sorts of supplies. My father was a scientist, hung up on realism. 'That doesn't quite look right,' he used to say. So I was always trying to get the drawings to 'look right.' My mom, on the other hand, was very free, liked abstract work, and argued endlessly with my dad about modern art. I was fascinated by their conversations and continually weighed the merits of their respective viewpoints.

"Another reason I'm drawn to detail is that in elementary school I had bad eyesight. In fifth grade I was fitted for glasses and was amazed by all the leaves on the trees, and I wanted to draw every one of them.

"My father, a physicist, worked on a Navy base in Southern California. During the early days of computers he started his own business, making all the components he had conceived. He was a master craftsman and a somewhat absent-minded inventor. He made a solar oven out of a huge disk with many mirrors, which he forgot to cover only to find that it had burned a line of fire across the patio. We were lucky it didn't burn down the house!

"My mother instilled a strong social consciousness in us. She worked for women's rights, world hunger, and a variety of other causes. Her art work was important, but came second to her responsibilities as the mother of four children. She had her own studio, an enormous kiln for high-fire ceramics, and exhibited her work. Her creativity carried over into all phases of our lives, not always to our liking, however. One Christmas she made our tree out of Chinese umbrellas she had decorated. We were absolutely horrified; we wanted a traditional Christmas tree! Looking back now, though, her idea seems marvellous.

"I doodled my way through school and was privileged to study the paintings at the Los Angeles County Museum and to take art classes at the Pasadena Art Museum. My talents were encouraged, nurtured and inspired. From the beginning, I think, there was a narrative bent to my art work. I would create a story in my mind and make images to bring the story to conclusion. During high school and college my art became socially oriented.

"I toured Europe and was profoundly moved by its cathedrals. In my youthful arrogance, I had the habit of looking at art, saying 'Yeah, I could do that.' But here I had to admit, 'No, I couldn't do this.' The spirit in these artists soared to astounding heights. I wanted to know what motivated their very special energy. It dawned on me that it was their faith in God. Having been raised an atheist, my leanings tended towards Communism. In Eastern Europe, the atheist exultation of man and his efforts was inspiring in its own way, but the mood was gray and leaden. The religious art exerted such a pull on me that for the first time I had to seriously examine the question of my belief in God. This was the first step in a major change in my life. Eventually I became a Christian.

"I registed as a conscientious objector to do alternate service to the draft. I had recently married (at the age of nineteen) and my wife and I ended up in Barnsville, Ohio, working on a Quaker dairy farm. Our first child was born, and we generally had a very fulfilling time. After a year they changed my status and we returned to Pasadena. I worked a variety of jobs, from welder to letter carrier, in order to support my family.

"Eventually I was hired by World Vision, a Christian humanitarian organization, to do graphic design, posters, publicity and art work for their magazine. At night I attended the Pasadena Art Center with the thought of eventually doing children's books. With three kids to support, I was in a continual struggle between supporting my family and finding ways to grow artistically.

"Hallmark Cards was a promising option. They hired me and flew us out to Countryside, Kansas, where we lived for four years. It was a great experience, somewhat like graduate school. Altogether they employed four hundred artists—painters, photographers, engravers, calligraphers, among others. I learned a great deal about color and techniques, and got some wonderful training painting flowers. It became oppressive, however. I like to experiment, but Hallmark was uncomfortable with that. Their highly skilled artists were hired to replicate colors, styles, forms of whatever was deemed 'hot' in fashion shows, art galleries in Paris and New York. I decided to freelance doing album covers, computer software, advertising illustrations and so on.

"Not long after our return to California in 1983, I attended a conference of the Society of Children's Book Writers. After that things started to fall into place quite rapidly. I sent some samples to Harcourt and to Harper, both of whom gave me work. My first assignment *Bronwen, the Traw, and the Shape-Shifter* by James Dickey was a plum." The book won two awards: Best Book Design from the American Institute of Graphic Arts and an illustration award from the Parents' Choice Foundation.

"The following year I was an Ezra Jack Keats Fellow at the Kerlan Collection at the University of Minnesota. For the first three months I went through many different versions of *Tom Thumb.* I put together various combinations and added new elements to create a new version. The illustrations then took approximately thirteen months to execute. The first three or four pieces were done in watercolor, a technique that normally is free and loose. But I was doing it very tightly, and soon realized that at that rate I would not finish the book in my lifetime. So I switched to egg tempera, which has a very similar look. Each color is comprised of a powdered pigment mixed with a binder, in this case egg yolk or egg white. I use the yolk for its durability. The whites tend to crack. The pigment-yolk solution is mixed with a little water and lends a

Bronwen looked out toward the rap. (Illustration by Richard Jesse Watson from *Bronwen, the Traw, and the Shape-Shifter* by James Dickey.)

Grumbong turned on Tom. (From *Tom Thumb,* retold by Richard Jesse Watson. Illustrated by the author.)

yellow tinge in reproduction. It makes it difficult to achieve purple (the opposite of yellow on the color wheel). Using egg yolk is helpful to me because I'm somewhat red/green color-blind and the yellow helps keep me on track somehow. I love the ritual entailed in using this medium. We live in the country, and I begin by getting eggs from the chickens. Then I prepare the pigments. The process is at once physical and contemplative, and requires both nature and the studio.

"Egg tempera was used in my recent book, *The High Rise Glorious Skittle Skat Roarious Sky Pie Angel Food Cake* by Nancy Willard. The illustrations are looser than those for *Tom Thumb* and are done on gessoed board rather than Strathmore illustration board. I used rabbit-skin glue to size the board, five or six coats of warmed gesso, then egg tempera in conjunction with water soluble pastel.

"My basic process doesn't change that much from book to book. I tend to begin every project with physical activity: hiking, splitting wood, burning brush. Gradually I focus on the story and gear up for research. Invariably I over-research, but that, too, seems to be part of my process. I'm extremely interested in the effects of light and often make approximate models of characters or scenes. For *Tom Thumb* my wife sewed costumes from which I worked—a real luxury. Usually, I'll make do with physical 'improvizations,' say a Nike sweatshirt turned inside out. The end of a book is always very hard. I work constantly, become quite unsociable (I have to admit), and feel at once exhausted and exhilarated.

"I paint for the child inside me—that true, unpretentious person who meets the world with wonder and awe and acceptance. Some people think that drawings for children should be very simple. Some should. Some shouldn't. As a child I loved highly detailed art. I want to create pictures in

which I can get lost and in which a child can wander and be transported to someplace new.

"I look ahead to many challenges. I had to wait fifteen years before I could devote myself to children's books, and am very gratified that at long last things have come together. I want to do work that brings joy to children and that addresses such social issues as: the devastation of the rain forest, conflicts between Jews and Palestinians, racial strife in South Africa, social tensions in our own country. I want to create art that causes people to think and to reach out across pain and bitterness. Creativity is a part of God. I want to share the joy of creating and thereby share in the love."[1]

FOOTNOTE SOURCES

[1]Based on an interview by Marguerite Feitlowitz for *Something about the Author.*

WECK, Thomas L. 1942-

PERSONAL: Born June 3, 1942, in Norwalk, Conn.; son of Frank A. (an actuary) and Wilnor (a teacher; maiden name, Neebe) Weck; married Sandra Larson (a teacher), August 19, 1969; children: David Scot, Peter Michael, Kathryn Ann, Andrew Alan. *Education:* Stanford University, A.B. (with distinction), 1964; Harvard University, M.B.A., 1969. *Home:* 9 Beverly Rd., Madison, N.J. 07940. *Office:* Louis Berger International, 100 Halsted St., East Orange, N.J. 07019.

CAREER: U.S. Peace Corps, Washington, D.C., volunteer in Ethiopia, 1965-67; Louis Berger International (consultants), East Orange, N.J., financial analyst, 1969-71, associate, 1971-73, director of environmental studies, 1973-76, vice-president, 1976-82, group vice-president, 1982—. Member of Madison Borough Environmental Commission, 1974-78, and Transportation Research Board of the National Academy of Sciences, 1978—. *Awards, honors:* Children's Book Award from the Catholic Press Association, 1985, and

THOMAS L. WECK

New Jersey Institute of Technology Author's Award, 1987, both for *Back-Back and the Lima Bear.*

WRITINGS:

Moving Up Quickly, Wiley, 1978.
Back-Back and the Lima Bear (juvenile; illustrated by Neil Taylor), Winston-Derek, 1984.

Contributor to professional journals.

WHITLEY, Mary A(nn) 1951-

PERSONAL: Born October 7, 1951, in Flint, Mich.; daughter of Herson L. (an office worker) and Amelia (a homemaker; maiden name, Leffler) Whitley; married Patrick A. Sebrey, September 16, 1972 (divorced January 7, 1982); married Craig S. Sanders (a journalist), November 9, 1985. *Education:* Attended Flint College of the University of Michigan (now University of Michigan—Flint), 1969-70; University of Florida, B.S.J. (with honors), 1973. *Politics:* Democrat. *Religion:* Protestant. *Home:* 3025 North Meridian St., 802, Indianapolis, Ind. 46208. *Office: Indianapolis Star,* 307 North Pennsylvania, Indianapolis, Ind. 46204.

CAREER: Brooksville Sun-Journal, Brooksville, Fla., writer and photographer, summers, 1970-72; *Gainesville Sun,* Gainesville, Fla., feature writer, 1973-75; *Louisville Times,* Louisville, Ky., copy editor, 1975-76; *Corydon Democrat,* Corydon, Ind., writer, photographer, and in layout, 1976-81, assistant editor, 1980-81; *Bloomington Herald-Telephone,* Bloomington, Ind., feature writer and member of layout staff, 1981-85; *Indianapolis Star,* Indianapolis, Ind., copy editor, 1986—. *Member:* National Federation of Press Women, Woman's Press Club of Indiana (second vice-president, 1984-85).

AWARDS, HONORS: Sixteen awards from Hoosier State Press Association, 1976-81, for work on the *Croydon Democrat;* First Place Award for Editorial Writing from the Metropolitan Louisville Journalism Awards, 1980, for editorials about the Crawford County School Board; eight awards from the Woman's Press Club of Indiana, 1982-87, for work on *Bloomington Herald-Telephone,* and *Indianapolis Star;* Children's Choice from the International Reading Association and the Children's Book Council, and selected one of Child Study Association of America's Children's Books of the Year, both 1986, both for *A Sheltering Tree.*

WRITINGS:

JUVENILE

A Circle of Light, Walker, 1983.
A Sheltering Tree, Walker, 1985.

WORK IN PROGRESS: A juvenile novel.

SIDELIGHTS: "When I was in junior high school, I realized I wanted to be a writer, but I knew that one doesn't just go out and start writing books for a living, so I decided that journalism would be a good choice for a career. Then I could write to earn a living and write books on the side.

"As a child I was horse-crazy, although I never owned a horse or learned to ride until I graduated from college. Instead, I read every horse book in the library in Flushing, Michigan. I had always wanted to write my own horse story, my own version of *The Black Stallion.* I knew it would have to be a children's book by virtue of the subject matter.

"Eventually I did write my long-dreamed-of story, *A Circle of Light.* The equine heroine of the book is a fictional version of my own horse, Giniz. If the book has a theme, it's that you should trust your intuition.

"My second book, *A Sheltering Tree,* is set in the small community of Milltown, Indiana, where I lived for five years. It is the story of a girl who is trying to find her long-lost sister who is in a foster home. It is also the story of a developing friendship. If there is a message in it, it's about the importance of people caring for each other.

"I'm still very much interested in horses and ride my mare, Giniz, several times a week. I am currently studying dressage, the classical method of riding, and have competed with my horse in competitive trail riding (long distance riding). I also have a five-year-old gelding, Nighthawk, which I have raised from a foal and which I am training and riding."

WHYTE, Mal(colm Kenneth, Jr.) 1933-

PERSONAL: Born February 26, 1933, in Milwaukee, Wis.; son of Malcolm K. (a lawyer) and Bertha K. (a writer and artist) Whyte; married Karen Cross (a writer), December 19, 1959; children: Malcolm K. III, Kirsty, Andrew. *Education:* Cornell University, B.A., 1955. *Residence:* Mill Valley, Calif. *Office:* Word Play, 1 Sutter St., San Francisco, Calif. 94104.

CAREER: Troubador Press, San Francisco, Calif., founder and president, 1959-82, chairman of board of directors, 1970-82, editorial director, 1983-88; Word-Play, Inc. (publishing consultants), San Francisco, Calif., founder and president, 1983—. *Military service:* U. S. Navy, 1956-59; communications officer. *Member:* Cornell Club of Northern California, San Francisco Symphony Association, Roxburghe Club, National Cartoonists Society, Cartoon Art Museum of California (founder, president, and chairman, 1984—). *Awards, honors:* Cover Award from the American Institute of Graphic Arts, 1975, for "Catch the Eye."

WRITINGS:

(With Ed Callahan and Bill Shilling) *The Original Old Radio Game,* Pisani Press, 1965.
(With John Stanley) *The Great Comics Game Book,* Price Stern, 1966.
The Fat Cat Coloring and Limerick Book (illustrated by Donna Sloan), Troubador Press, 1967.
Love Bug Coloring and Limerick Book (illustrated by D. Sloan), Troubador Press, 1968.
Mona Lisa Coloring Book (illustrated by Dennis Redmond), Troubador Press, 1970.
Dinosaur Coloring Book (illustrated by Winston Tong), Troubador Press, 1970.
Beasties Coloring Book (illustrated by Vernon Koski), Troubador Press, 1970.
North American Wildlife Coloring Album (illustrated by Gompers Saijo), Troubador Press, 1972.
North American Birdlife Coloring Album (illustrated by G. Saijo), Troubador Press, 1972.
North American Sealife Color Album (illustrated by G. Saijo), Troubador Press, 1973.

MAL WHYTE

Meanings of Christmas (illustrated by Varian Mace), Troubador Press, 1973.

(With J. Stanley) *Monster Movie Game,* Troubador Press, 1974.

(With Bill Blackbeard) *Great Comic Cats,* Troubador Press, 1981.

Huggs and Cuddles Teddy Bear Paperdolls (illustrated by Terra Muzick), Troubador Press, 1984.

Huggs and Cuddles Teddy Bear Funbook (illustrated by Maryanne R. Hoburg), Troubador Press, 1985.

Travels with the Happy Bears: Paper Doll Book (illustrated by T. Muzick), Troubador Press, 1985.

Dinosaur Action Set (illustrated by Dan Smith), Troubador Press, 1986.

The Second Dinosaur Action Set (illustrated by D. Smith), Troubador Press, 1987.

Great Whales Coloring Album (illustrated by D. Smith), Troubador Press, 1987.

Prehistoric Mammals Action Set (illustrated by D. Smith), Troubador Press, 1988.

Undersea Dinosaur Action Set (illustrated by D. Smith), Troubador Press, 1988.

Butterflies (illustrated by Andrea Tachiera), Troubador Press, 1989.

Farm Animals (illustrated by A. Tachiera), Troubador Press, 1989.

African Safari Action Set (illustrated by D. Smith), Troubador Press, 1989.

Sea Creatures (illustrated by A. Tacheira), Troubador Press, 1989.

Zoo Animals (illustrated by A. Tacheira), Troubador Press, 1989.

(With D. Smith) *Zoo Action I Set* Troubador Press, 1990.

(With D. Smith) *Zoo Action II Set* Troubador Press, 1990.

SIDELIGHTS: "A number of events tugged me along a career path, mostly without my realizing it—for instance, the first public appearance of my writing (other than scribbling on walls, floors, or sidewalks). In second grade a little poem I'd written about a clever field mouse appeared in our elementary school monthly paper. The attention the poem got my attention.

"Everyone has a teacher they'll never forget. For me it was Miss Dorothy Albrecht, third grade, Milwaukee University School. She was strict, but fair. She drilled us in writing, penmanship (remember penmanship?), arithmetic, and reading. Seemingly endlessly. But after she read aloud to us, and we were very quiet, she'd pass out little jujube candies to everyone.

"During the class art period I got caught up in making little three-dimensional scenes with paper, cardboard, crayons, scissors, and paste. I began these projects at home, making a tennis game with a candy box lid for the court and paper players, net, racquets, etc. I also made some small cityscapes. Miss Albrecht liked my idea so much she suggested that the whole class pick up on it and make a large, three-dimensional model of our fair city. Milwaukee was built in a week with lots of enthusiasm from the class, and praise from our teacher. The rest of the school happily took time off to visit our classroom to view the paper metropolis that Miss Albrecht gave me credit for inspiring. I'll never forget her.

"In sixth grade I combined art and writing for the first time in a series of hand drawn-and-colored comic books I produced for the class. 'Super Bunny Comics' starred a mild-mannered alien rabbit named Floppy who crash-landed on earth from his home planet of Carrota, and who became an avenging hero after downing a slug of carrot juice. With villains like the Practical Joker and the Thief of Bagmom (hey, I was only eleven years old!), the stories parodied mid-1940s comic books that were reaching what was later to be called their golden age.

"My first published cartoons appeared in the high school newspaper, and I improved on them in the college humor magazine, the *Cornell Widow,* while I pursued a degree in world literature. A lit major, reading tons of great books and writing millions of papers, is a perfect background for almost any job—especially if it involves tons of reading and writing.

"I thought I'd go into advertising after graduation in 1955, but not many companies wanted a draft-age employee who could be called to duty at any time. Luckily I got a job at a major box manufacturing plant back in Milwaukee. Its immense printing presses jogged me further towards a career.

"At the paperboard products company I was asked, as one of the staff artists, to design a six-pack for candy bars for Schuler Candy Company of Minnesota. There were actually three different boxes needed, one design for each of the three types of chocolate covered bars: Mint Humps, Cherry Humps, and Assorted Humps. It was fun and a challenge, but the greatest thrill of all was walking out to the printing plant and seeing my artwork reproduced by a hissing, clanking giant in quantities of 50,000 for each Hump! That image still plays in my mind.

"To avoid being drafted by the Army I joined the Naval officer's training program and post graduate school at Newport, R.I. I emerged five months later as a communications officer and was ordered to report to the aircraft carrier *U.S.S.*

Oriskany in San Francisco, where I met my to-be partner, Brayton Harris. We shared art and writing interests and decided to start a greeting card company which we called Troubador Press as we used Shakespearean quotes in the cards. We sold 350 dollars worth of cards that we had silkscreened to our shipmates that fall in 1956, then things went on 'hold' as Brady and I were each transferred to different ships overseas.

"By 1959, however, we reconvened in San Francisco to open Troubador Press full time as a greeting card and printing business. We worked with many, marvelous artists and writers, and did a large amount of printing for poet-publisher, Lawrence Ferlinghetti, producing books and broadsides for his City Lights Publications, while learning a lot about publishing in the process. Brady and I were now both married. After a year it became clear that Troubador's income was too slim for two families, so Brady went back into the Navy, from which he retired as a full captain. I kept the presses running at Troubador.

"While continuing with greeting cards and printing books for others, I had *my* first book published in 1965. Titled *The Original Old Radio Game,* ('What was the Shadow's everyday identity?' 'Name the Lone Ranger's faithful Indian companion.') it was the first trivia book ever published. It sold very well nationally thanks to its appearing on the Merv Griffin and Johnny Carson television programs. The sweet, heady feeling of doing this first book was so powerful that all three co-authors of the *Radio Game* went into book publishing. Bill Shilling became publisher of Pisani Press, a humorous book line; Ed Callahan founded Nitty Gritty Publications, an outstanding list of unique cookbooks; and two years later my turn came.

"But first I had another 'bestseller' to get published. Spurred by the success of *Radio Game* I contacted John Stanley, *San Francisco Chronicle* entertainment by-liner and noted comic book collector, to collaborate on another trivia classic: *The Great Comics Game Book.* Published by Price Stern Sloan in Los Angeles, the book was aimed at tying-in with the 1966 Batmania driven by the hit television show. However, it came out too late. The *Comics Game* was a bomb then, but it's a rare collectors' book now.

"Nevertheless, I found making books a lot more fun than greeting cards, so in 1967 I published the first Troubador book, *The Fat Cat Coloring and Limerick Book.* It was a unique format for a coloring book: Large size with heavy-duty, top quality paper and beautifully intricate illustrations by one of our greeting card designers, Donna Sloan. I wrote the limericks:

>A fat cat in his elegant house
>When asked what fancy foods he'd espouse
>Replied: 'I'm quite keen
>On Trout Amandine
>And I've lost my taste for the mouse.'

"The *Fat Cat* took off. It put Troubador on solid financial footing and stayed in print for fifteen years. In 1970 I quit greeting cards and job printing to become a full-time publisher and author. For the next twelve years I wrote or published art books, cookbooks, how-to books, and scores of game, coloring, and activity books, until I sold the company to Price Stern Sloan. I continued as Troubador's editorial director until 1988, when I became an independent book 'packager' (producer) and author, primarily for Troubador/Price Stern Sloan.

"Of the twenty-eight books that I've written (selling over two million copies), most of them are for youngsters. I love writing for children because what fascinates them still fascinates me: dinosaurs, sea life, exotic animals—all the color, grandeur, and magic of nature. Having my own children and grandchildren keeps me in touch, too.

"There's probably a little teacher hiding inside me. The toy-book format that I developed—coloring and activity books with substantial text and sophisticated art—delivers a lot of information in an entertaining way. The illustrations by the excellent artists with whom I collaborate create a rich, aesthetic excitement that rounds out the young reader's experience. It really tickles me to hear that one of my books has inspired a child to develop his or her own creative talent.

"Currently I am writing, and *artiste supreme* Dan Smith is illustrating, the Troubador 'Action Set' series. These are full-color, die-cut books that make into stunning, sturdy, three-dimensional scenes of animals in their natural habitats. They're perfect for classroom projects like Miss Albrecht's."

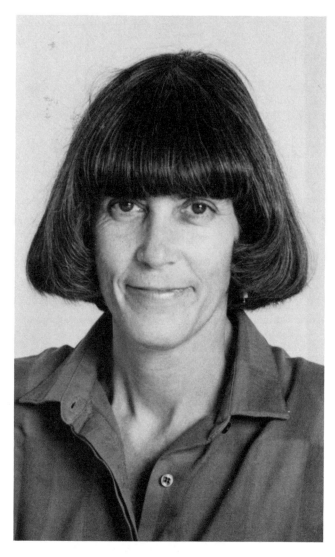

BARBARA WILLIAMS

WILLIAMS, BARBARA 1937-
(Barbara Wilson)

PERSONAL: Born October 21, 1937, in Ellesmere Port, England; daughter of Percy (a personnel officer) and Lucy (a homemaker; maiden name, White) Williams; married Michael R. Wilson (a doctor), July 31, 1961 (divorced, 1986); children: Matthew, Sophie. *Education:* Sheffield University, England, B.A. (general honors), 1959; Bristol University, England, certificate in education, 1960; Guelph University, Canada, M.A., 1973. *Home and office:* 43 Geneva Ave., Toronto, Ontario, Canada M5A 2J9.

CAREER: High school English and French teacher in England and Canada, 1961-71; helped establish a veterinary microbiology company, Guelph, Canada, 1975-82; freelance writer, 1975—. *Member:* Writers' Union of Canada, League of Canadian Poets (vice-chair, associated members, 1983), Canadian Society of Children's Authors, Illustrators and Performers. *Awards, honors:* Three Ontario Graduate Fellowships, 1972-73; Canada Council Research Grant, 1974, 1975; In-class Award from the University of Guelph, 1976, for best piece of writing produced in the course; Ontario Arts Council Grant, 1979, and 1980, for *ABC et/and 123;* Best Children's Poem and Best Collection of Children's Poems from *Cross-Canada Writers' Quarterly,* 1980, and runner-up in adult fiction category.

WRITINGS:

(Under name, Barbara Wilson) *ABC et/and 123* (illustrated by Gisele Daigle), Porcepic, 1980.

Poems for children have appeared in anthologies of the *League of Canadian Poets.* Contributor of short stories, articles, poems, and reviews to magazines in Canada, Australia, and the United States including, *Canadian Children's Annual, Magook, Jack and Jill, Wee Wisdom, Alive!, Westerly, Southerly, Ariel, Australian and New Zealand Studies in Canada, Descant,* and *Ahoy.* Columnist on Australian poetry, *Poetry Canada Review,* 1984-88.

WORK IN PROGRESS: Biography of Canadian pioneer woman, artist Anne Langton; several book length poetry sequences; book of interviews with Australian poets; editing letters of Richard Birley (1801-45), a pioneer who emigrated to Canada from Manchester, England in 1835.

SIDELIGHTS: "I began writing (mostly poetry) at the age of six or seven; had my first poems published in the 'Young Reader's League' section of a local newspaper at the age of eight or nine. I went on writing poetry until age fifteen, or so, then had one of the longest writer's blocks on record! Some twenty years or so as I completed my education, married, raised two children, emigrated to Canada, and helped establish a veterinary microbiology company, etc. But, I always wanted to write, and gradually I began to write again—part-time—from my mid-thirties, and for the last six years I've been writing almost full time. I never feel wholly 'centered' or 'grounded' unless I am writing, or mulling over what I'm going to write. My best ideas often come to me around dawn! Poetry often just fills my head then and has to be written down then and there (it may get revised later).

"I have always loved playing with words—waking or sleeping, working or relaxing. I find the creative process endlessly fascinating and, so, endlessly renewing. I consider myself very fortunate now to be doing what I *want* to do (there have been many struggles, much effort, to reach this point, but it's all been worthwhile); I only hope I can continue to do so for as long as I live.

"Writers are fortunate in that their imaginations enable them to be anyone, in any place, at any time, if they so wish. Sometimes, their writing also actually takes them into new territories—mine recently took me to Australia, a country that I had always wanted to visit. It was everything I'd always thought it would be—and much more! People were so friendly, vegetation so lush in tropical areas, or almost nonexistent in arid desert areas. A land of intriguing contrasts, mystery and, I believe, great future potential.

"I see writing as a continuous journey of exploration and discovery and then, further exploration. For me, it has been a 'serendipitous' voyage and I hope it will be so for my readers of all ages.

"In my bilingual (French and English), *ABC et/and 123,* I wanted to *delight* children from the very beginning of their encounter with words and pictures on the page. What magic that, from just twenty-six letters and ten ciphers, a whole world and history of art, culture and meaning (as well as everyday communication needs) have come into being and will go on developing, to offer rich nourishment to readers and viewers throughout their lives and throughout the centuries!

"My hobbies include gardening, especially growing herbs, which I love for their healing, culinary, and ornamental properties, but also often just for their names and associations with legend: 'Dittany of Crete,' 'Rue,' 'Rosemary,' 'Lemon Balm,' 'Pennyroyal,' 'Verbena'—to name only a few. It is said, for instance, that Rosemary's former white flowers changed to their present soft-blue when the Virgin Mary placed her blue cloak on a rosemary bush to dry after washing it and that she hid behind a rosemary bush to avoid detection during the flight into Egypt that she made with Joseph and the Christ child following Jesus' birth to escape from Herod's edict that all firstborn male babies should be killed. I also like listening to music, especially opera and my favourite musical instruments are the cello and the oboe. I find viewing art in books and exhibitions particularly 'nourishing.' And I *love* to dance! So, the arts and all things creative are very important to me: inspiring, nourishing, consoling."

FOR MORE INFORMATION SEE:

University of Guelph News Bulletins, November 7, 1974.
Daily Mercury (Guelph), November 13, 1980.
Tottenham Times, June 2, 1982.
Peterborough Historical Society Bulletin, April, 1983, September, 1986, October, 1986.
Fenelon Falls Gazette (Ontario), August 31, 1983.
Independent (Ontario), September 14, 1983.
North Kawartha Times (Ontario), September 14, 1983, August 1, 1984, July 8, 1986.
Post Vision (Ontario), July 14, 1984.
Fenelon Falls and Area Gazette, July 9, 1986.
Peterborough Examiner, September 17, 1986.
Free Press and Economist (Ontario), June 15, 1988.

Noontimes they lay in its shade. (Illustration by Nina Winters from *Carrot Holes and Frisbee Trees* by N. M. Bodecker.)

WINTERS, Nina 1944-

PERSONAL: Born March 10, 1944, in New York, N.Y.; daughter of Sidney R. (a stockbroker) and Gertrude Winters; married David Richard Brunoehler (an actor and director), September 14, 1984; children: Hauna Lee Sterra. *Education:* Cornell University, B.F.A., 1965. *Religion:* Scientologist. *Home:* 20 West 77th St., New York, N.Y. 10024.

CAREER: Nina Winters Illustration, New York, N.Y., president, 1980-88. *Exhibitions:* New York Art Directors Club, 1987. *Awards, honors:* Award from the New York Art Directors Club, 1987.

ILLUSTRATOR:

N. M. Bodecker, *Carrot Holes and Frisbee Trees,* Atheneum, 1983.

SIDELIGHTS: "I work free-lance for magazines, advertising agencies, doing book covers, record companies, etc. I work solely in water color."

WISTER, Owen 1860-1938

PERSONAL: Born July 14, 1860, in Germantown, Pa.; died of a cerebral hemorrhage, July 21, 1938, in North Kingstown, R.I.; son of Owen Jones (a physician) and Sarah (Butler) Wister; married Mary Channing Wister, in 1898 (died, 1913); children: six. *Education:* Harvard University, A.B. (summa cum laude), 1882; Harvard Law School, A.M., LL.B., 1887.

CAREER: Lawyer in Philadelphia, Pa.; writer.

WRITINGS:

The New Swiss Family Robinson: A Tale for Children of All Ages, University Bookstore (Cambridge, Mass.), 1882, another edition (illustrated by F. Nichols), Duffield, 1922 (first appeared in *Harvard Lampoon,* 1882).
The Dragon of Wantley, His Rise, His Voracity and His Downfall: A Romance (illustrated by John Stewardson), Lippincott, 1892.
Red Men and White (illustrated by Frederic Remington), Harper, 1896, reissued, Garrett Press, 1969.
Lin McLean, Harper, 1898, reissued, Literature House, 1970.
The Jimmyjohn Boss and Other Stories, Harper, 1900, reissued Garrett Press, 1969.
Ulysses S. Grant, Small, Maynard, 1900, second edition, 1901.
The Virginian: A Horseman of the Plains (illustrated by Arthur I. Keller), Macmillan, 1902, Harper, 1965, [other editions illustrated by Charles M. Russell and Frederic Remington, Macmillan, 1911, reissued, 1957, Citadel Press, 1984; Clarence Rowe, edited by James Fleming Hosic, revised by H. Y. Moffett, Macmillan, 1930; William Moyers, with an introduction by Struthers Burt, Limited Editions, 1951, Heritage Press, 1958; Sol Korby, adapted and abridged by R. J. Cohn, Grosset, 1963; Don Irwin, Childrens Press, 1968; another edition published with scenes from the all talking photoplay produced by Paramount, Grosset, 1925].
Philosophy Four: A Story of Harvard University, Macmillan, 1903.
A Journey in Search of Christmas (illustrated by F. Remington), Harper, 1904.

Owen Wister (right) and George Norman at the Mammoth Hot Springs, 1887. (From *Roosevelt: The Story of a Friendship* by Owen Wister.)

(With George B. Grinnell and Caspar Whitney) *Musk-Ox, Bison, Sheep and Goat,* Macmillan, 1904.
Lady Baltimore (illustrated by Vernon Howe Bailey and Lester Ralph), Macmillan, 1906, reissued, Buccaneer Books, 1977.
How Doth the Simple Spelling Bee (illustrated by F. R. Gruger), Macmillan, 1907.
Mother (illustrated by John Rae), Dodd, 1907.
The Seven Ages of Washington: A Biography, Macmillan, 1907.
Members of the Family (illustrated by H. T. Dunn), Macmillan, 1911.
Padre Ignacio; or, The Song of Temptation, Harper, 1911, another edition (illustrated by Zack Hogg), Harper, 1925.
The Pentecost of Calamity, Macmillan, 1915.
A Straight Deal; or, The Ancient Grudge, Macmillan, 1920.
(Compiler) *Indispensable Information for Infants; or, Easy Entrance to Education,* Macmillan, 1921.
Neighbors Henceforth, Macmillan, 1922.
Watch Your Thirst: A Dry Opera in Three Acts (illustrated by George Howe), preface by Samuel Johnson, Macmillan, 1923.
When West Was West, Macmillan, 1928.
The Writings of Owen Wister, Macmillan, 1928.
Roosevelt: The Story of a Friendship, 1880-1919, Macmillan, 1930.

High Bear galloped away into the dusk. (Illustration by H. T. Dunn from *Members of the Family* by Owen Wister.)

Two Appreciations of John Jay Chapman, privately printed, 1934.

Owen Wister Out West: His Journals and Letters, edited by Fanny Kemble Wister, University of Chicago Press, 1958.

The West of Owen Wister: Selected Short Stories, University of Nebraska Press, 1972.

That I May Tell You: Journals and Letters of the Owen Wister Family, edited by F. K. Wister, Haverford House, 1979.

Owen Wister's Medicine Bow, Lime Rock Press, 1981.

Owen Wister's West, University of New Mexico Press, 1987.

Contributor of stories and verse to periodicals, including *Harper's Weekly, Saturday Evening Post, Lippincott's, Atlantic Monthly, Harper's New Monthly, Outlook,* and *Collier's Weekly.*

ADAPTATIONS:

"The Virginian" (silent film), Lasky Productions, 1914, (silent film), starring Kenneth Harlan, B. P. Schulberg Productions, 1923; (motion picture), starring Gary Cooper, Paramount, 1929, (motion picture), starring Joel McCrea, Paramount, 1946, (sound recording), Armed Forces Radio and Television Service, 1975.

(With Kirke La Shelle) *The Virginian: A Play in Four Acts* (first produced in Boston, 1903) Tallahassee, 1958.

SIDELIGHTS: Owen Wister was born in Germantown, Pennsylvania, on **July 14, 1860,** the only child of Dr. Owen Jones Wister, a prominent physician, and Sarah Butler Wis-

ter, daughter of Shakespearean actress Fanny Kemble. Wister was very close to his socialite mother. When he was still very young, they began a correspondence that continued until her death in 1908. As Wister's daughter, Frances, remembered: "My father was taken to Europe very often for those days and when he was only eight his parents left him in boarding school in Switzerland while they traveled. Later he went to school in England for a short time .... [He] spoke French from childhood and all his life had a fluent and idiomatic use of that language which he could write as easily as English. He could read German and Italian and speak them moderately well [and] learned piano playing very young."[1]

His interest in music grew and, intent on becoming a composer, he entered Harvard in the fall of **1878** where he majored in both music and philosophy. He was a student at Harvard with Theodore Roosevelt. Wister's daughter recalled: "While at Harvard he wrote for the Hasty Pudding Club 'Dido and Aeneas,' both the words and music and sang in it. When it was given in New York the critics for the *Herald* reviewed it saying the music was in the manner of Offenbach and very pleasing, not like a college show at all."[1]

Wister graduated summa cum laude in the spring of **1882** and went to Paris for a year to study composition and piano at the conservatoire. His father, however, insisted he return home to accept a job, and in 1883 Wister went to work in the Union Safe Deposit vaults in Boston. His daughter wrote: "My father was very bored by the bank but that year the Tavern Club was founded in Boston by a group of painters, writers, musicians and doctors, with William Dean Howells as first president. My father became a member and all his life went regularly to Boston to its dinners at which celebrities of every kind were entertained. In 1923 he wrote his short light opera, 'Watch Your Thirst,' for the Tavern Club and played the piano while the club members sang and acted it. It was an anti-prohibition satire based on a Greek legend, as was 'Dido and Aeneas.'"[1]

For reasons unknown, Wister's health broke down in **1885,** and, on the advice of his doctor, he travelled to Wyoming. It was this first trip that inspired future trips and would fuel his writing for years to come. "One must come to the West to realize what one may have most probably believed all one's life long—that it is a very much bigger place than the East, and the future America is just bubbling and seething in bare legs and pinafores here. I don't wonder a man never comes back [East] after he has once been here for a few years.

"I can't possibly say how extraordinary and beautiful the valleys ... are. They're different from all things I've seen. When you go for miles through the piled rocks where the fire has risen straight out of the crevices, you never see a human

His undistracted eye stayed fixed upon the dissembling foe. (Illustration by Frederic Remington from *The Virginian: A Horseman of the Plains* by Owen Wister.)

being—only now and then some disappearing wild animal. It's like what scenery on the moon must be. Then suddenly you come round a turn and down into a green cut where there are horsemen and wagons and hundreds of cattle, and then it's like Genesis. Just across this corduroy bridge are a crowd of cowboys around a fire, with their horses tethered."[2]

"The sunsets ... are wholly magnificent. No hardness or uncanniness whatever. First the entire sky glows—then the mountains grow blue—then the crimson goes and a flood of golden saffron vapour seems to rise from some ocean of colour that lies just beyond the horizon then the mountains get violet and softer than the eyes of deer—then the prairie looks as if it was made of virgin velvet, purple & brown—and rolling passively & richly away till the eye returns to the mountains & finds they have become purple too—while through the darkening saffron one white star shines clear & steady, & the eyelash of the moon seems about an arm's length from the ground."[1]

Wister returned East to enter Harvard Law School. He then began a promising legal practice, but his continued trips West began to color his thinking. "This glorious, this supernatural atmosphere meets me again better, clearer, more magical, even than I remembered it. As for every word I could get together that would give the faintest notion of its beauty and its effect on the observer, that can't be done by me and hardly done at all, I think.

"Wish I could draw. Writing is so wretched. But I am bound on this trip to lose nothing. Former experience has taught that you can hardly make a journal too full. I hope I shall be able to keep it up and get down in notes, anyhow, all the things that are peculiar to this life and country."[2]

Wister shared, with his mother, his growing desire to write. "The only thing I do is to jot down all shreds of local colour and all conversations and anecdotes decent or otherwise that strike me as native wild flowers. After a while I shall write a great fat book about the whole thing. When I feel enough familiar both by time and knowledge. There's a story I've already begun, some fifty pages of manuscript lying at home. That is intended merely as a trial trip."[2]

By **1891** he had made five trips to the West. "Nothing can make me forget the homesickness I feel for it every day when I am in the East. Getting into court and arguing or doing some hard work of that sort does not cure the nostalgia; some only just stops it for the moment."[2]

Wister's daughter noted the moment her father finally decided to be a writer. "One night in the Philadelphia Club he was talking to his friend Mr. Walter Furness, the son of Horace Howard Furness, noted Shakespearean scholar. Mr. Walter Furness had also gone big game shooting. They were speaking of the articles Theodore Roosevelt had written about the West, which Frederic Remington had illustrated, and saying that there should be a Kipling to write about and preserve the West. 'I'm going to try it myself,' said my father. 'I'm going to start this very minute.' 'Go to it,' said Mr. Furness. 'You should have started long ago.' And that night in the library of the Philadelphia Club Owen Wister wrote 'Hank's Woman.' It was his first western story."[1]

In **1892,** he sold "Hank's Woman" and his second story, "How Lin McLean Went West" to *Harper's* magazine for one-hundred-seventy-five dollars.

(A. J. Keller's illustration for the original edition of *The Virginian: A Horseman of the Plains* by Owen Wister.)

Wister gave up his law practice and in **1894** *Harper's* magazine commissioned him to travel West and gather materials for a series of Western stories. "If I can write what is wanted of me, I shall certainly have eaten the cake and had it too. Alden [editor of *Harper's*] wants me to do the whole adventure of the West in sketches or fiction, as I find most suitable in each case—taking Indian fighting, train robbing, what I please. He suggests articles of 7,500 words on an average, and to pay me 250 dollars apiece—or on a basis of thirty to thirty-five dollars a thousand. He is at present paying me twenty dollars, which was an increase from twelve dollars. He also is willing to send Frederic Remington along with me if I desire it! He said that Remington was a very companionable fellow—but that I should do as I liked. He wanted the first MS by September 1. The series should begin through February, after 'Balaam and Pedro,' and continue through the year till at Christmas he should want—but here I interrupted and said that for Christmas, 1894, I had a Texas story in view called 'The Partners'—so there he acquiesced. I told him of my summer plans and how unwilling I was to relinquish them and why. And this resulted in his giving me a generous 'leeway,' and I am to try and give him a MS of this pure adventure sort by October 1—and stay West, if necessary.

"Events in my literary life have crowded so thick of late that I am a little bewildered. But one thing I plainly see—that one of my dreams to have Remington as an illustrator is likely to be realized in a most substantial manner. Alden wants my studies to pause for a while and says that after a series of pure adventure the studies will have a wider popularity . . . . So now my next duty is to hunt material of adventure voraciously.

"Remington is an excellent American; that means, he thinks as I do about the disgrace of our politics and the present asphyxiation of all real love of country. He used almost the same words that have of late been in my head, that this continent does not hold a nation any longer but is merely a strip of land on which a crowd is struggling for riches. Now, I am a thin and despondent man and every day compel myself to see the bright side of things because I know that the dark side impresses me unduly; but Remington weighs about 240 pounds and is a huge rollicking animal. So to hear him more caustic in his disgust and contempt at the way we Americans are managing ourselves then I have ever been was most unexpected . . . . During the journey to St. Paul, which was hot and odious, Remington and I discussed our collaboration and many other things. He made a good criticism on the first two pages of 'The Promised Land,' which I accepted and profited by. In fact Remington's artistic insight is quick and clear and forcible.

"How humiliating and damaging if I should fail as a declared and advertised writer of short fiction and go creeping back to the displeased law with my tail between my legs! But, thank heaven, no, it hasn't been that. Of eight stipulated manuscripts, five are safely complete and approved. The remaining three, short of a miracle, will be as readily done as the others. In fact, I know what they're going to be, for everything I need is to gather more of the original facts from the Army officers

(From the movie "The Virginian," starring Gary Cooper, produced by Paramount Pictures, 1929.)

I'm going to see—who have been writing me the most delightful cordial letters to come and revisit them.

"So far as the public goes, my readers, I have fallen into favor with an ease that suggests how easily I might fall out and be forgotten. Well, that shan't be, either, God willing. I'll deserve success anyhow by that capacity for taking infinite pains which some uninspired ass—Southey(?)—said was genius! Yes, I'm popular enough to have moved that purveyor of mere popularity the *Youth's Companion* to write me unsolicited for a story. That speaks more to the essence than even a good notice in a paper, one that's a genuine notice and not a publisher's 'ad.'

"The only people who, as a class, find fault with what I write are my acquaintances who live in the same town. This I suppose must always be so. The herd, who sees one of themselves eat his soup just like all the rest, can't conceive his doing some trick that perhaps all the rest cannot quite do. Then as for these acquaintances, there are a number of honorable exceptions who console and cheer me on, with discrimination, putting useful critical fingers on weak places and by so doing helping me often and exceedingly."[2]

Meanwhile, Remington was also enjoying success, and asked Wister to write the preface to his book, *Drawings.* "I am glad that we have Remington, one of the kind that makes us aware of things we could not have seen for ourselves. We have been scarce enough in native material for Art to let go what the soil

provides us. We have often failed to value what the intelligent foreigner seizes upon at once. And I think as the Frontier recedes into tradition, fewer of us will shrink from its details. If Remington did nothing further, already has he achieved: he has made a page of American history his own."[3]

In **1898,** Wister married his second cousin once removed, Mary Channing; together they had six children.

In **1902** *The Virginian* was published. Wrote his daughter, "Many of the chapters had appeared earlier as stories in *Harper's* with Remington illustrations. This runaway best seller made Owen Wister famous and is dedicated to Theodore Roosevelt. Over a million and a half copies have been sold and it stands among the ten most popular novels of the past fifty years. It has been translated into French, Czech, Spanish and Polish. It was acted in New York as a play, after trying out in Boston, the winter of 1903-4. My father first wrote five acts and Kirk La Shelle wrote parts of the third act and gave advice. His name is on the program as the dramatist. Dustin Farnum was the star. He played it the first winter and off and on for ten years, touring the whole country. His brother William Farnum played it in the first movie version in 1914 and it has been made into a movie three times since then. My father wrote the song 'Ten Thousand Cattle,' both words and music, sung by Trampas, the villain.

"Dozens of claims have been made by people saying that they were the Virginian, knew the Virginian, or had seen the

Wister in the 1930s. (From *Owen Wister: Chronicler of the West, Gentleman of the East* by Darwin Payne.)

Virginian. This is not true. The Virginian is a composite character drawn from several different men my father had either seen briefly or known well. In his preface to *The Virginian* in the collected edition of 1928, he says several different men were 'a ratification of a character already conceived and nearly rounded out.' My father mentions the gentle manners and gentle voice of a Virginian that he only saw once at a roadside ranch where the stagecoach let him off for his first night in Wyoming in 1885. In 1893 he met Corporal Skirdin, born in Arizona, who seemed to him a 'sort of incarnation of my imaginary Virginian.' Two Kansas boys he knew in New Mexico in 1894 were also a ratification of his imaginary character."[1]

Always eager for her opinion, Wister sent his mother a copy of *The Virginian.* She did not like it and told him so. Wister wrote back: "I wish this book was twenty times better than it is. I'd already like to have it back to make certain things better. But I think it is very much of an advance on its predecessors. And the *next* time I shall write a very big book indeed, if I can do it as I feel it in my bones. But never again can I light on a character so engaging. That only happens once, even to the great ones of the earth."[2]

The Virginian remained a best seller for a year and a-half. In 1902 literary editor William Morton Payne wrote in the *Dial:* "*The Virginian* is the story of a nameless hero. Throughout the book he is called 'the Virginian' and nothing else. But although nameless, as far as we are informed, he is one of the most distinct personalities that have appeared in American fiction. A Wyoming cow-boy, representing a phase of our civilization that has almost completely vanished—although it was real enough a quarter of a century ago,—uneducated and unskilled in the amenities of artificial society, he conquers our sympathies by his innate refinement of character and the clean manliness of his living. He represents an ideal that was probably never realized, yet the separate touches by which he is drawn for us bear the visible stamp of truth. His story is a series of episodes that may be enjoyed independently of one another, although they are held in a sort of unity by his relations with the New England girl who comes to Wyoming to teach school, and who promptly develops into as satisfactory a heroine as one could wish for. She gives him books to read, and his frank comments upon them are both humorous and refreshing. There are other humorous features, notably that which describes the mixing up of a dozen babies by changing their clothes—a prank not quite in keeping with the Virginian's character, but nevertheless irresistibly amusing. In the course of his career he finds himself a member of a lynching party, and the author makes the usual sophistical defense of this wild form of justice. *The Virginian* is a man's book, with not one touch of sickly sentiment, and must be regarded as a valuable human document because of the author's intimate acquaintance with the scenes and types which it portrays."[4]

Despite the success of *The Virginian,* and pressures from his publisher, Wister refused to write a sequel.

In later years, he ceased his Western excursions: "Too many ghosts are there for me. My first sight of it was in 1887. No: I don't want to see any of that country again. Too much nostalgia for past happiness. I have never enjoyed anything more than those camping days in Wyoming."[5]

Wister advised young writers to: "Let the subject of a piece of fiction contain a simple, broad appeal, and the better its art, the greater its success; although the noble army of readers will not suspect that their pleasure is largely due to the skill . . . . Clearly feel what you intend to express, and then go ahead, listening to nobody, unless to one who also perceives clearly your intention."[6]

Wister died of a cerebral hemorrhage on **July 21, 1938,** near Kingston, Rhode Island.

FOOTNOTE SOURCES

[1]Frances K. W. Stokes, *My Father, Owen Wister,* [Laramie, Wyoming], 1952.
[2]Fanny K. Wister, editor, *Owen Wister Out West: His Journals and Letters,* University of Chicago Press, 1958.
[3]Frederic Remington, *Drawings,* preface by Owen Wister, R. H. Russell, 1897.
[4]William Morton Payne, *Dial,* October 16, 1902.
[5]*Fifty Years of the Virginian: 1902-1952,* University of Wyoming Library Associates, 1952.
[6]Owen Wister, *Members of the Family,* Macmillan, 1911.

FOR MORE INFORMATION SEE:

Frederic Remington, *Done in the Open,* preface by O. Wister, Collier & Son, 1902.
Saturday Evening Post, January 3, 1903 (p. 13ff).
Stanley Kunitz and Howard Haycraft, *Junior Book of Authors,* H. W. Wilson, 1934.
Elizabeth Rider Montgomery, *The Story behind Great Books,* Robert McBride, 1946.
Southwest Review, summer, 1951 (p. 157ff).
American Literature, May, 1954 (p. 251ff).
Arizona Quarterly, summer, 1954 (p. 147ff).
Harper's, December, 1955 (p. 8ff).
Pennsylvania Magazine of History and Biography, January, 1959 (p. 3ff), January, 1977 (p. 89ff).
N. Orwin Rush, "Frederic Remington and Owen Wister," Tallahassee, 1961.
G. Edward White, *The Eastern Establishment and the Western Experience: The West of Frederic Remington, Theodore Roosevelt, and Owen Wister,* Yale University Press, 1968.
O. Wister (commentary), *The Illustrations of Frederic Remington,* Bounty Books, 1970.
Quarterly Journal of the Library of Congress, July, 1972 (p. 162ff).
New Republic, September 2, 1972 (p. 28ff).
Ben Merchant Vorpahl, *My Dear Wister—The Frederic Remington-Owen Wister Letters,* American West Publishing, 1972.
Richard W. Etulain, *Owen Wister,* Boise State College Western Writers Series, 1973.
Anne E. Rowe, *The Enchanted Country: Northern Writers in the South 1865-1910,* Louisiana State University Press, 1978.
Dictionary of Literary Biography, Volume 9, Gale, 1981.
Peggy Samuels and Harold Samuels, *Frederic Remington: A Biography,* Doubleday, 1982.
Western American Literature, fall, 1983 (p. 199ff).

This animal was thoroughly a man of the world. (Cover design by Tim Gaydos from *The Virginian: A Horseman of the Plains* by Owen Wister.)

Darwin Payne, *Owen Wister: Chronicler of the West, Gentleman of the East,* Southern Methodist University Press, 1985.
Sharon R. Gunton, editor, "Owen Wister," *Twentieth Century Literary Criticism,* Volume 21, Gale, 1986.
Robert Murray Davis, editor, *Owen Wister's West,* University of New Mexico Press, 1987.

COLLECTIONS

Library of Congress.
University of Wyoming Library.
Houghton Library, Harvard University.
American Academy of Arts and Letters.
Historical Society of Pennsylvania.
Alderman Library, University of West Virginia.
Arizona Pioneers' Historical Society.

WOLFSON, Evelyn 1937-

PERSONAL: Born April 24, 1937, in New York, N.Y.; daughter of Hugh C. (a salesman) and Catherine (a homemaker; maiden name, Biggane) Tweer; married William Wolfson (a venture capitalist); September 20, 1961; children: Jason, Dacia. *Education:* Framingham State College, B.A., 1976. *Politics:* Democrat. *Home and office:* 188 Pelham Island Rd., Wayland, Mass. 01778.

CAREER: Computer Control Co., Boston, Mass. and Los Angeles, Calif., secretary, 1955-57; Magnavox Research Laboratories, Los Angeles, Calif., secretary, 1957-61; Elbanobscot Environmental Education Center, Sudbury, Mass., teacher, 1972-78; Massachusetts schools and libraries, teacher and lecturer, 1978—; Wayland Preschool, Wayland, Mass., teacher, 1980—. Member, Wayland Conservation Commission, Outdoor Education, 1970-85, Castle Hill Archaelogical Excavation, Massachusettes Historical Commission, 1978-81, and Wayland Library Building Committee, 1983-88; president, Wayland Junior High PTO, 1974-76; board member, Arts Wayland Association, 1984-85; director, Wayland Historical Soicety, 1990—. *Member:* National League of American Pen Women (Wellesley branch, vice-president, 1984-86, president, 1986-88), Boston Authors Club (board member, 1987—), Society of Children's Book Writers, Boston Children's Book Collaborative, Woman's National Book Association.

AWARDS, HONORS: American Indian Habitats was selected one of Library of Congress' Best Children's Books, 1964-78; *From Abenaki to Zuni* was selected a Notable Children's Trade Book in the Field of Social Studies from the National Council for Social Studies and the Children's Book Council, and one of New York Public Library's Books for the Teen Age, both 1988.

EVELYN WOLFSON

WRITINGS:

(With Nancy Simon) *American Indian Habitats: How to Make Dwellings and Shelters with Natural Materials,* McKay, 1978.

American Indian Utensils: How to Make Baskets, Pottery, and Woodenware with Natural Materials, McKay, 1979.

American Indian Tools and Ornaments: How to Make Implements and Jewelry Using Bone and Shell, McKay, 1981.

(With Barbara Robinson) *Environmental Education: A Manual for Elementary Educators,* Teachers College Press, 1982.

Growing Up Indian (illustrated by William Sauts Bock), Walker, 1986.

From Abenaki to Zuni: A Dictionary of Native American Tribes (illustrated with photographs by W. S. Bock), Walker, 1988.

Touching the Past: Children of the Comanche, Hopi and Nipmuck, Walker, 1990.

Contributor of articles to periodicals, including *Canada Crafts, Homeowners How-to-Handbook, Horn Book, Cobblestone,* and *Country Journal.*

WORK IN PROGRESS: From the Earth to beyond the Sky: Native American Medicine, to be published by Houghton.

SIDELIGHTS: "My life-long interest in plants and animals led me to begin my college career as a biology major. However, I left school to get married and did not finish until 1976, by which time I had abandoned biology and settled for a B.A. degree in liberal studies. Our son, Jason, was born in 1963 and daughter, Dacia in 1964. My husband, a computer engineer turned venture capitalist, elected to semi-retire shortly after our children were born and for the past twenty-seven years our family has travelled extensively throughout the United States, Europe, Asia, Africa, and parts of the Mid East. These experiences broadened my view of both natural and man-made environments and led to an appreciation of world culture only brushed against in college.

"We have lived in the same community since our children were born and I have always been active in community affairs. In the early 1960s, when my children were toddlers, Rachel Carson's book, *Silent Spring,* appeared. This book caused a huge public outcry against the devastating effects of unregulated spraying of chemicals on plants to kill pesky insects. The public demanded controls and regulations and the environmental movement was born. I was so concerned about the kind of message chemical spraying gave our children and what it did to the environment that I became an active environmentalist and went to school to study how plants and animals interact and relate to each other and with the natural world. Before long I was teaching at the environmental education center where I studied. I also conducted workshops for teachers throughout Massachusetts.

"In 1972, an elementary school principal asked me to do out-of-doors teaching with two fourth-grade classes once a week from September to June. I agreed, even though I lacked a year-round environmental education curriculum. The idea challenged me and I was thrilled that an educator appreciated the importance of environmental literacy. I combed through my curriculum materials to find something that might capture the children's imagination. I was surprised to find the literature sprinkled with quotations by Native Americans who lamented the ruination of the land by whites. Many quotes were 100- to 150-years-old, yet they sounded very

Indian babies were often called "Little Girl," "Little Boy," or just plain "Baby" for the first five years. (Illustration by William Sauts Bock from *Growing Up Indian* by Evelyn Wolfson.)

much like what was being spoken by environmentalists in the 1970s. One quote went: 'How can the spirit of the earth like the white man. Everywhere he has touched it, the earth is sore. It is sick.'

"The widespread view of Native Americans was that we were ruining the earth. I realized that Native Americans HAD to know and respect the environment because they were totally dependent on it. I decided to examine the environment through the eyes of Native Americans who believed they were just another living organism—no more or less important than any other life form. To the students, I proposed living like Indians and using only the school grounds and the community to meet our needs. The curriculum I roughed out met with the approval of the principal who appreciated that while I did not know very much about Native Americans, I knew enough about the plants and animals on the school grounds to make reasonable deductions. (I assured him that I would research each project as I went along.)

"The program began in September, 1972. I explained my plans to the children emphasizing how little I knew about Native Americans. They knew we would be learning together—which turned out to be very contagious. Everyone wanted to learn with us— other students, teachers, and even parents. Over the course of the year we built a wigwam, a corn grinder, soapstone bowls, miniature canoes, and collected and prepared wild foods on the school grounds or in the community. The program was a great success. We discovered how the Indians of the Northeast used the environment to meet their needs. We also learned that if the environment of an area is examined and understood, it is simple to figure out how people meet their everyday needs in other regions of the country.

"My teaching focused on three important elements of nature: plants, animals, and minerals—topics which I later incorporated in my children's books. *American Indian Habitats: How to Make Dwellings and Shelters with Natural Materials* described how to build homes using plants. *American Indian Utensils: How to Make Baskets, Pottery and Woodenware with Natural Materials* described the need to find and use minerals such as clay, and plants, like wood and grass, to create cooking and carrying utensils. *American Indian Tools and Ornaments: How to Make Implements and Jewelry Using Bone and Shell* resulted from an obvious void in my writing. I had reams of research notes on Indians of the Great Plains but had not written about them. Why? Because they did not use plants or minerals to meet their everyday needs. Instead, they used all parts of the buffalo. Besides supplying them with meat, buffalo equipped them with materials for clothing, shelter, utensils, tools, and toys. In addition to tribes of the Great Plains, my third book described how other tribes of North America also met their needs using animals.

"In 1982 I co-authored with Barbara Robinson *Environmental Education: A Manual for Elementary Educators* which is used at teaching colleges and private education centers. Our manual includes directions on how to set up an environmental education program and how and what lesson plans might be included. It is a valuable tool for educators who are ready and willing to include this important subject in their curriculum.

"By 1986 I had accumulated enough experience teaching special programs about Native Americans to write a book which answered frequently asked questions. *Growing Up Indian,* published by Walker, describes how Indian children learned about the world from the time they were toddlers until they married—without ever going to school.

"*From Abenaki to Zuni: A Dictionary of Native American Tribes* was published in 1988 by Walker. It lists sixty-eight of the major tribes and includes information about where and how they lived and what happened to them from the time of European contact until the present—unhappy stories that are seldom told.

"My interest and concern for the environment never wanes, even though my curiosity about Native American culture dominates my life. The two subjects are closely intertwined and I continue to teach and lecture about the environment while viewing it through the eyes of Native Americans."

HOBBIES AND OTHER INTERESTS: Skiing, tennis, gardening, travel.

WOODBURY, David Oakes 1896-1981

PERSONAL: Born July 24, 1896 in South Berwick, Me.; died December 26, 1981; son of Charles Herbert (an artist) and Susan M. (an artist; maiden name, Oakes) Woodbury; married Ruth B. Ruyl (a homemaker), October 16, 1932; children: Peter Ruyl, Christopher John. *Education:* Harvard University, A.B., 1917; Stanford University, M.A., 1919; Massachusetts Institute of Technology, E.E., 1921. *Politics:* Republican. *Religion:* Episcopalian. *Residence:* Ogunquit, Me.

CAREER: Writer; lecturer. *Military service:* U.S. Navy, two years; achieved rank of Ensign. *Member:* Authors Guild, Creative Research (president, 1953-55).

WRITINGS:

Communication, Dodd, 1931.
The Colorado Conquest, Dodd, 1941.
What You Should Know about Submarine Warfare, W. W. Norton, 1942.
Beloved Scientist, Whittlesey House, 1944.
Builders for Battle, Dutton, 1946.
Battlefronts of Industry, Wiley & Sons, 1948.
The Glass Giant of Palomar (self-illustrated with Russell W. Porter), Dodd, 1948.
A Measure for Greatness, McGraw-Hill, 1949.

DAVID OAKES WOODBURY

Let Erma Do It, Harcourt, 1956.
Around the World in Ninety Minutes, Harcourt, 1958.
1001 Questions Answered about the New Science, Dodd, 1959.
Outward Bound for Space, Little, Brown, 1960.
The Great White Mantle, Viking, 1962.
When the Ice Came, Dodd, 1963.
Five Days to Oblivion (fiction), Adair, 1963.
Mr. Faraday's Formula (fiction), Adair, 1965.
Atoms for Peace, Dodd, 1965.
The New World of the Atom (juvenile), Dodd, 1965.
The Frigid World of Cryogenics (juvenile), Dodd, 1966.
Fresh Water from Salty Seas (juvenile), Dodd, 1967.
You're Next on the List (fiction), Western Islands, 1968.

Contributor of articles to periodicals, including *Reader's Digest* and *Saturday Evening Post.* Author of column "Your Life Tomorrow," for *Colliers.*